gratitude 34, 61, 71, 74, 97,
102, 103, 105, 124, 183, 245-247,
258

D1823428

43,

Free Markets and the Culture of Common Good

Ethical Economy. Studies in Economic Ethics and Philosophy

For further volumes:
http://www.springer.com/series/2881

Martin Schlag • Juan Andrés Mercado
Editors

Free Markets and the Culture of Common Good

 Springer

Editors
Martin Schlag
Pontificia Università della Santa Croce
Moral Theology
Piazza Sant'Apollinare 49
00186 Rome
Italy

Juan Andrés Mercado
Pontificia Università della Santa Croce
Philosophy
Piazza Sant'Apollinare 49
00186 Rome
Italy

ISBN 978-94-007-2989-6   ISBN 978-94-007-2990-2 (eBook)
DOI 10.1007/978-94-007-2990-2
Springer Dordrecht Heidelberg New York London

Library of Congress Control Number: 2012936559

Printed on acid-free paper

Springer is part of Springer Science+Business Media (www.springer.com)

Preface and Acknowledgments

In this book, we have put together a puzzle of very different pieces. The differences stem from the origin, the discipline, and the professional dedication of the authors. What they have in common is their interest in economics and their conviction that the functioning of a Free Market Economy depends on sound cultural and ethical foundations. We hope that the emerging picture, if not comprehensive, does offer a representative view of an interdisciplinary approach to economy and economics.

Interdisciplinarity as an approach responds to the growing uneasiness with the methodological fragmentation in the social sciences and the wish for a more holistic method that does not ignore human personality, motivations, and ethical interiority. Of course, interdisciplinarity has its limits. Just putting different methodologies next to each other does not necessarily result in a complete picture; in fact, it may actually just enhance the sensation of grasping at unconnected strands of research in the search for something more. However, we think that in this book we have brought together authors who have managed to communicate with each other because, even though they may work in different fields or come from different walks of life, they are united by a basically shared set of values. This is a fact, which is all the more remarkable since the contributors profess and practice different religions.

Each of the authors is outstanding in his or her field: philosophy (Rhonheimer and Hittinger), economics (Das Neves, Cañadas, Baroni, and Argandoña), social sciences (Zamagni and Donati), and theology (Cordes and Schlag). Theory without practice can become an "ivory tower." We, therefore, have invited well-known practitioners, many of them with academic affiliations, to give us their view on the subject in this book: experts in banking (Camdessus and Griffiths), politics (Buttiglione and Schneider), finance and social entrepreneurship (El-Khalil and Widmer), and journalism (Webber). This encounter between theory and practice enables a verification of scholarly learning, which otherwise might be endangered by too great an abstraction from reality.

This book is part of an ongoing endeavor of the Pontifical University of the Holy Cross in Rome to center attention and interdisciplinary study on an in-depth view of economy and ethics. Through research and an educational and cultural program involving the world of business and finance, we hope to contribute to changing the way the global economy works and to further developing the Catholic Church's moral teaching concerning social and economic questions. Therefore, Pope Benedict XVI's encyclical letter *Caritas in Veritate* appears frequently in the chapters.

In conclusion, we would like to make a few heartfelt acknowledgments. This book would not have been possible without the untiring work of Miss Jennifer E. Miller who not only corresponded with the contributors but also corrected and edited the manuscripts. She also put together the index. We are all indebted to her kind patience, and our first acknowledgment therefore goes to her.

We also cordially thank our publisher Springer for receiving our book in their prestigious house and for their patience in its production. Our thanks goes also to Prof. Peter Koslowski who has kindly accepted the book in his well-known series. Last but not least, we thank our contributors for entrusting their efforts and intellectual work to us. It has been lovely working together, and we think it was worthwhile.

Martin Schlag
Juan Andrés Mercado

Contents

List of Authors

Antonio Argandoña Professor at IESE Business School, Barcelona, Spain. He is Professor of Economics and Business Ethics "La Caixa" Chair of Corporate Social Responsibility and Corporate Governance. He is also a member of the Commission on Corporate Social Responsibility and Anti-corruption of the Paris International Chamber of Commerce, member of the Arbitration Tribunal of Catalonia (TATC), and member of the Ethical Standards Committee of AENOR. He also serves on the editorial boards of *Journal of Business Ethics*, *Business Ethics: A European Review*, and *Journal of International Business Education*. In addition, he is Director of *IESE Insight* and *IESE Alumni Magazine*.

Michel Baroni Professor at ESSEC Business School, Paris. He is a Fellow of the RICS (Royal Institution of Chartered Surveyors) and a member of the Continental Europe Standards Board of the RICS. Since 1989, he has been administrator for the European Institute of Cooperation and Development (l'Institut Européen de Coopération et de Développement, IECD), Strasbourg. Since 1991, he is advisor to the Agence Européenne pour le Développement Economique et Social, AEDES. He also has practical experience in the field as manager of SICE, a real estate investment company, and the administrator in charge of real estate issues for a limited liability company "Chaudronnerie Provençale" in Aix-en-Provence.

Rocco Buttiglione Professor at the S. Pio V University, Italy, Vice President of the House of Representatives of the Republic of Italy. Both an academic and a politician, he is president of the Unione dei Democratici Cristiani and the Democratici di Centro. He is also a member of the Senate commission regarding politics of the European Union and a member of the Pontifical Academy of the Social Sciences.

Michel Camdessus President of The International Monetary Fund (1987–2000), president of SRAEC, France. Michel Camdessus was Managing Director of the International Monetary Fund (IMF) from January 16, 1987, to February 14, 2000. He is currently president of the Semaines Sociales de France and is a member of the Commission for Africa established by Tony Blair. He is also a member of the Pontifical Commission for Justice and Peace. Camdessus is a member of the Africa

Progress Panel (APP), an independent authority on Africa launched in April 2007 to focus world leaders' attention on delivering their commitments to the continent.

Alejandro Cañadas Assistant Professor of Economics at Mount St. Mary's University. He also has the Msgr. Dennis Tinder Professorship and is a Visiting Scholar at the Center for Neurotechnology Studies in the Potomac Institute for Policy Studies, Arlington, VA.

Paul Josef Cardinal Cordes Former President of the Pontifical Council Cor Unum (1995–2010). He has also served as Vice President of the Pontifical Council for the Laity. He has been appointed by Pope Benedict XVI as a member of several congregations in the Roman Curia. These are the Congregation for the Causes of Saints, the Congregation for the Clergy, and the Congregation for the Evangelization of Peoples and the Pontifical Council for Justice and Peace. In November 2010, he was also appointed as member of the Congregation for Bishops.

João César das Neves Professor at the Universidade Católica Portuguesa, Lisbon, Portugal. He is currently the President of the Scientific Council of Faculdade de Ciências Econômicas e Empresariais (FCEE). He was economic advisor to the Portuguese Prime Minister from 1991 to 1995, advisor to the Portuguese Minister of Finance in 1990, and an economist at the Bank of Portugal in 1990–1991 and 1995–1997.

Pierpaolo Donati Professor at the University of Bologna, Italy. Since 1981, he is a Professor of Sociology in the Faculty of Political Sciences at the University of Bologna. He is also the Director of CEPOSS (Center of Studies for Social Politics and the Sociology of Health Care). Since 1997, he is a member of the Pontifical Academy of Social Sciences. Donati is also the Director of the National Observatory of the Family. He was recognized by the UNO as a distinguished expert member during the International Year of the Family (1994).

Youssef El-Khalil Senior CFO, Bank of Lebanon, Lebanon, visiting Professor at the London School of Economics. He is also President of the Association for the Development of Rural Capacities (ADR).

Lord Brian Griffiths of Fforestfach Vice Chairman of Goldman Sachs International, UK. He taught at the London School of Economics from 1965 to 1976. He held the position of Dean of the City University's Business School from 1982 to 1985, was Director of the Bank of England from 1983 to 1985, served as Head of the Prime Minister's Policy Unit from 1985 to 1990, and was the special advisor to the Prime Minister for Domestic Policy Making. He was made a life peer on leaving 10 Downing Street.

Francis Hittinger Professor at the University of Tulsa, USA. He is the William K. Warren Professor of Catholic Studies, Research Professor of Law, and the Chair of the Department of Philosophy and Religion. Since 2001, he is a member of the Pontifical Academy of St. Thomas Aquinas, to which he was elected a full member in 2004, and since 2009 he is a full member of the Pontifical Academy of Social

Sciences. He serves on several boards and boards of advisors, including *First Things*, the *American Journal of Jurisprudence*, *Nova et Vetera*, and the Notre Dame Center for Ethics and Culture.

Martin Rhonheimer Professor at the Università della Santa Croce, Italy. He is currently Professor of Ethics and Political Philosophy at the School of Philosophy of the Pontifical University of the Holy Cross in Rome. In addition to his scholarly activity, he is also dedicated to pastoral work in Zurich, especially for university students. Martin Rhonheimer is a member of the editorial boards of *The American Journal of Jurisprudence* (Notre Dame Law School) and member of the scientific board of *Acta Philosophica* (Pontifical University of the Holy Cross). In 2002, he was appointed as a corresponding academician to the Pontifical Academy of St. Thomas Aquinas.

Martin Schlag Associate Professor at the Università della Santa Croce, Italy. Presently, he teaches Social Ethics at the Pontifical University of the Holy Cross. He is Cofounder and Codirector of the project "Markets, Culture and Ethics."

Andrea M. Schneider Cabinet of the Federal Chancellor, Bundeskanzleramt, Germany. She has worked as Director of the Konrad Adenauer Foundation's economic policy group. Additionally, she is a member of the Central Committee of German Catholics, the preeminent organization for lay Catholics in Germany.

Alan M. Webber Cofounder of Fast Company, former Editorial Director and Managing Editor of *Harvard Business Review*, USA. He has also been active at local, state, and national political levels, serving as policy advisor for the mayor of Portland, Oregon, writing speeches for several governors, and working as special assistant to the United States Secretary of Transportation.

Andreas Widmer Chairman of SEVEN Fund, Inc. Andreas Widmer is the Cofounder of SEVEN Fund and the Pioneers of Prosperity Awards, a first-of-its-kind industry program that finds and promotes the best entrepreneurs in emerging markets. He currently serves on the advisory boards of the Templeton Foundation, Global Adaptation Institute, Spring Hill Equity Partners, and Karisimbi Business Partners. He was appointed by the Center for Interfaith Action on Global Poverty as a member of the Task Force to Advance Multireligious Collaboration on Faith, Health and Development, which presented its findings at the White House in November 2010.

Stefano Zamagni Professor at the University of Bologna, Italy. He is President of the Agenzia per le Onlus. In 1991, he became consultant to the Pontifical Council for Justice and Peace and successively a member of the Pontifical Academy of Social Sciences. As consultant to the Pontifical Council for Justice and Peace, between 2007 and 2009, he was one of Benedict XVI's primary collaborators in the elaboration of the encyclical *Caritas in Veritate*.

Part I
Free Market Economy
and the Role of State Authorities

Chapter 1
Capitalism, Free Market Economy, and the Common Good: The Role of the State in the Economy

Martin Rhonheimer

1.1 The Traditional Criticism of Capitalism and Laissez-Faire and the Call for State Intervention

In his famous and brilliantly written pamphlet *The End of Laissez-faire*, the great British economist, John Maynard Keynes, calls the essential characteristic of capitalism the "intense appeal to the money-making and money-loving instincts of individuals" (Keynes 2004, 43). In this same line, he somewhat contemptuously depicts an image of businessmen and entrepreneurs, governed by such capitalist instincts, whose evil economic consequences must be overcome by new forms of public business regulations. In his 1926 text, Keynes, somewhat surprisingly, contends that "progress lies in the growth and the recognition of semi-autonomous bodies within the state – bodies whose criterion of action within their own field is solely the public good as they understand it, and from whose deliberations motives of private advantage are excluded," returning thereby "towards medieval conceptions of separate autonomies." These bodies, Keynes continues, should be "subject in the last resort to the sovereignty of the democracy expressed through Parliament"

Preliminary Note: The following is a piece of moral and political philosophy – or political ethics – rather than of economics or political science. It tries to provide, however, a philosophical treatment of the topic embedded in, and – as I hope – enlightened by, basically sound economic thinking, as far as this can be successfully achieved by a noneconomist. At any rate, I am convinced that it is not possible to say something reasonable specifically from a moral point of view, which is also the viewpoint of political philosophy, about a topic like *Capitalism, Free Market Economy, and the Common Good* without respecting the logic proper to economic thinking. When speaking about so-called social justice, both moral philosophers and theologians should be always aware of this logic and the respect which it is owed. Economists reading this chapter, on the other hand, may indulge me for any misapprehension of economic issues, lack of clarity or undue simplifications they will possibly find.

M. Rhonheimer (✉)
Pontificia Università della Santa Croce, Rome, Italy
e-mail: rhonheimer@pusc.it

M. Schlag and J.A. Mercado (eds.), *Free Markets and the Culture of Common Good*, Ethical Economy 41, DOI 10.1007/978-94-007-2990-2_1,
© Springer Science+Business Media B.V. 2012

(Keynes 2004, 37). Such a solution, therefore, "would involve Society in exercising directive intelligence through some appropriate organ of action over many of the inner intricacies of private business, yet it would leave private initiative and enterprise unhindered" (Keynes 2004, 41).

This, in my view, somewhat utopian proposal appropriately describes a spirit of interventionism – although it pretends to "leave private initiative and enterprise unhindered"[1] – a position which was generally advocated after the First World War, albeit in different ways, both in democratic and nondemocratic societies. (It is known that Keynes' ideas not only inspired left-wing politics of government planning and regulation, but also fascist corporatism.) Government curbing of entrepreneurial initiative and bureaucratic state-regulation of business activity was considered to be the remedy for the principal failures of capitalism. Due to its monopolistic structure and increasing state interventions (which, rather than aiming at breaking the power of monopolies, tended to bureaucratically control and direct business activity), the former economic system was considerably degenerated at that time. After the 1929 New York stock exchange crash, caused by a speculative financial bubble, and the succeeding slump, such policies were increasingly recognized as beneficial and necessary.[2] However, as historians have argued on the basis of Milton Friedman's and Anna Schwartz's study of the financial history of the United States, these politics led to a mistaken, restrictive monetary policy by the Federal Reserve Board, suffocating the recovery of private business activity (Friedman and Schwartz 1963, 299–419). Others, however, most prominently Murray N. Rothbard, have argued against this idea on the grounds of the "Austrian" understanding of the business cycle as elaborated by Ludwig von Mises. They insist that the real cause of the depression was not restrictive money policy after the slump but rather continuous inflationary state intervention during the "roaring twenties (which because of permanent price stability remained unnoticed)" and the attempt by the Hoover administration to impede readjustment of the economy after the 1929 crash.[3] Rothbard

---

[1] Note, however, the formulation of Keynes (2004, 41) (emphasis added): "These measures would involve Society in *exercising directive intelligence through some appropriate organ of action over many of the inner intricacies of private business*, yet it would leave private initiative and enterprise unhindered." This sounds somewhat contradictory; I suppose, however, that what Keynes had in mind was something widely practiced some years later by one of the last German pre-Nazi governments, presided (1930–1932) by chancellor Heinrich Brüning, and afterward systematized by the Nazi Regime. This involved leaving business as such – the means of production and enterprise generally – as private property while the government regulated and directed concrete business decisions. This policy turned out to be fatally unsound; however, it provided the natural presupposition for Hitler's later war economy.

[2] A still useful summary and analysis of the international situation during these years is provided by W. Arthur Lewis's classic book, *Economic Survey 1919–1939* (London: Allan and Unwin, 1949, Ninth impression 1970); reprinted in the Routledge Reprint edition (London: Routledge Chapman & Hall, 2003).

[3] See Rothbard (2000). Both Rothbard's and Friedman's views, I think, do not strictly contradict each other since they perceive, although in different ways, the cause of the problem in the state's monetary policy and its grave distortion of economic equilibrium.

further argues that far from having followed a politics of laissez-faire, as a persistent myth continues to tell, the Republican administration of the 1920s, together with the Federal Reserve Board – in close, quasi-conspiratorial, coordination with the Bank of England and the British government (see Rothbard 2000, 131–145) – was in reality highly interventionist, causing continuous inflationary credit expansion. This policy necessarily brought about a depression and the final explosion of the malinvestment bubble in October (the consequence, not the cause, of the beginning of the depression, initiated already in July 1929). Moreover, the unfortunate protectionist measures taken by the Hoover administration (e.g., the Smoot-Hawley tariff in 1930) disintegrated the world economy and dramatically increased unemployment everywhere. Finally, under the successor to this administration, Franklin D. Roosevelt, these politics took the unprecedented form of "big government," famously called by its inventors the "New Deal" (although, in fact, it only continued the politics of the Hoover administration, pushing them to the extreme[4]).

Inspired by a Keynesian spirit – a line of thought much less original than is commonly believed as it primarily rationalized what at that time was widely en vogue[5] – Roosevelt's politics of the New Deal tried to overcome the economic depression not only by extensive public deficit spending and huge government programs like the *Tennesse Valley Authority* (TVA) but also by interventions into the price system, by meticulous bureaucratic regulations of entrepreneurial activity – with the justification of protecting society from greedy predators – and by imposing increasingly higher tax rates for the business profits of the wealthy (causing them to hoard rather than to invest their riches in business). As the economic historian Amity Shlaes has recently argued in her book, *The Forgotten Man: a New History of the Great Depression*, in reality Roosevelt's politics, though not *causing* the depression, "helped to make the Depression Great" (Shlaes 2007, 9) (although, provided the Austrians are right, this honor should already be attributed to President Hoover). With their bias for central planning and state regulation of productive activity through several government-run agencies, their public projects like the TVA, their interventions into the price system and the imposition of high taxes on the profits of the wealthy, the New Dealers, united in Roosevelt's "brain trust,"[6] were convinced that they were not only stimulating the economy but fighting against what they regarded as the cause of all evils: the capitalist's, and even ordinary businessman's, greed for money and profit. This was also the message Roosevelt effectively transmitted to the public through his regularly broadcasted "Fireside Chats," which additionally contributed to deteriorate the image of private business and those engaged in it. Roosevelt's policy, as Amity Shlaes points out, "made government into a competitor that the private sector could not match" (Shlaes 2007, 11; 262–268).

---

[4] For the details of the truly interventionist politics of the Hoover administration (e.g., its fight against the readjustment of price–cost relations by impeding the fall of wages, thereby causing heavy and persistent unemployment), see Rothbard (2000, 167–295).

[5] See for this argument Hazlitt (2007).

[6] This term was created and first applied to Roosevelt's board of consulters at this very time.

Although not all the measures taken by the Roosevelt administration were harmful – some actually were beneficial – most of them caused much damage. Their immediate effect was to strangulate entrepreneurial initiative and the readiness of businessmen and the rich to take risks, not only thereby withholding new prosperity from the economy, but also making simple recovery more difficult by interfering with the only forces which could have reestablished economical dynamics and innovation: entrepreneurial risk behavior in view of the reward of profit – that is, the alleged "evil" of capitalism – and a corresponding expansion of productive activity.[7] Contrary to encouraging this force of renewal, its interventionist character and strong belief in the superiority of state planning and regulation as well as its continuously experimental and volatile character caused arbitrariness and unpredictability. In this manner, the politics of the New Dealers made entrepreneurial risk calculation and long-term foresight impossible and thus greatly discouraged investment.[8] At the same time, Roosevelt, cherishing the myth of a society of classes – actually partially existing as a product of the failures of the first period of the New Deal – increasingly served interest groups. Basing his politics on constituencies, he was rewarded with votes and reelected twice. Hence, as Amity Shlaes concludes, "the New Dealer's economic failures were working to their own political advantage." (Shlaes 2007, 267).

This continues to be a well-known pattern: successful electoral politics united to generally harmful economic policies which, however, are held to be salutary by a majority of voters. This error is due to the strong influence of organized interest groups, who will gain from these policies, upon public opinion. This was first practiced systematically by the Roosevelt administration and greatly contributed to the following myth that the state – comprising public deficit spending and job creation by government-run enterprises – is not only the necessary and single remedy against slumps and similar economic crises, but the ordinary means to regulate economic cycles and to achieve social justice.[9]

---

[7] "The story of the mid-1930s is the story of a heroic economic struggling to recuperate but failing to do so because of perverse federal policy. The worst factor was Roosevelt's war on business. (…) The private sector, desperate, was incredibly productive – those who did have a job worked hard, just as our grandparents told us. But the government was taking all the air in the room. Utilities are a prime example. In the 1920s electricity was a miracle industry. There was every expectation even in the 1930s that growth in utilities might pull the country through hard times in the future. And the industry might have indeed done that, if the government had not supplanted it. Roosevelt believed in public utilities, not private companies" (Shlaes Afterword to the paperback edition 2008, 392–394).

[8] Some observers think that at present the Obama administration commits the same mistake: due to the unpredictability of government policy and the subsequent creation of a lack of confidence, private business and investment are discouraged so that the economy is not recovering as it should to decrease unemployment.

[9] One of the clearest European critics of the New Deal (and of Keynes), Wilhelm Röpke – after the Second World War he was among those greatly inspired by "neoliberalism" and the German *Soziale Marktwirtschaft* – remarked that if Keynes had only taught that as an incentive the state should contribute by some deficit spending to reanimate a depressed economy, he would have said

The effective economic failures of the politics of the New Deal were never fully realized, thanks to the outbreak of the Second World War and the transition to a war economy, strongly based on state regulation.[10] On the other hand, the New Deal has left to posterity what today is generally accepted as its most beneficial outcome: the Social Security system. This must not cause us to forget that the basis for the legitimization of the New Deal was a pro-socialist ideology of anti-laissez-faire, advocated by those members of Roosevelt's brain trust very much influenced by socialist ideas – at that time the Soviet Union still seemed to many of them to be an interesting experiment from which something could be learned. Moreover, joined to this socialist bias was the idea, openly supported by the President himself, that the government needed to bring morality into the immoral and selfish world of capitalist business by means of state regulation.

1.2 An Alternative View: Walter Eucken's *Ordo*liberalism

In the opening pages of his seminal work *Grundsätze der Wirtschaftspolitik* ["Principles of Economic Policy"], first published in 1952, the influential "*ordo*liberal" (or, as they were called at that time, "neoliberal") economist Walter Eucken extensively criticizes the nineteenth century idea of laissez-faire. In a short footnote (Eucken 1968, 27 note 1), Eucken remarks that Keynes, though having been quite right in criticizing pure laissez-faire, had not, however, understood the very essence of capitalism and, thus, the other side of the coin, that is, the positive and beneficial features of the idea of laissez-faire. These features were principally to be elaborated as the entrepreneurial freedom to make, on the basis of the information delivered by the price system in a free market shaped by the division of labor, decisions regarding the choice of what to produce, which factors of production to employ, and

something very reasonable and generally accepted. However, with this position, he certainly would not have gained the reputation he received by teaching that the medicine for an ailing patient should also be the ordinary nourishment for ordinary and healthier times; see Wilhelm Röpke. 1952. "Was lehrt Keynes? Die Revolution der Nationalökonomie." *Universitas* Dezember 1952: 1285–1295; reprinted in: Röpke. *Gegen die Brandung*. edited by Albert Hunold, 2. edition (Erlenbach-Zürich: Eugen Rentsch Verlag, 1959), 256–269. See also Röpke's devastating 1934 judgment about the first period of the New Deal, still worthwhile reading: "Die Nationalökonomie des 'New Deal'," first published in *Zeitschrift für Nationalökonomie*, V (1934), 577–595; reprinted in Röpke, *Gegen die Brandung* (quoted above), 60–84.

[10] Note that in September 1931, unemployment amounted to 17.4%; in July 1935, in the fifth year of the New Deal, it had risen to 21.3%, to come down in August 1937 to 13.5%, yet rising again to the initial amount of 17.4% in January 1938. In January 1940, when Roosevelt won reelection to his third term, it was still 14.6%. In the meantime, the Dow Jones Industrial Average was 140 (in 1931), 119 (1935), 187 (1937), 121 (1938), 151 (1940). Before the 1929 crash, it registered at 168 (1927) and 343 (October 1929, immediately before the crash). So, after 8 years of the Roosevelt administration, the New Deal generated only little recovery, and certainly no new prosperity. Moreover, as far as unemployment was concerned, its results were rather poor.

output numbers, as well as the unfettered freedom to invest privately owned monetary assets at one's own risk, motivated by the expectation of future profit.[11]

Contrary to what Keynes wrote, *as such* this entrepreneurial behavior of the real businessman has nothing to do with "money-loving." Even if in most cases love of money, personal enrichment, and what this actually involves are the innermost motive of a capitalist's undertakings – which, however, is by no means necessarily the case, but admittedly very natural and always most probable – it is simply flawed logic to assert that the *motives* or *intentions* with which people do what they are doing is equal to, and the essence of, *what* they are doing. Now, the essence of capitalism is to be seen in *what* a capitalist is actually doing, and not in *why* he does it or what *motivates* him to do it.[12]

Eucken dedicates many pages of his seminal book to criticizing nineteenth-century laissez-faire. However, he elegantly demonstrates that there are both sound and unsound elements in the idea of laissez-faire. The traditional laissez-faire political economy is completely correct in insisting on the freedom of entrepreneurial activity and personal responsibility and the freedom to make typical business decisions. Eucken further shows that this sound element of capitalistic laissez-faire is linked to the idea of free competition – which precisely contradicts

---

[11] With this description, which I admit is a simplification, it is not ignored that in modern, mainly big business companies, the capital owners – mostly shareholders – and those who take the concrete and current entrepreneurial decisions, the top managers, are not the same persons. Yet, this does not change the basic idea of capitalism; it only affects the way the idea is practically carried out. In fact, already in his 1926 anti-laissez-faire pamphlet, quoted earlier, Keynes had noticed that in big companies "the owners of the capital, *i.e.* the shareholders, are almost entirely dissociated from the management, with the result that the direct personal interest of the latter in the making of great profit becomes quite secondary" (Keynes 2004, 38). Keynes applauds this, thinking it to be a first step of big companies toward "socializing themselves," which, as he notes, is one of "the advantages of State Socialism" (Keynes 2004, 39; for other reasons, however, Keynes did not advocate what he called State Socialism). Today, we have come to understand the disadvantages of this kind of "self-socializing" of big companies, that is, of top managers being paid independently from the business success and profit of the companies they direct.

[12] A further differentiation should be made between the "real economy" market and financial markets; yet, as I understand the difference should not be stressed too much, because the nature and aim of financial markets is not just making money, as many people think, but in fact serving and making precisely the "real economy" (through financing, credit, insurance etc.) work. Therefore, financial markets and also speculative activity are, on principle, useful and necessary, and engaging in them is an absolutely honorable profession. In my view, the problem starts when finance transactions and speculation become totally uncoupled from any real economic substratum, that is, when they have no connection anymore to the world of the "real economy" which leads to the creation of economic value. Such a kind of financial speculation is far away from the real entrepreneurial spirit which is characteristic for capitalism; rather than being a long-term project for value creation, as it is typical for capitalism, its only "economical" function rather is to serve short-term personal enrichment. It has been proven to be very dangerous and detrimental to the international finance system to let it, without any further security measures, fall prey to these kind of financial sharks, who are lacking any real entrepreneurial spirit or are perverting this spirit from the inside of great firms (as banks, insurance companies, etc.), and thus are also tending to moral hazard and to taking exaggerated and irrational risks, which an authentic "capitalist" and classic entrepreneur would never take.

a monopolistic structure of the market – and finally depends upon an unfettered price-system as the *sole and unique* regulatory principle of decisions concerning production and consumption (according to the laws of supply and demand). Government intervention aimed at curbing, controlling, or fettering this entrepreneurial liberty, at partially annulling the regulatory role of the price system, or even at competing, through government-run companies, with private business, Eucken argues, is both economically and socially harmful. Hence, it is also essentially opposed to the common good.

On the other side, Eucken contends, the error of nineteenth-century laissez-faire was the conviction – based rather on philosophical, moral, or even theological assumptions (often also on popularized forms of Darwinism, or better: "Spencerism"), than on economic thinking – *that this entrepreneurial freedom alone* could positively establish a complete harmony between private interests and the common good. Therefore, even egoistic motivations were socially beneficial.[13] During the second half of the nineteenth century, united to the Industrial Revolution, capitalism undoubtedly led to unprecedented economic innovation and growth as well as to a constant rise of real wages and the affluence of all social classes (see, e.g., Mathias 1983; Braudel and Labrousse 1976). Yet, several factors, some intrinsic to the logic of the market – and the financial system – and others due to extrinsic causes, primarily harmful state interventions, led to fatal imbalances and distortions of the capitalist economy.

The free coordination of individual interests by market forces, without any ordering and correcting activity by the state, Eucken forcibly argues, does not necessarily and automatically lead to the common good. The free market needs a political framework developed by the state (*Ordnungspolitik*). Despite this, in Eucken's eyes the essential truth of laissez-faire and the insights of the classical theoreticians of economic liberalism remain valid: by undermining and even, although only partially, annulling the spontaneous market-forces through government intervention in the economic process itself, the common good is undermined and positively counteracted.

Thus, Eucken emphasizes, laissez-faire in the sense of entrepreneurial freedom and self-responsibility concerning production decisions, based on the information delivered by the price-system, undistorted by state regulations, is a *necessary* condition for obtaining the common good. Laissez-faire, however, is not a *sufficient* condition and therefore, if other conditions are not met, it cannot be in the public interest and may even be harmful (Eucken 1968, 360).

In other words: Adam Smith's "invisible hand" in fact does work. The invisible hand was actually Adam Smith's landmark discovery. Essentially, it is an argument against the mercantilist economic and trade policy of an absolutistic State, based on the idea that the *visible* hand of the state has to organize the whole economy, thus

---

[13] This was expressed in its purest form by the great French economist Frédéric Bastiat; see, e.g., Bastiat (1851). Note that also Keynes, in his aforementioned pamphlet, interprets capitalism in terms of the Darwinist – that is, "Spencerist" – "survival of the fittest."

creating the wealth and power of a nation.[14] For Adam Smith, instead, the pursuit of self-interest – which, as I argue in detail later, does not necessarily mean egoism – and the division of labor does create a spontaneous order of coordinated activities of supply and demand, regulated by the price system, and an optimal allocation of resources. Therefore, they also most forcefully promote the public interest and the common good. A "visible hand" of politicians and bureaucrats neither exists nor is it needed. There is no system of central planning or any superintelligent human mind which could possibly fulfill this task of coordination, because such coordination *can* only be achieved as the outcome of the whole *system* of, on the level of individual intentionality, uncoordinated and thus "spontaneous" economic transactions.

Now, the point of all this is that in a free market economy, as conceived by Adam Smith, *there is actually no such thing as an invisible hand at all*. The metaphor of the invisible hand only indicates what really and truly *happens* in a market economy. To those who do not understand the mechanism of markets, the division of labor, and free competition, an "invisible hand" *seems* to be there (they seek a "hand" which explains the otherwise seemingly miraculous outcome, according to the logic of conspiracy theories which always look for the "invisible hand": one single cause explaining complex patterns). Yet, in the free market economy, there is no "one hand" which explains the result. In reality, the invisible hand is the feedback system of the "many hands," that is, of the market which, through the price system, spontaneously coordinates private interests in such a way as to concur with an optimal allocation of resources. The hand, thus, is "invisible" because this indicates the market as a kind of black box: we know the result, but, despite knowing the basic mechanism, we are unable to comprehend all the steps having brought it about, precisely *because in none of these steps somebody actually intended to bring it about*.

Adam Smith was not an extremist; but he knew that an individual engaged in business does not, and cannot, intend to promote the public interest. Yet, when Smith writes: "By pursuing his own interest he frequently promotes that of the society more effectually than when he really intends to promote it," (Smith 1979, 456, Book IV, Chap. 2, IV.2) he not only simply describes what obviously happens, but also moderately and wisely says that this is the case only "frequently." In fact, nothing in the idea of the invisible hand denies that laissez-faire is only a necessary, *but not a sufficient*, condition for coordinating private interests, attaining thereby the common good. Further, there is not any denial that there are many circumstances

---

[14] Note that Mandeville's famous "Fable of the Bees" (with its moral "private vices are public benefits"), which is commonly held to be an authentic expression of the *laissez-faire*-ideology and of Adam Smith's invisible hand, actually is based on a mercantilist outlook. This is clarified at the end, where the author remarks that such private vices are certainly beneficial for the public good provided "that Private Vices by the dextrous Management of a skilful Politician may be turn'd into Publick Benefits"! Now, such "dextrous Management of a skilful Politician" is exactly the opposite of Smith's invisible hand! See Mandeville (2010, 371).

and cases in which the invisible hand would not work because some condition for its proper functioning fails.[15]

Unfortunately, there persists a confusing and detrimental attitude of those who, beginning from the insight into the insufficiency of laissez-faire and its unsatisfactory outcome if the market is left to itself, conclude that a free market is *intrinsically* harmful. Thus, entrepreneurial decisions and the regulatory force of the price system should *on principle* be checked by government intervention or even by directly converting the state into a competitor of private business to overcome its alleged egoism and greed of profit – of course by unjustly subsidizing economic state activity with taxpayers' contributions (also with those of citizens engaged in private business who thus are unjustly constrained to subsidize their often, even less efficient, state-run competitors). Such people think that capitalist laissez-faire, instead of being as it actually is, though very imperfectly, a cause of prosperity, is in reality a problem and a cause of misery. This is the great confusion to which Keynes, among economists – Marx, after all, was only a philosopher – has contributed certainly in the most influential way. This is not to deny that the capitalist or free market economy avoids causing problems or undesirable side effects. Yet, these should not be resolved by abolishing or fettering capitalism and the dynamics proper to it, but by making it work better and more efficiently, according to truly just rules so that it can develop its true potential.

1.3 The Free Market: An Order Both Natural to Man and Created, Which Should Be Supervised by the State

The popularity of the anticapitalist bias, which is actually an anti-free-market-economy bias, has survived right up to the present day. People who have no education in basic economics and, therefore, have difficulties in understanding economic logic, commonly believe, generally and as a matter of principle, that *the market is a problem* and that the state, however, is the solution. As Bryan Caplan has shown in his *The Myth of the Rational Voter* (Caplan 2007),[16] citizens of modern democracies apply economic thinking very well in their daily lives, but are much less able to understand it on the level of the public and democratic choice of government policies. Consequently, in crucial issues they vote for bad politics, which is opposed to their

---

[15] When I say *optimal* allocation this precisely does not mean *perfect* allocation. "Optimal" is always relative to concrete circumstances and their constraints. The outcome may also be *suboptimal*, due to market-distorting lacks of equilibrium. It seems to me reasonable to assert, however, that even the suboptimal allocation of resources is usually the best we can achieve in this real world, so that the difference between "optimal" and "suboptimal" becomes rather theoretical. On the other hand, to demand perfection, and to criticize the market economy on these grounds, is unrealistic and intellectually unsound.

[16] Bryan Caplan, *The Myth of the Rational Voter. Why Democracies Choose Bad Politics* (Princeton and Oxford: Princeton University Press, 2007).

own interests. By challenging the myth of the rational voter, Bryan also attacks the whole school of rational choice economics, based on its vision of a *homo oeco-nomicus* who is always and exclusively driven by pure economic rationality, even in his publicly relevant choices.

Bryan Caplan's argument is based on statistical evidence from the USA. (I suppose, however, that some of the biases mentioned by him may even be stronger in quite a few European countries because generally US citizens are much more pro–free market than Europeans who have a much stronger tradition of "state-devoutness" and, thus, of expecting solutions for public needs and social problems to come from the government.) Now, regarding US citizens, Caplan identifies four wide-spread biased beliefs concerning economics. First, he makes out an *antimarket bias*, which is a "tendency to underestimate the economic benefits of the market mechanism" (an expression of the most common error concerning the basic features of markets, trade and the logic of entrepreneurial activity). Secondly, Caplan states an *antiforeigner bias*, "which underestimates the economic benefits of interaction with foreigners," benefits which exist even if foreign countries are much poorer, and which leads to being sympathetic with protectionist policies. Thirdly, Caplan speaks of a *make-work bias*, which leads voters "to underestimate the economical benefits of conserving labor," ignoring that normally the destruction of jobs by bankruptcy of inefficient industries or by downsizing firms in order to increase efficiency and thus secure their survival, rather than being a loss, means economic growth (this bias favors state intervention in favor of maintaining and subsidizing with the taxpayers' money, inefficient enterprises). Finally, he sketches out a *pessimistic bias*, which is "a tendency to overestimate the severity of economic problems and underestimate the (recent) past, present, and future performance of the economy" – a bias readily used by politicians to enhance the agenda of govern-ment intervention, instead of spreading optimism in the creative and innovative forces of freedom (Caplan 2007, 30–49).

Because of the – at least at first glance – counterintuitive character of many basic economic truths, the idea that the market is the problem and the state the solution "is a deeply rooted pattern of human thinking that has frustrated economists for genera-tions" (Caplan 2007, 31) With most, perhaps not all, economists – from F. A. Hayek to Milton Friedman, Amartya Sen to Paul Krugman and even Joseph E. Stiglitz, independently of their belonging to the political right or left – I am convinced that, generally speaking and as a matter of principle, exactly the opposite is true: *normally* and *as a matter of principle* the solution is the market. The problems, however, are created by state and government policies aimed at checking and "correcting" the market mechanism, trying to at least partially replace it by bureau-cratic regulations, or even by the state's seeking to directly participate in the game.[17]

---

[17] Pointing out the failures of financial markets in recent times and taking advantage of the financial crisis, Joseph Stiglitz seems to me to somewhat demagogically overstate the defects and insufficiency of the free market. Also Stiglitz knows well that the State can never do what markets alone are able to do: to assure the optimal allocation of resources. State intervention can help markets to better attain this goal, or correct certain outcomes for political or moral reasons. So, despite his Keynesian view-point (pleading for the state having, as a primary economic goal, the task of assuring

Now, market failures are an obvious fact, but state failures are much more frequent and more harmful. State failures have a tendency to become institutionalized and thus an enduring solution for resolving the problems created by the very government interventions which claimed to remedy alleged market failures. Normally, state failures are less obvious and less perceived – for example, the huge failures of promoting and subsidizing real estate property by the US government through the huge mortgage associations of Fannie Mae and Freddie Mac, most probably one of the main causes, if not the condition sine qua non, of the recent subprime bubble and the following financial crisis. Hence, according to many who have commented on the crisis, the "underpricing of risk," which by providing biased information and nourishing the urges of greedy hunters of short-term gain distorted the financial markets, was greatly caused by previous state intervention (thus, provided this is a correct assessment of what happened, greed was not the *cause*, but already a consequence of, and a reaction to, a government policy creating the conditions to fuel such greed). As far as state failure is concerned, something analogous, although in a different order, seems to apply to the 1929 stock market crash and the following slump. What really caused the Depression and made it Great was not simply the greedy predators on the financial markets – they also had their part in causing the bubble and the 1929 stock exchange crash – but, as mentioned above, previous inflationary credit expansion during the "roaring twenties," causing a cluster of malinvestment and the subsequent state failure in reacting to the slump following the stock exchange crash. According to the Friedman-Schwartz-analysis, these latter failures, attributed to the actions of the Federal Reserve Board (contracting instead of expanding credit) (cf. Ferguson 2008, 158–165),[18] the fatal protectionist measures which converted the US depression into a worldwide economic crisis, the interventionist measures taken by the Hoover administration impeding the readjustment of price–cost relations (including wage rates) and eventually the aforementioned state

---

full employment) Stiglitz also, as an economist, in fact is much more an advocate of the free market than he seems to admit. To call (Stiglitz 2006, XVI) "pollution" or "too little basic research" market failures is not really to the point, because even the most liberal advocates of the free market admit that the market, by itself and without any state regulation, is not able to internalize external effects like pollution, or to provide sufficient resources for research and education. See also Stiglitz (2010), where it becomes rather evident that Stiglitz has no real alternative to offer to the market economy; his proposals are rather moral appeals than concrete proposals for institutional alternatives to the market economy.

[18] Ferguson also refers to Friedman and Schwartz (1963) (an explanation, however, not accepted by the adherents to the Austrian theory of business cycles). As Niall Ferguson argues, there were similar stock exchange crashes also after the Second World War, but they never caused a depression as the reaction of the government was quite different; the lesson of the period following 1929 had been well learned. But this also signifies that the catastrophic effect of the 1929 crash was not so much due to a failure of capitalism, but rather to state failures regarding government reaction to a speculative bubble, which periodically and perhaps inevitably occurs in societies in which the government together with central banks has control over the money supply, being able to inflate it for political reasons. This monetary system, as such, has nothing to do with capitalism or the market economy; both developed without it. It is rather a perhaps inevitable, but very dangerous, political decision.

activities and regulations of the New Deal, were the real causes of the disaster (though regarding this last point, perhaps also for obvious ideological reasons, there seems to be less consensus among historians). Contrarily, having at least partially learned from history, at present we are amazed at how rapidly and relatively spontaneously – at least outside the United States, in countries which have reacted with much less state stimulation of the economy – the market forces have succeeded in overcoming not only the 2008 financial crisis but also the worldwide recession and the contraction of international trade it caused (though it should be noted that it is not clear whether this recovery will be sustainable, considering not only the huge state-indebtedness of most European countries in the Euro-zone but also that of the United Kingdom and the structural imbalances among them, which are still a menace for the success of this monetary community, their economies, and the survival of their social security systems).

Now, to say that the market is the solution, admittedly, is not true for all economic und much less for all social problems. And it is certainly not to say that the state is *always* the problem while the market is *never* a problem. As liberals from Adam Smith to F. A. Hayek have noted, the logic of capitalism and the market mechanism certainly do not suffice for providing those public goods which are necessary, but cannot be provided by private initiative "because the profit could never repay the expense to any individual or small number of individuals, though it might frequently do much more than repay it to a great society" (Smith 1979, 688, IV.9; Hayek 2007, 87; see also Friedman 1982, 22–36). Therefore, no private businessman will reasonably engage in them. Something similar applies to external costs which can be internalized and thus managed only by legal measures and regulations imposed by the state.

Yet, there is more to say than what Adam Smith said – not in opposition to his basic insight into the nature of the free market as a system of *spontaneous* coordination of private interests in benefit of the public interest or common good, an outcome which, however, is *not intended by individual actors*. But Adam Smith – still living in a preindustrialized world dominated by agriculture, manufacture, and traditional trade and ignoring the effects of the Industrial Revolution and the antagonism of interests between employers and wage earners typical for the era of industrialized capitalism – still believed that by the market mechanism "the obvious and simple system of natural liberty establishes itself of its own accord" (Smith 1979, 466, IV.9). Better informed by historical experience and the intrinsic shortcomings, failures and imperfections of the market mechanism under conditions of industrialized capitalism, we have to add that the assertion that the market is the solution and the state is the problem is correct if, and only if, *there exists a real and functioning market*, that is, an order of competition not perverted by monopolistic structures (including the labor market!) and a price-system providing reliable information not only for the allocation of resources and entrepreneurial decision making, but also for the choices to be made by consumers. The most important insight of Walter Eucken's "ordoliberalism" (which in many aspects is close to Friedrich A. Hayek's "Catallactics" (see Hayek 1982) or even Milton Friedman's vision of capitalism as an order of freedom (see Friedman 1982), and certainly very close to what in Germany after the second World War successfully developed as *Soziale Marktwirtschaft*) is the following: *a market can only be a system of coordinating individual choices to the benefit of the common good if there exists a legal and economic order imposed and enforced by the state which creates and guarantees by legal and political measures an order of free competition.*

This is achieved not only by providing a legal framework – enforceable rules of the game – and the basis of a sound monetary and fiscal system with the corresponding institutions and policies, such as central banks which ensure the stability of the monetary system, even though this is the most important part. It also requires an active government politics of guaranteeing the functioning of the price-system and the existence of a functioning order of competition freed from the distortions caused by monopolistic concentration, cartels, and trusts. As Adam Smith already had remarked, it is intrinsic to business activity to try to overrule and even to eliminate competitors by collusion and creating cartels (this is most effectively and unjustly done by government itself, when it becomes a competitor of private business). According to Eucken, the market therefore possesses an intrinsic tendency to destroy itself. It does not naturally and necessarily tend to harmony between private and public interest, even though *the market mechanism* as such is precisely the means for bringing private and public interest into a certain correspondence – provided, to say it again, the market mechanism really works.

Eucken's main point is that in our real world and because of its inherent logic the market itself cannot guarantee the upholding of the functioning of its mechanism without support from public authorities. This is not properly a defect of the market mechanism, but a limitation due to a defect of the world in which this mechanism has to work and which it cannot remedy by itself. It is a consequence of the human condition. Freedom tries to use this mechanism against its proper logic of fair exchange, that is, unfairly or taking advantages of imperfect information or positions of power. Human beings tend to use – or abuse – good things in a way which renders them harmful for others and the community. Notice that this economic vision is embedded in wider anthropological presuppositions. Interestingly enough, it opens the way to seeing how human virtues and ethical behavior in general might and should be the necessary and salutary corrective of the factual forces of the market mechanism.[19]

Because of his deeply anthropological outlook, Eucken is very close to the perhaps most important twentieth-century representative of the Austrian school of economics, Ludwig von Mises, whose economic theory is a widely anthropological and action theory (Mises 1949). This is a truly humanistic approach to economics. Though being perhaps flawed and, in some respects one-sided,[20] nevertheless it provides an

---

[19] This is the basic idea of Peter Koslowski's excellently argued and, in my view, highly recommendable *Prinzipien der Ethischen Ökonomie* (Tübingen: J. C. B. Mohr – Paul Siebeck, 1988); English edition: *Principles of Ethical Economy*, (Dordrecht: Springer Netherlands, 2000). Koslowski, a disciple of Robert Spaemann, holds degrees both in economy and philosophy.

[20] See a good critique of these insufficiencies in Koslowski (1988, 205–207 *et passim*).

impressive corrective to rational choice-economists who, like Gary Becker – and unlike Adam Smith[21] – perceive human beings only as *homo oeconomicus*.[22]

The conclusion is thus: the goal of state politics ought to be to render the market an efficient tool by securing the correct functioning of the market mechanism.[23] This is not equal to creating "social justice" but to efficiently coordinating individual interests and the allocation of resources (the outcome of market processes is to be called neither "just" nor "unjust"; only the *rules* of the game can be just or unjust. The outcome, however, can be called "desirable" or "undesirable," also for moral reasons. Thus these outcomes can reasonably call for correction). Consequently, a functioning free market order is not a solution for problems of "social justice." Rather, it is a necessary and indispensable, or at least the best, presupposition for being able to achieve, with additional *political* measures, the maximum possible approximation of what we usually, but sometimes misleadingly, call the require-ments of "social justice" and should better be called demands of *solidarity*. Nobody is really able to clearly define the content of "social justice," because it is a matter which – in a world of limited and even scarce resources – is by its very nature highly controversial and about whose requirements reasonable people can certainly hold different views. Moreover, it seems to me difficult to reasonably hold that less well-off people and those in real need have properly a *right* to corrections of the outcome of market processes by redistributive measures – that is, that they properly have a *right* to get a share of the property of other people – and that such redistribution thus is a demand of *justice* properly spoken. I rather think that the correction of market outcomes by redistribution is to be grounded on an *obligation* – a *moral* obligation – of solidarity of the better-off toward the needy, an obligation citizens justly and reasonably delegate to democratically controlled public authorities to be carried out on their behalf by redistributive measures (whose amount and limitations are to be measured precisely by the criterion of the moral obligation of solidarity of those better-off toward the worse-off, not by the criterion of some pattern or program of an egalitarian "just society").[24]

As has been already mentioned, such a vision is based on essential anthropo-logical assumptions which, among other things, also involve the principle of sub-sidiarity. The market economy is *natural* to human beings (in the sense of *secundum*

---

[21] Amartya Sen argues very well against the view that Adam Smith favored the idea of *homo oeconomicus*; see Sen's (2009, 184ff.) recent book *The Idea of Justice* (Cambridge, Mass.: Harvard University Press, 2009), 184ff.

[22] An interesting comparison between the different liberal systems of Ludwig von Mises and Gary Becker can be found in Aranzadi (2006).

[23] I do not, as I should, differentiate between the "real economy" markets and financial markets: the latter are a special case and, as far as I can judge, need also, if ever, a different kind of regulation and protection.

[24] See more about this in Rhonheimer (1998, 57–122); an English version of this essay ("The Constitutional Democratic State and the Common Good") will be included in my forthcoming *The Common Good of Constitutional Democracy: Essays in Political Philosophy and on Catholic Social Teaching*.

naturam), but the market itself is not something "natural" in the sense of being "naturally given" (*a natura*). It must be organized, arranged, ordered, controlled and protected by the governing part of society, that is, the public authority of the state and its legal system. The market, though being based on the natural tendency of human beings to enter into relations of exchange and barter and thereby an attempt at a coordination of interests, is more than something spontaneously created by human natural inclinations: it is also and always *an institution* created by the legal system, by the obtaining culture, and by the ordering political framework activity of the state.[25]

In order to settle this point with conceptual clarity, Walter Eucken helpfully distinguishes between two fundamentally different kinds of economic action aiming also at pursuing two different goals: first, "the shaping of the *forms of order* of an economy" (*Gestaltung der Ordnungsformen der Wirtschaft*), and secondly, "the direction of the economic process" (*die Lenkung des Wirtschaftsprozesses*). The former task, that is, shaping the forms of economic order (like creating a legally ordered market and an order of free competition and guaranteeing this order with a policy aiming at maintaining such an order, not at *replacing* or *directing* its inner mechanism by state interventions and bureaucratic regulations), is properly the task of government, backed by the legal system and its coercive power. The latter, that is, directing the economic process itself, is the task of the market, the price system and the incentives it provides for the producer's and consumer's decisions, with the following allocation of resources according to the real needs of those who participate in the market.

This means that neither the state and state activity nor even state intervention *as such*, nor its amount and intensity, is a problem, but the *quality*, the meaning and the aim of such intervention.[26] The state transgresses the limits of its proper tasks when instead of organizing, ordering and – mainly by the suppression of monopolistic structures, collusion and cartels, as far as this is possible – protecting the market as a system of free coordination of the interests of free citizens and economic actors, it tries to take over part or the whole of the function of the market. The State does so by participating in the economic process itself, regulating entrepreneurial decisions or intervening in the price-system and thereby depriving it of its function of providing reliable information for produces and consumers; such a State, Eucken's ordo-liberalism contends, certainly acts in detriment to the common good. As far as I can judge, this position seems to me to be basically sound.

---

[25] Some of these features of the market are happily, though in my opinion also somewhat haphazardly, expressed in chapter three of Benedict XVI's encyclical *Caritas in veritate* to which I will briefly return below.

[26] This was already expressed by Ludwig von Mises (1929); Mises clearly distinguishes e.g., between the nationalization of some means of production or a railway company (which is not an "intervention" in his sense) and a state-induced change of the economic factors, that is, a state command which forces the private owners of means of production to employ them in a way which is different from the one they would have chosen if no such command existed (see Mises 1929, 5f.).

1.4   The Systemic Conflict Between Economic and Political Logic

Now, what has been outlined so far is not the whole story. One problem of Walter Eucken's vision of ordoliberalism is certainly that in the real world it will never be possible to have perfect competition: a market free from any monopolistic or oligopolistic structures. The idea that producers normally are bound to *take* the price for which they sell *from* the market, does not correspond to reality, or at least, it does not usually correspond to all sectors of a market economy. It is, therefore, important, not to have a too idealistic picture of a real market economy. In many cases, producers who have a factually monopolistic position can *give* or *dictate*, or at least *influence*, the price for which they sell their products. Thus, the market is not, and can never be, the perfect mechanism it should be. This in no way diminishes its real merits, however. Moreover, there is no reasonable alternative to the free market economy. As Milton Friedman noticed, even though monopolies are bad, they are sometime inevitable, and so we have to choose between three evils: private monopoly, public monopoly or public regulation. While Walter Eucken opted for public regulation, Friedman thinks that "private monopoly may be the least of the evils" (Friedman 1982, 28).

Yet, I wish to leave such questions to economists; this also applies to the burdensome question to what extent it is possible to neatly distinguish between acts of "shaping the forms of order" and acts of "directing the economic process" (much depends on whether one believes, as Keynes and his Keynesian followers did, in the possibility and efficiency of the macroeconomic steering of the concrete process of the economy). There is a second problem, however, which needs to be mentioned here and which I wish to briefly tackle. It is the *problem of democracy*, related to economics. Like markets, democracy is a very imperfect political system, though without a real alternative. Winston Churchill famously said: "Many forms of Government have been tried and will be tried in this world of sin and woe. No one pretends that democracy is perfect or all-wise. Indeed, it has been said that democracy is the worst form of government except all those other forms that have been tried from time to time."[27] This may be criticized as a common place complaint or a truism, justifying scandalous inequalities and the lack of social justice. Be that as it may, one of democracy's imperfections is that there is *a gap between the logic of economy and the logic of democratic politics*. Roughly speaking – and perhaps at a first glance this may sound odd – real and cold economic logic essentially and on principle aims at serving the common good, that is, the *long-term* outcome and interests of the *whole* of society while the logic of politics is rather focused on *short-term* outcome and *group* interests.

Let us not fool ourselves by appearances: apart from *Ordnungspolitik* in Walter Eucken's understanding (the politics of shaping and securing the form of

---

[27] Winston Churchill, Speech in the House of Commons 11.11.1947, in: *The Official Report, House of Commons* (5th Series), 11 November 1947, vol. 444, 206–207.

the economic order) and except for providing evidently necessary public goods, there is no such thing as an *economic* politics capable of directly aiming at and realizing the common good (I said *economic* politics, not excluding there being *other kinds* of politics, for example, social, or redistributionist, actually aiming at the common good). As seems to be now largely accepted by most economists, the Keynesian idea widely practiced in the decades after the Second World War, the macroeconomic steering of the economy, has been proven to be doomed to failure. As far as the allocation of material resources and the satisfaction of material needs is concerned – which up to a certain point is the supposition for satisfying higher human needs – only the economic logic of the market, that is, the logic of the coordination of individual plans pursuing individual interests regulated by the price system, can do the job.

For politics, however, it is typical to serve rather short-term goals, the interests and needs of determinate groups whose claims are perceived, sometimes by means of public persuasion, as being identical with the common good. This is not only a problem of modern democracies, but it also was the case during eighteenth century absolutism and its mercantilist politics. As Adam Smith forcefully criticized in his *Inquiry into the Nature and Causes of the Wealth of Nations*, the mercantilist system unilaterally served the interests of the state and the established groups of producers, manufacturers, tradesmen, etc. It did not, however, favor the interests of consumers, which were the needs of the broad population. Yet, as it seems to me, *the goal of the economy* is neither public enrichment, nor production, nor the satisfying of producers' interests; it is not even the creation of jobs and the provision of labor opportunities. The goal of the economy is *consumption*, that is, the satisfying of the needs of *all* the persons living in a determinate territory. Production, jobs, and the supply of produced commodities and services are supposed to serve concrete needs and the corresponding demand. Therefore, it seems to me to be unsound to conversely think of the economy as a system of demand or purchase power *with the goal of creating production, supply, and jobs*. This would be doing things back to front. In this manner, full employment cannot be a reasonable *goal* of the economy. About whether it is a reasonable means, *auctores disputant*, I would tend to rather adhere to the arguments of those who assert that it is not – not only for economic but also for moral reasons.

One may of course consider jobs and employment – opportunities to work – as a basic need of human persons, corresponding to their dignity, and even a moral right, and thus think of a policy of full employment as satisfying such a need and basic right of the human person. Yet, this would not be an *economic* policy, but one which is part of social politics, guided by moral principles. Even if it is believed to be politically or socially just, it can still be economically unsound. Consider, however, that also from a political, "social," or moral viewpoint, only the provision of *useful* and *economically efficient* jobs makes sense and thus corresponds to human dignity. Performing, even with the help of public funding, a useless job *is not dignifying*. Now, the politics of full employment are mostly based on the creation of jobs by inflating bureaucracies or work opportunities created by government programs, whose usefulness is at least very doubtful, or by supporting inefficient and ailing industries. This is both economically harmful and – precisely from the viewpoint of "social justice" – morally problematic, because it is tantamount to subsidizing with public funds inefficient and useless jobs *at the expense of other useful and efficiently working sectors of the economy*. Rather than subsidizing ailing industries or companies, it would be much more just, and thus morally upright in such cases, to let inefficient firms go bankrupt, and instead use public funds to help those who thereby lose their jobs in finding new and useful employment, even by subsidizing programs of retraining. This is why it seems to me possible to reasonably and in a morally justified way hold that a certain amount of unemployment is both economically healthy and socially just (to say it again: provided the unemployed are not simply forgotten, but rather supported in obtaining new jobs or in being retrained).

The problem is that this kind of economically sound logic aims at long-term and overall effects. Fighting for them is politically not very rewarding. Another example of politically unrewarding economic logic is the argument that *in the long run* free trade is always better than protectionism *for everybody*.[28] This is why Princeton's *emeritus* professor in International Political Economy, Robert Gilpin, has written that "Economists of every persuasion are convinced that free trade is superior to trade protection" (Gilpin 2001, 196) and why according to the rather left-wing liberal economist Alan Blinder, from Princeton as well, "enthusiasm for free trade is axiomatic to economists" (Blinder 1987, 111). Yet, in a short-term perspective, without considering all sectors of the economy, but only a determinate group, protectionism actually may be advantageous –for the time being. Politics, mainly democratic politics, aims at serving determinate groups of producers, industries, and their employees. They normally fail to serve the interests of consumers, and they certainly hurt other industries, which are not protected or aided by these measures. These protected interests are normally articulated in short-term perspectives and, in such a restricted perspective, may seem plausible and thus become popular.[29] But in the long run, policies of protectionism or the public subsidizing of ailing industries to conserve jobs also harm the interests of those they first pretended to serve. So, from the outset and on principle, as well as in regard to the *common* good, they are certainly harmful.[30] This is why political logic in so many cases does not promote

---

[28] The main arguments against protectionism and in defense of free trade can be found (apart from standard textbooks of international economics like Krugman and Obstfeld (2009)) in Irwin (2002) and Bhagwati (2002).

[29] In his 1926 pamphlet (page 33), Keynes also actually rejected protectionism – together with Marxian Socialism ("a doctrine so illogical and so dull") – as a "poor quality" opponent proposal to laissez-faire.

[30] So Alan Blinder – not a right-wing economist, nor a conservative, but a liberal (in the American sense) – says about protectionism: "… protectionism's allure stems not from the economics of the national interest, but from the politics of special interests. Politics turns trade policies that are economic turkeys into political peacocks. But to understand why, we must look beyond the abstract arguments for and against free trade to the specific lists of winners and losers from protection. Then we will see that trade protection secures concentrated and highly visible gains for a small minority by imposing diffuse and almost invisible costs on a vast and unknowing majority. That makes protectionism at once economically graceless and politically fetching" (Blinder 1987, 112).

the common good – even though politicians emphatically invoke the common good for advancing their agenda and denounce economic thinking as egoistic, serving only the interests of the rich. Again, according to Alan Blinder, the problem of politicians – and voters – choosing bad economic policies is not just "bad luck, bad judgment," or due to "human errors," but it is "rather systemic": "Economic policy is made by politicians, not by economists – which is just as it should be in a democracy. But politicians do not accept and reject economists' advice at random. They choose solutions that they perceive to be politically correct. Unfortunately, there seems to be a systematic tendency for good economics to make bad politics" (Blinder 1987, 3).

This is not the whole story, however. Sometimes and in some way, political decisions which run against economic logic may perhaps be justified or inevitable. The clearest case is wartime: a war economy is in itself an economic absurdity and economically harmful, yet it may be to a certain extent necessary as a short-term or emergency policy in order to win a war. Unfortunately, governments and the bureaucracies created by them like state-controlled war economy so they tend to conserve its structures also during peace time (this first happened, mainly in Germany, after the First World War, and in many countries, especially in the USA, it was repeated after the Second World War as well). Moreover, if they are big and important enough, the subsidizing or saving of ailing companies by the government with the taxpayers' funds is, more in Europe however than in the USA, very popular, though certainly opposed to the common good in terms of long-term and overall economic benefits (because, as aforementioned, helping a determinate industry or saving a determinate company inevitably hurts other sectors of the economy and other companies who by this are penalized for being more efficient). For example, maybe it would have been more advantageous for the world economy, for poorer countries, and for future generations if the US government had let General Motors go bankrupt and disappear. For obvious reasons, however, this would have been at the moment *politically* a very risky option because of the social problems it would have immediately caused. But there are good reasons to think that, regarding the *common good*, it would have been both economically more efficient and socially more just. In this special case, it would have possibly been even more popular, not in the Detroit region, but everywhere else in the United States, because US citizens are not happy about the government spending their money to save an inefficient and poorly managed industry (and are now – in August 2010, when this was written – expecting the government to sell the factually nationalized GM at a decent price on the stock market by its forthcoming IPO[31]).

As Henry Hazlitt noticed in his classic *Economics in One Lesson* – first published in 1946 – it was a mistake of classical economists not to perceive the deep divergence between economic and the political logic. This led them to overlook the endemic political inefficiency of economic arguments and, thus, to neglect trying to make economic thinking more accessible and more popular. "The art of

---

[31] "Initial Public Offering" (at the stock exchange).

economics" – Hazlitt explains – "consists in looking not merely at the immediate but at the longer effects of any act or policy; it consists in tracing the consequences of that policy not merely for one group, but for all groups" (Hazlitt 1979, 17). All economic fallacies, Hazlitt argues, "stem from one of two central fallacies, or both: that of looking only at the immediate consequences of an act or proposal, and that of looking at the consequences only for a particular group to the neglect of other groups." Hazlitt superbly illustrates this fallacy in all of its different variations, pointing out the counterproductive and sometimes even absurd consequences of widely accepted and practiced yet fallacious economic policies (like price fixing, the subsidizing of ailing industries, protectionism, etc.). Hazlitt, however, does not close his eyes to the political viewpoint and its merits. In fact, he remarks: "It is true, of course, that the opposite error is possible. In considering a policy, we ought not to concentrate *only* in its long-run results to the community as a whole. This is the error often made by the classical economists. It resulted in a certain callousness toward the fate of groups that were immediately hurt by policies or developments which proved to be beneficial on net balance and in the long run" (Hazlitt 1979, 17).

There actually exists a conflict, often ignored by free market economists, between the logic of economics and that of politics. Economics is grounded on a specific technical rationality aimed at optimizing overall benefits. As mentioned above, and perhaps somewhat ironically, an economics which is aimed at optimizing the *overall* and *long-term* effects of the economy *in its totality*, and not only regarding the interests of determinate groups, is in the highest degree focused precisely on the *common good*. Simultaneously, however, economic thinking seems callous and coldly contemptuous, as Hazlitt wrote, "toward the fate of groups that were immediately hurt by policies or developments which proved to be beneficial on net balance and in the long run." Politics, on the other hand, both democratic and autocratically plebiscitarian politics, aim at satisfying the needs of the moment and of those groups who are able to most convincingly persuade a majority that their interest is a common or public interest. This is why politicians rather focus on short-term effects and effects regarding determinate social groups and their actual problems (mainly the groups which hold out the prospect of the best election returns). *Long-term* common good and the interests of *all parts* of society, as well as the interests of *future generations*, tend to be taken into account only insofar as this is politically profitable – according to Keynes' well-known, somewhat cynical comment that, after all, "in the long run we are all dead." [32]

Economic and political logic, then, are often in mutual conflict. The political logic is in most cases *economically* unsound; but it is popular and promises to promote social justice. Unfortunately, though, it normally produces undesired long-term effects which run directly afoul of the original intentions of those who supported the corresponding policies and turn out to be neither social nor just. On the other

---

[32] The above quoted dictum "in the long run we are all dead" is considered cynical because future generations are not even born yet but will have to pay for what we are doing now.

side, economic logic is often rather counterintuitive and seemingly hard-hearted and "socially cold." The long-term advantages – even for the particular industries or sectors of trade that economic logic will hurt in the short-term – are not generally understood so that usually to advocate and promote the corresponding policies turns out to be politically suicidal.[33]

This is a real dilemma, which, however, is not to be understood as an argument against democracy. Nondemocratic regimes usually behave even worse in this respect, or at least *not sustainably* well (because dictators or otherwise authoritarian regimes systematically tend to undermine, or to neglect to build, the institutions warranting long-term sustainability of reasonable policies). After all, democracies are able to change majorities, and thus lead to a certain learning effect. At the very least, democratic politics tend to correct one error with its contrary, which is not the best of politics either, yet perhaps in many cases brings about acceptable results in the form of only limited harm. Moreover, liberal democracy, based on political freedom, participation, and majority rule, is still the best, if not the only appropriate, environment for a good and successful market economy. The market economy is an exercise in freedom and thus supposes institutions securing freedom.

We should never forget: both liberal constitutional democracy and the free, capitalistic market economy do not simply aim at maximizing "technical" efficiency. They first of all are based on, and aim at, securing freedom – individual freedom – convinced that only in a society in which this freedom is trump, social justice can finally be realized as much as possible in this broken and imperfect world.[34]

1.5 Capitalist Economy, Social Justice, and Catholic Social Doctrine: Traditional Misunderstandings and the Genesis of a New Vision of the Role of the State

The historical record seems to be clear: during the last two centuries, the capitalist free market economy and free trade without tariff barriers have continuously improved the conditions of life of *all social levels*, *always* and *everywhere*. Conversely, all kinds of state interventionism, bureaucratic planning of the economy,

---

[33] To have systematically studied these interconnections between the economy and democratic politics is the merit of the work of Bruno S. Frey and his school; see, e.g., Frey (1981); Frey (1983); Frey and Kirchgässner (2001).

[34] See for this the classical liberal "monument," F. A. Hayek. 2001 (*The Constitution of Liberty.* Chicago: The University of Chicago Press). Even if there may be considerable shortcomings and flaws from an anthropological viewpoint, and considering that Hayek is little sensitive to Hazlitt's above-mentioned caveat concerning "the error often made by the classical economists," that is, "a certain callousness toward the fate of groups that were immediately hurt by policies or developments which proved to be beneficial on net balance and in the long run," the merits of this book remain beyond discussion. In order to be able to criticize Hayek for such shortcomings, one has first to well understand the merits of his approach and to reach his level of learning and argument.

and socialism (or semi-socialism) have deteriorated conditions of life and welfare of *all social levels, always* and *everywhere*. Paradoxically, however, people generally think the opposite is true: that capitalism is good only for the rich, and that, if not checked and contained, it causes progressive pauperization of the masses. It was Karl Marx to have most effectively promoted this distorted view, based on a profoundly mistaken analysis of the capitalist economy – and not a few Christians as well as Catholics, "left-wing" and conservative, have been influenced by this view.

Yet, all the Marxist predictions about the pauperization of the working class as well as the *eherne Lohngesetz* (the *Iron Law of Wages*) formulated by the German socialist Ferdinand Lasalle (1825–1864) have been refuted by history. However, this prejudice still exists, working in the heads of a great many number of people although historians know perfectly well that it is not true. The same applies to the merits of free trade as it has been theoretically grounded by the English economist David Ricardo and his law of "comparative advantage" (a principle already known and expressed by Adam Smith). In practice, this principle was successfully promoted by the "Manchester school," another name for Richard Cobden's Anti-Corn Law League, which was later to be much defamed and condemned as "Manchester liberalism." During the second half of the nineteenth century, thus, free trade became a spectacular motor of economic progress, with a continuous rise of real wages at *all* social levels and a general increase in welfare. Where it created mutual bonds and interdependence between trading countries, it also secured peace in a way unknown in earlier periods. The renowned historian Eric Hobsbawm, himself a Marxist, writes that the spectacular expansion of world trade in the second half of the nineteenth century really benefitted all countries, "even if it benefitted the British disproportionately." It was the first and definitive step to globalization, "the creation of a single expanded world." At its root was "the liberation of private enterprise, the engine which, by common agreement, powered the progress of industry" (Hobsbawm 1997, 47–54). This was the presupposition to overcoming the living conditions of preindustrialized society which, we should not forget, sometimes and in some places were much more miserable than the sometimes miserable conditions during the process of industrialization (though, the first period of English industrialization – the period of so-called pauperism – cannot be compared with the second half of the nineteenth century, precisely the *liberal* "age of capital").[35]

So, as history teaches, a capitalist economy based on a free market, entrepreneurial creativity, and free trade without tariff barriers is more realistic and in the long run more beneficial for everybody. State interventionism, socialism, and protection of job opportunities by tariffs and strict regulations of the labor market (as exaggerated protection against wrongful dismissal), though they may look charitable, socially just, and benevolent, focus exclusively on a just and equal distribution of the cake. However, they are not concerned with the effective production and enlargement of this common cake. In reality, they rather tend to be harmful in the long-run, especially for the less advantaged, and thus to undermine the common

---

[35] As to living conditions in preindustrialized England – which were rather diverse according to the time and place – see Laslett (2000, especially Chap. 6 (122–152): "Did the peasants really starve? Famine and pestilence amongst English people in the pre-industrial past").

good – even if normally this becomes evident only to the next generations (or at least when the next election round approaches). This is not to say that in the past, socialist pressure, or pressure by the syndicates, creating legal protection of the workers and the improvement of working conditions, has not been necessary and beneficial precisely for relieving the often callous economic logic of capitalism toward determinate groups and their short-term needs. Yet, we have also to add that true and unfettered capitalism and free international trade has existed only during a very short period in history: between 1850 and 1870. We do not know how nineteenth-century laissez-faire capitalism would have developed without the First World War, which was the beginning of intense and lasting state interventionism in the economy of all countries, and of the modern welfare state (which in Germany began already with Bismarck's social laws, which, though being beneficial for workers, was in the first place meant to be a political tool for stopping the socialists).

One problem with economic progress is that it creates inequality. By sound economic transactions, the rich become even richer, even though the poor profit as well. If I have 100 and start trading with you who have only 10 and both of us thereby increase our wealth by, say, 10%, I will afterward have 110 and you 11. So, the gap between us has increased. Yet, the bargain may be beneficial for both: having now 11 instead of 10 increases your potential for sustainable growth and for doing business with others. Generally speaking, it is thus a question of promoting sound political and economic incentives and environments favorable for investment in order that the wealth of the rich may become the motor of progress for the poor. Yet, there is an egalitarian logic of envy which, against any economic logic, prefers to rather expropriate the rich by exaggerated measures of redistribution in order to create "social justice," instead of encouraging them to enlarge the cake by investment and entrepreneurial activity. This, again, is the fruit of the great confusion of thinking that capitalism as such is a *problem* which must be resolved by government intervention, checking the profit greed of capitalists. Again, this is not to deny that capitalism and the market economy do cause problems which have to be solved by government policies and, in the sense of basic solidarity, even redistributive measures (see Rhonheimer 1998). The problem is not material inequality but *inequality in rights and opportunities* which make it impossible for individual persons or whole social groups to participate in the market and the way in which economic inequality is managed so that, rather than harmful, it becomes beneficial also for the less well-off.

For several decades, anticapitalist and antimarket biases were rather typical for Catholic Social Doctrine. In 1931, in his encyclical *Quadragesimo anno*, Pope Pius XI rejected the idea that "in the market, i.e., in the free struggle of competitors" the economy has "a principle of self direction which governs it much more perfectly than would the intervention of any created intellect." The encyclical acknowledges that free competition is "justified and certainly useful provided it is kept within certain limits"; it however bluntly declares that free competition "clearly cannot direct economic life" and that therefore other principles of regulation of the economy must be sought. These are, as the encyclical teaches, "social justice" and "social love" which are "loftier and nobler principles" and which "public authority ought to be ever ready effectively to protect and defend" (Pius XI 1931, 88).

Now, the idea that it is not the market forces based on free competition and the price system, but the government, by implementing programs of social justice and love, which is to be the regulatory or directive principle of the economic process itself, seems to be economically unsound. We can, of course, read *Quadragesimo anno* in terms of ordoliberalism – the formulations used by the encyclical actually admit of a broad interpretation – but this is not what the text really says, and it is not as it was immediately understood.[36] Its critique of the monopolistic and "dictatorial" structure of capitalism at this time was certainly to a large extent justified. However the encyclical did not distinguish between "free competition" and such a system. The system Pius XI criticized was not exactly a system of free competition, but one of domination by monopolies and a high degree of political control by large firms. Now, the role of the state cannot be to *replace* competition and the price system by another regulatory principle like "social justice" and "social love" promoted by public authority; it is rather to destroy the monopolistic structure of the economy and to reestablish, as far as this is possible, a real order of competition. Afterward, and complementary to this, social justice and social love may come in and perhaps *correct* the outcome of market processes, or else *compensate* for their undesired side effects. They are unable, however, to replace free competition and the price system – and with them the laws of supply and demand – as the directing and regulatory principle of the economy without gravely damaging the common good.

As the 1931 encyclical *Quadragesimo anno* at least implicitly delegitimized the directive and regulatory role of competition and the price system on the free market of a national economy, the 1967 encyclical *Populorum progressio* by Pope Paul VI delegitimized it on the international level of free trade. Again, this is how the encyclical *was understood* when it appeared (something I remember perfectly: it was commonly praised by pro-socialists as a left-wing encyclical). Like *Quadragesimo anno*, *Populorum progressio* was right in rejecting a kind of economic liberalism which believed in the automatically harmonious self-regulation of markets. The evil, however, was again located in the wrong place, that is, in free competition and capitalist profit-making (cf. Paul VI 1967, 26). Here again it must be emphasized that free competition is good and beneficial. The problem is not *competition*, but the lack of an order provided by a legal framework and of just rules – in this case international treaties or a legal framework as provided by the WTO – by capital flows, caused by political instability, into more secure countries; by public indebtedness; by distorted market structures, typically caused by the anticompetitive behavior of global monopolies[37] and – most importantly – the protectionism of the rich countries

---

[36] See, e.g., the commentary on the encyclical by its main drafter (Nell-Breuning 1932, 166–173).

[37] See Stiglitz (2006, 200) (a nice example of how even a left-wing and Keynesian liberal cannot help emphasizing the importance of the competitive structures of a free market and even referring to Adam Smith who has clearly seen the problem): "The problem of anti-competitive behavior has been evident since the birth of economics: as Adam Smith put it, 'People of the same trade seldom meet together, even for merriment and diversion, but the conversation ends in a conspiracy against the public, or in some contrivances to raise prices.' When there is a lack of competition, the potential for abuses of multinationals grows much worse."

which closes their markets to the products of agriculture and manufacture of poorer countries (not always openly with tariffs, though, but sometimes by imposing so-called fair trade or antidumping laws, or by enforcing, even through WTO rules, environmental or labor standards and corresponding restrictions for imported products).[38] Profit as the "motor" of entrepreneurial activity is not the problem. Rather, it is state regulations and other factors which impede or discourage capital owners from taking the risk of investing in such economies. *Populorum progressio* unfortunately promoted the idea that free trade is not really beneficial for poor countries (Paul VI 1967, 58). It is true that not *only* the establishment of free trade is sufficient to secure the progress of poor countries. Free market and free trade *alone* do not do the job. The approach must be more complex and multifaceted.[39] But this does not negate the fact that free trade is always beneficial for everybody and a *necessary*, though not a sufficient, condition precisely for poor countries to develop economically and socially.[40]

Admittedly, Catholic social thinking contains an admirable outlook on solidarity and the fulfillment of the human person in all its dimensions. Moreover, the social doctrine of the Church rightly stresses the importance of the common good. These features, however strangely, combine with a long-lasting opposition against the soundness of economic logic and the logic of business. Among other things, this bias was certainly based on the confusion, in a way connatural for theologians but not confined to them alone (see the case of Keynes), between self-interest and egoism.[41]

We have to remember that for Adam Smith, self-interest was not the only motivation of human behavior. He clearly did not hold the idea of *homo oeconomicus*. Self-interest only dominates, according to him, in actions of *exchange*. But he also speaks of many other motivations underlying people's acts, like sympathy, humanity, justice, generosity, and public spirit (Smith 1976, 190f.).[42] Yet, as I will argue below, even self-interest is not necessarily selfishness or egoism, but rather the typically economic way most of us think in everyday life.

But before addressing this topic, let me try to make the following point: it seems to me essential to notice that already the very idea underlying "capitalism" is something *structurally* non-egoistic and rather social and beneficial for others (even if the concrete *motivations* of the capitalist may be egoistic and "money-loving" greed). Capitalism is the achievement of people who, instead of consuming and using their property and riches for themselves, postpone or partly renounce consumption in

---

[38] See for this rather complicated matter Irwin (2002, Chaps. 4 and 6).

[39] See, e.g., the many good arguments provided for this by Sen (2000, 126f.).

[40] I again refer to Irwin (2002) and Bhagwati (2002).

[41] See for this Novak (1989, 8ff.) and Novak (1993). Concerning the anticapitalist bias primarily in Catholic countries like Spain and France, see from a historical viewpoint Stark (2006).

[42] For a discussion of this topic I refer again to Sen (2009, 184ff.). See also the classical critique of the idea that economics is the characterization of *homo oeconomicus* by Ludwig von Mises; see Mises (1949, 62ff.).

order to invest *at their own risk* their riches in productive or otherwise entrepreneurial activity, therewith creating jobs, paying wages, and generating purchase power and demand. This in turn stimulates investment by more people, leading to the accumulation of capital which, through the public tax system, creates the possibility for state authorities to provide public goods like basic infrastructure, education, basic health care, etc. Again, this does not mean that capitalists are "good" or altruistic persons, or even that "renouncing consumption" means that they lead a modest and sober life (though there were and certainly still are many examples, mainly in the Puritan tradition, for which this was beyond doubt the case). Yet, by its very dynamics, capitalism and its competitive nature based on the division of labor has proven to promote innovation and to continuously increase productivity – the capacity of producing more and better things with less labor – and with this, welfare and opportunities for entire populations.

During this process some people, families, and countries will become richer than others, some of them very and even incredibly rich. Despite normally being beneficial – since it encourages investment – inequality sometimes also presents a political problem of uncontrolled and disadvantageous social and political power which needs to be solved, or at least mitigated, by adequate political and legal means. Much more harmfully, however, inequality creates quite another type of problem, a *psychological* problem: the tendency to equating "inequality" as such with "injustice." The origin of this error lies in considering economy and business as a zero sum game, that is, as if that great wealth was based on the rich having taken something away from those who remain worse off, or even poor. Yet, such an idea is wrong and harmful. A capitalist economy is not a zero sum game, in which one can only gain when others lose, but essentially a process in which *new wealth is created*. It is a common misunderstanding that wealth, also the "wealth of nations," consists in the possession of economic assets in the form of money, gold, silver, diamonds, or other things of value (whose amount at a given time is always limited and, therefore, can be possessed only in the degree in which others do not possess them). The belief that this possession, in opposition to a nonpossession, was what made a nation rich and powerful – i.e. to have, while others have not – was the main error of the economics of mercantilism, typical for the absolutist, and for this reason essentially imperialist, State. It was the error which Adam Smith set out to refute by his *The Wealth of Nations*. If anything, wealth consists in *capital*, that is, a productive asset, and therefore, apart from machines or technological know-how, it consists in the creativity and innovative potential of a social system of the division of labor, of productive labor, and of mutually beneficial exchange. I am rich only provided I am able to *sell* what I have or produce – for this, however, others must have purchasing power; thus they cannot be poor. Equally, I am rich only provided I am able to *buy* with my money something which is useful and necessary for me - and this again supposes others having something to sell. Money alone, in an environment where others are poor, is of no use. Thus, I am rich only to the extent that there are others who are rich as well.

If capitalism works – and throughout history it *has* indeed worked – this wealth, or its results, is distributed to all social levels, even though some gain disproportionally, and, of course in single cases, because of fraud or ruthlessness also unjustly, more than others. Others will not gain at all, but rather lose (be it by their own fault or by misfortune, discrimination, natural disadvantage, or handicap). Yet, the very existence of inequality tends to provoke irrational politics of exaggerated egalitarian redistribution, tantamount to the expropriation of the rich. As many examples show, in the long run this is mostly to the detriment of those who are not as well-off, because it hurts the dynamics of the economy by fettering the forces of creativity and innovation, even though it may be rewarding for those who are politically taking advantage of the forces of envy.[43]

Now, as mentioned above, self-interest, the motor of the capitalist market economy, is not equal to egoism or selfishness. Of course, there are many cases of the sheer love of money and greed. Morally speaking, this is detrimental in the first place to the capitalist himself, not materially perhaps, but for his spiritual well-being; it can be, and in the past very often was, harmful to workers. Yet, it can still be also economically advantageous. Many great and beneficial discoveries, inventions, and entrepreneurial achievements have had their immediate cause in some form of profit-seeking or greed.

More important, however, is that one can, and most people actually do, pursue *altruistic* self-interests, *because their self-interest is precisely to also promote the good of others.* This is not a paradox. Notice that those who care for their family will still act in their self-interest, that is, "economically": trying to obtain more or better things with less money or work. Businessmen will seek to produce more and better, more competitive products with less labor and for lesser costs; and consumers will always be interested in buying more and better things for a better price. Both in the first place care for making a living for themselves and those persons for whom they care. This is the sort of economic, truly self-interested thinking we all apply in our everyday calculations. It is "self-interested," not because it is selfish, but because it pursues the interest of the actor, and not some general or public interest for which the actor sacrifices what interests *him.* Just as the house-wife tries to make a good buy when shopping, without thinking thereby of the good of her neighbors, of the national textile industry, or of the agriculture of poor countries, the businessman will not produce with an eye on developing other countries, but in advancing the

---

[43] Once again, it provides a rather distorted view of free market economy to say, as does Joseph E. Stiglitz, that its advocates assume "that markets, by themselves, without government intervention, are efficient, and that the best way to help the poor is simply to let the economy grow – and, somehow, the benefits will trickle down to the poor" (Stiglitz 2006, XVI). Growth of the economy is truly a precondition of helping the poor; but those who defend this basic insight do not deny therewith that for various reasons also government policies, or other public minded organizations and institutions, should enable the poor to participate in the benefits of a growing economy (by providing opportunities for education, health care, etc., which are not produced by the mechanism of the free market, without at least some intervention of the State). But again, the fact that the market alone is not able to achieve this has nothing to do with a *market failure*, as Stiglitz seems to suggest; it simply shows the limits, but not failures, of the market (market *failures* are possible only in those sectors for which the market is supposed to be the solution, not in those which by its very nature – which is an exchange between equivalents – it cannot possibly be a solution).

good of his company in order to assure the income, jobs, and other goals he pursues – which are all a part of his self-interest, that is, economic calculation. Admittedly, and as already emphasized above, contrary to what rational choice economists contend, self-interest is not the only motivation of human beings. The *homo oeconomicus* is a limited, one-sided, and unrealistic model.

As such, self-interest and the behavior of the *homo oeconomicus* have nothing to do with egoism, and sometimes they have quite much to do with altruism and caring for others. To take Adam Smith's example (Smith 1979, 27, I.2): the butcher who delivers his meat, not driven by benevolence, but rather by self-interest (Adam Smith says: "self-love"), perhaps is the loving and caring head of a family who thinks of the well-being of his wife and the upbringing and education of his children. If he delivered to his clients the commodity he produces *by mere benevolence*, and not for making a profit, he most probably would violate both justice and charity toward his own family. Additionally, and this was Smith's main argument, this type of behavior is more advantageous for the client, because he knows that he will get his meat not only today, sometimes or once, depending on the benevolence and humanity of the butcher – who actually perhaps has no reason at all to be benevolent toward him – but that he will get it also tomorrow and in a continuous and *reliable* way (which enables him to enter into business too, because he can, within certain limits, foresee and calculate the future).

To be precise, Adam Smith does not say that *the butcher acts* not by benevolence but by self-love; what he says is that *we do not expect* our dinner from his benevolence and humanity, but from his self-love! So, Smith talks not about the *intentions of the butcher* but about the *reasonable expectations of the client*. If we really knew that we could reasonably and reliably expect our daily dinner on the grounds of the butcher's humanity and benevolence, this would certainly be a much better, but also a very different, world from the one in which we actually live. It would be a world of saints. In the real world, however, such an expectation is simply unreasonable. This does not exclude that a world and an economy in which butchers, though acting by economic logic and in their well-understood self-interest, do this *additionally* by benevolence toward their client – or are even saints – is a much better world and a much better economy as well (because it will generally improve the butcher's service and prevent him from fraudulently seeking profit). Yet, even if we should tend to improve our world exactly in this direction, this is not the point with which Smith was concerned.

The condemnation of self-interest and profit is at the basis of most confusion concerning capitalism and the free market economy. As I have argued, Church social doctrine in the past was not unaffected by this attitude. Moreover, it had a certain bias for state interventionism and regulations even though this was not in accordance with its own basic principles, for example, subsidiarity and property rights. It entirely overlooked the fact that the very idea of capitalism already included in a way, that is, *structurally*, a social commitment of private property since the capitalist is not simply an owner of property and riches, but of *capital*, that is, of means of production: he puts his riches at society's disposal. The profit of the capitalist is the reward he, or the shareholders of a company, is justly entitled to expect and to receive for taking their own risk. Even though reality does not always concord with this idea, it has been proven to be successful, leading to a real advantage for society as a whole. Therefore, even if a capitalist's profit is much more than he may seem to merit by standards of justice, his *expectation* of profit and the motivation following from it are highly useful for the entire society and, thus, serving the common good.

The overlooking of such logic can perhaps be explained by the fact that, as part of theology and made by theologians, the social teaching of the Church tends to be "charitable." It must show that it takes the side of the poor, the disadvantageous. Moreover, the Church's social magisterium has its starting point (with Leo XIII's encyclical *Rerum novarum*, 1891) in a time in which Catholicism was generally opposed to the modern world, namely, to the modern spirit of business and capitalism which by leading theologians and those in the Catholic press was commonly identified with an essentially unChristian, even "Jewish" spirit. Therefore, the widespread Catholic, socially motivated anti-Semitism was also intrinsically anticapitalist.[44] The fact is that not only among left-wing and pro-socialist Christians but also in more conservative ecclesiastical circles sound economic thinking, which is truly very advantageous for the poor, is still today often disregarded or even condemned as heartless, egoistic, and serving only the rich.

In this respect, however, and for many people very surprisingly, John Paul II's encyclical *Centesimus annus*, published in 1991, opened a new area. This encyclical contains a clear-cut argument in favor of "capitalism" insofar as it is conceived as "an economic system which recognizes the fundamental and positive role of business, the market, private property and the resulting responsibility for the means of production, as well as free human creativity in the economic sector" (John Paul II 1991, 42). It equally advocates the free market economy which "on the level of individual nations and of international relations, (…) is the most efficient instrument for utilizing resources and effectively responding to needs" (John Paul II 1991, 34). Moreover, the encyclical also adopts a vision of the rule of law, a separation of powers, democracy and the role of the state regarding the economy in the best tradition of liberal constitutionalism and ordoliberalism (John Paul II 1991, 44–48). With this promulgation, John Paul II actually abandoned the idea that the Church's social doctrine is "a 'third way' between liberal capitalism and Marxist collectivism" – as was already announced in his 1987 encyclical *Sollicitudo rei socialis* – "nor even a possible alternative to other solutions less radically opposed to one another: rather, it constitutes a category of its own" (John Paul II 1987, 41). Since *Centesimus annus*, thus, the Social Doctrine of the Church espouses the idea of a capitalist free market economy, rightly understood, including the "legitimate role of profit as an indication that a business is functioning well" and "that productive factors have been properly employed and corresponding human needs have been

---

[44] From the second part of the nineteenth century until the eve of the Second World War, this message was spread over and over again by the Vatican-authorized journal *La Civiltà Cattolica*, run by the Jesuit Fathers, which had also a great influence on the entire Catholic press at the time.

duly satisfied"[45]; it also understands the merits of free trade and opts for the rather limited role of the state.[46]

In *Centesimus annus*, John Paul II actually depicts a clear-cut conception of the role of the state in the economic sector. So, according to *Centesimus annus*, the state has first to guarantee "individual freedom and private property, as well as a stable currency and efficient public services." Secondly, the state has the role of "overseeing and directing the exercise of human rights in the economic sector," which, however, does not mean to "directly ensure the right to work for all its citizens," because this the state could only do if he "controlled every aspect of economic life and restricted the free initiative of individuals," which however would be harmful. Therefore, in the sense of subsidiarity, the state has rather "a duty to sustain business activities by creating conditions which will ensure job opportunities, by stimulating those activities where they are lacking or by supporting them in moments of crisis." Thirdly, the state must "intervene when particular monopolies create delays or obstacles to development." Furthermore, and "in exceptional circumstances the state can also exercise a substitute function, when social sectors or business systems are too weak or are just getting under way, and are not equal to the task at hand." Yet, "[s]uch supplementary interventions, which are justified by urgent reasons touching the common good, must be as brief as possible, so as to avoid removing permanently from society and business systems the functions which are properly theirs, so as to avoid enlarging excessively the sphere of state intervention to the detriment of both economic and civil freedom" (John Paul II 1991, 48).

It is obvious that this program is very close to, if not in a large part identical with, the best tradition of ordoliberalism (once called "neoliberal," a label which since some years has become a swearword, being identified with something totally alien to the original neoliberalism – a not only economic, but also social order of the purest and most extreme socially insensible laissez-faire, linked not with the names of the great economists of the postwar neoliberal tradition, but rather to names such as Margaret Thatcher and Ronald Reagan. These protagonists, though having unquestionable merits, were certainly not the champions of neoliberal economical *thinking*, but only of certain politics called Thatcherism or Reagonomics – while the Laffer-curve, after all, has nothing to do with "neoliberalism" either, but simply seems to be bad economics).[47] According to the *ordo*liberal outlook of *Centesimus*

---

[45] John Paul II (1991, 35) wisely adds however, that "profitability is not the only indicator of a firm's condition."

[46] For a synopsis of the main themes of this encyclical and an appreciation of its innovative character, see Rhonheimer (2003) (an English version will be contained in my forthcoming *The Common Good of Constitutional Democracy: Essays in Political Philosophy and on Catholic Social Teaching*, Washington D.C., The Catholic University of America Press).

[47] A telling example of how "neoliberalism" is seen by a left-wing, Marxist historian is provided by Harvey (2005), where one can find assertions such as (on p. 7) the "assumption that individual freedoms are guaranteed by freedom of the market and of trade is a cardinal feature of neoliberal thinking." No "neoliberal" economist or social theorist would maintain such nonsense (that "individual freedoms are *guaranteed* by freedom of the market"); they would rather say that freedom of the market and of trade *is an essential part* of individual freedom, which however has to be *ordered and guaranteed by the State and its legal system*.

annus, the state must create and secure the order of a real free market economy in which the forces of capitalism and free competition can develop and cooperate for the common good. So, the role of the state, rather than being an actor by bureaucratically intervening in the economic process and interfering with business decisions, is to be responsible for ordering the framework and regulating the parameters of the process as a whole while leaving its intrinsic forces to develop their proper potential. Hence, what *Centesimus annus* presents is actually a program of capitalist laissez-faire, but of laissez-faire – according to Eucken's differentiation – in the positive sense as economic liberty, spontaneity, and creativity embedded in an order of competition created, guaranteed, and actively overseen by the state and the rule of law. Most importantly, in *Centesimus annus* there is also a guiding principle for the role of the state in the economic sector: it is "economic and civil freedom." More than any previous document of the social Magisterium of the Church, *Centesimus annus* has definitively enriched Catholic social doctrine with the idea that the common good contains, and needs to be achieved by, both economic and civil freedom.

1.6 The Role of the State Regarding the Economy as Part of an Ethics of Institutions

In order to properly describe the role of the public authority of the state, it is necessary to emphasize the *importance of institutions*. The encyclical *Centesimus annus* presents a clear-cut doctrine about the state, democracy, and the capitalist market economy based on the insight that the first and principal task of state authorities is establishing and upholding institutions which are able to guarantee those freedoms of citizens. These citizens, in turn, cooperate for the common good – including the competitive order of a free market economy. The state is not viewed by *Centesimus annus* as a superior agency, equipped with a higher and privileged insight and wisdom into the concrete material requirements of this common good. Rather, the first and basic requirement of the common good is precisely held to be *the establishment and functioning of the basic political, legal, economic, and social institutions*.

At first glance, however, the last social encyclical of the Catholic Church, Benedict XVI's *Caritas in veritate*, seems to be less clear-cut. It focuses on so many topics that it is difficult to identify its main argument. Now, despite its title which gives the impression that the encyclical intends to focus on charity, *Caritas in veritate* actually stresses not so much "charity" but the ideas of *justice* and the *common good*. As the Pope argues, they are precisely what render charity *true* charity, and not only sentimental, taking the part of the poor and disadvantaged (Benedict XVI 2009, 6).

By focusing on justice and the idea of the common good – with the aim of making out what real charity demands – like *Centesimus annus*, *Caritas in veritate* also opens the way to integrating sound economic thinking into the *whole* of Catholic social doctrine, which is concerned with the human person in his integrity and the fullness of his earthly and eternal destiny. Now, what do "justice" and "common good" mean? In *Caritas in veritate*, there is actually a passage which seems to me to be crucial, and also quite innovative, in this respect. It is the affirmation that "[t]o take a stand for the common good is on the one hand to be solicitous for, and on the other hand to avail oneself of, that complex of institutions that give structure to the life of society, juridically, civilly, politically and culturally, making it the *pólis*, or 'city'" (Benedict XVI 2009, 7). The common good is not so much seen as a determined outcome, a social pattern or a pattern of distribution of wealth and opportunities, but as the *institutional framework*, which then generates, as a *result* of free cooperation of citizens, an outcome which is to be considered just and coherent with the common good. It is so because it has come about in a just and ordered manner.

Such perspectives might be the starting point for a missing piece of Catholic social doctrine: an *ethics of institutions* which does not focus on moral norms for personal conduct, but on *moral norms concerning the creation and securing of political, juridical, economic, and social institutions*, and this precisely as *moral* requirements. In this context, they would be requirements of justice and charity. That this is not entirely opposed to the meaning of the passage of *Caritas in veritate* quoted earlier as is shown by the astonishingly bold assertion which immediately follows (emphasis added): *"This is the institutional path – we might also call it the political path – of charity*, no less excellent and effective than the kind of charity which encounters the neighbor directly, outside the institutional mediation of the *pólis"* (Benedict XVI 2009, 7).

Admittedly, it might sound somewhat odd to talk in this context about "charity," mediated by the institutions of the *polis*. Yet, I think one of the profound inspirations of *Caritas in veritate,* expressed in its profoundly theological Introduction, was precisely to bring Christian charity down to the conditions of its concrete application to the real world in which we are living. This includes indicating that Christian charity is not only what is commonly called "charitable" actions, but that this charity must be concretized as justice and social and political *institutions* able to bring about what personal, private, and privately organized "charity" is not able to achieve.

Some commentators, such as George Weigel, have seen in this encyclical a clear left-wing or "red" antithesis to the rather right-wing liberal or "golden" *Centesimus annus* (Weigel 2009). This is perhaps correct regarding some formulations which might seem to be a kind of retraction from *Centesimus annus'* advocation of the free market economy. Yet, *Caritas in veritate* must not necessarily be understood in this way. Perhaps Weigel had in mind some propositions contained in the encyclical aiming at correcting or complementing the logic of exchange of equivalents ("giving in order to acquire") typical for the market economy, by a "market of gratuitousness." As the encyclical says, this market is characterized by solidarity and communion (Benedict XVI 2009, 39) as well as by "the *principle of gratuitousness* and the logic of gift as an expression of fraternity" which "in *commercial relationships* can and must *find their place within normal economic activity"* and is even "demanded by economic logic" (Benedict XVI 2009, 36). I am not sure how exactly this is to be understood. There seems to be a clear allusion to the late medieval and Renaissance tradition of civic humanism as it has recently been retrieved by some

Italian economists.[48] In any case, when *Caritas in veritate* speaks of the "continuing hegemony of the binary model of market-plus-State" which "has accustomed us to think only in terms of the private business leader of a capitalistic bent on the one hand, and the State director on the other" (Benedict XVI 2009, 41), it should be remarked that this "binary model of market-plus-State" does not necessarily belong to the best of liberal tradition. The best of liberal tradition has always claimed that the binominal of market and state must be complemented by other forms of relationships and forms of solidarity, rooted in civil society. Twentieth-century liberals have stressed the importance of recognizing that a free market economy must be embedded in a system of values which the market itself cannot create but presupposes. Thus, in his last book *Jenseits von Angebot und Nachfrage* ("Beyond Offer and Demand"), one of the leading neoliberal German economists and social philosophers, Wilhelm Röpke, emphasized that in order for it to work properly and in a human and freedom-enhancing way, the market mechanism, based on the laws of supply and demand, actually depends on what is *beyond* supply and demand (Röpke 1966). Liberals have usually also stressed the importance of the *corps intermédiaires*, public-spirited yet neither state-run, economically spirited or profit-seeking institutions, charities, and other organizations, arising from and located in civil society, many of them also run by the Church and different religious communities. They have even pleaded for many publicly relevant services, for example, in the field of education, research, or health care, to be privately organized and funded (as are most of the best universities in the USA). It also seems that in societies with a rather more developed market economy and less developed state-run welfare institutions, civil society is more creative and there is an especially high intensity of volunteering (which is the case in the USA[49] while people in countries like Italy, Spain, or Germany rely much more on state-run aid[50]).

---

[48] See, for example, Bruni and Zamagni (2004); as is well known, Stefano Zamagni, as consultor for the "Pontifical Commission for Justice and Peace" – charged by Benedict XVI with drafting this encyclical – was one of the main contributors to this work and one of those who officially presented the new document to the press.

[49] See, e.g., the detailed report *Volunteering in America: State Trends and Rankings 2002–2005*, edited by the Corporation for National and Community Service, Office of Research and Policy Development, Washington, DC, June 2006; www.nationalservice.gov. A 2010 fact-sheet indicates as the most recent key findings: "Approximately 1.6 million more volunteers served in 2009 than in 2008, making this the largest single-year increase in the number of volunteers since 2003 (annual data collection for volunteering statistics started in 2002). A total of 63.4 million volunteers contributed 8.1 billion hours of service in 2009, equaling an estimated dollar value of approximately 169 billion for their services. The volunteering rate increased in 2009 to 26.8%, up from 26.4% in 2008" (www.nationalservice.gov/pdf/10_0614_via_2010_fact_sheet_6_10_10.pdf).

[50] See data for European countries on the website of the "The European Volunteer Centre" (CEV) in Brussels: www.cev.be/66-cev_facts_e_figures_reports_-EN.html. According to the information provided by the CEV, Italy had in 2003 a total of 825,995 persons engaged in volunteering (USA: 65 million in 2005), which, taking into account the difference in population size (Italy about 58 million, USA 307 million) – and provided the figures are correct and comparable – signifies that the percentage number of persons engaged in volunteering in the USA (22%) is about 15 times higher than in Italy (1.45%).

However, as far as the state and its relation to the economy is concerned, it is important to thoroughly understand the role of the state as precisely both *fundamental* and *limited*. It is equally important to recognize the establishment and the upholding of the institutions which are fundamental as part of the political ethics involved in the economic order of the free market. In my judgment, with the idea of an ethics of institutions – political, juridical, economic, and social institutions as basic *moral* requirements of justice and Christian charity – *Caritas in veritate* has complemented the fundamental vision of *Centesimus annus*, concerning the role of the state in the economic sector, in an important and promising way.

1.7 Conclusion: The Trade-Off Between Economic Efficiency and Equity and the Necessarily Limited Role of the State

As was said above, the outcome of the capitalist economy and the market is neither morally good nor evil, neither just nor unjust; it can, however still be considered more or less *desirable*, and thus demands correction precisely for moral reasons. Provided the market mechanism really works, the market is certainly the most efficient way of coordinating human energies, resources and their allocation. As Peter Koslowski in his *Ethics of Capitalism*[51] has convincingly argued, capitalism, which he strongly defends as an economic order, cannot, however, also be a *social order* because the market itself is unable to decide between preferences of goals and values. In other words, the totality of the social order cannot be understood solely as a market, and the market cannot be conceived of as the whole of society (see Koslowski 1998, 55–72). The idea of the market and free competition (F. A. Hayek's "Catallactics") form an ideal of coordination, but they are not yet a complete theory of society. Moreover, not all human needs are "marketable," that is, possible objects of exchange transactions of equivalents. There are people who first must be helped in order to become players in market relations; there are others who never will be able to participate. No one of the often defamed important "neoliberal" – or *ordo*liberal – economists has ever denied this. Moreover, the goal to attain and the values to realize are certainly not the market itself. The market is an optimal, if not the only working, mechanism for allocating resources in the most efficient way and therefore specifically regards the common good of the most beneficial *economic* order. But the efficiency of allocation, although a *condition* for social justice, does not yet select the goals that human beings living together and cooperating in a determinate society desire to attain. Economic efficiency and legally correct procedures are not yet sufficient criteria for just distribution (Koslowski 1998, 55f.). In the same

---

[51] I refer to the original German edition: Peter Koslowski, *Ethik des Kapitalismus. Mit einem Kommentar von James M. Buchanan*, 6th edition (Tübingen: Mohr Siebeck, 1998). The English edition is part of: Peter Koslowski, *Ethics of Capitalism and Critique of Sociobiology: Two Essays with a Comment by James M. Buchanan* (Berlin: Springer, 1996).

way, the goal of freedom and self-choice cannot be mere freedom. "Self-choice as an ideal makes sense only because some *issues* are more significant than others... Which issues are significant, *I* do not determine. If I did, no issue would be significant. ... So the ideal of self-choice supposes that there are *other* issues of significance beyond self-choice" (Taylor 1992, 39). The common good cannot simply be an ideal of freedom and self-choice; it must also contain the conditions which render possible the realization of one's freedom in view of *valuable* goods (see Raz 1986, 400ff.). Social or redistributive justice is thus sometimes required to realize the goals and the "common good" we aim at, to a certain and prudent measure, even at the expense of long-term and overall economic efficiency.

It must be clear, however, that there is a trade-off between the freedom of the market and social justice, between economic efficiency and equity, though, as Alan Blinder thinks, it is not necessarily inevitable (see Blinder 1987, esp. 30f.). What seems to be certain, however, is that social justice will never be attained by *systematically* contravening economic efficiency. Social justice at the expense of freedom and self-responsibility, as is the case in the paternalistic Welfare State or the "Social Assistance State," deplored and criticized also by *Centesimus annus* (John Paul II 1991, 48), is not a desirable ideal either. It leads to a society with less solidarity, because when citizens know that the state taxes away a great amount of the fruits of their labor, returning it in the form of social security, public health care, etc., they will be less motivated to show personal solidarity or engage in volunteering. Rather, they will try to use for themselves the best of what the state does not tax away. "By intervening directly and depriving society of its responsibility" – John Paul II wrote rather prophetically in *Centesimus annus*– "the Social Assistance State leads to a loss of human energies and an inordinate increase of public agencies, which are dominated more by bureaucratic ways of thinking than by concern for serving their clients, and which are accompanied by an enormous increase in spending. In fact, it would appear that needs are best understood and satisfied by people who are closest to them and who act as neighbors to those in need" (John Paul II 1991, 48). Extreme Welfare State plus capitalism is not an ideal combination at all. Besides systematically violating the principle of subsidiarity, it also provides a justification for employers, entrepreneurs – if they still exist – businessmen, and citizens in general to act more egoistically. Today, as we know, the Welfare State is not any more affordable: it has turned out to be too expensive, causing an ever-increasing state indebtedness. Understandably, however, politicians are reluctant to call these problems by their real name.

Anticapitalism is as unsound as thinking that capitalist economic efficiency alone does the job. Therefore, even if government intervention may be required to sometimes protect weaker social groups from the immediately damaging effects of sound economic policy, it should not be concerned *too much* or *primarily* with this kind of social justice; otherwise, it will tend to advocate structural economic inefficiency, which in turn will undermine all the efforts to achieve precisely the social justice one intends to attain.

Unfortunately, there are and will always be politicians who take advantage of the economic inefficiencies of the market economy; this legitimizes their advocation for more government interventionism, thus creating even more market failures. This was, as mentioned above, the sort of self-fulfilling-prophecy-policies first practiced in the USA during the 1930s by the Roosevelt administration. Hopefully, however, responsible politicians and responsible citizens with a better education in basic economics will in the future see better through such political calculations and correspondingly penalize such politicians by refusing to cast their vote for them.

But notice again that defending economic liberalism means to defend not only, or in the first place, *economic efficiency*. Liberalism is not a political and economic doctrine aiming at money making, maximum productivity, and profit. It is part of a vision of society based on freedom and which sees in freedom an essential part of the common good. Liberals, more than in economic efficiency, believe in freedom. This is a strength, but also an obvious weakness, of liberalism. Traditional liberalism is somewhat reductionist, one-sided, and in some respect flawed in its anthropology. As a purely secular mode of thinking, it most importantly lacks the knowledge of what is basic for any Christian approach to human and social problems: not only the awareness of the real condition of mankind as a consequence of sin, but also its real and eternal destiny. Such knowledge, of course, is not immediately relevant for economics and politics. It does, however, help to see things in another perspective. I think it is mainly here, and not in trying to find better economic models, that the social teaching of the Church can contribute to economics– not by being anticapitalist, but by complementing the idea of a capitalist and free market economy with a vision of the common good that is not simply economic, but much more integral.

I am convinced that Catholic Social thinking can also learn much from the liberal tradition, namely, the insight that for those who are pursuing the common good, freedom, and not only justice and peace, is both an essential basis and a goal. On the other hand, the perennial and most valuable insights and achievements of the liberal tradition will certainly be supported and even enhanced by being integrated into a wider anthropology and vision of society, characteristic of the tradition of Catholic social doctrine.

Bibliography

Aranzadi, Javier. 2006. *Liberalism Against Liberalism. Theoretical Analysis of the Works of Ludwig von Mises and Gary Becker*. London/New York: Routledge.
Bastiat, Frédéric. 1851. *Harmonies économiques*. Paris: Guillaumin et Cie.
Benedict XVI. 2009. Encyclical *Caritas in veritate*. Vatican: Libreria Editrice Vaticana.
Bhagwati, Jagdish. 2002. *Free Trade Today*. Princeton/Oxford: Princeton University Press.
Blinder, Alan S. 1987. *Hard Heads, Soft Hearts. Tough-Minded Economics for a Just Society*. Cambridge, MA: Perseus Books.
Braudel, Fernand, and Ernest Labrousse. 1976. *Histoire économique et sociale de la France, 1789 – années1880*, vol. III. Paris: Presses Universitaires de France.
Bruni, Luigino, and Stefano Zamagni. 2004. *Economia civile. Efficienza, equità, felicità pubblica*. Bologna: il Mulino.
Caplan, Bryan. 2007. *The Myth of the Rational Voter. Why Democracies Choose Bad Politics*. Princeton/Oxford: Princeton University Press.

Churchill, Winston. 1947. Speech in the House of Commons 11.11.1947. In *The Official Report, House of Commons* (5th Series) 444: 206–207.

Eucken, Walter. 1968. *Grundsätze der Wirtschaftspolitik*, 4th ed. Tübingen/Zürich: J.C.B. Mohr – Paul Siebeck/Polygraphischer Verlag.

Ferguson, Niall. 2008. *The Ascent of Money. A Financial History of the World*. London: Penguin.

Frey, Bruno S. 1981. *Theorie demokratischer Wirtschaftspolitik*. München: Vahlen.

Frey, Bruno S. 1983. *Democratic Economic Policy*. New York: Palgrave Macmillan.

Frey, Bruno S., and Gebhard Kirchgässner. 2001. *Theorie demokratischer Wirtschaftspolitik*, 2nd ed. München: Vahlen.

Friedman, Milton. 1982. *Capitalism and Freedom*. Chicago/London: The University of Chicago Press. Originally published in 1962.

Friedman, Milton, and Anna J. Schwartz. 1963. *A Monetary History of the United States, 1867–1960*. Princeton: Princeton University Press.

Gilpin, Robert. 2001. *Global Political Economy. Understanding the International Economic Order*. Princeton/Oxford: Princeton University Press.

Harvey, David. 2005. *A Brief History of Neoliberalism*. Oxford: Oxford University Press.

Hayek, F.A. 1982. *Law, Legislation and Liberty. A New Statement of the Liberal Principles of Justice and Political Economy*, Complete Edition in one volume. London: Routledge & Kegan.

Hayek, F.A. 2001. *The Constitution of Liberty*. Chicago: The University of Chicago Press.

Hayek, F.A. 2007. The Road to Serfdom. In *The Collected Works of F. A. Hayek*, vol. II, ed. Caldwell Bruce. Chicago: The University Press of Chicago. Originally published in 1944.

Hazlitt, Henry. 1979. *Economics in One Lesson*. New York: Three Rivers Press. First edition in 1946.

Hazlitt, Henry. 2007. *The Failure of the "New Economics." An analysis of the Keynesian fallacies*. Auburn: Ludwig von Mises Institute. Originally published by D. Van Nostrand Company, Inc. (1959).

Hobsbawm, Eric. 1997. *The Age of Capital 1848–1875*. London: Abacus. Originally published in 1975.

Irwin, Douglas A. 2002. *Free Trade Under Fire*. Princeton: Princeton University Press.

John Paul II. 1987. Encyclical *Sollicitudo rei socialis*. Vatican: Libreria Editrice Vaticana.

John Paul II. 1991. Encyclical *Centesimus annus*. Vatican: Libreria Editrice Vaticana.

Keynes, John Maynard. 2004. *The End of Laissez-Faire (1926), republished in: Keynes, The End of Laissez-Faire/The Economic Consequences of the Peace*. New York: Prometheus Books.

Koslowski, Peter. 1988. *Prinzipien der Ethischen Ökonomie*. Tübingen: J. C. B. Mohr/Paul Siebeck. English trans: 2000. *Principles of Ethical Economy*. Dordrecht: Springer.

Koslowski, Peter. 1998. *Ethik des Kapitalismus. Mit einem Kommentar von James M. Buchanan*, 6th ed. Tübingen: Mohr Siebeck. English edition: 1996. *Ethics of Capitalism and Critique of Sociobiology: Two essays with a comment by James M. Buchanan*. Berlin: Springer.

Krugman, Paul R., and Maurice Obstfeld. 2009. *International Economics: Theory and Policy*, 8th ed. Boston: Pearson/Addison Wesley.

Laslett, Peter. 2000. *The World We Have Lost: Further Explored*. London: Routledge. Originally published in London: Methuen (1965).

Lewis, W.Arthur. 2003. *Economic Survey 1919–1939*. London: Routledge Chapman & Hall. Originally published in London: Allan and Unwin (1949), Ninth impression (1970).

Mandeville, Bernard. 2010. *The Fable of the Bees: Or Private Vices, Publick Benefits*, edited with an introduction by Philip Harth. London: Penguin Books.

Mathias, Peter. 1983. *The First Industrial Nation. An Economic History of Britain 1700–1914*, 2nd ed. London/New York: Routledge.

Mises, Ludwig von. 1929. *Kritik des Interventionismus. Untersuchungen zur Wirtschaftspolitik und Wirtschaftsideologie der Gegenwart*. Stuttgart: Gustav Fischer Verlag.

Mises, Ludwig von. 1949. *Human Action. A Treatise on Economics*. London: William Hodge & Company.

Nell-Breuning, Oswald von. 1932. *Die soziale Enzyklika. Erläuterungen zum Weltrundschreiben Papst Pius' XI über die gesellschaftliche Ordnung*. Köln: Katholische Tat-Verlag.

Novak, Michael. 1989. *Catholic Social Thought and Liberal Institutions*, 2nd ed. New Brunswick/ Oxford: Transaction Publishers. Originally published as *Freedom with Justice*.

Novak, Michael. 1993. *The Catholic Ethic and the Spirit of Capitalism*. New York: The Free Press.

Paul VI. 1967. Encyclical *Populorum Progressio*. Vatican: Libreria Editrice Vaticana.

Pius XI. 1931. Enyclical *Quadragesimo anno*. Vatican: Libreria Editrice Vaticana.

Raz, Joseph. 1986. *The Morality of Freedom*. Oxford: Clarendon.

Rhonheimer, Martin. 1998. Lo Stato costituzionale democratico e il bene comune. In *Ripensare lo spazio politico: Quale aristocrazia? Con-tratto – Rivista di filosofia tomista e contemporanea*, vol. VI (1997), ed. E. Morandi and R. Panattoni, 57–122. Padova: Il Poligrafo.

Rhonheimer, Martin. 2003. La realtà politica ed economica del mondo moderno e i suoi presupposti etici e culturali. L'enciclica Centesimus Annus. In *Giovanni Paolo teologo. Nel segno delle encicliche*, ed. G. Borgonovo and A. Cattaneo, preface by S. Em. Camillo Card. Ruini, 33–94. Roma: Edizioni Arnoldo Mondadori.

Röpke, Wilhelm. 1966. *Jenseits von Angebot und Nachfrage*, 4th ed. Erlenbach-Zürich: Eugen Rentsch Verlag; English edition: 1960. *A Humane Economy*. Chicago: Henry Regnery Company.

Rothbard, Murray N. 2000. *America's Great Depression*, 5th ed. Auburn: The Ludwig von Mises Institute. Originally published in 1963.

Sen, Amartya. 2000. *Development as Freedom*. New York: Anchor Books/Random House.

Sen, Amartya. 2009. *The Idea of Justice*. Cambridge, MA: Harvard University Press.

Shlaes, Amity. 2007. *The Forgotten Man: A New History of the Great Depression*. New York: HarperCollins.

Smith, Adam. 1976. *A Theory of Moral Sentiments*, ed. D.D. Raphael and A.L. Macfie. Oxford: Oxford University Press.

Smith, Adam. 1979. In *An Inquiry into the Nature and Causes of the Wealth of Nations*, ed. R.H. Campbell and A.S. Skinner, Textual editor: Todd, W.B. Oxford: Oxford University Press.

Stark, Rodney. 2006. *The Victory of Reason: How Christianity Led to Freedom, Capitalism, and Western Success*. New York: Random House.

Stiglitz, Joseph. 2006. *Making Globalization Work*. New York: Norton.

Stiglitz, Joseph E. 2010. *Freefall: America, Free Markets, and the Sinking of the World Economy*. New York: Norton.

Taylor, Charles. 1992. *The Ethics of Authenticity*. Cambridge, MA: Harvard University Press. Originally published as *The Malaise of Modernity* (Canadian Broadcasting Corporation, 1991).

Weigel, George. 2009. Caritas in veritate in gold and red. The revenge of justice and peace (or so they may think). *National Review Online*. http://article.nationalreview.com/399362/icaritas-in-veritatei-in-gold-and-red/george-weigel. Accessed 7 July 2009.

Chapter 2
Divisible Goods and Common Good: Reflections on *Caritas in Veritate*: Response to Martin Rhonheimer

Francis Hittinger

2.1 Introduction

In this chapter, I will not attempt to expound *Caritas in Veritate* (2009) thoroughly or at the proper level of detail and complexity. Instead, I will use the encyclical as an occasion to remove a few impediments to serious dialogue between economists and Catholic social doctrine. I admit at the outset that this is a risky way to proceed, because I must bring into view certain impediments not from the standpoint of an economist but as someone who works within the tradition of Catholic social doctrine. However, there is no other way. I do not know the soft spots and the obscure corners of economic theory while I do have a trained sense of where they exist in Catholic social doctrine.

First, I have to say a few things about how to read a social encyclical. An economist, or any social scientist, deserves at least a rough idea of what can be reasonably asked and expected in documents of this kind. Second, and somewhat cautiously, I want to examine the distinction between a market, an economy, and a society. I say cautiously because although social encyclicals are usually very clear about what is meant by a society, they are not always so clear about the terms market and economy. Third, apropos of the title of my presentation, I will offer some concluding reflections on the distinction between divisible goods and a common good.

F. Hittinger (✉)
University of Tulsa, Tulsa, USA
e-mail: francis-hittinger@cox.net

M. Schlag and J.A. Mercado (eds.), *Free Markets and the Culture of Common Good*, Ethical Economy 41, DOI 10.1007/978-94-007-2990-2_2,
© Springer Science+Business Media B.V. 2012

2.2   Hermeneutical Issues

You will have noticed that I used the word "doctrine" rather than "thought." "Thought" is a more academically respectable term; if nothing else, it avoids the *odium theologicum* (the allergic reaction to things theological, including doctrines). While all doctrines are thoughts, which encompass still other thoughts, definitions, and dialectics, not all thoughts are doctrines, and not all schools of thought are doctrinal. The reader who has no truck with doctrines will find it useful to keep the term intact, just as a reminder of the literary genre that he or she is trying to interpret and to understand.

Caritas in Veritate is a teaching letter. There are several standards internal to the practice of teaching letters. Two are especially important: (1) it should speak truthfully and coherently on a subject matter within the competence of the author's office and (2) it should speak in light of a tradition of such teaching. In the case of *Caritas in Veritate*, putting to one side the many references to Scripture, we find about two hundred discrete references to previous documents reaching back to the nineteenth century. It is not so easy to interpret which ones are documentary tracks of support and which ones are pivotal, which is to say that they are the very points at issue for purpose of clarification, or extension, or application to some new set of facts. The salient point is that the first principle (to speak truthfully and coherently on a subject matter) is very much complicated by the second principle (doing so in the light of a tradition).

Although the analogy is imperfect, take the federalist papers, originally penned by John Jay, Alexander Hamilton, and James Madison over a 10-month period, between 1787 and 1788. Imagine subsequent authors who endeavor, over two centuries, to perpetuate the original lines of their predecessors. What does the adjective "federalist" signify? Even the seasoned interpreter will admit that it is not easy to distinguish between recurrent paradigms and changing circumstances and that it is even more difficult to say whether the later lines of thought ought to be interpreted in light of the former, or vice versa. Does the silence of a particular document indicate that the issue has already been solved? Or, does it suggest that the present author is not prepared to tackle the issue head on?

Social encyclicals are especially apt to be read out of context because they refit the tradition within the terrain of historically contingent things: wars, economic crises, and religious persecutions, to name only a few. It goes without saying that most people already have their own opinions about these things. Hence, the mischievous piece of Jesuit doggerel about Pope John XXIII's encyclical *Pacem in terris* (Peace on Earth):

> By now we know the simple trick;
> Of how to read Pope John's encyc.;
> To play the game, you choose your snippet;
> Of "Peace on Earth" and boldly clip it (Cogley 1963, 709).

Here, I will limit myself to one example of the "clip it" method. Grappling with the meaning of the adjective "social" when used in the term "social doctrine," the generation of Catholic thinkers who came of age in the wake of the economic turmoil of the 1930s and 1940s was inclined to adopt a restricted use of the word. In a restricted sense, social means economic activity and the diverse social relations which ensue upon it.[1] That having been done, these phenomena are brought to the bar of morality, chiefly justice. For the generation that came of age in the 1960s, in the wake of decolonization and the emergence of what was then called the "third world," the "social" was restricted to the political and economic policies needed for international aid and development. This was the era of Paul VI's *Populorum Progressio* (1967), the 40th anniversary of which Benedict XVI's *Caritas in Veritate* was meant to celebrate. (It is useful to know that most of the encyclical was written prior to the 2008 economic crisis.)

However well-intentioned, the restricted meaning caused more than a little confusion among Catholics and who knows who else who might have come upon the encyclical letters. The subject matter, along with the terms of art by way of definitions and distinctions, were cut and trimmed for the purpose of advancing policies on issues of political economy. So, for example, Leo XIII's encyclical *Rerum Novarum* (1891), which was chiefly about the natural right to form voluntary societies, especially those which constitute a kind of social membrane around the family, became, on the "restricted" meaning, simply a teaching about labor unions and just wages. While Leo XIII was examining social relations which ensue upon the family, many of his commentators assumed that he must have been speaking of relations which ensue upon economic activity. On this view, one *might* finally arrive at the family but only as the terminal object of work, collective bargaining, a just wage, and state law.

This habit of interpretation not only turned the subject matter of social encyclicals upside down but also created the impression of a ready-made pontifical account of economics and economic policy. This violates both principles internal to the practice of teaching letters – speaking within a certain competence on a given

---

[1] Calvez and Perrin were influential in this regard and were, to my knowledge, the first interpreters to use the term "restricted sense." The term *social* should be limited to "those human relationships which grow out of the economy." (Calvez and Perrin 1961, 3–4). This is, they note, a "restricted use of the word 'social,'" but, nonetheless, one that is historically justified. See also the Introduction: "we shall be dealing with the question of 'economic society' and of the diverse social relations to which economic life gives rise" (Calvez and Perrin 1961, xiii). The restricted meaning for Calvez and Perrin has one important qualification. Catholic social doctrine is not an economic doctrine per se but a treatment of social relations ensuring upon economic activity analyzed from the standpoint of a moral anthropology. Calvez and Perrin's restricted definition of the *social* is due, in large part, to the debates located first in the Great Depression era and then in the political and economic reconstitution of Europe after the Second World War. These issues might be an example but certainly are not the core pattern itself. On the Calvez and Perrin interpretation, almost all of the encyclicals prior to *Quadragesimo Anno* (1931) would become irrelevant. It is dubious that *Rerum Novarum* (1891) would neatly fit their understanding of the *social*, because this encyclical dealt mainly with the rights of the family and the right of workers to form associations. Moreover, if we look over the horizon, 10 years after the Calvez and Perrin work, human life issues become more prominent. They will not fit the restricted definition of *social* either. Note, for example, that in the new *Compendium of the Social Doctrine of the Church*, issued by the Pontifical Council for Justice and Peace (2004), economic issues represent only two of twelve chapters.

subject matter and the continuity of tradition. To be sure, individual economists and social scientists might have agreed with the moral and political gist of a particular encyclical read in the restricted sense, but they could see perfectly well that the documents contained very little economic theory. The restricted sense of the word "social", therefore, obscured rather than clarified dialogue between economists, social scientists, and Catholic social doctrine.

For more than a century, popes warned that this restricted sense was mistaken. Leo XIII, the father of the Catholic social doctrine tradition, wrote: "For, it is the opinion of some, and the error is already very common, that the social question is merely an economic one, whereas in point of fact it is, above all, a moral and religious matter" (Leo XIII 1901, 10). Pope Benedict makes the same point at the outset of *Caritas in Veritate*. Catholic social doctrine, he warns, does not pretend to be merely an analysis of social scientific "data" (Benedict XVI 2009, 10). In fact, long before he became pope, Cardinal Ratzinger had registered the complaint that social doctrine was being transformed into a second-rate social science, muting distinctively Catholic insights into history and society.[2]

Indeed, the title of his encyclical – *Caritas in Veritate in re sociali* – indicates clearly enough the proper location and meaning of the adjective "social" (Benedict XVI 2009, 5). Not "social" in the restricted sense of relations ensuing upon economic activity but rather, in social matters, love rooted in truth. Social therefore signifies the diverse modes and levels of human fraternity (friendship, communion), natural and supernatural.

It is always important to understand what a thinker is *looking through* and what he is *looking at*. Whereas the restricted meaning of "social" attempts to locate social relations and issues of justice *after* economic activity, Benedict is interested in modes of friendship "*within* normal economic activity, and not only outside it or 'after' it" (Benedict XVI 2009, 36). The subject matter therefore is social relationships. Moreover, as Benedict repeatedly insists, social relations are not being considered exclusively under the aspect of justice but more broadly or deeply under the aspect of friendship.

On the surface, the restricted meaning will look more agreeable to economists, but it should be eschewed for two reasons. First, it promises more than what can be delivered in either empirical or abstract economics. Second, it obscures the subject matter of Catholic social doctrine, which is not a good way to engage in dialogue. These problems come from the Catholic side, not that of social scientists.

---

[2] Henri de Lubac, a generation ago, worried that the social aspects of dogma would be lost in doctrines about social things: "It is social in the deepest sense of the word: not merely in its applications in the field of natural institutions but first and foremost in itself, in the heart of its mystery, in the essence of its dogma. It is social in a sense which should have made the expression 'social Catholicism' pleonastic." (Lubac 1988, 15). This book has the English title, *Catholicism: Christ and the Common Destiny of Man*, but note the title of the French original: *Catholicisme: les aspects sociaux du dogme*. The French subtitle brings out more clearly de Lubac's method – the social through the doctrinal, which is to say, through theology. In his Introduction to a new edition, Cardinal Ratzinger wrote: "The social dimension which de Lubac saw rooted in deepest mystery has often sunk to the merely sociological so that the unique Christian contribution to the right understanding of history and community has disappeared from sight. Instead of a leaven for the age, or its salt, we are often simply its echo" (Lubac 1988, 12).

I will return to Benedict's understanding of friendship within, and not after or outside economic activity, later. First, however, I need to remove another impediment to constructive dialogue between Catholic social doctrine and social science.

2.3   Markets, Economies, Societies

When we consider the political morality of state interventions in the market economy, the beginning of wisdom is to "find a path between uncritical apology and presumptuous moralism" (Koslowski 1996, 7). For the better part of the past two centuries, this path has been difficult to locate, and in times of economic crisis, the voice of "presumptuous moralism" about the failures of the market economy are liable to be the loudest and the most insistent.

I commend Martin Rhonheimer, whose essay, while not uncritical of certain features of the market economy, does not give into superficial indignation about its flaws.

According to the Austrian school, a spontaneous or catallactic order is not the entirety of an economy, much less the entirety of a social order. The so-called invisible hand refers chiefly to the market part of a much more complex order. As Martin Rhonheimer, a Catholic moral and social thinker in the liberal tradition, puts it: "In reality, the invisible hand is the feedback system of the 'many hands', that is, of the market which, through the price system, spontaneously coordinates private interests in a way which concurs to an optimal [but not necessarily a perfect] allocation of resources" (Rhonheimer 2012, 10).

Indeed, Friedrich Hayek was at pains to insist that spontaneous order must not be confused with what we ordinarily understand by an economy. "An economy, in the strict sense of the word, in which a household, a farm, or an enterprise can be called economies, consists of a complex of activities by which a given set of means is allocated in accordance with a unitary plan among the competing ends according to their relative importance" (Hayek 1976, 107–109). According to this view, while a spontaneous order under a rule of law becomes dysfunctional if someone should put their thumb on the scale to game the system, every economy has someone's thumb on the scales, for economy requires judgment about a particular order of goods to be pursued, achieved, and distributed in accord with a particular social body or enterprise. When we predicate "free" of a market and "free" of an economic enterprise and "free" of a particular social body enjoying a common life, we are using that word in quite different – although, admittedly, interrelated – senses. We hope, of course, that these distinct sectors can be kept in equilibrium, but keeping or restoring an equilibrium presupposes that we can sort out the things to be harmonized. Historically, efforts to do so have not always yielded happy results.

Martin Rhonheimer argues that although "market failures are an obvious fact," history testifies that "state failures are much more frequent and more harmful" (Rhonheimer 2012, 13). On this score, the lesser-known Austrian economist, Karl

Polanyi, in *The Great Transformation* (1944), showed how market failures can give rise to political pathologies. His thesis is succinctly stated at the beginning of the book:

> Our thesis is that the idea of a self-adjusting market implied stark utopia. Such an institution could not exist for any length of time without annihilating the human and natural substance of society; it would have physically destroyed man and transformed his surroundings into a wilderness. Inevitably, society took measure to protect itself, but whatever measures it took it impaired the self-regulation of the market, disorganized industrial life, and thus endangered society in yet another way (Polanyi 2001, 4).

For Polanyi, who was writing during the Second World War, the utopian dream of markets functioning without the rule of law, and completely untethered from other social concerns, ignites political passions which move the hand of the state to restore an equilibrium between market, economy, and society – usually, rather brutally, driven by what Rhonheimer aptly calls short-term interests of constituencies. He famously called this the "double movement," which can be personified as two organizing principles: one, the fecundity of a self-regulating market and the other, the principle of social protection against the market (Polanyi 2001, 138). Polanyi believed that Fascism was born in that double movement of an avenging state exacting retributive justice for the sins of laissez-faire economics. In any event, he was skeptical that the passion for retribution is liable to produce an equilibrium between markets, economies, and societies.

During the same era, Catholic social doctrine also worried that the heavy hand of state intervention would homogenize society rather than produce equilibrium throughout the various sectors. Both the totalitarianism and the democratic imperatives of the post-1929 economic crisis made precarious the predicate "social." It was practically inevitable that there would be a confusion of three things: a just distribution of resources on the part of the state; the rule of law, which puts a legal and political limit on state action; and the principle of subsidiarity, which puts a specifically social limit on that same project.

I take a more favorable view of *Quadragesimo Anno* (1931) than does Rhonheimer. Pius XI maintained that "social justice" is not the justice of exchange nor the justice of distribution, redistribution, or retribution. Social justice marks the justice of actions maintaining a common good that transcends goods commuted and distributed – the right order of a society both within itself and among its subsidiary societies. Politically, "society" exists as a union of other social unions. Whereas particular justice acts are ordered to the good of another singular person (relations equalized by exchange or distribution), general justice – what came to be called social justice – orders actions to the common good. It considers individuals, of course, but insofar as they are members of a whole, about which we can say that what is good for the whole is good for each of its parts (Aquinas 1999, II-II, q.58, a.9, ad. 3).

Furthermore, it was in terms of social justice (not distributive justice) that Pius XI emphasized the principle of subsidiarity, namely, that actions taken by a superior society should not displace, or absolutely replace, the common good of other societies within the body politic. Importantly, subsidiarity does not merely require that extraordinary intervention by the state ought to be temporary but that even temporary interventions may not absorb or destroy families, churches, and the array of associations that we call "civil society."

Unfortunately, the principle of social justice, originally intended to mark the importance of a specifically *social* common good, was interpreted in the "restricted" sense as a principle chiefly informing political and economic policies of distribution and redistribution. This is the version of social justice that Hayek ruthlessly criticized.[3] The upshot was that social justice could no longer be a regulative ideal of common good distinct from exchange and distribution – instead, all of the cards were

---

[3]Hayek's problem, at least in part, is due to the fact that he assumes that "social justice" is nothing other than distributive justice – and what is worse, an inauthentic one. It is, he avers, a "slogan used by all groups whose status tends to decline" (Hayek 1976, 141). Thus conceived, social justice is the opposite of institutional justice, and it amounts to nothing more than special interests and the special pleading of a "part" against what is good for the entire social order.

On this score, we are reminded of the danger of equating social justice, considered as Hayek does, with what Aristotle and Thomas meant by "general justice." General justice, later dubbed social justice in Catholic teaching, means the virtue of referring action to the common good. It is not solely the virtue of legal authorities.

Aquinas writes: "For just as charity may be called a general virtue in so far as it directs the acts of all the virtues to the Divine good, so too is legal justice, in so far as it directs the acts of all the virtues to the common good. Accordingly, just as charity which regards the Divine good as its proper object, is a special virtue in respect of its essence, so too legal justice is a special virtue in respect of its essence, in so far as it regards the common good as its proper object" (Aquinas 1999, II–II, q.58, a.6).

Eight years before *Quadragesimo Anno*, Pius XI insisted that Thomas is to be studied in order "to formulate exactly *de justitia legali aut de sociali, itemque de commutativa aut de distributiva*" (Pius XI 1923, 322). Clearly, for Pius XI, social justice is distinct from commutative and distributive justice. Carefully read, the distinction is maintained in *Quadragesimo Anno*:

> Hence, the institutions themselves of peoples and, particularly, those of all social life (*Quapropter ipsa populorum atque adeo socialis vitae totius instituta*) ought to be penetrated with this justice, and it is most necessary that it be truly effective, that is, establish a juridical and social order which will, as it were, give form and shape to all economic life (Pius XI 1931, 88).
>
> Free competition, kept within definite and due limits, and still more economic dictatorship, must be effectively brought under public authority in these matters which pertain to the latter's function. The public institutions themselves, of peoples, moreover, ought to make all human society conform to the needs of the common good, that is, to the norm of social justice. If this is done, that most important division of social life, namely, economic activity, cannot fail likewise to return to right and sound order (Pius XI 1931, 110).

Once confused with distributive justice, it became all too easy to regard social justice as chiefly concerned with economic commutations and distributions. Pius XI's dictum,"[I]t is of the essence of social justice to demand from each individual all that is necessary for the common good," could only be obscured (Pius XI 1931, 51). For one thing, it is needlessly redundant. Distributive justice is inherently social. This would seem true whether the apportioning is done in a small social body, like a family, or in a larger social body, like a polity. Commutative justice also exists in this general sense of "social" as reciprocities between two or more individuals. Both of these, in quite different modes, are justices about divisible things. Social justice, on the other hand, was originally meant to mark justice about something common.

For my account of this issue in Catholic social doctrine, see Hittinger (2008). Roger Aubert surveys some of the more important opinions, including the judgment of Vermeersch: "unless we are going to identify social justice with general justice, there is no *special* virtue that could merit that name" (Aubert 2005, 175). For the debate in the French, German, and Swiss intellectual world, it is important to read Talmy (1961) and Palhaus (1983). For full tilt studies, see Shields (1941) and Ferree (1997).

put in the deck of state action. Accordingly, subsidiarity itself had to be reinterpreted to mean the residue of free action that must remain at the lowest level. The price paid is that the social principle was either lost altogether or collapsed into the state or whatever residue of liberty was left to private law.

This is precisely what *Caritas in Veritate* rejects (Benedict XVI 2009, 39, 41). Benedict is quite clear:

> The Church has always held that economic action is not to be regarded as something opposed to society. In and of itself, the market is not, and must not become, the place where the strong subdue the weak. Society does *not have to protect itself from the market*, as if the development of the latter were *ipso facto* to entail the death of authentically human relations. Admittedly, the market can be a negative force, not because it is so by nature, but because a certain ideology can make it so. It must be remembered that the market does not exist in the pure state (Benedict XVI 2009, 36).

Among the causes given for the "negative force," Benedict XVI emphasizes (2009, 34) how a mistaken understanding of human autonomy is projected onto economic processes, as though immanent dynamisms are merely automatic and therefore by right, or in any event in the interests of efficiency, need to be shielded from moral direction. "The economic sphere," he writes, "is neither ethically neutral, nor inherently inhuman and opposed to society. It is part and parcel of human activity precisely because it is human" (Benedict XVI 2009, 36).[4]

> In a climate of mutual trust, the *market* is the economic institution that…is subject to the principles of so-called *commutative justice*, which regulates the relations of giving and receiving between parties to a transaction. But the social doctrine of the Church has unceasingly highlighted the importance of *distributive justice* and *social justice* for the market economy,[5] not only because it belongs within a broader social and political context, but also because of the wider network of relations within which it operates. In fact, if the market is governed solely by the principle of the equivalence in value of exchanged goods, it cannot produce the social cohesion that it requires in order to function well. *Without internal forms of solidarity and mutual trust, the market cannot completely fulfil its proper economic function* (Benedict XVI 2009, 35).

In the real world, exchange and distribution presuppose human fraternity, albeit along a broad and differentiated spectrum. Friendships, he says, are conducted within and not merely outside or after economic activity.

As I said earlier, I am reluctant to ascribe the Hayekian notion of a catallactic market order to Catholic social doctrine. Perhaps, the notion is compatible with Catholic social doctrine, perhaps not. What we can confidently say is that Benedict and his predecessors do not imagine a pure catallactic cosmos, but by the same token, they do not disparage a robust sector of private law. If this sector can be called spontaneous in Hayek's sense of the term, then the Catholic side of that understanding

---

[4] If it were true that market economy is a robotic order, then society would justifiably demand that the state controls, if not opposes, it, because such an order would be unworthy of free action.

[5] Notice that *et* is a coordinating conjunction that functions discretively. Social justice is not equated with distributive justice, for its object is the "social" from another point of view. Presumably, Benedict XVI means to speak of actions constituting and maintaining "internal forms of solidarity." Alas, the exposition is foggy and confusing.

would be that "spontaneous" is not the opposite of either "intentional" or "social." Rather, it is the opposite of "planned" or "commanded."

I read Benedict in this way. Exchange and distribution do not, and cannot, create from scratch what he calls "internal forms of solidarity." The absence of justice in an exchange of distribution can certainly destroy societies. Works of love and friendship require works of justice, but works of love and friendship are not reducible to commutation and distribution. From my point of view, this is a deliverance of moral and social realism and could just as well be found in Aristotle or Augustine.

In this light, we can interpret Benedict's assertion that "the exclusively binary model of market-plus-State is corrosive of society" (Benedict XVI 2009, 41). That model depicts human action along two fronts and reduces justice to the moral issue of their collision. Along one front, we find human action ordered to exchange, productivity and profit, and along another front, human action is ordered to cleaning up the mess by way of distributing or redistributing (Benedict XVI 2009, 39, 41). This confused collision is the specter that haunted Polanyi.

For Benedict's part, what is being left out of this picture is the fact that friendship is anterior and posterior to the logic of exchange and distribution. In an article on *Caritas in Veritate*, John Breen has captured the point quite nicely and succinctly: "Solidarity is not something that is exchanged, nor can it be compelled" (Breen 2010, 1019). A marriage can be ruined by defects in commutation and a family by defects in distribution. Yet, neither of these internal solidarities can be created or recreated by justice without an intention to form a union on the part of the acting persons, who really do go on to perform just the kind of acts which have union as their end.

2.4 Common Goods and Common Good

In the space remaining, I want to say a few things about the notion of the common good and how it differs from common goods. Roughly, this is the Catholic social doctrine version of the distinction between a common good and common utilities. I apologize in advance for having to do more work defining and stipulating than philosophically unpacking all of features of this very complicated distinction. But it is important because here we see most clearly why Catholic social doctrine rejects methodological individualism – namely, that social unities and relations among members can be reduced to nonsocial properties of members or composites thereof.

When two or more persons engage in a common structure of action for a common end, and where the common action (what Aristotle would call the "form of order") is an intrinsic good, we have something like a common good in the strict sense of the term. The union of the members in common activity is not an end that comes after some other purpose but is the good being continuously aimed at and sought. The scholastic philosophers called such a union *bonum commune*, always in the singular. The salient mark of a *bonum commune* is that it cannot, just as such, be distributed or divided in exchange but only participated by its members. Take the example of a marriage. The civil law might entitle the spouses to a writ of divorce and then distribute the properties, but the law certainly cannot distribute the marriage itself, sending each spouse on his or her way with 50% of the matrimonial common good.

In divisible things, justice requires that the right things be apportioned to the right people. A common good might include divisible things – monies, properties, and other important instruments – but the common good is *indivisible*. Therefore, it requires a different social logic and scheme of justice. A common good is impeded or destroyed when, for instance, the state attempts to distribute what can only be shared or participated. This is very likely to happen in times of economic crisis, when the passion for distributive justice reaches too far and disturbs the order of the "commons."

The common good is an analogous notion. The "common" that is participated rather than distributed varies considerably, depending upon the end and the mode of order through which the end is sought. Marriages, teams, and polities differently instantiate a common good. Hence, a common good can also be impeded or destroyed by trying to force a family, for instance, to instantiate a common good that pertains uniquely to the polity, and vice versa.

It is important, too, to distinguish common good, in the way we have just outlined it, from common *goods*, in the older scholastic parlance, *bona communia* – always in the plural (Froelich 1989). Take, for example, a water system or a group portfolio of mutual funds. Here, we have common ends, like health or the accumulating value of a common investment, along with a shared structure through which those ends are attained. To be sure, "the common" in such cases is destined for private yield, perhaps – but not necessarily – in unequal portions. The common water system, after all, must terminate in my or your kitchen spigot and into this or that glass, to be consumed and enjoyed by each one privately. Such utilities have an aspect of indivisible order. The rule of law governing commercial transactions is logically not the kind of thing that can be distributed – for one agent cannot be given more of the rule of law than another. Even so, the law is *about* divisible things, which is to say goods that can be exchanged or distributed.

The organization of things in a common "pool" takes considerable social cooperation and imagination. It is neither asocial nor antisocial. In fact, it is impossible or at least very difficult to imagine a *human* common good in the absence of common goods destined for private enjoyment. However, they do need to be distinguished and mutually ordered.[6] A *bonum commune* (always in the singular) denotes a society enjoying a common end and an intrinsic common good of shared action. It is fully compatible with individual participation but not with private possession.

---

[6]We are speaking of what the canonists somewhat woodenly distinguish as a *universitas personarum* rather than a *universitas rerum*. The principle of unity consists primarily in the unity of the persons rather than in the unity of the things which are organized, or, as we just said, "pooled."

In a fully common good, each member can say *Mihi sed non propter me* – "for me, but not for my sake." This is a fully social instantiation of the "commons."[7]

Based upon friendship and not just a cooperation through a common instrument, we are speaking now of societies that cannot reach their end without their appropriate mode of communion.[8]

Take the example of a queue in front of a credit union: the individuals are *parts* of the queue, *partners* in the credit union, and *members* of St. Rita's parish. To be sure, human persons related as parts and partners exhibit sociability, but it is only in their relation as *members* that it is possible to speak of "society." A social union, as John Paul II insisted, is something more than a relation *alter apud alteram*, a side-by-side intersubjectivity. It is also something distinct from cooperation in creating a common pool. It will enjoy a common good – a form of reciprocal action – that is, intrinsically valuable to each of its members.[9]

Precisely, when "society" most strenuously demands that certain results be achieved by way of distribution is when we are less able to think *sub specie societatis*.[10] Wars and economic crises are usually the excuse for state action that produces "results" incompatible with the human liberty essential for this wide range of common goods as well as a truly common good: the catallactic order of a market, the free cooperation in the economic sphere, the rule of law, and a host of societies enjoying a true common good. Precisely, in times of crisis, the people and their government will be less cautious in respecting the fragile goods of the "commons."

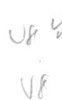

This is the problem that animates *Caritas in Veritate*. It is not the end of the story. What we have outlined are principles of social communion that "emerge from the common human experiences of love and truth" (Benedict XVI 2009, 54). There is more to be said in the light of the specifically Christian understanding of divine.

---

[7] In this way what we nowadays call the principle of solidarity, the validity of which both in the internal order of each nation and in the international order I have discussed in the encyclical *Sollicitudo Rei Socialis*, is clearly seen to be one of the fundamental principles of the Christian view of social and political organization. This principle is frequently stated by Pope Leo XIII, who uses the term "friendship," a concept already found in Greek philosophy. Pope Pius XI refers to it with the equally meaningful term "social charity." Pope Paul VI, expanding the concept to cover the many modern aspects of the social question, speaks of a "civilization of love" (John Paul II 1991, 10).

[8] Society, for Thomas, is not a thing but a communication. He quotes Augustine's *De Doctrina Christiana*: "Everything that is not lessened by being imparted, is not, if it be possessed without being communicated, possessed as it ought to be possessed." *Contra Impugnantes*, I.4. §14 A83 1265–70.

[9] Thus, Cajetan's dictum: *Mihi sed non propter me* – "for me, but not for my sake." Cajetan, *in IIa IIae*, q.17, a.5, no. 8: "Et cum dicitur *quia non potest amari Deus propter nos*, respondetur quod non potest amari *propter nos*, sed *nobis*."

[10] Thus does Pope Benedict XVI insist that social assistance is not just a question of getting the job done. Catholic charity is "an action of the Church, as such" (Benedict XVI 2005, 32). Here, Benedict reconnects with one of the main points of *Quadragesimo Anno*. Social assistance is not an undifferentiated delivery system. It must respect the good of distinct social forms – family, church, and so forth.

Bibliography

Aquinas, Thomas. 1999. *Summa Theologiae*, 3rd ed. San Paolo: Cinisello Balsamo.

Aubert, Roger, and D.A. Boileau, ed. 2005. Development of the Social Teaching of the Church in Europe. In *Catholic Social Teaching: An Historical Perspective*, with preface by Charles E. Curran, 161–180. Milwaukee: Marquette University Press.

Benedict XVI. 2005. Encyclical *Deus Caritas Est*. Vatican: Libreria Editrice Vaticana.

Benedict XVI. 2009. Encyclical *Caritas in Veritate*. Vatican: Libreria Editrice Vaticana.

Breen, John M. 2010. "Love, Truth, and the Economy: A reflection on Benedict XVI's *Caritas in Veritate*". *Harvard Journal of Law and Public Policy* 33: 987–1029.

Calvez, Jean-Yves, and Jacques Perrin. 1961. *The Church and Social Justice: The Social Teachings of the Popes from Leo XIII to Pius XII (1878–1958)*. London: Burns & Oates.

Cogley, John. 1963. "How to read an encyclical". *America* 108(20): 709.

Lubac, Henri de. 1988. *Catholicism: Christ and the Common Destiny of Man* (trans: Lancelot C. Sheppard and Sister Elizabeth Englund), with foreword by Joseph Cardinal Ratzinger. San Francisco: Ignatius Press. Originally published in French Edition: 1947. *Catholicisme: les aspects sociaux du dogme*. Paris: Les Editions du Cerf.

Ferree, William J. 1997. *Introduction to Social Justice*. Arlington: Center for Economic and Social Justice. Originally published by Paulist Press (1948).

Froelich, Gregory. 1989. "The equivocal status of *Bonum Commune*". *The New Scholasticism* 63: 38–57.

Hayek, Friedrich A. 1976. *Law, Legislation and Liberty*, The mirage of social justice, vol. 2. Chicago: University of Chicago Press.

Hittinger, Francis. 2008. "The Coherence of the Four Basic Principles of Catholic Social Doctrine: An interpretation. Keynote address Pontifical Academy of Social Sciences, XVIII plenary session". In *Pursing the common good*, ed. Margaret S. Archer, and Pierpaolo Donati, 75–123. Vatican: Pontifical Academy of Social Sciences.

John XXIII. 1963. Encyclical *Pacem in Terris*. Vatican: Libreria Editrice Vaticana.

John Paul II. 1991. Encyclical *Centesimus Annus*. Vatican: Libreria Editrice Vaticana.

Koslowski, Peter. 1996. *Ethics of Capitalism and Critique of Sociobiology: Two Essays with a Comment by James M. Buchanan*. Berlin: Springer.

Leo XIII. 1891. Encyclical *Rerum Novarum*. Vatican: Libreria Editrice Vaticana.

Leo XIII. 1901. Encyclical *Graves de Communi*. Vatican: Libreria Editrice Vaticana.

Paulhus, Normand Joseph. 1983. *The Theological and Political Ideals of the Fribourg Union*. Ph.D. Dissertation, Boston: Boston College.

Pius XI. 1923. Encyclical *Studiorum Ducem*. Vatican: Libreria Editrice Vaticana.

Pius XI. 1931. Encyclical *Quadragesimo Anno*. Vatican: Libreria Editrice Vaticana.

Polanyi, Karl. 2001. *The Great Transformation: The Political and Economic Origins of our Time*, forward by Joseph E. Stiglitz. Boston: Beacon Press. Originally published in 1957.

Pontifical Council for Justice and Peace. 2004. *Compendium of the Social Doctrine of the Church*. Vatican: Libreria Editrice Vaticana.

Rhonheimer, Martin. 2012. "Capitalism, Free Market Economy, and the Common Good: The Role of the State in the Economy". In *Free Markets and the Culture of Common Good*, ed. Martin Schlag and Juan Andrés Mercado. New York: Springer.

Shields, Leo W. 1941. *The History and the Meaning of the Term Social Justice*. Notre Dame: Notre Dame Press.

Talmy, Robert. 1961. "La Justice Légale". In *Aux Sources Du Catholicisme Social: L'École De La Tour Du Pin*, Bibliotèque De Théologie, Série IV, vol. 3, ed. Robert Talmy, 73–89. Belgium: Desclée.

Chapter 3
Market and Common Good

João César das Neves

Do markets have ethical dignity? In the deep and vast financial crisis the world is facing, many old questions about the moral justification of markets resurface. More importantly, the political and social interventions aimed at solving the crisis raise many questions about the level of intervention which could improve the role of the market in both the development and equity aspects of society.

Although these are serious, complex, and encompassing problems, a few basic and simple ideas go a long way toward a solution. It is always very important, particularly in moments of turmoil and bafflement, to reaffirm the basic principles of reasoning.

3.1 Two Serpents in Paradise

The ability of markets in achieving common good was a decisive element in the birth of economics. The crucial intuition which gave prominence to Adam Smith's *Wealth of Nations* was precisely the surprising conjecture that the tumultuous forces of competition could be beneficial to prosperity. This, which was later ambiguously and erroneous called "*invisible hand*," is present from the initial phrases of the 1776 treatise:

> The greatest improvement in the productive powers of labour, and the greater part of the skill, dexterity, and judgment with which it is any where directed, or applied, seem to have been the effects of the division of labour. (…) As it is the power of exchanging that gives occasion to the division of labour, so the extent of this division must always be limited by the extent of that power, or, in other words, by the extent of the market (Smith 1776, book I, Chap. 1 and paragraph 1: I.1.3).

J.C. das Neves (✉)
Universidade Católica Portuguesa, Lisbon, Portugal
e-mail: jcn@ucp.pt

M. Schlag and J.A. Mercado (eds.), *Free Markets and the Culture of Common Good*, Ethical Economy 41, DOI 10.1007/978-94-007-2990-2_3,
© Springer Science+Business Media B.V. 2012

Smith was no extreme liberal and was very much aware of the dangers and distortions market forces could create in society. But, at the same time, he saw their global effect as sound and beneficial.

> The manufacturers of a rich nation, in the same manner, may no doubt be very dangerous rivals to those of their neighbours. This very competition, however, is advantageous to the great body of the people, who profit greatly besides by the good market which the great expense of such a nation affords them in every other way (Smith 1776, IV.3.40).

This idea turned out to be one of the most influential in the last two centuries. Although much of our institutions still rely on the positive effects of markets upon common good, we are now very much aware of the countervailing aspects which, maintaining the relevance of competition in society, moderate and qualify the original Smithian optimism. Subsequent analysis has been stressing the need for a social equilibrium which includes "market, the State and civil society" (Benedict XVI 2009, 38).

The obstacles disturbing the achievement of common good by the raw market forces are many and diverse. But they may be classified in two very general groups as operational and coordination problems. Moreover, these may be symbolized in the basic intuitions behind the works of two of the most influential economists in history, Thomas Malthus and Karl Marx. After their contributions, which captured very deep and influential traits of the economic system, the candid and naïve initial optimism about competition was no longer tenable.

Even in a well-functioning society, production and distribution processes may be plagued by some operational traits. The main point of Malthus' analysis was not specifically the limits of natural resources. Smith was very much aware of those and had included them in his investigation. A rebuttal from that side would be unnecessary and redundant. The real poisonous aspect of the Malthusian system is the influence of decreasing returns, which make those limits so relevant. If, as society increases its size, both in physical and welfare levels, marginal productivity is reduced, the results become oppressed by the very dynamic that creates them. As many new forms of decreasing returns have been faced as history evolved, successive generations of Malthusian ghosts have surged.

Another source of market obstacles is to be found in coordination issues. This may be connected to the Marxian criticism, where a similar precision is necessary. The most quoted aspect, the greed and personal wickedness of the investors and managers, is also something Smith repeatedly mentioned and incorporated in his approach. Marx's basic intuition is the incentive structure arising from the distinction between property and use of the means of production. He clearly understood that this separation of ownership and operation, which is crucial for the remarkable productivity and dynamics of capitalism, is at the same time responsible for many social and economic misunderstandings and confrontations. The fact that those which own the capital and, consequently, the returns of production, are not those which operate daily those instruments of production and produce those returns, is a very real source of trouble in the workings of the forces of competition.

These two problems, decreasing returns and ownership-operation distinction in capital, are at the very center of most of the socioeconomic problems which have plagued progress, at least since the Industrial Revolution. They are also being invoked today, as causes for our present crisis. It is arguably possible to see them as the seed and origin of most of our economic debates and conflicts. At the same time, most institutional and cultural solutions created in these last centuries have tried to access and moderate their bad consequences. Although never completely eradicating their noxious influence, society has achieved important progresses toward a sound social equilibrium.

All these considerations, both by Smith, his subsequent critics and modern efforts of reform, are centered in the functioning of institutions. This is a natural trait of the scientific and political approaches, which must limit themselves to objective elements. We should never disregard these central issues. Good institutions are valuable assets in the search for common good. The results of this kind of approach are remarkable, and society owes a lot to them. But at the same time, we are now facing its limits.

> In the course of history, it was often maintained that the creation of institutions was sufficient to guarantee the fulfillment of humanity's right to development. Unfortunately, too much confidence was placed in those institutions, as if they were able to deliver the desired objective automatically. In reality, institutions by themselves are not enough, because integral human development is primarily a vocation, and therefore it involves a free assumption of responsibility in solidarity on the part of everyone (Benedict XVI 2009, 11).

3.2 Original Sin

As aforementioned, present discussions on the ability of market forces to achieve common good, and consequently assessments of their ethical dignity, have primarily stressed both operational and coordination issues. However, although these are very influential, the real problem is to be found at a much deeper level. The most serious questions concern not so much the functioning of the means but the purposes and ends of economic activity. This crucial aspect was formulated many centuries before the *Wealth of Nations*.

Aristotle's analysis of the economic process in the first book of *Politics* is not his most important contribution to the theory of economics. That is to be found in the fifth book of *Nicomachean Ethics*. But the former treatise includes what may be regarded as the most influential piece on axiological evaluation of the economic forces by the old Greek master: Aristotle's ethical condemnation of both commerce and lending.

The reasoning supporting such a drastic judgment is centered upon a crucial and famous distinction between two types of economic activity, *household management* (οικονομικη, "oikonomikê") and *wealth getting* (χρηματιστιχη, "chrematistikê").

Oikonomikê is the natural version of economics and is related to the management of a family or state: "One kind of acquisition therefore in the order of nature is a part of the household art, in accordance with which either there must be forthcoming or else that art must procure to be forthcoming a supply of those goods, capable of accumulation, which are necessary for life and useful for the community of city or household" (Aristotle 1932, 1256b.26).

When a change of attitude occurs, *chrematistikê* arises, separating economic efforts from the natural needs of a household: "When currency had been now invented as an outcome of the necessary interchange of goods, there came into existence the other form of wealth-getting, trade, which at first no doubt went on in a simple form, but latter became more highly organized as experience discovered the sources and methods of exchange that would cause most profit" (Aristotle 1932, 1257b.1–5).

The main difference between the "natural wealth-getting" (*oikonomikê*) and the unnatural one (*chrematistikê*) is that the second ignores the intrinsic limits of the former (Aristotle 1932, 1256b.30, 1257b.30). "*These riches, that are derived from this art of wealth-getting, are truly unlimited*" (Aristotle 1932, 1257b.25). In a thinker as deep as Aristotle, this lack of limits must have a profound origin. It is crucially connected to the desire for life: "*as therefore the desire for life is unlimited, they also desire without limit the means productive of life*" (Aristotle 1932, 1257b.40). The inevitable and drastic consequence of such distinction is the famous condemnation of trade and usury,[1] as activities unlimited and disconnected from the natural household needs.

Such a clear-cut and provocative analysis by Aristotle established a dual connection between markets and common good. In themselves, money transactions are not necessarily bad. However, they turn into unnatural and perverse actions if they become ends in themselves.

This model was very influential for many centuries. Yet, in the new scientific climate of Enlightenment soil where economic science was to be born, Aristotle's influence was much effaced. It is thus hard to find references to *chrematistikê* in modern economic authors. Adam Smith never mentions the Aristotelian analysis of the "*kinds of acquisition.*"[2] Nevertheless, we may find some considerations which seem reminiscent of the ancient elaboration, in particular in the analysis of the much criticized mercantile system.

> Consumption is the sole end and purpose of all production; and the interest of the producer ought to be attended to only so far as it may be necessary for promoting that of the consumer. The maxim is so perfectly self-evident that it would be absurd to attempt to prove it. But in the mercantile system the interest of the consumer is almost constantly sacrificed to that of the producer; and it seems to consider production, and not consumption, as the ultimate end and object of all industry and commerce (Smith 1776, IV.8).

---

[1]These condemnations follow immediately in Aristotle (1932, 1258b.01, 1258b.2–8). See the now classical discussion in Gordon (1975), Lowry (1987), Lowry, and Gordon (1998).

[2]Actually, the Greek philosopher is not a frequent reference of the Scott at all. In *The Wealth of Nations*, Aristotle is mentioned in only six paragraphs of the massive treatise. In the total of the six volumes of the *The Glasgow Edition of The Works and Correspondence of Adam Smith*, Aristotle is mentioned in just 51 paragraphs, with 23 of these in *The History of Astronomy*, one of the *Essays on Philosophical Subjects* in volume 3.

Other early economists, like Thomas Malthus, David Ricardo, John Stuart Mill, and even Alfred Marshall and Maynard Keynes, simply ignore Aristotle's analysis and distinction. The only classical economist to include it in his system was Karl Marx. The German author uses explicitly the Greek philosopher's elaboration as part of the justification for his own theory on the process of transforming money into capital.[3]

Although avoiding the explicit structure of the *Politics'* model, many classical, medieval, and modern authors present an explicit or latent suspicion about the motives and purposes of economic actors. Even when the nature of the problem is clearly identified as operational or coordination issues, as seen above, the analysis is frequently poisoned by doubts about the real aims of the intervening agents. Malthusian and Marxian elaborations also include implicit criticisms of motives and purposes. Do the investors or managers care about the household management or merely about wealth-getting? This is even today a recurrent, if not always explicit, question in economic debates.

As mentioned, most of the contemporaneous proposals concerning the problems markets have shown in achieving common good are centered upon institutions. But, even if frequently neglected in scientific and political debates, everyone is very much aware of the influence of subjective and spiritual elements.

> Development is impossible without upright men and women, without financiers and politicians whose consciences are finely attuned to the requirements of the common good. Both professional competence and moral consistency are necessary (Benedict XVI 2009, 71).

3.3   Redemption by Christianity

What does the Christian doctrine have to say about the essential relation between markets and common good? The rich and vast Christian literature on economic issues has greatly evolved during the two millennia of the Church. However, by means of a direct comparison of the Gospel to Aristotle's *Politics*, it is possible to identify two aspects which summarize the issue.

In the first place, there is a very visible similarity of approach. Many considerations in the teachings of Jesus Christ point in the same direction as Aristotle, considering the moral dangers of money when used as a final end. Some of the most famous of Jesus' teachings present an even more clear, forceful, and insightful presentation of the theme in Aristotle's text.

> No one can serve two masters. Either he will hate the one and love the other, or he will be devoted to the one and despise the other. You cannot serve both God and Money (Matt. 6:24).
>
>   I tell you, use worldly wealth to gain friends for yourselves, so that when it is gone, you will be welcomed into eternal dwellings. Whoever can be trusted with very little can also be trusted with much, and whoever is dishonest with very little will also be dishonest with much. So if you have not been trustworthy in handling worldly wealth, who will trust you with true riches? And if you have not been trustworthy with someone else's property, who will give you property of your own? (Lk. 19:9–12).

---

[3] See Marx (1867), volume I, part II, Chap. IV, paragraph 19, note 6, and Chap. V, paragraph 18.

On the other hand, this analysis is not followed by the specific moral condemnation of any practical activities. Jesus omits all denunciation of trade and usury, frequent in many ancient and religious masters, assuming these institutions as normal and even commendable.

> The kingdom of heaven is like a merchant looking for fine pearls (Matt. 13:45).
>   You should have put my money on deposit with the bankers, so that when I returned I would have received it back with interest (Matt. 25:27).

The evolution these concepts have throughout the history of the Church is both vast and interesting.[4] But it is enough to point to one of the most insightful and profound analysis of the ethical legitimacy of markets, to be found in St. Augustine. In his *Exposition* on Psalm 71, after having formulated a harsh and severe condemnation of trade, the African bishop presents a brilliant fictional debate between himself and a trader, in which the latter attempts to justify his own activity. The result is a profound and shrewd ethical analysis of markets, with a conclusion much richer than the Aristotelian system.

> I then, the merchant, do not shift mine own fault to trading: but if I lie, it is I that lie, not the trade. (…) A trader might thus speak to me – Look then, O Bishop, how thou understand the tradings which thou hast read in the Psalm: lest perchance thou understand not, and yet forbid me trading. Admonish me then how I should live; if well, it shall be well with me: one thing however I know, that if I shall have been evil, it is not trading that maketh me so, but my iniquity. Whenever truth is spoken, there is nothing to be said against it (Augustine 1888, Ps. LXXI, n. 15).

3.4   Conclusion

Economic science provides a rich and powerful understanding of the functioning of market forces, crucial for any ethical evaluation. Moreover, axiological aspects have existed since its origin because this scientific approach always stressed the deep relationship between competition and common good, even if some limits and obstacles were to be taken into account.

On the other hand, all of these elements are simple instruments for human decisions. Personal attitudes, moral identities, and ethical aims are irreplaceable aspects for any evaluation of social institutions.

> The Church has always held that economic action is not to be regarded as something opposed to society. (…) Society does not have to protect itself from the market, as if the development of the latter were ipso facto to entail the death of authentically human relations. Admittedly, the market can be a negative force, not because it is so by nature, but because a certain ideology can make it so. (…) it is man's darkened reason that produces these consequences, not the instrument per se. Therefore it is not the instrument that must be called to account, but individuals, their moral conscience, and their personal and social responsibility (Benedict XVI 2009, 36).

---

[4] See, among many others, Kaye (1998); Langholm (1983, 1992, 1998), and Noonan (1957).

Bibliography

Aristotle. 1926. *Nicomachean ethics* (trans: H. Rackam). Cambridge, MA: Harvard University Press (The Loeb Classical Library, vol. XXI).

Aristotle. 1932. *Politics* (trans: H. Rackam). Cambridge, MA: Harvard University Press (The Loeb Classical Library, vol. XXI).

Augustine, Saint. 1888. Exposition on the book of Psalms. In *Nicene and post-nicene fathers*, First series, vol. 8, ed. Philip Schaff. Buffalo: Christian Literature. http://www.newadvent.org/fathers/1801.html.

Benedict XVI. 2009. *Encyclical caritas in veritate*. Vatican: Libreria Editrice Vaeicana.

Gordon, Barry. 1975. *Economic analysis before Adam Smith*. London: Macmillan.

Kaye, Joel. 1998. *Economy and nature in the fourteenth century – Money, market exchange and the emergence of scientific thought*. Cambridge: Cambridge University Press.

Langholm, Odd. 1983. *Wealth and money in the Aristotelian tradition – A study in scholastic economic sources*. Bergen: Universitetsforlaget.

Langholm, Odd. 1992. *Economics in the medieval schools. Wealth, exchange, value, money & usury according to the Paris theological tradition*, 1200–1350. Leiden: E.J.Brill.

Langholm, Odd. 1998. *The legacy of scholasticism in economic thought. Antecedents of choice and power*. Cambridge: Cambridge University Press.

Lowry, S.Todd. 1987. *The archaeology of economic ideas – The classical Greek tradition*. Durham/London: Duke University Press.

Lowry, S.Todd, and Barry Gordon (eds.). 1998. *Ancient and medieval economic ideas and concepts of social justice*. Leiden: Brill.

Marx, Karl. 1867. *Das kapital*, 4th ed. Chicago: Charles H. Kerr. 1906. http://www.econlib.org/library/YPDBooks/Marx/mrxCpA.html.

Noonan Jr., John T. 1957. *The scholastic analysis of usury*. Cambridge: Harvard University Press.

Smith, Adam. 1976. *An inquiry into the nature and causes of the wealth of nations*, The Glasgow edition of the works and correspondence of Adam Smith, vol. 2. Oxford: Oxford University Press. http://oll.libertyfund.org/index.php?option=com_staticxt&staticfile=show.php&title=197

Chapter 4
Beyond the Market/State Binary Code: The Common Good as a Relational Good

Pierpaolo Donati

4.1 A Premise

Caritas in Veritate (Benedict XVI 2009, 39) states: 'The exclusively binary model of market-plus-State is corrosive of society, while economic forms based on solidarity, which find their natural home in civil society without being restricted to it, build up society. The market of gratuitousness does not exist, and attitudes of gratuitousness cannot be established by law. Yet both the market and politics need individuals who are open to reciprocal gift.'

In this paper I wish to elaborate on this statement, and show that, in order to go beyond the present domination of the binomial market-State (*lib-lab* in my language), which destroys sociality, we need much more than good, altruistic individuals: we need a societal configuration able to generate *relational goods*. Relational good is the name of the common good in a highly differentiated and globalised society.

4.2 What is Behind the World Economy's Crisis? There is a Problematic and Obsolete View of the 'World System'

4.2.1 Attempts at Explaining the Financial Crisis

The financial economy's crisis that broke out in September 2008 has been interpreted in many different ways, mostly from a strictly economic point of view. Basically, the crisis has been attributed to a 'malfunctioning' of financial markets,

P. Donati (✉)
Università di Bologna, Bologna, Italy
e-mail: pierpaolo.donati@unibo.it

M. Schlag and J.A. Mercado (eds.), *Free Markets and the Culture of Common Good*, Ethical Economy 41, DOI 10.1007/978-94-007-2990-2_4,
© Springer Science+Business Media B.V. 2012

obviously widely resorting in the process to moral considerations concerning economic actors failing to behave ethically. Solutions have been looking to identify new rules capable of moralising markets.

Politics has been assigned the task to find practical solutions, that is, measures implemented by national States and formulated by international agreements among States. International monetary authorities have been called upon by governments to act as fire brigades (i.e. to bail out banks and financial agencies from bankruptcy). Governments have adopted measures to limit the crisis' effects on unemployment as well as an increase in national poverty rates.

We are still short of a sociological interpretation of the crisis per se, differing from interpretations centred upon economic, moral and political factors. Sociological analyses have often been confused with moral ones. Take, for instance, the proposals regarding a new economy with a 'human face', drawing economic behaviour from anthropology (in particular from a personalistic anthropology rooted in both Catholic and Islamic thought).[1] Such philosophical proposals fall short of making the link between anthropology and economics by considering the specifically social factors that are the subject of sociology.

In fact, the interpretations that have shown how the crisis was determined by a lack of ethics in the economy have also shown that ethics on its own – that is seen as a call upon economic actors to act according to moral principles – can do very little, not to say nothing. It has been observed that only political coercion can introduce rules into the economy, whose ethical quality is always debatable. Instances of ethical self-regulation on the part of economic actors and financial markets have been rare in for-profit sectors. This in turn has highlighted to an even greater extent the weakness of the ethics-economy match as a remedy for the crisis.

In my view, we need a sociological analysis to show how the crisis stemmed from a certain set-up of the so-called 'global society'. Such a set-up is the product of a long historical development, which goes beyond the financial crisis' outbreak in 2008.

The question we ask is the following: from a sociological standpoint, why did this crisis break out? And what remedies can be put in place?

Luhmann's sociological analysis turns out to be very useful to understand the situation in question. Luhmann (1984) holds that highly modernised societies act as a *world system* (a *world society*) of a functional kind, in which each sub-system, for instance the economic one, is self-referential and autopoietic. The financialisation of the economy has emerged precisely out of that (Luhmann 1998). This means that in Western societal systems, representing the paradigmatic model of modernisation processes for the rest of the world, political power can enforce some limitations to economic systems. These limitations, however, are only contingent, merely

---

[1] It is certainly remarkable that Catholic anthropology has been associated with the Islamic Ummah on the grounds that Islamic finance is reported to use money only as a means and not as a goal, which would explain why Islamic financial institutions were able to avoid being crashed by the world crisis of September 2008 (cf. Milano 2010).

functional and they cannot meet normative imperatives beyond economic and political action. Ethics is turned into an *exaggerated steering mania*, which proves to be practically ineffective when challenged by real incidents (Luhmann 1997a, 50).

In other words, it is clear that modernised societies cannot resort to any solid moral values, least of all to a *business ethics*, simply because this goes against the modernisation idea itself. Modernised societies are constructed in such a way as to be immunised from ethics. As Luhmann put it bluntly and brutally (1984, 1990, 354), 'man is no longer the yardstick of society'.

I am not going to expound Luhmann's theory here: I will have to take it as known. I will get straight to the point: the thing is that sociological theory nowadays converges on the idea that world society is bound to face a future bristling with risks, uncertainties, disorientation, and even chaos (in the technical sense of the word). A future which, as Luhmann put it, *cannot* even *begin*. 'Reflexive modernisation' theory (Beck et al. 1994), though with different emphases, has in essence legitimised such an analysis of the current situation and of future prospects.

What, then, is/lies behind the world financial crisis started in 2008? There is certainly a very different crisis from that of 1929. The historical circumstances are totally different. At the time capitalism was scarcely regulated and lacked a substantial welfare State structure. Nowadays markets are far more regulated and benefit from of more developed social security systems.

As national States play a much larger part than 8 years ago, the measures that are now put in place to solve the crisis amount to three kinds of action: (1) incentives to and enforcement of market best practices by political-administrative systems, (2) ban on 'dirty' financial products and on fiscal heavens and (3) greater public commitment in terms of social expenditure, to nurture the real economy's virtuous cycles (by supporting family expenses, by limiting unemployment damages, by protecting poorer segments of the population).

And yet is that the solution? Personally, I doubt it. My analysis, then, proposes an interpretation of the crisis and of its solutions that is different from the most widespread ones.

The measures adopted these days cannot solve the crisis, but, for a number of reasons, they can at most provide temporary stoppers and remedies.

First of all, all these remedies remain within the 'economic-political system', which would confirm Luhmann's arguments by which the market + State system will keep on working even during a constant endemic crisis (I call it '*lib-lab*' configuration).[2] My argument, then, is that if we want to avoid a permanent crisis – more or less 'under control' as the case may be – then remedies have to break away from the self-referential logic of economic-political systems. In Luhmann's conceptual framework, this is not possible. We then have to accept the challenge posed by having to prove that an alternative societal set-up is not only abstractly possible, but

---

[2] As I have described and analysed the *lib-lab* set-up in many works, I simply have to refer to here: cf. Donati (2000, 2001, 2009).

is also necessary and realistic, if we really want to get out of a system producing a chronic crisis.

Secondly, the ethics that is called upon to correct the markets' malfunctioning has no credible sociological foundations, for the ethical principles one would like to uphold have nowhere to be generated or regenerated in this societal configuration, since neither the market nor the State is the source of ethical standards. If ethical corrections are to work, one needs to think of a different way of organising society. Such a new set-up (1) has to be capable of allowing for the emergence of social subjects (namely 'social environments' for the economic and political system) that can generate and adopt certain ethical standards of conduct and uphold them in economic-political systems and (2) has to meet such a condition in a structural manner and not by way of an occasional voluntary commitment. Luhmann would say that this is not possible, because – in his view – society's multiple spheres cannot in any way influence one another, least of all exchange ethical services. I propose to meet the challenge of proving that this is as possible as it is necessary, if we want to avoid a permanent crisis.

4.2.2   A Sociological Explanation

My argument, of a sociological kind, is that '*the set-up of world society is a critical and unstable set-up; it is impossible to get out of except by reforming its own lib-lab basic structure*'. Let me explain this.

Societies that have been or are in the process of being modernised are based on a structural (systemic) compromise between market (*lib*) and State (*lab*). By 'market' I mean free competition and capitalistic production theories and practices that refer to liberalism as an economic doctrine (it is the *lib* side, on which we find, for instance, the Chicago school). By 'State', I mean the State intervention theories and practices, aimed at guaranteeing equal opportunities and a welfare bare minimum as a citizenship right, which is generally supported by socialist-oriented political doctrines (it is the *lab* side, on which we find, for instance, the doctrines going back to J.M. Keynes, Lord Beveridge, R. Titmuss).

In brief, modernised systems are a mix of *lib* and *lab*, that is, *lib-lab* systems. Whenever the market (*lib*) is insolvent, one resorts to the State (*lab*); whenever the State (*lab*) is insolvent, one resorts to the market (*lib*). This is the game of modern economy, which attained its most accomplished model in the second half of the twentieth century.

Our societies are still working on the basis of this framework, looking to stabilise economic cycles and a fairer resource distribution through *lib-lab* regulations.

What is wrong with this societal configuration?

On the one hand, it is to be said that the *lib-lab* set-up has so far offered remarkable advantages, in as much as it has guaranteed freedom and more extensive political and social citizenship rights. In fact, we can say about this set-up what is said about liberal democracies, that is that although this system is full of defects, it is the best one human history has produced so far. On the other hand, though, we have to point out that its structural faults are not insignificant, but they concern some mechanisms which produce intrinsically and inevitably recurrent crises. In other words, *lib-lab systems are not sustainable as long-term systems*.

What are the mechanisms that make this society unsustainable? I would like to analyse the problematic aspects of *lib-lab* systems and verify whether there can be a societal configuration that can overcome these limitations.

4.2.3   The Lib-Lab Structure

Let us first look at intrinsic faults of the *lib-lab* set-up.[3]

(a) According to the *lib-lab* approach, *society is an intertwining of economics and politics against which the rest is seen as insignificant for the common good and for citizenship*. In particular, life worlds are conceived as a merely 'private' sphere. I myself would rather point out that, from a sociological point of view, what lies outside the market-State pair is not insignificant for the achievement of the common good, for citizenship and for the workings of both market and State. If life worlds are conceived as 'left overs', the *lib-lab* system falls into a chronic crisis it cannot remedy.

(b) For the *lib-lab* system, *there is no alternative to the combination of liberalism and socialism*.[4] Such a societal configuration, though, essentially considered as a problem of *balancing* between (anti-systemic) freedom and equality (in view of extending individual freedoms), refrains from tackling the *social integration* problems[5] posed by such an approach. Even though one may agree that society's systemic planning is not a workable regulatory response, still it is clear that the *lib-lab* combination says almost nothing on social integration problems in contemporary social systems. To put it another way, *lib-lab* systems generate increasing social integration deficits (the so-called 'modernity pathologies')[6] for which they provide no remedies.

(c) The *lib-lab* set-up seeks to tame the 'competition-profit versus solidarity-social redistribution' conflict without providing alternatives to the permanent opposition between these two contradictory needs. The conflict is seen and dealt with as an

---

[3]For a more detailed analysis cf. Donati (2000, 229–260), Donati (2001, 202–227).

[4]A champion of this approach, Ralph Dahrendorf (1994) sees citizenship as a gift granted (*octroyée*) by an enlightented political élite, including entitlements guaranteed by the State versus other provisions offered by the free market.

[5]I am using the phrase 'social integration' here to distinguish it from 'systemic integration' (Lockwood 1992, 1999).

[6]The well-known expression was first proposed by J. Habermas (1981), who deals with such pathologies in terms of communicative forms and not as a more complex problem. At the cultural level it has been employed by Charles Taylor.

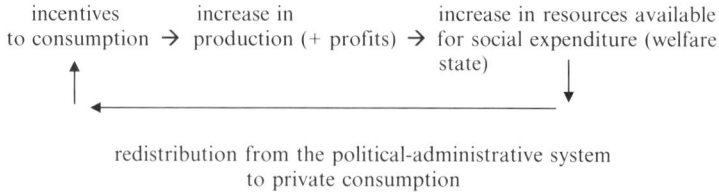

incentives   increase in   increase in resources available
to consumption → production (+ profits) → for social expenditure (welfare
                                                                    state)

redistribution from the political-administrative system
to private consumption

Fig. 4.1 *Lib-lab* systems' economic logic (an evolutionary model which is supposed to bring us to 'progress')

insoluble opposition, which may only be kept under control through political democracy, especially in the form of neo-corporativistic democracy. The two oppositions, though, bring about a structural imbalance. In the USA, the competition-profit side has the upper hand over social citizenship rights, which entails serious social inequality and poverty indexes in Third World contexts. In Europe the solidarity-redistribution side prevails on the basis of a citizenship principle that seeks to be unconditional without actually succeeding in that.

The *world system* (or globalisation), marked by the economy's financialisation, is the outcome of this current worldwide societal *lib-lab* structure.

The recurrent crises are not those predicted by Karl Marx. The polarisation process setting the leading world imperialist bourgeoisie against the proletarian masses does not occur on a worldwide scale, but in limited geo-political-economic areas, where it is restrained by *lib-lab* systems, looking, despite all their shortcomings, to reduce social inequalities. Furthermore, globalisation gives rise to many other intermediary economic actors between the two poles envisaged by Marx.

What determines the crises occurring in systems based on the *lib-lab* compromise between State and market is the very 'economic logic',[7] which is not purely capitalistic, but is based on the intertwining of market and State, and thus embraces society as a whole (starting with the market). Such an economic logic has unexpected effects, side effects and negative external effects which erode the civil society on which the lib-lab system is based. What is this logic about?

Let me summarise it in Fig. 4.1. The economic logic I am talking about consists in using political power to increase consumption, which in turn will foster productivity and profits, so as to be able to draw on fiscal drag for the financial resources needed to push consumption. The rest is irrelevant. Banks and financial systems serve this logic.

Such a systemic logic, with all its internal mechanisms, cannot be extended over certain thresholds, because great social problems arise once certain economic growth levels are exceeded. The present societal model proves functional to break

---

[7] The term 'economic' here is used in an analytical generalised sense: cf. Donati (1991, Chap. 4).

away from poverty and under-development, whereas it becomes dysfunctional for a welfare society. In particular:

(a) Consumerism generates a broad range of problematic or pathological human conditions since consumption needs are artificially induced and technologies, especially the media, are misused;
(b) The social inclusion model that is supported by this logic (founded on a simple extension of the typical twentieth-century welfare State) makes beneficiaries ever more passive and produces distorted effects: for instance, it creates various 'traps' (the poverty trap, the 'crystal roof' limiting women's social mobility and distorting equal opportunities on the basis of gender, etc.) and, above all, immunises individuals from social relations.

Many will point out that there are no alternatives to the systemic logic I am talking about (Fig. 4.1) because (a) if you curb consumption, you also stop economic growth and (b) if you cut social expenditure (the welfare State), you create poverty.

What shall we do then?

The proposals put forward are centred on introducing two kinds of correcting tools:

1. Putting '*more ethics into the market*', as proposed by some, in the hope of making actors more responsible[8]: two examples of this are 'business ethics' at the production stage and a 'fairness ethics' in the distribution of goods – such proposals are especially aimed at correcting the *lib* side of this set-up.
2. Extending citizenship, as proposed by others, to make it 'more inclusive' to embrace the weakest social segments, in order to reduce poverty and social problems – such proposals are especially aimed at correcting the *lab* side of this set-up.

I note that such corrective measures do not modify the systemic logic of *lib-lab* systems. As generous as the above proposals may be, they do not stand many chances of succeeding. They do not stand many chances of succeeding because it is the *lib-lab* system itself which makes them ineffective. The system continues to work in such a way as to be functional to a moral order centred upon individual, instrumental and utilitarian values and criteria. Though sensitive to the need for personal honesty and greater social justice (in the form of equal opportunities), these values and criteria fail to meet the need to create a civil society capable of supporting honest and fair behaviour. On the whole, it is a self-contradictory model, because it is the economy that drives morality and not vice versa.[9] We have to modify the *lib-lab* logic. I shall now attempt to present these arguments in more detail.

---

[8] On the issue of finance ethics, see Gotti Tedeschi (2005, 2007).
[9] In the AGIL terms, the Adaptation function prevails on the Latency function.

4.3   Should We Yield to Evolution Laws?

4.3.1   Lib-Lab and Evolution

The *lib-lab* view of the *world system* urges us to let society run in accordance with its own evolutionary tendencies. Such an approach is implemented through a so-called reflexive modernisation model, which in essence chronically questions itself. As Beck et al. (2003, 3) put it, 'Reflexive" does *not* mean that people today lead a more conscious life. On the contrary, "reflexive" does not signify an "increase in mastery and consciousness, but a heightened awareness that mastery is impossible". Simple modernity becomes "reflexive modernization" to the extent that it disenchants and then dissolves its own taken-for-granted premises'. This leaves the referent, the purpose and the point of 'reflexivity' highly ambiguous.

The society envisaged by the *lib-lab* way of thinking is a society which suffers from a permanent identity crisis, pervaded as it is by insoluble social and personal risks. Reflexive modernisation is seen as a radical uncertainty affecting every sphere of social life.[10]

According to my argument, on the basis of modernity's own assumptions, the abovementioned correcting measures (i.e. a. ethical injections into the market and b. extension of citizenship rights and their beneficiaries) do not work because (a) the *lib-lab* logic is relativistic from an ethical point of view and neutralises any attempts to replace economic criteria by 'non-negotiable' ethical criteria and (b) the extension of citizenship rights (in terms of more rights and more beneficiaries) is always unstable and problematic and, at any rate, if it is viewed according to the typical twentieth-century *lib-lab* welfare State model, faces increasing failures (fiscal crises, inclusions generating exclusions, etc.).

In short, the present modernisation processes do not tolerate any restrictive, external regulations of the *lib-lab* logic (in the three stages summarised in Fig. 4.1: consumption, for profit production and redistribution through the welfare State). The only regulations this logic can endure are functional ones, that is functional to its own reproduction.

Neo-functionalism, though, does not ensure any society capable of avoiding the dilemmas and social pathologies produced by such a societal model. It cannot produce any stable social system, it can only determine the same problems again and again. *Neo-functionalism turns to be just 'another way', only outwardly non-ideological, of describing the commodification of the world and an evolutionary adaptation of the whole society to such commodification processes.*

Basically, the *lib-lab* model proposes us to live in a society that adapts to Darwin's evolutionary laws, lacking any finalism and pushed by its competition and survival skills. This is globalisation's own *world system*.

---

[10]On a critique of the reflexive modernisation theory: cf. Archer (2007), Donati (2011).

There seem to be no alternatives to this State of affairs. Utopias have fallen. And yet, perhaps, a careful analysis of the situation may reveal ongoing societal morphogenetic processes which question the functionalistic view of economic rationality as configured in the *lib-lab* model (Fig. 4.1). Sociology has consecrated this model first with Talcott Parsons' theory and later, faced with the former's failure, with Niklas Luhmann's one. We now see a new version in place, which we had better look at: it is a version of functionalism proposing an interpretation of markets, particularly financial ones, through key 'reflexive truths' (Soros 2000).

4.3.2   Reflexivity and Reality

George Soros, the international magnate, has pointed out that financial markets' workings follow their own 'reflexivity' (or reflexive rationality) marked by evolutionary mechanisms, which are self-referential and have uncertain outcomes. These 'mechanisms' are rooted in the particular reflexivity of economic actors who 'discount' the future. They shape reality (what actually happens in society, not only in markets) through investments that anticipate the future and pre-empt future reality in the shape desired by financial operators. Reality is transformed through the financial operators' own 'reflexive truth'.

However, our question is: to what extent can society – interpreted as daily life's social texture – be configured in the same way as financial markets and their 'reflexive' logic promoting an evolution without finalism? The thing is that society – if we see it as a social relationships network properly – is not a *stock exchange*. There are other types of reflexivity to shape society (Archer 2003, 2007, ed. 2010; Donati 2009, 2011).

The argument I would like to hold is that it is these 'other' forms of reflexivity that can get us out of the crisis started in 2008 and beyond the *lib-lab* systems' own chronic crisis.

4.4   Is There an Alternative to an Evolution Without Finalism?

Can we think of an alternative to the functionalist and evolutionist model I have been discussing? I think that the world needs a post-functionalist, indeed an *after-modern* development model (Donati 2011), that is based on the assumption of definitely overcoming functionalism – theoretical and empirical – as its intellectual infrastructure.[11]

---

[11]I take it that modernity corresponds to a society spirit and model of a functional type (as has been clarified very well by Niklas Luhmann's own theory). I see functionalism as the root of the scientific-technological approach typical of the West and of Western modernity, as Davis (1959) described it.

However, a word of caution is needed here. Functionalism cannot be overcome by a backward-looking humanistic view, unable to match the competitive skills of functionalism. It has to be a humanism proving capable of taking functionalism into account while overcoming its limitations.

Such a post-functionalist development configuration or logic ought to be able to do two things:

(a) At a macro level, to reduce systemic determinisms, in favour of organisational networks capable of self-steering;
(b) At a micro level (i.e. of individual action), to modify life styles, that is consumption habits, according to more austere value guidelines, to avoid functionalistic commercialisation mechanisms. Life worlds, that is primary (face-to-face) relations and interactions, taking place within families, small groups, associations' networks based on interpersonal relations, have to be given a chance to speak. One has to take into account the decisive role of *personal* reflexivity, seen as inner conversation (Archer 2000, 2003) and the role of *social* reflexivity as a quality of relations' networks (Donati 2011).

It is clear that such changes are not possible within a consumption economy whose only ruling principle is the GNP growth imperative (as it is in Fig. 4.1). They become possible, though, as soon as one takes on board the fact that GNP has been a useful well-being parameter when used for developing countries with quite a low average income and with widespread poverty problems, but it becomes hardly significant for societies that have reached a certain well-being threshold, such as post-industrial countries. In these countries, GNP has to be replaced by other units of measure, such as Gross National Well-Being (GNWB), which should be adopted not only by developed countries, but also by developing countries.

An austere life-style does not mean a 'poor' economy that reduces aspirations to a greater well-being. It does not mean, for instance, a mere de-industrialisation or a demise of medical services or schooling as proposed in the past, nor does it mean rejecting technology. It does not mean going back to a naively 'naturalistic' way of life. These are utopias without any hope or sense. A different economy is made possible by a different notion, relational and not merely materialistic, of well-being and of happiness.[12] We need another economic logic, if we realise the relational character of society which follows from the 'happiness paradox' (according to which the well-being in the advanced countries does not increase over time, or even declines, in spite of the rising trend of income, while people continue to strive for money).

We have to ask ourselves if and how it is possible to envisage an economy centred upon the human quality of individual and social life and focused on humanising social relations.

---

[12]Cf. Diwan (2000) and Donati (2009).

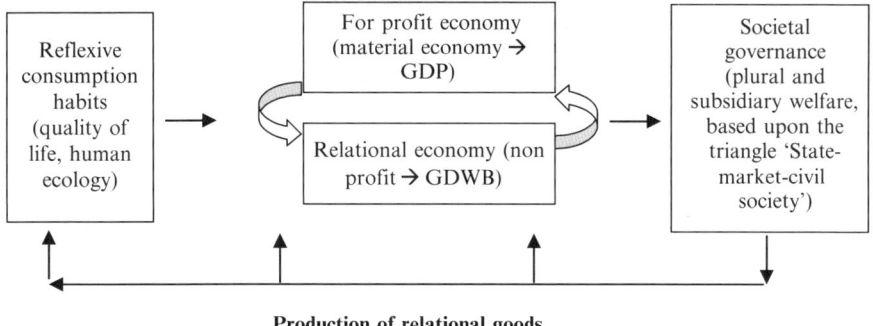

Production of relational goods

Fig. 4.2 The economic logic of a relational society

The crisis that emerged in 2008 is at the root of the following novelties (see Fig. 4.2):

– Consumption habits are becoming more reflexive.
– We are seeing an expansion of an economy that we may call relational because it envisages the economic stages of production-distribution-consumption of goods and services in terms of social relations and aims at producing a synergy between profit and non-profit.
– The rule of the welfare State is gradually replaced by a societal governance (plural and subsidiary welfare, featuring a market-State-third sector triangle).
– Societal governance seeks to operate reflexively both on consumption and on market differentiation (for profit, non-profit, civil economy, etc.) in order to produce relational goods.

Such changes point to the rise of another type of societal configuration, as outlined in Fig. 4.2.

It is important to emphasise the role of the social spheres commonly called 'third sector'. Not only does the influence of their economic role increase (in terms of turnover and workforce), but above all such spheres operate as an 'engine of a civil society' that is alternative to the market underpinning the *lib-lab* set-up (as described in my Fig. 4.1).

It is the vast world of co-operation (social co-operation, social enterprises), of voluntary associations, of ethical banks and of various forms of microcredit, of fair trade, of NGOs, of multiple forms of enterprises which we call 'civil'. Such bodies create their own financial markets, such as the *Bolsa de Valores Sociales y Ambietais* (BVS&A) in Brazil, SASIX *(South African Social Investment Exchange)* in South Africa, the KIVA project in the USA, the Asian *Impact Investment Exchange (IIX)* managed by the *Social Stock Exchange Asia (SSXA)* in Singapore, GEXSI *(Global Exchange For Social Investment)* in the UK, MYC4 in Denmark and *Social Stock*

Exchange Ltd. in the UK, involving the Rockefeller Foundation, and finally the *FacciaperFaccia* [Face for Face] event at the *Falacosagiusta* fair in Milan. Others have proposed to create a 'social stock exchange', aimed at managing *'social and welfare business'*, which would become an integral part of a horizontal subsidiary set-up a State could not ignore. And this might happen by setting up a sort of AIM (*Alternative Investment Market*), whose financial instruments would be shares (issued by low profit enterprises and non-profit social enterprises) and debt bonds (equally issued by for profit and non-profit bodies).

Such new enterprises as *low profit limited liability companies* and *community interest companies*, as well as new financial markets, can produce a different response to the world economic crisis, not merely by adapting themselves but by giving moral standards priority in economic and social action and by being able to modify life, work and consumption styles. Compared with traditional capitalist enterprises, such enterprises have a number of peculiar features: for instance, they produce relational goods (and more generally *intangibile goods*), they show greater flexibility, value sideways social mobility, rather than upward or downward job mobility.

These new economic entities do convey a new model of society, but to implement it they have to overcome a number of obstacles: (1) internally, they have to develop their own reflexivity and (2) externally, they have to get rid of their structural dependence on the State (above all in Europe) and on the for-profit market (above all in the USA).[13]

4.5   Rethinking Civil Society and Its Economic Foundations

4.5.1   Civil Society and Globalisation

The problem with modernity having reached the globalisation stage is that civil society is still seen as a capitalist economy tending to financialise real economy. The 2008 crisis has revealed this way of seeing civil society and has at the same time started to elaborate a new way of interpreting civil society. In other terms, the 2008 crisis has highlighted the difference (a real *splitting*) between the old and the new civil society. We may have reached a turning-point between one and the other.

On the one hand, the old civil society is still amongst us, tending to subject every good to the sequence by which money is invested in goods which in turn are used to make more money [Money-Good-Money (M-G-M)]. Actors, that is, invest money in a good they have no need for, but which is only instrumental to making more money. At first, they attribute to that good a monetary (functional) value and then trade it to make more money. It is important to understand that this mechanism

---

[13] As an indicator that a *lib-lab* configuration is prevailing in the USA too (and not only in Europe), it can be reminded that 97% of the private debt in the States passes through the State (Sinn 2010, Chap. 11).

Table 4.1 Two paradigmatic set-ups of economy

	In a 'modern' society	In an 'after-modern' society
A (means)	Money = currency	Money ≠ currency
G (goals)	The only constraint set by money is for it to provide more money	Functional constraints are set for the use of money (in its various monetary and non-monetary forms)
I (social responsibility)	Enterprises only have an internal social responsibility to their employees	Enterprises also have an external responsibility (to the community's stakeholders)
L (values)	Value motives are individualistic, instrumental, acquisitive	Value motives are relational (inspired by subsidiarity and solidarity to produce goods seen as relational goods)

presides over the whole *lib-lab* system. The State also uses it in its relationship with the market: the State uses the market to get the money to pay for public welfare, which in turn is the source of votes, the political system's own money. In this context, civil society is identified with the market.

On the other hand, a new civil society has emerged, which is identified with real economy. In real economy, in contrast with the previous case, the good is evaluated in itself and money (also in forms different from currency) is only used by actors as a tool to acquire the goods they need [according to the sequence: Good-Money-Good (G-M-G)]. A good is translated into the money needed to obtain another necessary good (for instance: work provides the money used by actors to buy the goods they want).

Rethinking civil society means understanding whether, and how, it is possible, and necessary in the first place, to shift from the M-G-M sequence to the G-M-G sequence. This shift requires a more complex view of society than modernity's own view. At the core of this view lies the relational nature of goods. Indeed, if it is true that the distinctive feature of a modernising economy is to erase the relational nature of goods and economic processes, the building blocks of a new economy will be precisely the new needs for individual and social relationships. It is not by accident that we see gifts coming back into so many social spheres and in many different forms (Donati 2003): from a sociological point of view, gifts point to the pursuit of social bonds and to the need for social relations to be forged to cement the sense of community.

4.5.2   Modern and After-Modern Societies

Let me explain the distinction I have been drawing between the two societies: the modern one and the one I call after-modern, in more detail (Table 4.1).

The key element of this distinction is the fact that after-modern society is confronted with the need to produce a variety pool of options (in goods consumption and production, in life styles, in welfare measures) which cannot be 'accidental', or amount to a merely functional monetary equivalence (as Luhmann holds), but has to be endowed with sense, permitting the creation of common goods, by which I mean relational goods (Donati 2008).

This results in the rise of a new *Zeitgeist*. Whenever we say that future society will have to be inspired by the ethical criterion of 'sustainability', we have many different things in mind, the first being that instruments, such as finance, technology, etc., must match human needs and not vice versa, which in turn implies that means have to be used only as means and not as self-standing ends or goals.

I summarise the distinction between modern and after-modern set-ups in a table (Table 4.1).

1. In modern society:

   (A) Financial economy is based on the equation: money = currency.
   (G) Money is an end in itself, because of the functional culture which makes all goods and services subjectable to monetary equivalence.
   (I) Enterprises have no broader social responsibility than that strictly associated with their own employees.
   (L) The motives of economic action are individual, instrumental, acquisitive.

2. In after-modern society, on the other hand:

   (A) Means economy assumes that money does not only amount to currency, but there can be other forms of money, meaning by money an entitlement to access goods and services [money ≠ currency]. This economy, therefore, draws a distinction between monetary and non-monetary forms of money, by connecting them to 'real economy' (in which many goods and services do not allow for monetary equivalents). Hence arises an observable multiplication of forms of money, labour and capitals (not only financial capital, but also political, social and human) and also a multiplication of contracts, in brief, of all the goods needed to pursue an economic objective (Donati 2001);
   (G) Money is subjected to social constraints, which may be usage or functional constraints (as, for instance, is the case of vouchers).
   (I) Corporate social responsibility is extended outside the company to the surrounding community and to stakeholders (profits do not only or entirely go to shareholders); social responsibility is also broadened with regard to employees with forms of conciliation between work and family, with relational contracts, as well as corporate citizenship.
   (L) The motives of economic action relate individual interests to principles of subsidiarity and solidarity which are necessary to produce common goods, which will be relational goods.

4.5.3   The Structure of After-Modern Society

The new societal configuration (as outlined in Fig. 4.3) does not erase modernity, but sees the modern *lib-lab* set-up only as a particular case, that is as a way of

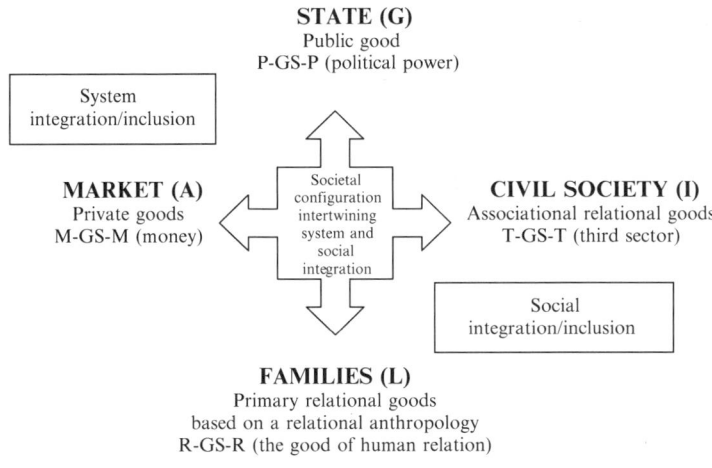

STATE (G)
Public good
P-GS-P (political power)

System
integration/inclusion

MARKET (A)
Private goods
M-GS-M (money)

Societal
configuration
intertwining
system and
social
integration

CIVIL SOCIETY (I)
Associational relational goods
T-GS-T (third sector)

Social
integration/inclusion

FAMILIES (L)
Primary relational goods
based on a relational anthropology
R-GS-R (the good of human relation)

Legenda:
AGIL (A=adaptation; G=goal-attainment; I=integration; L=latency)
Symbols: M (money); GS (goods and services); P (political power); T (third sector, civil
society associations); R (social relations)

Fig. 4.3 The new configuration of after-modern society

operating (of organising economy, politics, etc.) which is no longer general and which cannot be generalised throughout all social actors and spheres (i.e. AGIL), but is only applicable to ever more limited action areas. Earlier on modernisation was seen as potentially extendable throughout all spheres of society. This in turn legitimised the fact that the compromise between State and market was able to turn life worlds into commodities. The new set-up that I call after-modern is not characterised by a logic of dominance of a pole (market or State) over the other or by commercial negotiation logics between sub-systems or social spheres,[14] but by a *network-like logic* which is forced to make the different societal spheres more cooperative, or at least to follow a mutually non-destructive competition logic, within a world-system's global sustainability project.

To implement such a set-up, one needs a relational configuration that modernity was unable to tolerate, because it was overwhelmed by cultural movements seeing modernity as a denial of sociality.[15]

---

[14] I am referring to individual A, G, I, L sub-systems with the institutions thereof.

[15] J. J. Rousseau's works, for instance, provide a paradigmatic example of this position, which has justified an apolitical individualism and at the same time State dictatorships within modernity (cf. Spaemann 2009).

4.5.4   The Interpretation of Caritas in Veritate

The encyclical *Caritas in Veritate*, in my opinion, is to be read and interpreted in this light. I shall make a few remarks on the encyclical to highlight how this document paves the way to the view of society that I have summarised in Fig. 4.3. We shall thus be able to grasp even better what societal configuration will be functional to get out of the long-term crisis that broke out in 2008.

Caritas in Veritate has been the subject of many comments, both written and oral. These have rightly focused on its central issue, that is that charity lived out in truth 'is the principal driving force behind the authentic development of every person and of all humanity' (Benedict XVI 2009, 1). The Pope's call to rediscover the deepest meaning of human actions in the true love of God (who is Truth) and of others certainly lies at the heart of the encyclical. It is undoubtedly the guiding star for the analysis of both complex economic, social and political problems and of their possible solutions.

In the present essay, I would like to underline an aspect of the encyclical which has not yet been discussed in depth. I am referring to the 'way of thinking' Pope Benedict XVI proposes in this text. It is a way of thinking which is centred on *relationality* as a central category to interpret human condition and the ways to achieve a full genuine development of the person and of humanity: 'Thinking of this kind requires a *deeper critical evaluation of the category of relation*' (Benedict XVI 2009, 53).

Pope Benedict XVI proclaims that 'charity is at the heart of the Church's social doctrine' with the following justification: as 'it gives real substance to the personal relationship with God and with neighbour, it is the principle not only of micro-relationships (with friends, with family members or within small groups) but also of macro-relationships (social, economic and political ones)' (Benedict XVI 2009, 2). From the very beginning, it is clear that the turning point of the encyclical is found in the quality of relations, micro and macro, through meso-relations (those of civil society's median bodies which are dealt with at length in Chaps. 3, 4, 5).

This approach is based on the idea that, while the eternal truth by which human dignity consists in being children of God still holds, it is also true that today there is a change in the sense (historical, cultural and contextual) of what 'human' is. The scenario shows us a range of degradations of every kind, especially in the area of human life and family manipulations, and also presents many emergencies in education, unemployment, denial of fundamental human rights in so many areas of the globe. This new scenario cannot be addressed without an adequate anthropology ('*the social question has become a radically anthropological question*', (Benedict XVI 2009, 75)) and without this anthropology being able to cast its light on the whole society, that is on all the social relations in which human life is in question.

In my view, the way Benedict XVI proposes can be called 'relational', given the fact that it is in the category of relation that a solution is to be sought. 'As a spiritual being, the human creature is defined through interpersonal relations. The more authentically he or she lives these relations, the more his or her own personal identity matures. It is not by isolation that human beings establishes his worth, but by placing himself in relation with others and with God. Hence these relations take on fundamental importance. The same holds true for peoples as well. *A metaphysical understanding of the relations between persons is therefore of great benefit for their development*' (Benedict XVI 2009, 53). And a little further: 'The Christian revelation of the unity of the human race presupposes a *metaphysical interpretation of the "humanum" in which relationality is an essential element*' (Benedict XVI 2009, 55).

That is then the *fil rouge* running through the encyclical: interpreting the 'humanum' through relationality and hence moving on to carry out an analysis suited to our times of the various difficult questions with which we are confronted.

The quality of social relations is identified with what people love most, the 'ultimate' concerns they express in their relations. Love is a gift of God, but it is also an ultimate concern of human persons. Its presence or its absence justifies the problems we endure and paves the way to their possible solutions. Yet love is not a nice feeling, but rather *a certain relation* with oneself, with neighbours and with God. The encyclical precisely insists on the fact that charity cannot be interpreted as a generic feeling, affection or emotion. The charity discussed here, precisely because it is relation, cannot be a 'private' fact (deprived of social responsibility). It is conversely the source of every good, as a relational good. This is why love can and must become a principle of social organisation (the civilisation of love). '*the decisive issue is the overall moral tenor of society*' (Benedict XVI 2009, 51). Humans have to 'weave networks of charity' (Benedict XVI 2009, 5). 'The *earthly city* is promoted not merely by relationships of rights and duties, but to an even greater and more fundamental extent by relationships of gratuitousness, mercy and communion. Charity always manifests God's love in human relationships as well' (Benedict XVI 2009, 6).

Hence, then, can be drawn all the operational consequences. In sum: the idea that the relations in which charity is made concrete, such as gifts and fraternity, can and must turn from marginal and marginalised occurrences in modern society into principles occupying a primary place in most practical matters, such as the way of organising and managing economic enterprises, consumer associations, unions, social service networks, the welfare State, the relations among peoples and so on. Right up to supporting the articulation of society, the way of 'setting up societies' (associations in the broad sense of the word), based on a *governance* of a societal and plural type, which realises the common good through a solidarity and subsidiarity combination between all society's parts. This holds true from a family organisation right up to international relations.

What, though, can push men and women along this path, given the present globalisation process led by a rampant capitalism, by ever more pervasive individualism, by clear signs of separation and fragmentation of the social fabric?

It is at this point that truth comes into play, so that charity may not be reduced to mere emotions: 'Without truth, charity is confined to a narrow field devoid of relations. It is excluded from the plans and processes of promoting human development of universal range, in dialogue between knowledge and praxis' (Benedict XVI 2009, 4);

and again: 'Truth frees charity from the constraints of an emotionalism that deprives it of relational and social content' (Benedict XVI 2009, 3).

Here again emerges the importance of the relational key as a 'novelty' of the encyclical. In fact, beyond well-known issues (call to an integral human development, to fight old and new poverties, etc.), its specific contribution lies in highlighting *the mutual interchange between charity and truth configured as thinking of them 'relationally'*. It is from such relationality that can arise blueprints for a new humanism open to transcendence. There is no truth without charity and there is no charity without truth. Truth needs charity, just like charity needs truth. This *unbreakable link* is the relation that characterises the 'humanum'. In it find their roots all the qualities we may define as authentically human, which are indispensable to achieve a 'society of the 'humanum', that is an economy and politics, a technology, a bioethics with a human face.

The relational link between love and truth is always necessary, but its forms and content are always contingent due to the peculiarities of contexts, in space and time.

The outcome of this new perspective is the development of 'a new vision' (Benedict XVI 2009, 78) which responds to Paul VI's cry: 'the world is in trouble because of the lack of thinking' (Benedict XVI 2009, 53). The encyclical letter *Caritas in Veritate* invites us to embrace a new vision opening up a precise path, which stems from a theological vision, but is able to speak to and fertilise all human and social sciences.

The Church does not claim to provide cookery book recipes, but points to a new way of thinking which has its source in *relationality*, rooted in the simultaneously transcendent and immanent reality of the Trinity. Such a perspective is particularly voiced as a dialogue with human and social sciences in paragraphs 53–55 (see a comment by Archer 2009), and adds substance to all the other more 'practical' considerations concerning the configuration of economic relations (a new civil economy), of political relation (a new plural, subsidiary, relational welfare), of family relations and life care (a new relational bioethics), and so on.

The deepest message of the encyclical, I believe, lies then in betting on a new ethical interaction between consciences and intellects, on a relational vision, which may be up to the challenge of the new interdependences among individuals and among peoples. Human development will be the emergent effect of this new vision of socialising and of the resulting practices. For instance, it will no longer be feasible to see and practice artificial procreation as an expression of a private desire or (emotional) feeling expressed by one or more individuals, because what matters is the dignity of the relation which bears the child, a dignity on which depends the *humanum* in the identity of the child him/herself. Pope Benedict's call to 'reciprocity of consciences and liberties' is a call to rethink our lives in this direction, that is as a relation in what it has of human. Life is human in so far as it is a 'relational reality' in a specific sense (Donati 2011). From this way of thinking can arise a new society.

In view of this perspective the common good is reinterpreted as a relational good, which can only be achieved by making an appropriate and combined use of the solidarity and subsidiarity principles, on the basis of a relational anthropology and a relational view of society as a whole, starting from the family.

Particularly important is the statement according to which: 'The exclusively binary model of market-plus-State is corrosive of society, while economic forms based on solidarity, which find their natural home in civil society without being restricted to it, build up society. The market of gratuitousness does not exist, and attitudes of gratuitousness cannot be established by law. Yet both the market and politics need individuals who are open to reciprocal gift' (Benedict XVI 2009, 39).

In my sociological language, this means that we have to see social inclusion as relational inclusion and social differentiation as not merely functional but as relational differentiation (Donati 2009).

I therefore propose to interpret the encyclical in a relational perspective enabling us to make it lively and practicable. This means that twenty-first century society has to take a new departure from civil society. Which nowadays entails the fact that the New Deal no longer only rests on the State or only on the market, or on a combination of the two, but on the network between State, market and civil society (third sector organisations). Such a network is to be observed and implemented therein as a relational network, not as a knot structure (Fig. 4.3). But surely a decisive role is assigned to relational economy, with its prototypical, though not exclusive expression in the Third Sector, capable of providing ethical inputs to State and market. Yet, as demonstrated by empirical sociological research (Donati and Tronca 2008), the Third Sector in turn needs inputs to devise a culture capable of upholding goods and services as social relations, rather than as means to make money. Such inputs come from the primary networks of families and of interpersonal relations.

4.6 In Conclusion: A New 'Way of Making Society'

The *world system* based on the financialisation not only of economy but, we may well say, of all social relations experiences a chronic crisis and has to be reconverted. But how?

In the present essay, I have argued that we do not have to resort to an abstract societal 'model', but rather to facilitate some ways of life (forms of a *modus vivendi*), that is ways of operating and making society, which may trace the original practices of a civil society that is not subordinate to the compromise between State and market.

It is possible to apply to the paradigmatic civil society a notion of 'reconversion' by analogy with what happened to market reconversion, when we shifted from an economy based on large industrial concerns to the information and knowledge economy. It can be defined as a reconversion of *civil* society if we think of it as a 'bottom up' promotion of networks of social relations which do not respond to imperatives of functional service and to monetary equivalence criteria, but meet the need to create relational goods.

The reconfiguration of civil society according to the scenario I have outlined (Figs. 4.2, 4.3 and Table 4.1) will redefine the ways of being of State and market as well.

Certainly, present societal configurations are characterised by great disparities between countries. The gap between the two sides of the Atlantic is well-known. In the USA, the market is typically *lib* and is celebrated as such. In Europe (EU), conversely, the market proclaims itself as 'social' and is celebrated as such. In actual fact, though, in both cases the societal model pursued is the *lib-lab* one, as proved by the continuing State and Federal intervention in the USA (in particular under the Obama administration, even though Ronald Reagan and Bill Clinton had already widely implemented Keynesian policies) and by the increasing practice of resorting to market privatisations (disguised as applications of the subsidiarity principle) in Europe.

My view is that not only Europe and North America but every continent needs the new development model I have tried to outline.

Bibliography

Archer, M.S. 2000. *Being human. The problem of agency*. Cambridge: Cambridge University Press. Italian translation: 2007. *Essere umani. Il problema dell'agire*, ed. Prandini, R. Genova-Milano: Marietti.

Archer, M.S. 2003. *Structure, agency and the internal conversation*. Cambridge: Cambridge University Press. Italian translation: 2006. *La conversazione interiore. Come nasce l'agire sociale*. Trento: Edizioni Erickson.

Archer, M.S. 2007. *Making our way through the world: Human reflexivity and social mobility*. Cambridge: Cambridge University Press. Italian translation: 2009. *Riflessività umana e percorsi di vita. Come la soggettività umana influenza la mobilità sociale*. Trento: Erickson.

Archer, M.S. 2009. L'enciclica di Benedetto provoca la teoria sociale. *Vita e Pensiero XCII* 5: 52–56.

Archer, M.S. (ed.). 2010. *Conversations about reflexivity*. London/New York: Routledge.

Beck, U., Giddens, A., and S. Lash. 1994. *Reflexive modernization*. Cambridge: Polity Press. Italian translation: 1999. *Modernizzazione riflessiva*. Trieste: Asterios.

Beck, U., W. Bonss, and C. Lau. 2003. The theory of reflexive modernization. Problematic, hypotheses and research program. *Theory, Culture and Society* 20(2): 1–33.

Benedict XVI. 2009. *Encyclical caritas in veritate*. Vatican: Libreria Editrice Vaticana.

Dahrendorf, R. 1994. The changing quality of citizenship. In *The condition of citizenship*, ed. B. van Steenberger, 10–19. London: Sage.

Davis, K. 1959. The myth of functional analysis as a special method in sociology and anthropology. *American Sociological Review* 24(6): 757–772.

Diwan, R. 2000. Relational wealth and the quality of life. *Journal of Socio-Economics* 29(4): 305–340.

Donati, P. 1991. *Teoria relazionale della società*. Milano: FrancoAngeli.

Donati, P. 2000. *La cittadinanza societaria*. Roma/Bari: Laterza.

Donati, P. 2001. *Il lavoro che emerge. Prospettive del lavoro come relazione sociale in una economia dopo-moderna*. Torino: Bollati Boringhieri.

Donati, P. 2003. Giving and social relations: The culture of free giving and its differentiation today. *International Review of Sociology* 13(2): 243–272.

Donati, P., and L. Tronca. 2008. *Il capitale sociale degli italiani. Le radici familiari, comunitarie e associative del civismo*, Milano: FrancoAngeli.

Donati, P. 2008. Discovering the relational character of the common good. In *Pursuing the common good: How solidarity and subsidiarity can work together*, ed. M.S. Archer and P. Donati, 659–683. Vatican: PASS.

Donati, P. 2009. Welfare e globalizzazione: fra mercificazione e demercificazione. *Studi di Sociologia* 47(1): 3–31.

Donati, P. 2011. Reflexivity after modernity: From the viewpoint of relational sociology. In *Relational sociology. A new paradigm for the social sciences*, ed. P. Donati, 192–210. London/New York: Routledge.

Gotti Tedeschi, Ettore. 2005. *Denaro e Paradiso*. Casale Monferrato: Edizioni Piemme.

Gotti Tedeschi, Ettore. 2007. *Spiriti Animali. La concorrenza giusta*. Milano: Università Bocconi Editore.

Habermas, J. 1981. *Theorie des Kommunikativen Handelns*. Frankfurt: Suhrkamp. Italian translation: 1986. *Teoria dell'agire comunicativo*, vol. 2. Bologna: il Mulino.

Lockwood, D. 1992. Social integration and system integration. In *Solidarity and schism. 'the problem of disorder' in Durkheimian and Marxist sociology*, ed. D. Lockwood, 399–412. Oxford: Clarendon.

Lockwood, D. 1999. Civic integration and social cohesion. In *Capitalism and social cohesion: Essays on exclusion and integration*, ed. I. Gough and G. Olofsson, 63–84. Basingstoke: Macmillan.

Luhmann, N. 1984. *Soziale Systeme. Grundriss einer allgemeinen Theorie*. Frankfurt: Suhrkamp. Italian translation: 1990. *Sistemi sociali. Fondamenti di una teoria generale*. Bologna: il Mulino.

Luhmann, N. 1997a. Limits of steering. *Theory, Culture and Society* 14(1): 41–57.

Luhmann, N. 1997b. Globalization or world society: How to conceive of modern society? *International Review of Sociology* 7(1): 67–80.

Luhmann, N. 1998. Politics and economy. *Thesis Eleven* 53: 1–10.

Milano, Riccardo. 2010. *Finanza islamica e finanza etica. Il denaro al servizio dell'uomo*. newsletter@benecomune.net.

Sinn, H.W. 2010. *Casino capitalism*. Oxford: Oxford University Press.

Soros, G. 2000. Reflexivity in financial markets. In *Open Society. Reforming global capitalism*, ed. G. Soros, 58–90. New York: Public Affairs.

Spaemann, R. 2008. *Rousseau. Mensch oder Bürger. Das Dilemma der Moderne*. Stuttgart: Klett-Cotta. Italian translation: 2009. *Rousseau cittadino senza patria. Dalla 'polis' alla natura*. Milano: Edizioni Ares.

Chapter 5
Paradigm Shift in the Social Doctrine of the Church: From Rerum Novarum (1891) to Caritas in Veritate (2009)*

Paul Josef Cardinal Cordes[†]

The sociohistorical context and ideas that served as the backdrop of the Catholic Church's first social encyclical *Rerum Novarum* (1891) are well known. The initial desire was for *Rerum Novarum* to respond to the dramatic economic tensions caused by the so-called Industrial Revolution. A few names may suffice to remind us of the difficulties of this era: Karl Marx, the German Bishop Wilhelm Emmanuel von Ketteler († 1877), *Les Miserables* by Victor Hugo, *A Tale of Two Cities* by Charles Dickens, and *Tom Sawyer* by Mark Twain. Against the despondency of the working class, the Church raised her voice.

5.1 The Beginning

Leo XIII's social encyclical arose from a memorandum summarizing varying reflections and ideas of different groups in Europe. Its reasoning is not derived from a global scientific theory but is instead oriented toward practical improvement. It strives for change by means of arguments capable of general consensus – for the good of all. Using neo-Scholastic as well as natural law concepts, it sums up solutions stemming from preexisting theories and practices.

The encyclical condemns the idea of class conflict: "[C]apital cannot do without labor, nor labor without capital. Mutual agreement results in the beauty of good order" (RN 19). This connection is then punctuated within the ambit of the Church, the State, and the workers. The Pope clearly opposes the capitalistic-liberal positions where the State does not accept regulators' duties but only a simple role of "night

---

*Translation by Colin Howell.

[†]Former President of the Pontifical Council Cor Unum

P.J.C. Cordes (✉)
e-mail: cardcordes@gmail.com

watchman." The chapter continues by addressing the regulation of labor contracts regarding work hours, salaries, and work conditions in addition to proposing reflection on issues of law and justice.

With similarly generalized guidelines, the Church presents herself not as a director or commander but rather as a teacher. This is the first conclusion drawn from a retrospective look at *Rerum Novarum*. The social doctrine of the Church aims to raise awareness and accountability with respect to a specific historical situation. Nevertheless, the central issues addressed by the first papal encyclical are the timeless concerns of the social life of man, making them, therefore, irresolvable with one magisterial decision. Thus, it would become confusing if one tried to equate the social doctrine of the Church with dogmatic theology, for example, or with the central assumptions of moral theology. Instead, these exhortations are to be put into concrete action at the level of the individual conscience.

There is a second point in *Rerum Novarum* worthy of attention. The ecclesial doctrine found therein primarily appeals to secular intelligence and reason. Its elements had, as their model, the universally accepted rights and duties of man and therefore relied heavily on principles derived from natural law. Accordingly, the Church's viewpoint of social doctrine, regarding the prescribed social order, is fundamentally inspired by philosophy, and, more accurately, by philosophical anthropology. It was from this standpoint that the natural order of human society was discussed, delineating new principles of order. The references to Sacred Scripture remained relatively marginal.

New impulses, with a wealth of possibilities to be developed, were to come into existence only during the second half of the past century. These impulses became apparent during the pontificate of John XXIII. In 1963, he published his encyclical dedicated to peace, *Pacem in Terris*. Therein, he does not limit himself primarily to classic philosophical arguments in order to elucidate the dignity of man. Rather, he bases his arguments upon divine Revelation. The ultimate foundation for the dignity of the human person – as he taught – is found in the divine filiation of the human being, saved by means of the blood shed by Christ on the Cross.

Through a framework similar to that implemented by John XXIII, additional factors for analysis were added to the social doctrine of the Church. The papal magisterium, from a merely philosophical-rational position – albeit unmistakably enlightened by faith – moved to embrace a perspective derived directly from Revelation, and therefore from faith, creating a shift from the philosophical to the theological perspective. This paradigm shift should be noted as well as promoted.

Contemporaneous with Pope John XXIII's first steps guiding the Church's social doctrine into the field of theology, the Council Fathers of the Second Vatican Council were engaged in the drafting of the Pastoral Constitution, "*The Church in the Contemporary World – Gaudium et Spes* (GS)." Herein, we find elements of faith used for the proper understanding of society, and the categories of social doctrine begin to more closely conform with the guiding principles of faith. *Gaudium et Spes* makes it clear in numerous passages how it is Christ, the new Adam, who "fully reveals man to man himself and makes his supreme calling clear." Such expressions, chiefly inspired by the theology of the Incarnation, reveal an opening to the theology of the cross: "By suffering for us He not only provided us with an example for our imitation, He blazed a trail" (GS 22).

Words like these attest to how the Church's social doctrine has grown into an entirely new line of thought: the philosophical tendency has been relativized while its theological position is strengthened. Revelation and reason together form the foundation of the Church's social doctrine, mutually determining one another in both the Church's internal and external relations.

5.2 A New Keyword

Of course, these changes of perspective did not occur overnight. Already at the time of the Second Vatican Council, there existed lengthy and controversial arguments in their regard. An initially significant impetus, worthy of consideration for underscoring the existence of theological truths in the Church's social doctrine, came from the French Dominican Marie-Dominique Chenu. His argument focused on the expression of the Biblical "signs of the times" (Matt. 16:3). He argues that it is in those "signs" that God reveals His presence, here and now, in the history of human civilization. For this reason, Chenu awards such "signs" the high theological rank of a *locus theologicus*, an epistemological source of theology. His ideas were promptly published within and outside of the Council.

Chenu's impetus has deeply influenced the social doctrine of the Church. Even some theologians in the conciliar sessions desired to use the expression "signs of the times" for a completely new reading of the theological sources. They affirmed that it should, as an anchor for a clearer understanding of the teaching of the Church, provide guarantees concerning the revealing character of nature and, in any event, be more than a mere figure of speech.

Still, some of Joseph Ratzinger's observations in 1968[1] with respect to the Constitution *Gaudium et Spes*, would have warned against similar suggestions. In fact, we read that:

> The expression 'signs of the times' goes back to a preliminary draft in the 'Text of Zurich' (1964). At the time of its being singled out, one desired to express that the times are a sign and a voice, manifesting the presence or absence of God; as such, the voice of the times needs to be interpreted as the voice of God.

We read from Joseph Ratzinger that this assertion was the focus of heated criticism in the course of subsequent sessions:

> Equating the Roman proverb (sc. 'vox temporis – vox Dei'), which seeks to recognize the voice of God in time, with Jesus' eschatological warning in regard to the blindness of his people – who, though searching for signs, could not recognize him nor his teaching as an eschatological sign sent by God to this age – such an equation was perceived not only as inadmissible from an exegetical point of view but also objectively problematic.

---

[1] Cf. Das Zweite Vatikanische Konzil, Bd. III, Freiburg 1968, 313ff.

This critique of Joseph Ratzinger concerning the Constitution *Gaudium et Spes* displays once again how the insertion of the Catholic social doctrine into the framework of Revelation promises to be an extremely complex task and yet needs to be tackled. One can only agree with Fr. Chenu when, during the course of the Council sessions, he cautioned that contemporary social analysis could not continue to rely exclusively on the principles of natural philosophy.

However, the new foundation he desired to proffer to social doctrine reveals a twofold theological misunderstanding. The first concerns the concept of Revelation. The Constitution of the Second Vatican Council *Dei Verbum* (DV) teaches that after the death and resurrection of Christ, "we now await no further new public revelation" (DV 4). It is therefore ruled out that God should send to humanity, through certain events in the lives of individuals or groups of persons, new Revelations ("*loci theologici*"). For the same reason, certain forms of liberation theology, when they intend to replace Revelation with actual events, lack theological legitimacy.

A Christian scholar of social ethics reaches extreme conclusions when he says that social doctrine is convergent with the empirical social sciences and that an eventual link to Revelation is consequently irrelevant for social doctrine. (cf. Möhring-Hesse and Emunds and Hengsbach 1993).

The second theological misunderstanding is found in the nullification of uniqueness that distinguishes the social teachings of the Church, maintaining that one can no longer speak of a single "doctrine," but only of "doctrines" particular and varied. It is not surprising then that at the time and in the context of said arguments (cf. Nell-Breuning 1972) – after the Council – the identity and charism of social doctrine became heavily obscured in the thinking and catechesis of the Church: an incorrect interpretation of the Second Vatican Council rendered the social doctrine of the Church superfluous.

The Second Vatican Council's *Constitution on the Church in the Modern World* has left the social doctrine of the Church the task of considering this discipline within the context of faith. It was the Magisterium itself which continued the work of clarification.

5.3   Epistemological Limits

There is no doubt that the Church's social doctrine must rely upon empirical data, as it concerns economic, social, and political systems. Social doctrine establishes certain norms aimed at guaranteeing justice in these areas; this justice must in turn derive its proper measure from the truths about the human person and the common good. Consequently, social doctrine needs a precise knowledge of reality as well as a philosophical wisdom pertaining to the human person and justice. Natural law has not lost its relevance, and the very Constitution *Gaudium et Spes* continues to reference the natural law, pointing it out to citizens as the limit within which it is lawful to defend one's rights (cf. GS 74).

Can Church teaching be satisfied exclusively with a philosophical foundation? Is "pure reason" sufficient? A negative response is found in the simple fact that "a" universally valid philosophy no longer exists. Moreover, is it legitimate to ignore a possible contribution of Revelation concerning the foundation of an important teaching of the Church? Do we therefore believe that the social commitment of the Church to the world is inspired by mere philosophical or political beliefs?

The tradition of the Church's social doctrine dates back to Pope Leo XIII, who founded it on the "recta ratio" (right reasoning, righteous reason) and its certainty, immediately evident to everyone. He believed that the evidence of the arguments was recognizable by "recta ratio"; he believed in the accuracy of reason and in its "truth." The course of history has only partially confirmed the view of Pope Leo. Given our painful experiences with the reality of "original sin" (for example, Nazism, Communism, Marxism, terrorism in the name of religion, etc.), we are forced to admit that the evidence of the "recta ratio" is not accessible to all and that pure reason is insufficient for a general consensus of truth and justice.

For this reason, the social doctrine of the Church cannot renounce the truth of Revelation – despite its indispensable and firm correlation with empirical truths. The Church of the incarnate Logos will definitely not forget the "ratio" of reason; in fact, the Church will seek to confront herself with it, but she cannot deny the source of light that gives certainty and balance to the judgments of human reason. To date, certain ecclesial statements give the impression that the realization of a just world is sufficiently possible with the consensus of men of good will, inspired by right reasoning. Faith looks like a pretty ornament, a second floor – decorative but superfluous. However, it is difficult to deny that reason and good will are always darkened and hampered by original sin; it is not only faith that suggests this but also the experience of past centuries. We cannot help but recognize that Revelation is indispensable for the social doctrine of the Church: only in this manner will the source of our certainty of "justice" continue to be the Logos who became man.

5.4   John Paul II

During the Second Vatican Council, the Archbishop of Krakow, Karol Wojtyla, spoke decisively in the chamber regarding the preparatory work for the Constitution *Gaudium et Spes*. He was also a member of the "Signs of the times" subcommittee that made a significant contribution to the formulation of this draft. However, the passages of the Constitution *Gaudium et Spes* seemed to him to be clearly insufficient for a collocation of social doctrine within the truths of the Church's faith. Robed later as Pope, in his encyclical *Sollicitudo Rei Socialis* (SRS 1987) he strongly urged the reemphasis of some indispensable theological data.

In SRS 35–40, the programatic title already makes his intentions clear: "*A Theological Reading of Modern Problems.*" The Pope felt called to act since the evils and sufferings in the world apparently had not diminished since the publication of Paul VI's encyclical *Populorum Progressio*. He concluded that the origin of these evils must be considered more than merely economic. He spoke about the political world and the people responsible for this situation, and in doing so, he no longer primarily focused on technical and specific intraworldly issues. More than once, he regretted the failure of those responsible. By their actions, they had created the "structures of sin" that impeded the poor from asserting their rights. He then touched upon concepts and statements clearly belonging to the realm of Revelation: the Ten Commandments, evil, and forms of idolatry.

Faced with so much distress, the Pope exhorts: "For Christians, as for all who recognize the precise theological meaning of the word 'sin,' a change of behavior or mentality or mode of existence is called 'conversion,' to use the language of the Bible (cf. Mk. 13:3, 5, Is 30:15)" (SRS 38). According to the Pope, this pertains to the individual as well as the community. John Paul II no longer believed in the efficacy of appealing strictly to goodwill and human understanding. He goes beyond the strictly philosophical and naturalistic argument by basing a desired solution on divine salvific acts, proclaiming: "It is God, in 'whose hands are the hearts of the powerful' and the hearts of all, who according to his own promise and by the power of his Spirit can transform 'hearts of stone' into 'hearts of flesh' (cf. Ezek 36:26)." Later, the chapter identifies the Gospel itself as a source of Catholic social doctrine and speaks of the Church's evangelizing mission, in which individuals and institutions have a prophetic character. To the Church's social doctrine, he attributed a precise *locus epistemologicus* ("epistemological source") within the theological and canonical categories: it "belongs to the field, not of ideology, but of theology and particularly of moral theology" (see SRS 41ff.).

The theological references, to someone with only a scarce knowledge of papal social doctrine, may appear sporadic. But anyone dedicated to the profound study of the intellectual evolution of social doctrine cannot help but note them. With the successor to John Paul II on the papal throne, the change of perspective will become evident.

5.5   Benedict XVI

Already in his first encyclical *Deus Caritas Est* (DCE), Benedict XVI, had contributed original and profound ideas concerning the Church's commitment to safeguard and guarantee the dignity of the human person. As we already have mentioned, he had ruled out the possibility that the Church's task could consist in enforcing political solutions. The Pope, following the footsteps of his predecessor, denies a political identity to the Church by pointing out that her central task is evangelization. A complete announcement of man's salvation cannot do without the Gospel. The proclamation of the death and resurrection of Christ, which forms the basic mission of the Church, is also of great importance to the life of and in society.

The Church's social doctrine therefore does not represent a "third way"; it does not make any claim to implement a political program in order to create a perfect society. "A just society must be the achievement of politics, not of the Church. Yet the promotion of justice through efforts to bring about openness of mind and will to the demands of the common good is something which concerns the Church deeply"

(DCE 28a). Those who would understand the Church in another manner paradoxically run the risk of encouraging a "theocracy," in which the principles of faith would inevitably become the ordering principles of social life – valid for believers and nonbelievers alike and to be imposed by force if necessary. Facing such arguments, the Second Vatican Council expressed itself in favor of religious freedom and of the rightful autonomy of the created order.

Pope Benedict also – contrary to the exhortations of previous popes appealing almost exclusively to groups and classes – primarily turns to the responsibility of the individual. He pits himself against the illusion that a "state of providence," which is practiced by some dictatorships, may eradicate all evil from this world; as he notes, "there will never be a situation where the charity of each individual Christian is unnecessary, because in addition to justice man needs, and will always need, love" (cfr. DCE 29). In the same manner, he addressed the staff of Caritas organizations as individuals, rejecting *a priori* any misleading collectivism (DCE 33).

With the social encyclical *Caritas in Veritate* (CV) published in 2009, Benedict XVI harks back to his first doctrinal text DCE. In CV, he once again puts love at the core and maintains a theocentric point of view. "Everything has its origin in God's love, everything is shaped by it, everything is directed towards it" (CV 2). As he did in DCE, in CV, Pope Benedict XVI from the very beginning ties the "love" he encourages to the history of salvation realized in Christ.

It is Christ's redemption that enables and inspires the thought and action of the Christian in the world. Truth and love are conditions of one another. "*Only in truth does charity shine forth*, only in truth can charity be authentically lived," and the Pope teaches us that in truth, "charity reflects the personal yet public dimension of faith in the God of the Bible, who is both *Agápe* and *Lógos*: Charity and Truth, Love and Word" (CV 3).

Once again, in his explanation of charity, we observe the Pope's intention to ascribe unequivocal theological parameters to the perspective of social doctrine:

> Charity is love received and given. It is 'grace' (*cháris*). Its source is the wellspring of the Father's love for the Son, in the Holy Spirit. Love comes down to us from the Son. It is creative love, through which we have our being; it is redemptive love, through which we are recreated. Love is revealed and made present by Christ (cf. Jn. 13:1) and 'poured into our hearts through the Holy Spirit' (Rom. 5:5). As the objects of God's love, men and women become subjects of charity, they are called to make themselves instruments of grace, so as to pour forth God's charity and to weave networks of charity. (CV 5)

The love of the Father, God the Creator, and of the Son, the Redeemer, poured into us by the Holy Spirit, enables us to live the social life on the basis of certain principles. The encyclical elucidates how "the centrality of charity" is foundational to the development of the human being (CV 19). Knowledge capable of directing man – the text continues – "must be 'seasoned' with the 'salt' of charity" (CV 30). Such statements, seemingly simple and predictable, bear important implications: separated from the Christian experience, social doctrine degenerates into a utopian ideology or, worse still, a soulless political manifesto. Instead, social doctrine commits Christians to put into practice and to live out their faith in society. As stated in the encyclical: "Charity always manifests God's love in human relationships as well, it gives theological and salvific value to all commitment for justice in the world" (CV 6). Later, the Pope underscores that the transcendental end of the mission of the Church cannot be ignored, despite its relevance for earthly realities (CV 9).

Once again, the individual is addressed, despite the appeals of a pragmatic nature made to groups, to encourage politics, legislation, and communal commitment. In fact, the desired changes must originate within the individual; thus, by turning his attention to the independent actors, the Pope behaves in a pedagogically sound manner. We actually see that in the central part of his encyclical, relating to the various problematic areas, Benedict XVI never deals only with the pertinent questions but also and always with the individual man or woman affected by and active in those fields. The perspective shifts from that of an objective treatise to that of a pastoral exhortation.

The style and tone of the final section are therefore surprising only at first glance. Certainly, the literary form of doctrinal reflections addressing problems in the world, justice between individuals and peoples as well as specific appeals to a better society, usually is different. But those who know how to recognize the cardinal design of the Pope cannot but implement the turning toward God with which Benedict XVI concludes his social encyclical: "*Development needs Christians with their arms raised towards God* in prayer, Christians moved by the knowledge that truth-filled love, *caritas in veritate*, from which authentic development proceeds, is not produced by us, but given to us. Christians long for the entire human family to call upon God as 'Our Father!'" (CV 79).

5.6   Response

The publication of Pope Benedict XVI's social encyclical was followed by the usual expressions of discontentment and anger. Especially north of the Alps, the Pope's stance promptly became a pretext for critical manifestations. However, those who thoroughly understand the subject will recognize the continuation and conclusion of an important process: the linking of the elements of natural philosophy with the data of Revelation. Moreover, in such intellectual progress can be recognized a joyful approach of Catholic social teaching to Protestant social ethics.

Unexpected applause to the encyclical came instead from another quarter. Certainly, no one would suspect the *New York Times* of servility or pandering to the Catholic Church. Yet the reaction of the *New York Times* to the encyclical was a highly positive comment, published July 13, 2009, on the front page:

> For liberals and conservatives alike, "*Caritas in Veritate*" is an invitation to think anew about their alliances and litmus tests. Why should being pro-environment preclude being pro-life? Why can't Republicans worry about economic inequality, and Democrats consider devolving more power to localities and states? Does opposing the Iraq war mean that you have to endorse an anything-goes approach to bioethics? Does supporting free trade require supporting the death penalty?
>
> These questions, and many others like them, are the kind that a healthy political system would allow voters and politicians to explore. But for now, at least, you're more likely to find them being raised in Benedict XVI's Vatican than in Barack Obama's Washington.

The clear theocentrism with which Pope Benedict formulates his indications for social doctrine has so far attracted little attention; even Catholic ethicists have shown little interest in the opening of his arguments to divine Revelation and its applications. We see, however, that politicians, society, and public opinion seem to have less difficulty in rooting human life and Church teaching in the faith. The days in which the Church remained silent regarding the real and binding foundation of her messages to the world seem to be over.

5.7 A "Qualitative Leap"

Gaudium et Spes, Pope John Paul II, and Benedict XVI point to the social doctrine of the Church as the road to postmodern reality. They postulate a correlation between reason and faith (cf. CV 31). The current pope highlights this relationship in some of his initial theological research.[2] The paradigm shift is realized by the unmistakable placement of doctrinal statements in the light of faith. Church statements on social concerns cannot be read or vocalized irrespective of the saving word of God. They find their fullness only in the light of Revelation and must be interpreted in this fashion. At the same time, the light of Revelation illuminates their natural traits. It gives greater realism to the earthly hopes for desired social changes. The conscious rapprochement of social doctrine and Biblical message makes clear the fact that human beings should no longer be perceived as mere *objects* but as the *bearers* of a better future. Any human progress can only arise from a humanity that is more human, and the individual not only requires better social structures and better opportunities; the individual also needs salvation and sanctification in the Church.

5.8 Lived Theocentrism

Today, we cannot limit ourselves to an extrinsic perspective in dealing with social doctrine, one that is only concerned with the question of its relevance, asking whether it outlines current political and economic issues, if it offers real answers to poverty in the world, or whether it tends to the right or the left. This would be a mere academic "l'art pour l'art." We could moreover be certain of the contempt of the Danish philosopher Soren Kierkegaard, who criticized such couch philosophers as "aesthetic existences." He described thus those intellectuals who do not apply the truth to themselves, who only see "possibilities" without ever becoming personally engaged in decisions

---

[2] For his acute analysis of their mutual relationship, see Ratzinger (1999, 63ff). Also in DCE 28, he tackles the topic once again in depth. According to his interpretation, there is no alternative to these two forms of perception of the truth; it follows that the social doctrine enlightened by faith can never give up the teachings of natural philosophy.

and relationships, who maintain an ambiguous relationship with respect to the seriousness of the real world.

If we wish therefore to distance ourselves from a social doctrine as "l'art pour l'art," we must ask ourselves what could be the existential link for each of us. What responsibility are we asked to assume here and now? Reflection upon its historical development clearly shows us the focal point: it is the weight we give to God in our lives and our commitments, not as an element which we take for granted, since we are already practicing Christians, but rather moved in the center of our hearts by the Holy Spirit.

During the Christmas celebration of 2009, Benedict XVI remarked in his sermon on the Gospel that the "shepherds make haste": "For most people, the things of God are not given priority, they do not impose themselves on us directly. And so the great majority of us tend to postpone them. First we do what seems urgent here and now. In the list of priorities God is often more or less at the end. We can always deal with that later, we tend to think. The Gospel tells us: God is the highest priority. If anything in our life deserves haste without delay, then, it is God's work alone. (…). Time given to God and, in his name, to our neighbour is never time lost. It is the time when we are most truly alive, when we live our humanity to the full."

Bibliography

Möjromg-Hesse, Matthias and Bernhasd Emunds and Friedhelm Hengsbach. 1993. *Jenseits Katholis cher Soziallchre. Neue Entwürfe christilcher Gesellschaffsethik*. Patmos: Düsseldorf.
Nell-Breuning, Oswald von. 1972. Krise der katholischen Soziallehre. *Stimmen der Zeit* 189: 86–98.
Ratzinger, Josef. 1999. *Wahrheit, Werte, Macht. Die pluralistische Gesellschaft im Kreuzverhör*. Knecht: Frankfurt.

Chapter 6
The Encyclical *Caritas in Veritate*, Christian Tradition and the Modern World

Martin Schlag

6.1 Introduction

In 1895, Georg Jellinek published the first edition of his book *The Declaration of the Rights of Man and of the Citizen.*[1] Its content gave rise to a heated debate. Jellinek argued that both the 1789 French Declaration of the Rights of Man and of the Citizen and the analogous bills in the United States (as well as similar declarations issued in the Western world) were ultimately the product of the struggles to safeguard religious freedom. "The idea of legally establishing the unrenounceable, innate and sacred rights of man did not have a political but a religious origin. What until then had been considered the work of the revolution is, in reality, a product of the Protestant Reformation and its ensuing conflicts." (Jellinek 2006, 57) Although the scope of this chapter does not permit a full investigation of this thesis and the many interesting questions it raises, I would like to focus here on one question that Jellinek's work entails: "Is there a substantial continuity between the Christian tradition and the modern world? Or, on the contrary, is modernity the result of a rupture and discontinuity with this Christian tradition?"[2]

---

[1] I have used the 2006 edition of Georg Jellinek's *Die Erklärung der Menschen- und Bürgerrechte: Ein Betrag zur Modernen Verfassungsgeschichte*, third posthumous edition, revised and completed by Walter Jellinek, 1919. VDM Dr. Müller, publisher, Saarbrücken.

[2] Trutz Rendtorff discusses the work of Jellinek in light of this question in Rendtorff (1987). The following reflections on Max Weber and Jellinek are indebted to Rendtorff.

M. Schlag (✉)
Associate Professor. Università della Santa Croce, Rome, Italy
e-mail: schlag@pusc.it

M. Schlag and J.A. Mercado (eds.), *Free Markets and the Culture of Common Good*, Ethical Economy 41, DOI 10.1007/978-94-007-2990-2_6,
© Springer Science+Business Media B.V. 2012

When Max Weber wrote *The Protestant Ethic and the Spirit of Capitalism*,[3] he was greatly influenced by Jellinek. Weber argued that it is not just material and economic but also religious forces that change the world and that the latter played a significant role in the evolution of Western industrial society (see Rendtorff 1987, 98).

Pope Benedict XVI's encyclical, although not drawing explicitly upon the work of Max Weber, accepts many of his main points. While its line of argument is not easy to grasp in a single reading,[4] we will argue here that in *Caritas in Veritate*, Benedict XVI seeks to highlight elements of the Christian tradition that can be of value for the modern economy. The goal of this economy, according to the Pope, must be the integral development of mankind.

Caritas in Veritate is the longest social encyclical in history and, in terms of content, one of the richest. It offers many suggestions that could generate a change in the way of thinking in the area of social doctrine and lead to innovative points of view.

In this introduction to the encyclical, I would like to stress two of these points that seem particularly important to me. The first is the so-called anthropological orientation of the Church's social doctrine stressed by *Caritas in Veritate* (cf. Campanini 2009, 25ff; Cordes 2009). Indeed, Benedict affirms that "the social question has been radically converted into an anthropological question" (Benedict XVI 2009, 75).[5] An excessive reliance on mathematics and the exaggerated use of econometric methods in economics have at times obscured the obvious human meaning of work, exchange, and other economic phenomena as a consequence of the methodological shift of economics toward an empirical science (cf. Bauer 2009, 87). This shift reflects the desire to create an "exact" science modeled on the natural sciences in an area where this is not possible without a methodological reduction, that is, in the sphere of the human person, of his or her social and economic activity, of integral human development, etc. Economics studies economic reality as it is, not necessarily as it ought to be. However, human reality is much richer than anonymous aggregate forces of demand and supply. Personal motivations, wishes, and desires underlie the social mechanisms. All of these realities call for a different, more holistic method. In the end, it should be the object studied that decides which method is to be employed and not the method that decides what object should be studied (cf. Koslowski 1994, 2002).

The second point I would like to consider here is the epistemological status of the Church's social doctrine (cf. Campanini 2009, 21). This body of teaching certainly belongs to theology and more specifically, to moral theology. However, it is not only theology (insofar as it is based on Revelation) but also anthropology (as a philosophy based on human reason). And since it speaks in the name of reason, the

---

[3]Published for the first time under the title: "Die protestantische Ethik und der 'Geist' des Kapitalismus," in *Archiv für Sozialwissenschaft und Sozialpolitik*, vol. XX and XXI (1905).

[4]For an introduction and a first approximation, see Roos (2009); Beretta et al. (2009); Campanini (2009); Brambilla et al. (2009); Melé and Castellà (2010).

[5]Perhaps to highlight this aspect, rather than the publication date of *Rerum Novarum*, Benedict XVI chose the anniversary of *Populorum Progressio* for his social encyclical.

Church can demand a public forum. Moreover, "the social doctrine of the Church was born to revindicate a 'status of citizenship' for the Christian religion"(Benedict XVI 2009, 56).

We will now turn to the relationship between Christian tradition and the modern world, considering the aspects of continuity and discontinuity found in the Church's social teaching.

Pope Benedict XVI writes in his encyclical:

> The link between *Populorum Progressio* and the Second Vatican Council does not mean that Paul VI's social magisterium marked a break with that of previous Popes, because the Council constitutes a deeper exploration of this magisterium within the continuity of the Church's life. In this sense, clarity is not served by certain abstract subdivisions of the Church's social doctrine, which apply categories to Papal social teaching that are extraneous to it. It is not a case of two typologies of social doctrine, one pre-conciliar and one post-conciliar, differing from one another: on the contrary, there is *a single teaching, consistent and at the same time ever new*. It is one thing to draw attention to the particular characteristics of one encyclical or another, of the teaching of one Pope or another, but quite another to lose sight of the coherence of the overall doctrinal corpus. Coherence does not mean a closed system: on the contrary, it means dynamic faithfulness to a light received. The Church's social doctrine illuminates with an unchanging light the new problems that are constantly emerging.[6] (Benedict XVI 2009, 12)

The footnotes to this paragraph cite, together with the encyclical *Sollicitudo Rei Socialis*, Benedict XVI's address to members of the Roman Curia on December 22, 2005. In this address, the Pope referred to the correct interpretation of the new focus given by the Council. His main concern is the problem of transformation and permanence. He contrasts a "hermeneutic of discontinuity and rupture" with a "hermeneutic of reform," maintaining the underlying continuity of the Church. This second type of hermeneutic was the one desired by the Second Vatican Council, to be used in clarifying the relationship between the Church and modernity.

The Council certainly saw the need to carry out a process of major reform. In his December 2005 address, the Pope highlighted three important reference points: the relationship of the faith and the Church to the natural sciences, to the modern state, and to other religions.

> It is clear that in all these sectors, which all together form a single problem, some kind of discontinuity might emerge. Indeed, a discontinuity had been revealed but in which, after the various distinctions between concrete historical situations and their requirements had been made, the continuity of principles proved not to have been abandoned…The Second Vatican Council, with its new definition of the relationship between the faith of the Church and certain essential elements of modern thought, has reviewed or even corrected certain historical decisions, but in this apparent discontinuity it has actually preserved and deepened her inmost nature and true identity (Benedict XVI 2005).

In this context, Benedict also referred to the right to religious freedom. All of these steps were taken in full accord with Christ's teachings, passing on a heritage deeply rooted in the Church's own life.

---

[6] Italics in the original text.

6.2   Catholic Social Doctrine and the Modern Economic Order

Thus we can ask: If the Pope referred explicitly to the relationship with the natural sciences, with the modern state, and with other religions, what importance does the modern free economy have here? Did Pope Benedict XVI include this implicitly when speaking about modernity? Or did he rather omit it deliberately? Does the Church not have to be concerned about the *modernity of the economy?*

At first sight, it might seem that the Pope excluded economics from the topics in which a reconciliation between faith and reason has been attained. This could be inferred, perhaps, from the lecture he gave on November 23, 1985. In this conference, Joseph Ratzinger showed himself to be decidedly critical in regard to economic liberalism (Ratzinger 1986, 13ff). He argued that the capitalist economic system cannot be accepted in an uncritical way, not even if one adopts all the corrections that have been introduced since its inception. At the same time, the future Pontiff also rejected Marxism. His criticism of economic liberalism was directed against a tradition going back to Adam Smith, maintaining that ethics and the market economy cannot be reconciled. According to this theory, moral decisions were opposed to the laws of the market: moral economic activities – according to the view criticized by Joseph Ratzinger – had no chance of surviving in the world of the market. Ethics and the market were seen as irreconcilable, given that in the economy what matters is efficiency, not morality. Ratzinger pointed to the determinism hidden in this position. The laws of the market alone, in a necessary and absolute way, were seen as leading to the good of mankind and to progress, independently of the moral qualities of the acting persons.

However, the truth that needs to be defended is that the laws of the market have an autonomy and a validity that is only *relative.* They fulfill their function if they are grounded in a culture of ethical responsibility oriented to the common good, that is to say, in a context of consensus in regard to values. The economy is not put into effect solely by laws, but by persons. A simple adaptation to the "reality of the market and economic facts" would not recognize the true nature of man and therefore would be false.

In the encyclical *Centesimus Annus* of May 1, 1991, Pope John Paul II employed a terminology much closer to the modern liberal tradition. Basing himself on the Second Vatican Council, John Paul II gave a definitive right of citizenship to the modern political culture in the teaching of the Church, including the model of the free market economy; however, this latter was not to be exempted from social concern. Reinhard Marx writes in this regard:

> This interior logic of the functioning of the market economy was first discovered by Adam Smith, who described it systematically: this is a great contribution that cannot be denied. Economic liberalism was a great advance, as has been the entire development of freedom found in modern life. Nevertheless, it is now worthwhile emphasizing once more that in the face of economic liberalism, the Church has maintained a great reserve for a long time – for a longer time than in regard to political liberalism. (Marx 2008, 82; cf. also Rhonheimer 2003, 142ff)

In the aforementioned encyclical, John Paul II also asked himself whether capitalism was the victorious social system and the model to be followed. The response is obviously complicated. It is not just a question of a new terminology. The Pope took a stand in favor of profit, the free market,[7] and of a "good capitalism" – an economic system that recognizes the positive role of business enterprises and human creativity, of the free market and private property, and a corresponding responsibility in the use of the means of production. Furthermore, he specified in regard to this "good capitalism" that "it would perhaps be more appropriate to speak of a 'business economy,' 'market economy' or simply 'free economy'." He rejected with the same force a "bad capitalism," that is, the "system in which freedom in the economic sector is not circumscribed within a strong juridical framework which places it at the service of human freedom in its totality, and which sees it as a particular aspect of that freedom, the core of which is ethical and religious" (John Paul II 1991, 42).

The goal of *Caritas in Veritate* is different from that of *Centesimus Annus*. John Paul II wanted to provide orientation for the period that followed the collapse of the Soviet Bloc. Benedict XVI finds in the world economic crisis a pressing call for reflection and seeks to provide an anthropological and Christian grounding for progress in the free economy. The two Pontiffs are speaking different languages. However, despite possible initial impressions, their message is not contradictory. *Caritas in Veritate* does not cancel anything in *Centesimus Annus*; on the contrary, it presupposes and confirms it.

Still, at first sight, one's attention is drawn to the differences between *Centesimus Annus* and *Caritas in Veritate*. Benedict XVI defends a strengthening of state sovereignty (Benedict XVI 2009, 24, 41), he does not praise capitalism, not even in its most moderate and positive form, nor does he particularly underscore the value of the free market. Aspects of the free economy, such as interest, international commerce, the financial markets, speculation, etc., are viewed by the Pontiff with a certain caution and reserve. He also employs terminology that an economist might find unsettling, leaning toward introducing elements of what is called the *gift economy* into the market economy. The *gift economy* is a situation typical of so-called primitive civilizations (made up primarily of farmers and hunters), with a social structure in which goods and services are produced and given without an explicit accord of "*do ut des*". The *gift economy* is not a market economy in the modern sense. The Pope, of course, is not at all proposing a return to economic forms prior to the modern era; rather, he is extending an invitation to "broaden our outlook" and to introduce a new logic into the economy: the logic of gratuitousness and gift. This invitation merits a deeper explanation.

---

[7] John Paul II (1991, 34): "It would appear that, on the level of individual nations and of international relations, the free market is the most efficient instrument for utilizing resources and effectively responding to needs."

6.3 Fundamental Goals Proposed by the Encyclical
Caritas in Veritate

6.3.1 The Epistemological Question of Economics

In *Caritas in Veritate*, Pope Benedict XVI speaks of "the excessive segmentation of knowledge" (Benedict XVI 2009, 31) in fields that have reached a high degree of specialization, such specialization paid for with a loss of the human meaning of the object studied. Confronted with this situation, the Pope calls for "a further and deeper reflection on the meaning of the economy and its goals" (Benedict XVI 2009, 32).

The problem to which the Pope refers is parallel to the epistemological problem in the relationship between faith and the natural sciences. If a scientist consciously and *a priori* excludes all that is not material, the method he employs can never reach anything that transcends the material world. J. B. S. Haldane, a biologist of the last century, wrote: "My practice as a scientist is atheistic. That is to say, when I sct up an experiment I assume that no god, angel, or devil is going to interfere with its course" (Haldane 1934, vi). We could expand his words: neither persons, nor sentiments, nor ethical reflections will be allowed to interfere in the course of his experimentation. If a scientist works within the limits of this empirical method and deliberately remains within those limits, then the method might be justified. On the other hand, if one seeks to demonstrate the nonexistence of something that the very choice of the method excludes, one falls into an obvious vicious circle.

This is particularly important when dealing with human actions because in this case, the voice of conscience makes itself heard. Economic activity is a free human activity, an action judged by our conscience and guided by our convictions and virtues or vices. Moral principles are not bothersome limitations opposed to economic benefits: what is ethically bad is also an error in terms of the economy and vice versa; what is an error in regard to the economy is also such from the ethical point of view because it would constitute mistaken human behavior. As Benedict XVI writes: "the conviction that the economy must be autonomous, that it must be shielded from 'influences' of a moral character, has led man to abuse the economic process in a thoroughly destructive way. In the long term, these convictions have led to economic, social and political systems that trample upon personal and social freedom, and are therefore unable to deliver the justice that they promise"(Benedict XVI 2009, 34).

When economics, both theoretically as well as practically, opens itself to a broader concept of reason – as Benedict XVI hopes – then it will discover new solutions for attaining integral human development (Benedict XVI 2009, 31).

The Pope's concern here connects with a current in the social sciences born in Italy but not yet sufficiently well known elsewhere. We are speaking of the so-called school of "civil economy."[8] Although a detailed explanation is beyond the scope of

---

[8]Cf. for a general survey: Bruni and Zamagni (2004, 2009).

this study, this school stems from certain historical facts. For centuries, there has existed what one might call a "Catholic antagonism" toward economics, finance, money, etc., that is, toward the fundamental factors of the modern economic system. We shall briefly try to sketch this development.

The Church Fathers in general had a positive or neutral attitude toward trade. In fact, presupposing the admissibility of commerce and trade, they did not often treat the subject. The Fathers' use of these themes is rather of a theological and moral nature. The monetized and commercial society of the Roman Empire (see Walbank 1987) in which they lived supplied their lexicon, and thus they used a commercial language to explain redemption, praised as "*sacrum commercium*"[9]: Christ has bought us for the price of his own blood. Ambrose dramatically describes the devil as a usurer who gives sin to Eve as a loan. She in turn indebts all of mankind. Christ is the "redeemer" who – as this Latin word expresses – buys our freedom back from the devil at an exorbitant price, his blood (Ambrose 1845, 770f). In the Patristic Christian tradition, "economy" even came to mean "redemption", as the perusal of any Patristic dictionary will reveal. What the modern concept of economy implies was dealt with under the concepts of *negotium* or *commercium*.

The social concerns of the Church Fathers had to do with the protection of the poor against exploitation, with social aid to the sick, the widows and orphans, the foreigners, etc. Consequently, they preached against irresponsible luxury and wealth and against usury understood as oppressive interest rates on loans to the poor (Nuccio 1984, 411). Ambrose opposed all interest on loan, qualifying it as theft. Although Leo was skeptical about trade, he mentions it in the context of canonical penance. Penitents, he advises, should not engage in trade, because it is hardly possible to avoid sins in selling and buying (Leo 1957, 294f). In this warning, he merely echoes words of the Bible (Sir. 26:20-27:2).[10]

A negative attitude toward commerce grew out of feudalism. In the feudal system, the merchants were ambiguous figures. On the one hand, they were useful and even indispensable for society; on the other, they were held in suspicion because they worked for their own pocket and not with the aim of enhancing public well-being. This critical attitude is reflected by the *Sentences* of Peter Lombard (ca. 1158) and in one of the texts added to the *Decretum Gratiani* (ca. 1140) in the twelfth century and called "*palea Eiciens.*"[11] These texts declare trade to be an illicit profession for a Christian. In the Medieval commercial revolution of the twelfth to the

---

[9] Preface of the Christmas Mass which goes back to the fifth century using words of Leo I.

[10] The Bible passage Leo I echoes is: "A merchant can hardly remain upright, nor a shopkeeper free from sin; For the sake of profit many sin, and the struggle for wealth blinds the eyes. Like a peg driven between fitted stones, between buying and selling sin is wedged in." For the negative attitude of Leo I to usury see his Sermon 17, 3, in Leo (1996, 63ff).

[11] For more details, see Wood (2002, 112); Langholm (1992, 102ff). The Decretum Gratiani, C. XXIV, q. 3, c. 23, however, also protects merchants from "unusual" taxes and road fares. "Si quis (…) mercatores novis teloneorum et pedaticorum exactionibus molestare temptaverit, donec satisfecerit, conmunione careat Christiana."

fourteenth century, such an evaluation no longer made any sense. From the thirteenth century onward, Scholastic teachers underscore that commerce is a necessary and useful social function. In support of this position, they were able to quote Augustine as witness: the vices usually associated with merchants are not to be blamed on the profession but on the people who exercise it (Augustine 1970, 747ff: Psalm 70, verse 15).[12] Augustine was utilized by both of the great Medieval schools (the Dominicans and the Franciscans) but in different ways.

Around the year 1260, the Dominicans Albert the Great and Thomas Aquinas, as the earliest commentators on Aristotle, could dispose of the Latin translation of *Politics* by their confrère William of Moerbeke. In the first book of his *Politics*, Aristotle distinguishes *oikonomiké* (procuring the necessary material means for the household) from *chrematistiké* (quest of money as an end to itself). Aristotle refers to trade (*kapeliké*) as a despicable form of "*chrematistiké*". However, in his translation, Moerbeke erroneously translates *kapeliké* as *campsoria* which means money changing. Through this "happy error", trade is not condemned in the Latin translation of Aristotle's *Politics*. There is consequently no condemnation of merchants in Albert or Thomas. Procuring the necessary material means for a dignified life according to one's social status is good and natural, says Thomas; however, this activity does not pertain to the merchants (*negotiatores*) but rather to the *oeconomici* and the politicians who manage the household and the city. Commerce is not well considered, and justly so, writes Thomas, as it serves the desire for profit. By essence, commerce has no honorable or necessary aim, but, on the other hand, Thomas goes on to say, profit in no way is vicious or contrary to virtue. Thus, commerce is neither good nor evil. Through this surprising maneuver, Thomas is able to justify profit (and consequently commerce) through its aims (Aquinas 1999, q. 77, a. 4 c). There does remain, however, a certain attitude of doubt. Clerics, he writes, should refrain from commerce because they must not only avoid what *is* evil but also what *seems* to be evil, as is the case with commerce (Aquinas 1999, q. 77, a. 4 ad 3; also q. 187, a. 2).

In the Franciscan School, from Alexander of Hales onward, the general tenor throughout Medieval Scholasticism was that commerce was necessary and useful but fraught with moral dangers. In his *Summa Theologiae*, Alexander of Hales diverted criticism of commerce as such to a number of circumstances which render trade and commerce sinful. Commerce can be sinful if the wrong persons engage in it (clerics or religious), the merchants are guided by a sinful purpose (cupidity), and trade is conducted at the wrong time (Sunday, holidays) or in the wrong place (in the Church); certainly, commerce becomes sinful if the means employed are evil (fraud, deception) or if improper business associations are formed (monopolies) (Langholm 1992, 135). St. Bonaventure is of the same thought (Langholm 1992, 158). This position became increasingly enthusiastic in the course of the Middle Ages. Richard of Middleton found merchants praiseworthy, and in the Franciscan authors of the fourteenth century, the merchants were seen as the builders of public happiness. Diana Wood has summarized this development in the Scholastic attitude toward

---

[12]Quoted e.gr. by Aquinas (1999), q. 77, a. 4 sed contra.

commerce and the merchants in different consecutive steps: condemnation, justification, and exaltation (Wood 2002, 111–120).

Another difficulty the Christian tradition had to cope with in connection with the modern forms of economy was its condemnation of any kind of interest on loans as usury. Charging interest as the price paid for the use of financial capital is an essential element of monetized economies. Roman law had permitted interest on loans, establishing a legal maximum of the interest rate in order to avoid exploitation. The Council of Nicea had accepted this regulation for the Church; it had, however, prohibited all members of the clergy to charge interest. This discipline was maintained in the Oriental Churches (Wittreck 2009). In the meantime, in the Catholic Church, the development was different.[13] In Carolingian times, the prohibition of interest as usury was extended to all Christians. No one was allowed to demand more in return than the sum given as a loan. By the time the Scholastics began work on the subject of usury, Church doctrine had become a secular tradition. They encountered and shared the solid conviction that taking interest was a mortal sin. In a feudal and agricultural economy, in which loans are only meant for consumption and are asked for in times of urgent need, such a condemnation may be easy to understand. A modern monetized economy cannot do without interest. The great scholar of Medieval economic thought, Raymond De Roover, while being critical of the theoretical Scholastic justifications of the ban of usury, has been able to state that this ban did not brake or hamper the economic development of Europe. It actually indirectly catalyzed the invention of instruments of cash-free financial exchange and other forms of investment, for example, bills of exchange, commercial partnerships, rent contracts, government bonds, etc. (De Roover 1974, 332).

The theoretical "antagonism" to the economy, however, continued and was nourished from roughly four sources: Aristotle, who considered money as a medium and a measure of exchange, therefore rejecting the view that money could be used to increase money, a form of "unnatural enrichment" (this attitude in the subsequent reception of Aristotle was condensed into the adage *nummus non facit nummum*: "money does not produce money")[14]; the Biblical prohibition of usury, which was extended to include any type of interest[15]; some of the Fathers of the Church[16]; and

---

[13]For a complete analysis, see Noonan (1957); a synthetic explanation in Wood (2002, 160ff).

[14]See Aristotle, *Politics*, I (A), 1258 b, 2–8: "The most detestable sort (of wealth getting) and with the greatest reason, is usury, which makes a gain out of money itself and not from the natural object of it. For money was intended to be used in exchange but not to increase at interest....Wherefore of all modes of getting wealth, this is the most unnatural." On this topic, see Schefold (2008, 39); for a detailed analysis of Aristotle's attitude toward economy and money, see Wittreck (2002, 173ff).

[15]The principal texts of the Old Testament are *Ex* 22:24; *Lev* 25:35–37; *Deut* 23:20–21; cf. also *Ps* 15:5; *Prov* 28:8; *Ezek* 18:8; 13:17; 22:12. In the New Testament, there is *Lk* 6:35. For an exegetical commentary, see Tosato (2002). For the history of usury in Catholic teaching, see Noonan (1957) and Le Bras (1950).

[16]Cf. for example Lactantius, *Institutiones divinae* 6, 18; Ambrose (1845, 759ff); Leo I (1996, 63ff).

some statements of the Magisterium, in particular the canons of ecclesiastical law. As late as 1745, Benedict XIV, in his encyclical *Vix Pervenit*, severely condemned the charging of interest while at the same time he permitted the establishment of parallel contracts that *de facto* made possible the payment of sums equal to interest (Denzinger and Hünermann 2003, 2546–2550). This teaching was finally abandoned at the beginning of the nineteenth century.

It was specifically in the Franciscan School of the fourteenth and fifteenth centuries and in the School of Salamanca of the sixteenth century that the foundations were laid not only for a new understanding of economic activity in the Church but also for the beginning of the modern science of economics. It is correct to say that the basic concepts of modern economic thought were formed during the Scholastic period and reached Adam Smith and modern economics through the works of late Scholasticism, which come "nearer than does any other group to having been the 'founders' of scientific economics" (Schumpeter 1954, 97).[17] The concept of "capital,"[18] for example, was coined and developed by friars who had themselves taken a vow of poverty: money was converted, thanks to man's work, into *caput*, that is, into a source of benefits. It was the Franciscans who, for the first time, opened a chain of more than 150 *Montes Pietatis*. Bearing some similarities to modern-day "pawnshops," these were places where one could take out a loan at very low interest against some type of bond or surety. This practice was established all over Italy to provide credit accessible to craftsmen and poor farmers in moments of crisis (microfinance). These friars were in constant contact with the poor, who frequently ended up the victims of usurers. The latter paradoxically, and precisely because of the canonical prohibition against giving loans with interest, fell outside all regulation and therefore, at times, demanded exorbitant interest. At the same time, the poor were often forced into greater indigence because their work instruments and their livestock were impounded by the usurers. This situation was reversed, thanks to the *Montes Pietatis*, for which the Franciscan theologians, overcoming great difficulties, had to create the necessary theoretical framework.[19]

This phenomenon occurred wherever the "paleo-capitalistic" tendency was strongest: first in the city-states of the early Renaissance (fourteenth and fifteenth centuries) and later, in the period of the Enlightenment, in the chairs at the Universities of Naples and Milan.

This cultural movement came to be known as "civil economy." From this school of thought stem the concepts in the Pope's social encyclical that we might find surprising in the context of economic theory: gratuitousness, the logic of gift, fraternity, reciprocity, and relationality.

---

[17]Cf. also Melé (1999); De Roover (1974); Todeschini (2004, 7f); Bazzichi (2008).

[18]For the history of the term, see Hilger (2004).

[19]The Bull *"Inter Multiplices"* (May 4, 1515) promulgated by Leo X recognized the *Montes Pietatis* as charitable institutions, with an interest rate that had to be reasonable (i.e., covering the running costs). The prohibition of requiring interest remained in force even after the publication of this Bull, unless the interest of the loan was to be used for the salaries of the employees and to cover the other costs of the *Montes Pietatis* and not simply to pay for the loan as such. Cf. Denzinger and Hünermann (2003, 1442–1444).

6.3.2 The Principle of Gratuitousness, Gift, and Fraternity

Benedict XVI seeks in *Caritas in Veritate* "to make room for the *principle of gratuitousness* as an expression of fraternity" (Benedict XVI 2009, no. 34). This "principle of gratuitousness" does not exclude justice nor is it extrinsic to it, and this is true also of the "logic of gift." "While in the past it was possible to argue that justice had to come first and gratuitousness could follow afterwards, as a complement, today it is clear that without gratuitousness, there can be no justice in the first place" (Benedict XVI 2009, no. 38).

"Gift" is not the same thing as a "present." Rather, it flows from the fact that commerce is always an exchange of merchandise or other material goods between *persons*. This exchange is possible only in the context of a personal relationship, which may be of various kinds (human or inhuman, friendly or exploitive, loyal or fraudulent, etc.). To ensure that this relationship is a human one, first of all, there needs to be a "pre-gift" (*Vorgabe*), the recognition that the other is our "neighbor," with intrinsic dignity. One needs to have confidence in the other persons and put oneself in their shoes. This "pre-gift" confers a specific meaning on the commercial relationship: the relationship will be human or inhuman, exploitive or loyal, etc., depending on the way in which one views the commercial partner or neighbor to whom the commercial activity is directed. The "pre-gift" is, at the same time, a "gift of meaning" (*Sinngebung*). Where this fullness of meaning is lacking, the relationship becomes inhuman. Therefore, the gift in the context of a spirit of gratuitousness is a sign of the actual development of a society.[20]

It is difficult to define gratuitousness. Living together in a human way is impossible without gratuitousness. Without gratuitousness, there is no truly human encounter with one's neighbor. Without gratuitousness, there is no trust, an indispensable element for the stability of the market and of society.

The concept of "gratuitousness" should not be understood as "giving things away for free." Gratuitousness is not "distribution at a zero price" but rather "unpayability", giving "something that has no price". It is what Kant tried to express with his concept of "human dignity": man has dignity, which means he does not have a price. Human dignity is the basis and the source of all human rights. The human person is called to live in a society but is not dissolved into it. Each person is unique, unrepeatable, indispensable, incommensurable, and incommunicable. The person is an end in itself, never a means. "Gratuitous" behavior in the economy consists, therefore, in having truly human relationships, which are not just instruments for purposes of benefit or efficiency.[21]

---

[20]Cf. Pierpaolo Donati, under the heading of "Dono" ["Gift"], in Bruni and Zamagni (2009, 279–291).

[21]Cf. Luigino Bruni under the headings *Fraternità* and *Gratuità* in: Bruni and Zamagni (2009, 439–444 and 484–488); also from a juridical point of view: Galasso and Mazzarese (2008).

In the ancient and Medieval *communitas*, one could not conceive of an ethical life outside of the *polis*: the community was the whole of which the person was merely a part. In the Aristotelic-Thomistic tradition, the essence of the part was analyzed from the whole, analogous to the way in which the essence of a body organ can be defined sensibly as being part of a living organism. Thus, the individual human being was seen as part of the community to which he or she belonged, and the common good was essentially and gnoseologically prior to the individual good. All economic insights of the Medieval schoolmen (the institution of private property, the usefulness of commerce, the reason why civil law did not punish usury, etc.) were derived from the common good, not from the individual natural rights of the individual persons. Private ownership, for instance, was seen as convenient to the common good because owners work better and take greater care of their own things than in a system of collectivism. Commerce and economic exchange were justified because they advance public wealth and well-being. Thus, in the Medieval Scholastic view, there was not any need, as in modern political philosophy, to reconcile the various and antagonist individual rights and to recompose the common good with the fragmented parts of social life. In modern times, this process of recomposition is brought about by "social justice" and "social charity". The content of modern common good is defined as peace, freedom, and justice, not virtuous life as such.

The modern age and the overcoming of the Medieval perspective in which the community prevails over the individual have led to the birth of the individual with his or her rights, even against the community. A new foundation for life in common was therefore necessary since the concept of the totality of the community had been lost. In the economy, this was found in the market. In economic exchange, it does not matter, in principle, what one's religion, culture, or ethnicity, etc., might be. Rather, the system of prices, as a mediator of relationships, sterilizes the elements that might give rise to clashes: everyone who is able to pay or exchange goods or services is included in the market system.

The solution of establishing a market, however, results in two antithetical effects: one of inclusion or union and a second that produces loneliness and unhappiness since modern economics denies the relevance of love and fraternity in the economy. Modern economics is an empirical science which formulates descriptive laws about how things are, not prescriptive rules about how things ought to be. Empirical economics uses the hypothesis that self-interest is the factual motor of economy. In his most frequently quoted sentence, Adam Smith writes that we expect our dinner not from the benevolence of the butcher, the brewer, or the baker, but from their self-interest (Smith 1979, Book 1, Chap. 2). However, would it not be more appropriate to expect our dinner from the justice of the butcher, the brewer, and the baker? It is the virtue of justice which leads them to fulfill their contracts. In certain cases, self-interest alone could lead to avoid fulfilling contracts. A system based solely on self-interest could easily disintegrate. Moreover, we expect our dinner also from their benevolence because in order to agree to a price both buyer and seller usually have to yield a little.

True fraternity in modernity is restricted to the private sphere. Universal fraternity is too dangerous for the public sphere because – by being a manifestation of *agape* (disinterested love) – it creates a crisis for the apparent equilibrium of the market economy.[22] "The great deception of the humanism of the market was thinking that one could preserve something authentically human even while eliminating the relationship of fraternity, with all its tragic weight of sorrow and suffering."[23]

The great question which social ethics with a Christian inspiration has to tackle is if and how to introduce fraternal love (one could also say solidarity or charity or gratuitousness) into the public sphere and into the market. Can love be institutionalized? That is the central question behind the idea of love as social principle ("social charity").[24] Once love is institutionalized in governmental or societal institutions, it has stopped being love and turns into justice; individuals acquire rights to standardized courses of action. A structure of social ethics emerges. In a certain sense, social ethics aims at making charity unnecessary. Take the parable of the Good Samaritan: Social ethics aims at creating a police force, public health care, etc., instead of relying on uncertain individual aid. Even so, solidarity remains necessary as the "heart" of a society that discovers and puts remedy to new needs. Social charity is not a "fifth social principle" beside human dignity, common good, subsidiarity, and solidarity but is a part of each of these. Love makes injustice visible and overcomes it. It is not the case that a free market economy is intrinsically opposed to fraternity or that our market economy has to be replaced with a nonmarket economy. Rather, we need to discover and strengthen many gratuitous elements that already exist, for example, blood and organ donations, social volunteer networks, open source software and, above all, the gratuitous services that take place within the sphere of the family. All these activities help to make our life and society more human (Chirinos 2006).

6.3.3   Reciprocity and Relationality

Gratuitousness is connected with another aspect the Pope wishes to highlight as important for the economy: that of reciprocity and relation. "As a spiritual being, the human creature is defined through interpersonal relations. The more authentically he or she lives these relations, the more his or her own personal identity matures. It is not by isolation that man establishes his worth, but by placing himself in relation with others and with God" (Benedict XVI 2009, 53).

---

[22] Luigino Bruni, under the heading *Communitas* in Bruni and Zamagni (2009, 202–208).

[23] Luigino Bruni, under the heading *Fraternità* in Bruni and Zamagni (2009, 442).

[24] See, for example, Benedict XVI (2009, 2): "Charity is at the heart of the Church's social doctrine. Every responsibility and every commitment spelt out by that doctrine is derived from charity which, according to the teaching of Jesus, is the synthesis of the entire Law (cf. Mt. 22:36–40). It gives real substance to the personal relationship with God and with neighbor; it is the principle not only of micro-relationships (with friends, with family members or within small groups) but also of macro-relationships (social, economic and political ones)."

Reciprocity is the internal law of the web of relationships that governs a society. There exists a "negative" reciprocity (conflicts, wars, revenge, etc.),[25] but there is also a "positive" and constructive reciprocity that makes collaboration and social development (contracts, the market, friendship, love, etc.) possible. Positive reciprocity represents a fundamental act of recognition of the other as my equal (cf. Rhonheimer 2000, 289ff).

Benedict XVI studies four aspects of economic life in which the principle of reciprocity and relation is effective: the market, the business enterprise, the managerial activity, and the political authority. Applied to the market, reciprocity means considering the market as a meeting between persons who enter into a mutual relationship: "In a climate of mutual trust, the market is the economic institution that permits encounter between persons, inasmuch as they are economic subjects who make use of contracts to regulate their relations as they exchange goods and services of equivalent value between them, in order to satisfy their needs and desires" (Benedict XVI 2009, 35).[26]

The market "does not exist in the pure state," the Pope says.

> It is shaped by the cultural configurations which define it and give it direction. Economy and finance, as instruments, can be used badly when those at the helm are motivated by purely selfish ends. Instruments that are good in themselves can thereby be transformed into harmful ones. But it is man's darkened reason that produces these consequences, not the instrument per se. Therefore, it is not the instrument that must be called to account, but individuals, their moral conscience, and their personal and social responsibility (Benedict XVI 2009, 36).

The Church's social doctrine "holds that authentically human social relationships of friendship, solidarity and reciprocity can also be conducted within economic activity, and not only outside it or 'after' it. The economic sphere is neither ethically neutral, nor inherently inhuman and opposed to society. It is part and parcel of human activity and precisely because it is human, it must be structured and governed in an ethical manner" (Benedict XVI 2009, no. 36).

6.4 Conclusion

Pope Benedict XVI, in his encyclical *Caritas in Veritate*, has expanded and developed the content of his predecessor's *Centesimus Annus*. He does not eliminate the possibility of reconciling the faith with modernity, but he calls on modernity to take a step forward. The Pope seeks to free reason from the prejudices and narrow methods which sometimes characterize modern economics, in order to make room for the deepest human realities. But what does all this mean in connection with the

---

[25]Cf. Luigino Bruni, under the heading "*Reciprocità*", in Bruni and Zamagni (2009, 652–660).

[26]For a preliminary look at the different concepts of "market" from a historical perspective, see Röttgers (1980).

question we raised at the outset? Has the Church reconciled itself with the modern economy? And in doing so, has it returned to the roots of its own faith?

Yes, in my opinion, the Church has accepted the modern economic system, rejecting its negative aspects while underscoring the importance of immaterial values, solidarity, fraternity, etc. On the other hand, as regards the second question concerning the Church's return to the roots of its faith, it is still too early to answer with a clear, affirmative yes, because this is an ongoing endeavor. I will try to explain.

To evaluate the historical continuity of the social doctrine of the Church, we have to go back to a period much earlier than the beginning of liberalism in 1789, even to the time of the Fathers of the Church. In this article, this historical review has been performed schematically. The Fathers of the Church, and with them the Christian Scholastic tradition, stressed the centrality of the person and his or her freedom and dignity and moral calling, even in regard to economic and commercial concerns. At the same time, they placed clear limits to the conformity of Christian conduct in the public sphere with the dominant spirit of the times, the *Zeitgeist*. Thus, they gave clear indications, relevant also for the modern economic system, of what a "purification of reason by the faith" might mean. The encyclical *Caritas in Veritate* continues the discussion beginning with this point. In this sense, returning to the roots of Christian tradition does not mean repeating a static system of rules or ideas of the past but taking up and responding in a Christian spirit to the new challenges posed by present circumstances. The Christian spirit inspires action through principles, especially those of human dignity and freedom combined with social responsibility. Freedom and social responsibility are complementary.

Bibliography

Ambrose, Saint. 1845. De Tobia. In *Patrologiae cursus completus, series prima*, vol. 14, ed. Jacques Paul Migne. Paris: Vrayet de Surcy. 759ff.

Aquinas, Thomas. 1999. *Summa theologiae II-II*. Cinisello Balsamo: San Paolo.

Augustine, Saint. 1970. Enarrationes in Psalmos, Psalm 70, verse 15. In *Opere di Sant'Agostino, Esposizioni sui salmi. Nuova Biblioteca Agostiniana*, vol. XXVI. 747ff. Roma: Città Nuova Editrice.

Bauer, Peter T. 2009. *Dalla sussistenza allo scambio: Uno sguardo critico sugli aiuti allo sviluppo*. Turin: IBL Libri.

Bazzichi, Oreste. 2008. *Dall'usura al giusto profitto. L'etica economica della Scuola francescana*. Torino: Effatà.

Benedict XVI. 2005. Speech to the cardinals, archbishops, bishops, and prelate superiors of the Roman Curia on 22 Dec 2005. www.vatican.va. Accessed 22 Aug 2011

Benedict XVI. 2009. Encyclical *Caritas in Veritate*. Vatican: Libreria Editrice Vaticana.

Beretta, Simona, Virginio Colmegna, Flavio Felice, Bortolomeo Sorge, and Stefano Zamagni. 2009. *Amore e verità. Commento e guida alla lettura dell'Enciclica Caritas in veritate di Benedetto XVI*. Milano: Paoline.

Brambilla, Franco Giulio, Luigi Campiglio, Mario Toso, Francesco Viola, and Vera Zamagni. 2009. *Carità globale: Commento alla Caritas in veritate*. Vatican: LEV.

Bruni, Luigino, and Stefano Zamagni. 2004. *Economia civile. Efficienza, equità, felicità pubblica*. Bologna: Il Mulino.

Bruni, Luigino, and Stefano Zamagni. 2009. *Dizionario di economia civile*. Rome: Città Nuova.
Campanini, Giorgio. 2009. *Benedetto XVI, Caritas in Veritate, Linee guida per la lettura*. Bologna: EDB.
Chirinos, Maria Pia. 2006. *Claves para una antropología del trabajo*. Pamplona: EUNSA. Italian edition: 2005. *Un'antropologia del lavoro: il "domestico" come categoria*. Rome: EDUSC.
Cordes, Paul Josef. 2009. Kirchliche Soziallehre und Offenbarung: Zur Enzyklika *Caritas in Veritate*. *Die Neue Ordnung* 5: 234–332.
De Roover, Raymond. 1974. Scholastic economics. Survival and lasting influence from the sixteenth century to Adam Smith. In *Business, banking, and economic thought in late medieval and early modern Europe. Selected studies of Raymond de Roover*, ed. Julius Kirshner. Chicago/London: The University of Chicago Press. 306ff.
Denzinger, Heinrich, and Peter Hünermann. 2003. *Enchiridion symbolorum*. Bologna: EDB.
Galasso, Alfredo, and Silvio Mazzarese (eds.). 2008. *Il principio di gratuità*. Milano: Dott. A. Giuffrè Editore.
Haldane, John Burdon Sanderson. 1934. *Faith and fact*. London: Watts.
Hilger, Marie-Elisabeth. 2004. Kapital, Kapitalist, Kapitalismus. In *Geschichtliche Grundbegriffe. Historisches Lexikon zur politisch-sozialen Sprache in Deutschland, Studienausgabe*, vol. 3, ed. Otto Brunner, Werner Conze, and Reinhart Koselleck, 399–428. Stuttgart: Klett-Cotta.
Jellinek, Georg. 2006. *Die Erklärung der Menschen und Bürgerrechte: Ein Beitrag zur modernen Verfassungsgeschichte*. Saarbrücken: VDM Dr. Müller. Reprint of the third posthumous edition, revised and completed by Walter Jellinek in 1919. First published 1895.
John, Paul II. 1991. Encyclical *Centesimus annus*. Vatican: Libreria Editrice Vaticana.
Koslowski, Peter. 1994. *Prinzipien der ethischen Ökonomie. Grundlegung der Wirtschaftsethik und der auf die Ökonomie bezogenen Ethik*. Tübingen: J.C.B. Mohr. Paul Siebeck. (1988, RP 1994).
Koslowski, Peter. 2002. Economics as ethical economy and cultural economics in the historical school. In *The Historicity of Economics. Continuities and Discontinuities of Historical Thought in 19th and 20th Century Economics*, ed. Heino H. Nau and Bertram Schefold. Berlin/Heidelberg/New York: Springer. 139ff.
Langholm, Odd. 1992. *Economics in the medieval schools. Wealth, exchange, value, money & usury according to the Paris theological tradition, 1200–1350*. Leiden/New York/Köln: E.J.Brill.
Le Bras, Gabriel. 1950. Usure, La Doctrine ecclésiastique de l'usure a l'époque classique (XXIIᵉ-XVᵉ siècle). In *Dictionnaire de théologie catholique*, XV/2. 2336ff. Paris: 8n Marcel Marion.
Leo, I. 1957. Letter 167. In *The Fathers of the Church. A New Translation. St. Leo the Great, Letters* (trans: Brother Edmund Hunt). C.S.C. Washington: The Catholic University of America Press.
Leo, I. 1996. Sermon 17. In *The Fathers of the Church. A New Translation. St. Leo the Great, Sermons* (trans: Jane Patricia Freeland, C.S.J.B., and Agnes Josephine Conway, S.S.J.), 63ff. Washington: The Catholic University of America Press.
Marx, Reinhard. 2008. *Das Kapital. Ein Plädoyer für den Menschen*. München: Pattloch. Italian trans: 2009. *Il capitale. Una critica cristiana alle ragioni del mercato*. Milano: Rizzoli.
Melé, Domenec. 1999. Early business ethics in Spain: The Salamanca School (1526–1614). *Journal of Business Ethics* 23(3): 175–189.
Melé, Domenec, and Josep Maria Castellà. 2010. *El desarrollo humano integral. Comentarios interdisciplinares a la encíclica Caritas in veritate de Benedicto XVI*. Barcelona: Iter.
Noonan Jr., John T. 1957. *The Scholastic Analysis of Usury*. Cambridge: Harvard University Press.
Nuccio, Oscar. 1984. *Il pensiero economico italiano, vol. I, tome 1., Le fonti (1050–1450). L'etica laica e la formazione dello spirito economico*. Sassari: Edizioni Gallizzi.
Ratzinger, Joseph. 1986. Market Economy and Ethics. In *Church and Economy in Dialogue*, ed. Lothar Roos, 13ff. Köln: Bachem. (www.ordosocialis. de). The German original: "Marktwirtschaft und Ethik." In *Stimmen der Kirche zur Wirtschaft*, ed. Lothar Roos, 50ff. Köln: Bachem. Italian trans: 2008. Chiesa ed economia: Responsabilità per il futuro dell'economia mondiale. *Communio* (Italian edition) 218. 83ff.
Rendtorff, Trutz. 1987. Menschenrechte als Bürgerrechte: Protestantische Aspekte ihrer Begründung. In *Menschenrechte und Menschenwürde: Historische Voraussetzungen – säkulare Gestalt – christliches Verständnis*, ed. Ernst-Wolfgang Böckenförde and Robert Spaemann. Stuttgart: Klett-Cotta. 93ff.

Rhonheimer, Martin. 2003. La realtà politica ed economica del mondo moderno e i suoi presupposti etici e culturali. L'enciclica Centesimus Annus-1.V.1991. In *Giovanni Paolo teologo. Nel segno delle encicliche*, ed. Graziano Borgonovo and Arturo Cattaneo, 142–161. Milan: Mondadori.

Rhonheimer, Martin. 2000. *La perspectiva de la moral. Fundamentos de la Ética Filosófica*. Madrid: Rialp. In English edition: 2008. *The perspective of the acting person: essays in the renewal of thomistic moral philosophy*. Washington: Catholic University of America Press.

Roos, Lothar. 2009. *Menschen, Märkte und Moral: Die Botschaft der Enzyklika Caritas in veritate*. Köln: Bachem.

Röttgers, Kurt. 1980. Markt. In *Historisches Wörterbuch der Philosophie*, vol. 5, ed. Joachim Ritter and Karlfried Gründer, 753–758. Basel/Stuttgart: Schwabe.

Schefold, Bertram. 2008. Platon (428/427-348/347) und Aristoteles (348-322). In *Klassiker des ökonomischen Denkens. Von Platon bis John Maynard Keynes*, ed. Joachim Starbatty, 19–55. Hamburg: Nikol.

Schumpeter, Joseph A. 1954. *History of Economic Analysis*. New York: Oxford University Press.

Smith, Adam. 1979. In *An Inquiry into the Nature and Causes of the Wealth of Nations*, eds. Campbell, R. H., and A. S. Skinner; textual editor Todd, W.B. Oxford: Oxford University Press.

Todeschini, Giacomo. 2004. *Ricchezza francescana. Dalla povertà volontaria alla società di mercato*. Bologna: il Mulino.

Tosato, Angelo. 2002. *"Vangelo e ricchezza." Nuove prospettive esegetiche*. Rubbettino: Soveria Mannelli.

Walbank, Frank William. 1987.Trade and industry under the later Roman empire in the west. In *The Cambridge economic history of Europe, vol. II, Trade and industry in the middle ages*, ed. Postan, M.M., and Edward Miller, 71ff. Cambridge: Cambridge University Press.

Wittreck, Fabian. 2002. *Geld als Instrument der Gerechtigkeit. Die Geldlehre des Hl. Thomas von Aquin in ihrem interkulturellen Kontext*. Paderborn: Schöningh.

Wittreck, Fabian. 2009. *Interaktion religiöser Rechtsordnungen. Rezeptions- und Translationsprozesse dargestellt am Beispiel des Zinsverbots in den orientalischen Kirchenrechtssammlungen*. Berlin: Duncker & Humblot.

Wood, Diana. 2002. *Medieval economic thought*. Cambridge: Cambridge University Press.

Chapter 7
From a "Culture of Greed" to a Culture of Common Good

Michel Camdessus

As a central banker, all of my experience confirms the basic statement: "The functioning of a free market economy depends upon sound cultural and ethical foundations." Using this statement as a starting point, the present chapter will try to answer two fundamental questions:

1. How is a collective "culture of greed" at the origin of the disastrous end of a "heresy of the market economy"?
2. Remembering that international monetary stability is one of the public common goods which must be pursued, how could ways toward a new monetary system based upon values and the promotion of common good be identified?

7.1 The Disastrous End of a "Culture of Greed"

An annual meeting of the International Monetary Fund and the World Bank took place in October 2010. It is difficult to summarize all that was said, but three major observations were shared by many of the delegates:

- We are at a juncture full of uncertainties.
- This crisis has hurt the world economy severely, and the recovery will take years.
- The perversion, by a culture of greed, of a well-established model of market economy is at the origin of this unexpected crisis.

This last remark was made several times, and thus reflection upon the dramatic trial and challenge this crisis represents for our societies is necessary.

M. Camdessus (✉)
President of The International Monetary Fund (Washington, 1987–2000), President of SFEF, Société de Financement de l'Économie Française (Paris, 2008-2010), Honorary Governor of the Banque of France, Code Courrier 09-1060, 75049 Paris Cedex 01, France
e-mail: lyliane.huot@banque-france.fr

M. Schlag and J.A. Mercado (eds.), *Free Markets and the Culture of Common Good*, Ethical Economy 41, DOI 10.1007/978-94-007-2990-2_7, © Springer Science+Business Media B.V. 2012

The crisis struck in August 2007, and the virus from which it sprang soon mutated into a global economic crisis that has produced human ravages everywhere:

- Unemployment is close to 10% in the United States and 20% in Spain.
- More than 50 million people in Africa are falling back into the extreme poverty from which they had so painfully begun to emerge.
- There has been an enormous cost in terms of public finances and indebtedness in advanced countries due to containment measures, leaving "the king with no clothes" to face new potential major shocks.
- Increases in all forms of insecurity are visible.

Moreover, as is always the case, all these forms of devastation strike first and foremost the poorest among us.

This crisis has many dimensions. This is not yet another crisis in a globalized world, but it is the first true crisis of globalization itself. It is undoubtedly about finance and that dimension is what we must, first and foremost, master. But, just as the Hydra of mythology had seven heads, it is systemically part of at least six other crises: the poverty of the third world, the climate crisis, the food crisis, the energy crisis, the crisis of multilateralism, and the crisis which dominates them all: the crisis of ethics and culture. There are seven crises altogether. All of these must be taken into account if anyone of them is to be addressed.

Let the cultural and ethical roots of the crisis be clearly understood. The chain of events since the late 1980s, up until the subprime disaster in the United States, then the collapse of major American, British, and other financial institutions, and the following spread of the crisis, demonstrate that they have spilled over into a world in which the principal leaders had been more or less convinced that the self-regulating forces of the market would always produce the adjustments that were necessary. Hence, they were convinced not only that all public interventions that might counter market forces should be rejected[1] but also that to try to subordinate the market to ethical principles was just nonsense.

As a matter of fact, this approach is very far from the views of Adam Smith and of the founding fathers of the market economy and capitalism. "[T]he conviction that the economy must be autonomous, that it must be shielded from 'influences' of a moral character" (Benedict XVI 2009, 34), as the Pope writes in *Caritas in Veritate*, was also a heresy of the market economy as conceived by Adam Smith, not to mention the idea of the more recent European promoters of the Social Market Economy. In this context, the international financial market which had been created over the past 20 years was left to its own devices without rules or monitoring institutions. The IMF itself was not allowed to broaden its mandate from monetary to financial issues; in fact, it was denied the right to enter into this field until the crisis. It is hardly surprising, therefore, that a good number of actors began to behave like people without faith or laws. Their behavior came to serve as a reference point, even

---

[1]"The State is the problem, not the solution," said President Reagan.

when more and more voices echoed in warning. The end result was what Alan Greenspan in 1996 called "irrational exuberance" (Greenspan 1996), but his characterization did not shake the global consensus that urged unbounded laissez-faire. This inexorably led not only toward deregulation, which was at times desirable, but also to a refusal to interfere with the practices developing in this climate of euphoria, including ever more risk-taking business, frequently with serious technical flaws and grave moral lapses. The list of these moral lapses is long, and they can be observed at every stage of the crisis.

The fact that the world settled into this "irrational exuberance," that no true social reaction materialized, that no sufficiently vigorous and organized citizen opposition emerged, and that the leaders who were responsible allowed themselves to be carried along on this collective wave raises questions that continue to haunt those active in the financial market: how was it possible? There is only one convincing explanation: these behaviors were deeply rooted in a cultural context where the seduction of money was so strong that it produced a collective blindness, disarming all forms of vigilance.

This context has prevailed despite all sorts of protests against the commercialization of the world. Since the 1960s, the more developed countries, imitated by transitional and emerging countries, have allowed a culture to take root whose drive "to earn more, always to consume more" became, although certainly not exclusive, clearly the dominant force. Man was reduced to his simple economic function. Consumption became destiny; life was emptied of meaning. The cupidity which President Obama so vigorously denounced in his inauguration speech (Obama 2009) surreptitiously had become subliminally, politically correct, fixed at the heart of the collective culture. The world began to worship the golden calf, gripped as it was by this culture in which the countries had immersed themselves. Like the Jewish people after the death of Joshua, settled in heathen lands, these countries allowed themselves to be governed by the collective culture which, little by little, took over, so that they came to "serve Baal and Astarte" (Joshua 2: 11–13).

The surrounding culture surreptitiously binds a people. "The little mother," said Kafka, speaking about culture, "has claws." It grips those within range. In the cultural environment, there was fertile ground for all of the abuses committed in the financial sphere. In this manner, an ethical pit was created in which the world economy was engulfed until large parts of the global financial pyramid began to crumble.

In summary, there are three major failures that explain the origin of the crisis: the absence of necessary rules, the inadequacy of monitoring institutions, and very fundamentally, collective behaviors that result from this culture of having. It is the task of governments, led by the G20, to mitigate the first two, those that touch on regulations and institutions. They are busy with that, working also to reboot a dynamic economy. But beware: if the underlying cultural challenge is not addressed, the same causes will produce tomorrow, perhaps with far greater damage, the same effects. Hence, of paramount urgency is the need for this cultural and ethical challenge to be addressed. The action of governments will not suffice in this role. It is here that religious leaders, together with all those enjoying some influence on education and culture, are confronted with an immense responsibility.

By means of the inspiration of the admirable encyclical letter, *Caritas in Veritate*, there is not only the possibility of creating a new conception of a global monetary and financial system, no longer dominated by greed and solidly rooted on a culture of common good, but also of taking the few first steps in that direction. Certainly, this is the proper moment: "The financial crisis and the threat to the Euro are an opportunity to reintroduce a moral dimension to economics"(Benedict 2010).[2]

The following is an examination of possible key features of a new global monetary and financial system based on values and on the promotion of common good.

7.2   A New Global and Monetary Financial System Based on Values and on the Promotion of Common Good

For an understanding of the common good, its definition as provided by *The Compendium of the Social Doctrine of the Church* should suffice: "The sum total of social conditions which allow people either as groups or as individuals, to reach their fulfillment more fully and more easily" (Pontifical Council for Justice and Peace 2004, 164).

These remarks focus on what will be central in the agenda of the G20 in 2011, the reform of the global monetary and financial system, and on what feasible steps can align this objective it with the global common good. Succeeding in this reform after the disruptions of the culture of greed, which has prevailed since the 1970s, is all the more important as international monetary stability is recognized by the United Nations as one of the key public common goods.

As this task seems impossible to many key actors, it is important for Christians to meditate on the message of *Caritas in Veritate*, particularly pertinent to this matter and contrary to the frequently held opinion that monetary issues are of a purely technical character. One can find in this text a most welcome invitation to hope and confidence. The Holy Father sees formidable potential for renovation in this world ruined by the crisis. Falling into an empiricist and skeptical view of life should be avoided since openness to God will bring us to "an understanding of life as a joyful task to be accomplished in a spirit of solidarity" (Benedict XVI 2009, 78).

Beginning with this conviction, the encyclical letter opens perspectives particularly relevant to the present circumstances of the financial market economy since in a more and more globalized universe, "the common good and the effort to obtain it cannot fail to assume the dimensions of the whole human family, that is to say, the community of peoples and nations" (Benedict XVI 2009, 7).

---

[2]My friend Onno Ruding called my attention to these words of the Holy Father, while traveling to Portugal, which are quoted from the International Herald Tribune (12.05.2010). The literal quotation is not to be found in the original discourse, but it is expressive of the Pope's thought.

The encyclical letter devotes its fifth chapter to the new forms of collaboration that globalization requires, with a particular emphasis on the necessary interaction between the two key principles of subsidiarity and solidarity. Here, as his predecessors, the Pope enters a timely plea in favor of international development aid. This is of particular importance since one of the perverse consequences of the crisis has been probably to make the financing of the development of the poorest countries and of the millennium development goals more precarious.

Paragraph 67, particularly devoted to the problem of the reform of the international organizations, is especially important in this new idea. Applied to the global monetary and financial system, its broad principles call for immediate major changes. The immediacy of their application is imperative not only due to the damages that the sheer refusal of ethical prescriptions can create but also since retaining the old paradigm would be a recipe for a new crisis sooner rather than later. The same causes could not but produce the same effects.

Reforming the global monetary and financial system will be the indispensable complement without which the valuable work which has been initiated in the prudential and regulatory field would lack its basic foundation. The task of the G20 will be nevertheless a difficult one. What then could be the basic tenets of this reform?

A precondition to these changes in the field of regulation and institutional reforms is to be identified in respect to behaviors and cultures, notably the way in which countries interact with the central institution of the system, the International Monetary Fund. A major change in the attitudes and the behaviors of countries must be elicited if the institution is to be in a position to more effectively serve the common good. If there is to be universal trust in the system as well as in its central institution, this change must begin with a recognition that, over time, the multilateral spirit of cooperation has been eroded. Too many times nationalist concerns have prevailed over the global purposes of the membership, major powers frequently forgetting their particular responsibility for exemplarity attached to leadership. Reform would be to no avail if it were not to be accompanied by a new spirit of partnership among the key actors of the system. At the same time, the reform of the institution should be ambitious enough to generate a new spirit of ownership, a stronger political commitment of all countries, without any privileged status, and the shared conviction by all that each one can contribute to the common good, accepting the price and the sacrifices that such contributions require. In a word, conditions for real universal ownership must be created together with the shared sense of the new responsibilities that ownership implies. This is what is needed for the reform of the system to make sense. Now, if progress in that direction could be accomplished, what would be the practical elements of the reform of the governance of the International Monetary Fund? The key findings of a so-called group "of eminent persons," including Amartya Sen and chairman Trevor Manuel, former minister of finance of South Africa, are summarized as follows (Committee on IMF Governance Reform 2009).

The group began by recognizing that the IMF, thanks to its experience and the quality of its staff, must be entrusted with the task of steering the process of global monetary reform, thus continuing to be the machinery for the collaboration necessary to respond to the needs of the system during the next decades. The key reforms recommended to this effect were the following:

- The expansion of the Fund's surveillance mandate beyond exchange rates and macroeconomic policies in order to provide appropriate coverage of prudential issues and financial spillover.
- The activation of a very high political caliber council made of ministers and governors, to provide a political forum for coordination and to make the strategic decisions critical to global stability while retaining them in the hands of civil servants.
- An accelerated quota revision process and an amendment to the Articles of Agreement that would eliminate appointed chairs, thereby allowing for a necessary consolidation and a reshuffling of constituencies, including those of EU countries, in order to reflect current economic realities and to "achieve a better balance between advanced and emerging market/developing countries" (Committee on IMF Governance Reform 2009, 24) in shared decision-making.
- The lowering of the voting threshold on critical decisions from 85% to 70–75%, de facto eliminating any United States or European veto right, along with a consideration of extending double majorities to a wider range of decisions, thus ensuring that decisions affecting key aspects of the institution command the support of a broad majority of members.
- The introduction of an open, transparent, and merit-based system for the appointment of the managing director and deputy managing directors.

Further reflection on the problem of the relationship of the IMF with the G20 is also justified. This problem can be summarized in rather simple terms: the IMF Board, and tomorrow hopefully its Council with their 24 members, finds in the Bretton Woods Treaty the necessary legal instruments but still lacks political clout. The G20 – de facto the G26 or more – is in the opposite situation: its decisions are only binding for its own members, even if it has obviously a broader influence.

An adjustment of the memberships of the two bodies would more easily allow for the combination of legal power and political influence. One could easily imagine similar changes being introduced into the governing bodies of the World Bank, aiding the G20 by providing a stronger leverage over these institutions and, when needed, over their coordination. These questions remain open in the absence of a decision concerning the desirability of these changes – preferably by a reduction of the membership of each – the desirable timing, and their practical modalities. It goes without saying that such a change should keep in place a system of "constituencies" as presently exists in the Bretton Woods Institutions but not in the G20. This would be of major importance in more firmly establishing the democratic legitimacy of the renovated G20 (whatever the number of its members).

All of the aforementioned suggestions may appear relatively straightforward. Nevertheless, taken together they amount to an ambitious program providing the system with the anchor and the institution it needs. This profound change would necessarily take time, as it would transform the IMF into a truly global monetary and financial fund. It would become the "World Fund," to put it simply.

One could expect that the adoption of these institutional changes would create the conditions for the emergence of a renewed spirit of collaboration. A few more technical changes could help also to make further progress in the pursuit of the global common good and the promotion of the stability of the financial and monetary system. Five can be mentioned here:

1. At the global level, one of the most significant changes required would consist in establishing a system of incentives and sanctions strong enough to promote a global discipline which has so far been absent. De facto, the prescriptions of the global surveillance were only binding for countries in need of conditional multilateral financing. Countries prefer carrots rather than sticks, but they are both necessary. In 1991, John Paul II, addressing ambassadors, reminded them of the necessity that "the rules of international law be more and more effectively supported by constraining devices able to guarantee their implementation" (John Paul II 1991a). Renewed efforts must be undertaken also so that these instruments of surveillance are more effectively applied to exchange markets; the failures of the past are not a good enough reason to avoid creating new approaches. This area as well is in need of a certain discipline providing stability and in particular forms of competitive devaluation.

2. A set of universally accepted rules to discipline private financial activities since "justice requires rules." Governments as well as regional organizations must actively continue the task they have undertaken by following the comprehensive program adopted at the G20 meeting in November 2008 in Washington. They should not allow the pressure of lobbies to detract them at a time when the work has become more and more difficult as the details are being discussed. The Pope reminded the world of the powerful warning of his predecessor in *Centesimus Annus*, where he condemns "a system in which freedom in the economic sector is not circumscribed within a strong juridical framework which places it at the service of human freedom in its totality" (John Paul II 1991b, 42).

3. A significant strengthening of the prudential organizations, a field in which Europe has, at least on an institutional level, recently introduced useful instruments based on a report by Jacques de Larosière.

4. Two fundamental reforms in the provision of international liquidity:

   • The first is the immediate establishment of an effective monitoring of the present liquidity overhang, which contributes to generating disorderly capital flows responsible for destabilizing effects on emerging countries.
   • The longer term perspective requires a progressive renovation of the system for the provision of reserve currencies in the world, which is today almost exclusively dependent upon the domestic requirements of the United States monetary policy. Such a change necessitates the development of a multilaterally

managed international reserve currency, which could over time provide the system with the anchor of stability it is currently lacking. It is believed that the present Special Drawing Right could be the embryo of such a world currency unit.

5. Last, but not least, the reform of the global monetary and financial system must be part and parcel of a broader reform of the entire United Nations system, having in mind the principles which John XXIII, in a prophetic statement almost 50 years ago Paul VI and Benedict XVI have clearly laid out in calling for a public authority with universal competence (John XXIII 1963, 137; Paul VI 1967, 78; Benedict XVI 2009, 67).

Some progress in this direction is being made with the present work of the G20. More is needed, of course, primarily by establishing a more precise institutional relationship between this informal group, the Bretton Woods Institutions and the United Nations. Suggestions to that end were made, at the request of the COMECE, at the beginning of this decade. They deserve to be revisited in view of the experience gained since the beginning of the crisis, taking into account in particular the need to establish an effective cooperation and coordination with newly created bodies, such as the Financial Stability Board, the new European institutions, and of course, the entire family of the United Nations.

Could such a new framework – at least in the field of finance – contribute to creating "better conditions" for a single human family working together in full partnership, if not yet in true communion? It is certainly a possibility, and this recent crisis has provided the opportunity for such an attempt.

Would it be effective? This is also certainly possible, provided that a major prerequisite is fulfilled: men with a strong sense of social and political responsibility must be willing to devote their energies and talents. Tocqueville's principle applies here (cfr. Tocqueville 2002, 351ff): harmony in human societies rests on the quality of the couple linking institutions with behavior guided by ethics. Freedom in the economy does not work without social responsibility.

Bibliography

Benedict XVI. 2009. Encyclical *Caritas in Veritate*. Vatican: Libreria Editrice Vaticana.
Benedict XVI. 2010. Interview of the Holy Father Benedict XVI with the Journalists on the Flight to Portugal. http://www.vatican.va/holy_father/benedict_xvi/speeches/2010/may/documents/hf_ben-xvi_spe_20100511_portogallo-interview_en.html. Accessed 11 May 2010.
Committee on IMF Governance Reform. 2009. Final report.
Greenspan, Alan. 1996. *The Challenge of Central Banking in a Democratic Society. Annual dinner and Francis Boyer Lecture of the American Enterprise Institute for Public Policy Research*. Washington, D.C.: Federal Reserve Board.
John XXIII. 1963. Encyclical *Pacem in Terris*. Vatican: Libreria Editrice Vaticana.
John Paul II. 1991a. Discorso di Giovanni Paolo II ai membri del corpo diplomatico accreditato presso la Santa Sede. http://www.vatican.va/holy_fatherjohn_paul_ii/speeches/index_spe-dip-corps.htm. Accessed 12 Jan 1991.

John Paul II. 1991b. Encyclical *Centesimus Annus*. Vatican: Libreria Editrice Vaticana.

Obama, Barack. 2009. Inaugural Address. Washington, D.C. http://www.whitehouse.gov/blog/inaugural-address/. Accessed 20 Jan 2009

Paul VI. 1967. Encyclical *Populorum Progressio*. Vatican: Libreria Editrice Vaticana.

Pontifical Council for Justice and Peace. 2004. 2004. *Compendium of the Social Doctrine of the Church*. Vatican: Libreria Editrice Vaticana.

Tocqueville, Alexis de. 2002. *Democracy in America*, vols. 1 and 2. (trans: by Henry Reeve). University Park: Pennsylvania State University.

Chapter 8
Free Markets and the Common Good: A Few Methodological Remarks

Rocco Buttiglione

8.1 The Necessity of Law for Free Markets

Free markets do not exist in nature. To have a free market (and, in general, a free economy), we must have a rule of law determining the private property of each one of the agents in the market and forbidding the acquisition of the property of another agent through the use of force or deception. The exchange of equivalents is not the only way in which one may acquire property. Stealing, pillaging, and plundering have had a glorious history in times past and (who knows?) perhaps will have also in the present and in the future as more or less legitimate forms of acquiring property. Tacitus tells us that the ancient Germans considered property acquired through the use of force more honorable than property acquired through labor or through commerce (Tacitus 1942, Chap. 14).

In order to have a free market, you must have a law regarding the ways in which property may be acquired and transferred. As a rule, economists take these presuppositions for granted. As a matter of fact, they cannot. You cannot put a kind of economic discovery at the beginning of the free market, as occurs, for instance, in *An Inquiry into the Nature and the Causes of the Wealth of Nations* by Adam Smith. You must recognize a certain primacy of law, and especially of Roman law. The first presupposition of a free economy is the contract, that is, an act in which two free wills converge in accepting an exchange. I accept a transfer of my rights on a certain object to you in exchange for your rights on another object.

The contract presupposes two free subjects. Here, you are confronted with the ethical value of a free economy before you consider its properly economic

R. Buttiglione (✉)
Vice-President of the House of Representatives of the Republic of Italy
Università degli Studi S. Pio V, House of Representatives, Rome, Italy
e-mail: buttiglione_r@camera.it

M. Schlag and J.A. Mercado (eds.), *Free Markets and the Culture of Common Good*, Ethical Economy 41, DOI 10.1007/978-94-007-2990-2_8,
© Springer Science+Business Media B.V. 2012

advantages. The free economy presupposes free men and is a component element of a free society. Nobody can take what is mine without paying a fair price, and fair is the price to which I give my consent. The free economy arises as an alternative to the command economy where somebody (the powerful, the noble, the baron, or the robber) can take what is mine without paying any price or paying merely the price he is willing to pay. This ethical value of the free economy is in one sense in dependent of the fact that this is the best possible way to organize social cooperation and the division of labor. Some theorists say that at the beginning of the free market stands greed and a unilateral acquisitive mentality. Of course, when you make men free, they can make a good or a bad use of their freedom. A world with freedom and also greed is, however, better than a world without freedom. Would a world without a free market be a world without greed? Most likely not. We know command economies and have seen that their greed conditions the lives of men not through market mechanisms but through the arts of war and the sheer use of force.

8.2   Free Markets and Preferences

I shall not deal at length with the well-known fact that markets register the preferences of the customers much better than any planning bureaucracy. Ludwig von Mises (1975, 87–130) has given a definitive demonstration of the impossibility of economic calculation without the market, and I shall not repeat his arguments here.

8.3   Economics as an A Priori Science

Carl Menger has shown that economics is an a priori science. There are some fundamental economic truths that are in themselves self-evident. We do not learn them through experience or through history although these truths give us invaluable instruments with which to understand and to organize our empirical experience (1985, 69). In order to understand that lower prices will stimulate an increased demand, we do not need to have any experience of commerce. This truth is evident in itself. The science of economics is based on these self-evident truths.

8.4   Other A Priori Sciences

Economics is not the only a priori science. Mathematics, ethics, and politics (to a certain extent) are also a priori sciences (Menger 1985, 86, 158).

8.5 Reality and A Priori Sciences

But does reality conform itself to a priori laws categorized by a priori sciences? Not always.

A priori sciences deal with a simplified reality that is not the same as the real world we experience everyday. This will become more apparent through an example. We all recognize the truth of the a priori law we have just stated: lower prices stimulate an increased demand. We also know, however, instances in which a decrease in prices does not produce the desired effect. If we all have more bread than we need, we will not buy additional bread, even if the price is reduced to nothing. A priori laws should always be stated with a *caveat*: all other things being equal. All other things being equal, lower prices will stimulate an increased demand. When we formulate an a priori law, we isolate a certain phenomenon from all others and create what the scholastics would call a formal object. The real object is subject not only to one a priori law but to many, and these laws do not belong only to the realm of economics but also to other realms (for example, to the realm of morals and to the realm of politics).

8.6 Political Economy for the Common Good

I propose to reserve the name "political economy" for the empirical science that studies the way in which different a priori laws influence a material object and the decisions that have to be taken in order to promote the common good of a particular community. Let us consider some concrete examples.

After the Second World War, important economic decisions had to be taken in order to shape the post-war economies of Europe. The pure science of economics suggested that what we needed was a thorough going liberalization of restricted and overregulated markets. The political leaders of that time were confronted with the necessity of winning the consent of the majority of voters for these policies. Some concessions had to be made. To win the support of the farmers, a system of protection for agricultural products had to be devised. The compromise has produced good results. A free economy was developed. A different choice would have been better accepted by the theorists of pure economy but would have failed and consigned our countries to communist governments.

Let us consider now the issue of globalization. It is not necessarily a zero-sum game. It is quite possible that in the end it will result in better living conditions for all. In the short run, however, emerging countries enter into comparatively low-technology markets where a large part of people from more developed countries previously held their jobs. This results in the destruction of many jobs and may bring misery to many families. However, it would be unwise to stop globalization. It would mean sending to emerging countries the following message: we do not recognize your right to a human life, and if you want a better destiny, you will have to conquer it with weapons raised against us. We must try to steer globalization by adjusting its pace to the demands of different peoples. We must develop policies in more developed countries by which we substitute the jobs lost in traditional sectors with new jobs created in new high-technology sectors, upgrading the capabilities of our people to produce new goods and services that emerging peoples cannot produce (yet). With time, they will reach our same level of technology, but by that time, they will also pay salaries that we consider acceptable. We need international cooperation and political wisdom in order to orient this process. In this, as in other cases, pure economy is like a compass that helps a pathfinder to determine the direction in which he has to move. It helps, but it is not enough. To circumnavigate obstacles that cannot be surpassed, he needs a more detailed map. To provide this map is the task of applied economics and of politics. The political decision has to take into account the a priori laws of economics but also those of ethics and of politics. It must be oriented toward a result that satisfies the demands of economics but also finds a concrete way toward this result that is ethically acceptable and politically viable.

8.7   Social Justice or Distributive Justice?

A controversial issue is the debate whether to implement either social justice or distributive justice. Shall we defend the thesis that to all men is due the same amount of the general product of society? Should we implement policies redistributing income and equalizing the income of all persons, of those who worked and of those who did not, and of those who worked well and of those who worked not so well? This would be not only economically incorrect but also morally unjust and politically impossible. The exchange of equivalents is not only an economic principle but also a moral principle. Shall we say then that social justice demands the equality of the starting points and not that of the points of arrival? It seems that this formulation also does not correspond to the true meaning of social justice. I shall now try to approximate this meaning through three different avenues.

The first one is provided by the encyclical *Dives in Misericordia*. There is something that is due to man as a human being, quite irrespective of a capacity of giving anything in exchange. Man is not only an individual and a market agent, but man is also a person and a member of a community. In a community, the exchange of equivalents is not the only form of exchange. There is also a gratuitous exchange as, for example, in the family, where the children are raised and cared for out of love. Those who are out of the market cannot be left there to die but have a right to be supported and, if possible, reequipped to go back to work (John Paul II 1980, 14).

We derive the second avenue from a current discussion in Austrian economics on minimum salary. Many economists reject the idea of a minimum salary, because they say that many less well-paid jobs will be destroyed by a minimum salary law. This is of course true, if the minimum salary is too high. On the other hand, if the salary does not cover the minimal needs and demands for a human life, those who receive that salary will be compelled to drop out of the market and to struggle for life by means of rebellion, force, crime, and revolution. The economic law telling us that minimum salary laws eliminate less well-paid jobs from the market must find a point of encounter with a physiological and sociological law, stating that a salary that does not cover basic needs will be a cause of social unrest and end in a civil war.

The third inroad into our concept is here derived from the so-called civil economy and can be seen as a kind of mediation or unification of the first two. If I were a rich man, I would not like to have to move around always escorted by bodyguards in order to be protected against the outrage and the desperation of the poor. I would like to live in a city adorned by beautiful monuments with solid civic institutions that extend, in a certain measure, the system of gratuity that dominates in the family to the public space. It is not just a principle of humanity. In the long run, it also has an economic meaning. It is not wise to expect the delivery of our sausage just from the sympathy and goodwill of our butcher and not from his enlightened self interest. But what is wrong if I enter into a relation of civil friendship with my butcher? In principle, this does not exclude the exchange of equivalents. It may, however, happen that one day, I stand in need of help. On that day, the sympathy of my neighbors, of those who hold a stake in my business, of my creditors, and of my suppliers can make the difference between going bankrupt and having a second chance. The experience of being members of a community can also have an economic meaning that strengthens a company and allows it to flourish. Solidarity is (also) an economic asset. Social justice is the system of relations holding a community together. It must not be identified with redistributive policies (although under circumstances, they can be a part of it). I wonder whether Hayek would extend to this definition of social justice the hostility he manifests against the concept of social justice in general.

It seems to me that the hostility of Hayek is rather motivated by the fact that to him social justice seems to be entrusted solely to the state, enlarging the scope of state activity and state control of human activity almost without boundaries. It is of course impossible to know what he would have thought of a social justice that is entrusted, in different forms, to all of society, of course without excluding a responsibility as a last resort which also belongs to the state.

Bibliography

John Paul II. 1980. Encyclical *Dives in Misericordia*. Vatican: Libreria Editrice Vaticana.

Menger, Carl. 1985. *Investigation into the Method of the Social Sciences with Special Reference to Economics* (trans: Louis Schneider). New York: New York University Press.

Mises, Ludwig von. 1975. "Economic Calculation in the Socialist Commonwealth". In *Collectivist Economic Planning*. ed. F.A. Hayek. London: George Routledge & Sons 1935, reprint by Augustus M. Kelley, 87–130. Originally published as *Die Wirtschaftsrechnung im sozialistischen Gemeinwesen*. Archiv für Sozialwissenschaften, vol. 47. (1920).

Smith, Adam. 1776. *An Inquiry into the Nature and the Causes of the Wealth of Nations*. London: Methuen.

Tacitus, Cornelius. 1942. "Germany and Its Tribes". In *Complete Works of Tacitus*, ed. Alfred John Church, William Jackson Brodribb, and Lisa Cerrato. New York: Random House.

Chapter 9
A Multidisciplinary Model of Economics: An Essential Framework for Building a True Integral Human Development

Alejandro Cañadas

9.1 Introduction

Even though the last financial crisis officially began in December 2007 and ended in June 2009, we still suffer from high levels of unemployment, abrupt international disruption in economic growth, disinflation of asset prices, and crippled credit markets. The financial crisis also created a crisis in the theory of economics and finance, which I believe could – and perhaps should – affect the ways that economics is addressed, studied, and taught. As a true crisis – a point and time of change – it would thus be necessary to examine existing methods and paradigms, identify, and analyze current gaps in theory, practice and pedagogy, and develop and articulate new approaches that delimit and compensate for the deficiencies in economic discipline that have been highlighted in *Caritas in Veritate* (CV) by Benedict XVI. In fact, I suggest that economics, as a profession and practice, requires an ever more multidisciplinary approach so as to more effectively ground its theory and outcomes in the realities of the human condition in which it is enacted. Such a multidisciplinary framework will enhance the capacity of economic theory to encounter and sense the real complexities of the human condition and will enable a more truthful, and comprehensive orientation to economics, both at present and in the future.

This chapter first presents the main problems of human development presented in *Caritas in Veritate*. With this foundation, it describes a philosophically based model of economics, and it gives an example of a multidisciplinary framework with a spiritual dimension. Finally, it ends with conclusions about the value and viability of such an approach.

A. Cañadas, Ph.D. (✉)
Assistant Professor of Economics
Mount St. Mary's University, Emmitsburg, USA
e-mail: canadas@msmary.edu

M. Schlag and J.A. Mercado (eds.), *Free Markets and the Culture of Common Good*, Ethical Economy 41, DOI 10.1007/978-94-007-2990-2_9,
© Springer Science+Business Media B.V. 2012

9.2   The Importance of *Caritas in Veritate* in Rethinking the Role of Economics

From a macro point of view, economists of almost all persuasions agree that the main goals for economics are a stable growth of real Gross Domestic Product (GDP), a relatively stable level of prices (low inflation) and a high level of employment (low unemployment). However, the same group of economists would disagree about how these goals can be achieved or the economic policy by which those goals should be delivered in any given economy. So, I argue that the three main goals of economics should be trying to promote human development by increasing the (material) standard of living of every society, by preserving the purchasing power of currency, and by promoting the personal realization of every person in society through work.

It is very important to recognize that in neoclassical economics, the main framework of economic thought applied in business and taught in the majority of modern universities, there is a particular meaning of human development different from the one explained in Catholic Social Teaching. There are three main characteristics of the neoclassical framework. First, the way in which we know the truth about economics is by investigating the mathematical structure of human choices by applying ad hoc models. Second, the definition of the human being who makes decisions in economics is called *homo economicus*, a purely rational and materialistic being who pursues self-interest by maximizing his utility or profits based on the availability of perfect information. Finally, economics is a positive discipline and, as such, it is a value-free science; therefore, it has no ethical implications. Thus, in pure neoclassical economics, integral human development is associated with material human progress, and it is measured and related by maximizing Gross Domestic Product (GDP).

Benedict XVI in *Caritas in Veritate* reminds us of Paul VI's teaching that integral human development concerns the whole of the person in every single dimension, not only the materialistic one. Thus, without the perspective of eternal life, human progress runs the risk of being reduced to the mere accumulation of wealth. What is more, integral human development is a vocation; it requires a transcendent vision of the person, and it needs God. Hence, it involves a free assumption of responsibility in solidarity on the part of everyone.

> Man does not develop through his own powers, nor can development simply be handed to him. In the course of history, it was often maintained that the creation of institutions was sufficient to guarantee the fulfillment of humanity's right to development. Unfortunately, too much confidence was placed in those institutions, as if they were able to deliver the desired objective automatically. In reality, institutions by themselves are not enough, because integral human development is primarily a vocation, and therefore it involves a free assumption of responsibility in solidarity on the part of everyone. Moreover, such development requires a transcendent vision of the person, it needs God: without him, development is either denied, or entrusted exclusively to man, who falls into the trap of thinking he can bring about his own salvation, and ends up promoting a dehumanized form of development. Only through an encounter with God are we able to see in the other something more than just another creature to recognize the divine image in the other, thus truly coming to discover him or her and to mature in a love that "becomes concern and care for the other" (Benedict XVI 2009, 11).

In order to reconcile the deficiencies of the neoclassical view of economics with Catholic Social Teaching, I propose a philosophically based model of economics that enables a multidisciplinary framework and approach. The philosophical domain is characterized by three essential tasks: an epistemological task that tries to address how knowledge is acquired and the ways such knowledge is used, an anthropological task that seeks to orient the use(s) of such knowledge within the dimensions of human activity, and the ethical task that attempts to develop and employ formal systematic analysis of moral decisional processes and the use of such formal systems in moral activities focused upon achieving individual and social "good."

9.3   The Philosophically Based Model

9.3.1   The Epistemological Component

How do we make decisions? A recurrent problem in economics and other disciplines is that the interpretation of the realities of the field is contingent upon the strength of the underlying theoretical base. Therefore, if a discipline is built upon weakly established foundations, then any interpretation of reality within that discipline's focus may be distorted. Current economic theory is based upon a set of ad hoc assumptions regarding consumer psychology that are drawn from a set of axioms, a mathematical structure. However, Anderson and McShane (2002) have shown that these assumptions cannot be verified in real subjects. Moreover, mainstream economics attempts to establish macroeconomically relevant premises based upon the summation of decisions extracted by individual agents or actors. This poses the epistemological question of whether it is possible to derive a modeled totality by summating and/or integrating the components of its parts. In other words, is economics intertheoretically reducible? Neoclassical economists (such as Lucas) have claimed that such reducibility is both possible and valuable (Hoover 2001) by viewing the systematic relations between macroeconomic aggregates. Although this might be theoretically possible, it assumes that economies work in a vacuum.

In order to appreciate the importance of reflecting upon the epistemological component of economics, I will review its origin, evolution, and limitations. Neoclassical economists (e.g., Samuelson, Arrow, and Debreu) began to investigate the mathematical structure of consumer choices and behavior in conceptual markets in the 1930s. In doing so, they created models with a strong normative component by focusing upon idealized choices and the efficient allocation of resources rather than describing the realities of individual choice and market contingencies. The result was the weak axiom of revealed preference (WARP) developed by Samuelson (Samuelson 1938), that began from a set of very simplistic assumptions (i.e., axioms) that would integrate a theory (e.g., utility) using formal language. Surprisingly, the theory could make sharp predictions about what kinds of choice patterns should or should not be observed. It is important to note that the theory predicted which new choices could possibly follow from an observed set of previous choices (e.g., responses to changes in prices, taxes, or income; see Glimcher 2002). Following WARP, additional theorems were developed that extended the scope of the revealed preferences approach to choices with uncertain outcomes whose likelihoods are known,[1] and in which outcomes may be spread over time (e.g., discount utility theory). These theories demonstrated that if one obeys particular axioms, then such behavior will likely reflect both a continuous utility function and "as if" actions aimed at maximizing total obtained utility. These theorems established foundations for much of game theory, and by the end of the 1930s, neoclassical economics possessed considerable concept, construct, and theoretical influence. As a result, these axioms of consumer choice became the basis for the demand component of the Arrow-Debreu theory of competitive "general" equilibrium, a system in which prices and quantities of all goods were simultaneously determined by equating supply and demand. This allowed economists to "predict" or anticipate the consequences of policy change, resulting in a style of analysis that both became unique to economics and was increasingly important to economic regulation and policy. In reality, such an approach provides an example of how clever axiomatic systems can be used to infer properties of unobservable preference from observable choice; the revealed preferences approach suppressed interest in the psychological nature of decision-making and individual and group preference(s) (Bruni and Sugden 2007). Pareto (1897) noted that:

> It is an empirical fact that the natural sciences have progressed only when they have taken secondary principles as their point of departure, instead of trying to discover the essence of things...Pure political economy has therefore a great interest in relying as little as possible on the domain of psychology (quoted in Busino 1964: xxiv).

In the 1950s, Milton Friedman's important book, *The Methodology of Positive Economics*, advanced the argument that assumptions underlying a prediction about market behavior could be wrong, but that the predictions drawn could be (approximately) true. According to Friedman, for example, even if a manager does not actually calculate a total profit maximization, the prices in that market evolve "as if" such calculations have been made, due to the underlying forces of the market. Friedman's argument provided license for economists to ignore considerable evidence of the ways and instances that economic agents violate rational-choice principles. In response – and contradiction – Maurice Allais designed a series of pairwise choices which led to reliable pattern of revealed preferences violating the central "independence" axiom of expected utility theory (called the "Allais Paradox" 1953). Subsequently, Daniel Ellsberg described another paradox that, together with Allais' effect, raised the possibility that the specific functional form of Expected Utility (EU) and subjective EU implied by simple axioms of preference were generally wrong (Ellsberg 1961). Kahneman and Tversky (1979) showed that the range of phenomena that fell outside classical expected utility theory was even broader than

---

[1] For example, Neumann and Morgenstern (1944) on expected utility theory, EUT, and Savage's subjective EU theory.

Allais' and Ellsberg's paradoxes. This work led many scholars of both economics and psychology to criticize simple axiomatic approaches. Counterexamples led to more general axiomatic systems more sensibly rooted in principles of psychology (Glimcher 2003). This represented the dawn of behavioral economics, which in many ways exemplifies the concept of "collective intelligence" by arguing that evidence from psychology can improve the model of human behavior inherited from neoclassical economics. Behavioral economics is based upon the presupposition that psychological principles are important in improving economic analysis. Similarly "Experimental Economics" presumes that incorporating psychological methods (e.g., highly controlled experiments of behavioral choice) will enhance the testability of economic theory.

This brief review of the epistemological component of economics shows that the limited epistemic basis of economic theory could be effectively revised and improved as long as economics could tend to be more integrative (i.e., human ecology) and open to interactions with other disciplines (i.e., the social and natural sciences). Moreover, even though neoclassical economics has been taught in many undergraduate programs all over the world, its limitations are very well known, and many attempts (e.g., behavioral economics, experimental economics, or neuroeconomics) have been developed to bring economics out of its theoretical (neoclassical) vacuum. Therefore, it is the principal responsibility of every professor of economics, especially within introductory courses, to address the epistemological limitations of neoclassical economics and to highlight the efforts in which neoclassical economics is open to creating synergies with other disciplines.

9.3.2   The Anthropological Component

A part of the problem lies in a lack of a core construct of the human being; the absence of this significant concept has both practical and moral consequences for disciplines, such as economics, that arise from or depend upon a scientifically valid model of the human person to describe or predict the cognitions and activities inherent to a particular endeavor. This can be seen in the emphasis that economics and finance have afforded to the neoclassical theoretical assumption that perfectly rational subjects prescribe economic interactions. I opine that this is an erroneous assumption, inconsistent with currently accepted models of human cognition, emotion, and behavior(s). Furthermore, I posit that the basic premises of neoclassical theory fail to account for the periodic irrationality and emotionality inherent to humans – as the subject(s) of economic discourse.

Neoclassical economics views the human person as *homo economicus*, that is, one who is purely rational and who pursues self-interest by maximizing his/her utility or profits based upon the acquisition and use of perfect information. I claim that there are more contemporary and more complete philosophical theories that define the human being as an amalgam of rational intelligence, emotional, and spiritual sensitivities within a responsible environment. Such a multipartite construct obtains a more realistic definition of the human being and, in this way, provides a more accurate description of the human decisional processes, influences, and capabilities. This distinction is neither trivial nor uncertain, because the terms and constructs used to define the human being (and its predispositions, cognitions, and actions) will sustain different practical and moral implications in any attempt to understand economic intent and behaviors (i.e., decisions) and to operationalize systems of moral analysis and articulation (i.e., ethics) of these intents and actions. Thus, it is important to use current epistemic capital in defining both the human being (in my view, a biopsychosocial organism) and the environment(s), nature, and applications of human actions. Such a definition requires humility that recognizes the limitation of the current view and a open mind to learn from other sciences (even theology) in order to construct a "collective intelligence" through the synergy of knowledge.

9.3.3   The Ethical Component

That economics can and should be framed as an anthropologically based, ethical human enterprise is neither a new nor novel concept. In the Aristotelian and Scholastic traditions, economics (and politics) was studied under a broader rubric and was aligned with ethics in constituting the *philosophia moralis* (Alvey 1999). This tradition was preserved within the European universities of the 1700s (Canterbery 1995), but as the economist and Anglican scholar Lord Griffiths has suggested, the intellectual tenor of the Enlightenment encouraged a more abstract, even amoral (i.e., not necessarily immoral, but rather nonmoralistic) manner (Griffiths 1984). Lionel Robbins defines economics as "the science which studies human behavior as a relationship between ends and scarce means that have alternatives uses" (Robbins 1952, 16). Thus, one of the goals of economics is to determine the effects of different choices in relation to the possible uses of scarce goods and resources. For Mises, economics is a "theoretical science. It is not its task to tell people what ends they should aim at. It is a science of the means to be applied for the attainment of the ends chosen, not... a science of the choosing of the ends. Science never tells a man how he should act; it merely shows how a man must act if he wants to attain definite ends" (Mises 1966, 10). These definitions suggest that economics is a positive discipline, because it entails studies of cause–effect relationships with a high degree of empirical validity. Yet, it is important to recognize that even as a science (as consistent with a formal definition of science qua *scientia*), economics is not simply the acquisition of knowledge for its own sake but rather, as adherent to its underlying philosophical tenets, engages in the attainment of knowledge so as to foster an understanding of field(s) of human endeavor. Indeed, Samuel Gregg claims that "economics is the study of how free persons choose to cooperate through voluntary exchanges to satisfy their own and other's needs in light of the reality of limited resources" (Gregg 2001, 9) and any such regard for the needs, values, and actions of others would vest economics – as a science, profession, and practice – with the construct of human ecology that philosopher Owen Flanagan claims is intrinsic to any naturalistic ethics (Flanagan 2002).

But unless we fall into the *ought vs. is* trap of the naturalistic fallacy, it is important to acknowledge that economics, as a science, has not necessarily embraced this trajectory, and economic ethics often fail to take into account foundational epistemic capital (that enables a current understandings of the human being as a biopsychosocial organism) and/or its anthropological dimensions (that situate human activities as ongoing interactions of biological, social, and psychological dimensions). Thus, while economic ethics *ought* to address, assess, and describe the articulation of the "good" of resource-based decisions and practices relative to the biopsychosocial aspects and exigencies of the human condition, in reality, it has neither uniformly attempted nor accomplished this undertaking. In this regard, it is noteworthy that the political philosopher, Thomas Carlyle, described economics as the "dismal science," referring both to the dire consequences of unchecked population growth predicted by Malthus and to economists' embracing a "pig philosophy" in their study of the production, distribution, and consumption of scarce goods and services.

In a practical way, how economists implement their ideas will depend upon the difference between positive and normative economics. On the one hand, normative economics or political economy is what Carl Menger referred to as "basic principles for the suitable advancement (appropriate to conditions) of national economy on the part of the public authorities" (Menger 1963, 211). Critical to Menger's argument is the notion of suitability – here defined as what is appropriate when philosophical, political, and ethical implications are duly considered. Normative economics is focused upon objects, opinions, moral, and/or political judgments and the effects of potential or actual economic policies. Samuel Gregg (2001) specifies that even when considering positive economics, it is important to note that not all assumptions are philosophically neutral. According to Ricardo Crespo, this reveals that "economics is not a value-free science" after all (Crespo 1998, 201).

In discussing the moral implication of economics, Hayek posits that "economic activity provides the material means for all our needs" (Hayek 1962, 49). This explicates that the subject of economics *is* the human being. Any interpretation of Hayek's claim will therefore be based, at least in part, upon what philosophical (namely, epistemic, anthropological and ethical) definition(s) of the human being is assumed to be valid and/or valued. If, for example, one presumes that the human being is simply a material, physical body, then any economic activity will only be dedicated to – and reflective of – material needs. However, if one holds that the human being is an embodied brain and mind that is nested within and vested with sociocultural environments, then, psychological, social as well as biological/material needs will figure into the decision processes (and moral sentiments) oriented toward acquiring, distributing, and utilizing resources. Moreover, if the biopsychological and social dimensions are inclusive of some "spiritual" aspects, then a more expansive, somewhat transcendent set of needs might be germane and influential to the moral and practical decisions involved in resource utilization. Therefore, if economics is to be pragmatically apt and ethically sound, I opine that economics as a science must appreciate current and complete definition(s) of the human being. I believe that this will create a more realistic "collective intelligence," improving the interpretation of the complexities of both the human organism and its condition, guiding economic activities, and at the same time, better informing pragmatic and ethical decision making in light of potential ethical, legal, and social consequences.

Benedict XVI reminds us in paragraphs 36 and 37 of *Caritas in Veritate* that economics and finance are instruments and as such they are good in themselves; it is the human being who can transform them into harmful tools. Therefore, "it is not the instrument that must be called to account, but individuals, their moral conscience, and their personal and social responsibility. The economic sphere is neither ethically neutral nor inherently inhuman…precisely because it is human; it must be structured and governed in an ethical manner. Thus, every economic decision has a moral consequence."

9.4   The Biopsychosocial (BPS) Model with a Spiritual Dimension

It is in this light that I offer a biopsychosocial model of economics with a spiritual dimension and economic ethics to describe and better intuit the multidimensional contingencies that derive from – and impinge upon – the human being in the discourses relevant to practical, moral decisions and actions of resource allocation and use. The biopsychosocial (BPS) model was first proposed by George Engel in 1977 to provide a more realistic orientation to the factors that affect human health, wellness, and illness. To be sure, a multidimensional orientation to the human person – and human condition – is not new, as such multifocal conceptualizations are evident in ancient Asian (2600 B.C.) and Greek (500 B.C.) philosophies. Yet, Engel's BPS was unique in that it offered a holistic, more integrated construct of human function and as such stood apart from prior depictions of physiological systems and their effects. Formally, as applied to medicine, Engel's BPS model claims that biological components of human function provide particular predispositions, tendencies, and substrates that establish mechanisms and baselines affected by social and psychological factors, both during development and throughout the lifespan. Psychological components reflect potentially positive and negative neurocognitive and emotional responses to both the biological and environmental condition, and social components constitute those effects incurred by factors of the external environment, including "culture," social group dynamics, socioeconomic status, and technology.

As so conceived, the BPS model is one of complementarities and permits conceptualization of both body-brain/mind (i.e., "bottom-up") effects and brain/mind-body (i.e., "top-down") effects (Giordano et al. 2008; Giordano 2009, 2010). In this way, the BPS paradigm has been increasingly used as a technical term for the proverbial mind–body connection, in contrast to other less integrative biomedical models (Sarno 1991). Within the BPS paradigm, persons can be considered beings in relationship, and, therefore, any meaningful approach to the human person – and her activities – must consider and address this relationality and its effects at physical, psychological, social, and spiritual levels (Fábrega 1997; Sulmasy 2002; Ben-Arye et al. 2006).

Cañadas and Giordano (2010) have been the first to propose the application of the biopsychosocial model to economics as a complement to the limited neoclassical framework. They have explained that integral human progress is something more complex than only material progress, and the BPS model applied to economics could help us explain human progress more accurately. Operationalizing this model to the realities of economic decision making would establish the premise that individual persons are complex, dynamic (biopsychological) systems that function as agent/actors possessing individual intelligence, nested and embedded within environmental (biosocial) systems.

Finally, given the fact that integral human development should include every dimension of the human being and requires a transcendental vision of the person that needs an encounter with God, I propose that the biopsychosocial model of economics should include a spiritual dimension as well. Benedict XVI reminds us in paragraph 30 of *Caritas in Veritate* that the complexity of this human reality "requires a commitment to foster the interaction of the different levels of human knowledge." So, it is precisely in view of this complexity that "various disciplines have to work together through an orderly interdisciplinary exchange." However, it is essential to recognize that "knowledge is never purely the work of the intellect; it must be seasoned with the salt of charity." At the end, we should pursue "charity in truth" which is complementary and not in opposition, because "the demands of love do not contradict those of reason."

9.5 Conclusions

The last financial crisis not only incurred an international disruption in economics but has also shown the weaknesses of economic theory as being overly dependent upon the neoclassical assumptions and philosophical interpretation of the human being as purely rational. Moreover, the financial crisis serves to highlight the importance of economics as a "social science" with ethical responsibilities. Because of this, I view the financial crisis as a "real crisis" – a time of change – and thus perceive an opportunity to reconsider the constructs and role(s) of economics. Philosophical inquiry is critical to the discourse of economics, and given that humans are the (practical and moral) actors – and subjects – of economics, then any such philosophical reflection and analysis must begin with a valid and accurate construct of the human being. Moreover, it has to take into account humans' spiritual dimension which is necessary to have a transcendent vision of the person and his encounter with God.

I suggest that the philosophical principles of neoclassical economics fail to account for the most contemporary epistemic, anthropological, and ultimately ethical views of the human being and, in this way, are insufficient to provide explanatory, predictive, and/or directorial guidance to economics. Furthermore, I argue that if positive change in economics is to occur, any such change must begin with a reinterpretation of facts, so as to avoid anachronism and the repetition of past mistakes.

In this chapter, I have tried to explicate how neoclassical economics offers a rather incomplete epistemology of human decision-making processes and activities. As well, I have suggested that the neoclassical assumption that human beings become "*homo economicus*" when they make decisions does not afford a realistically spiritual concept of the human, claiming that the absence of this core construct has both practical and moral consequences. Hence, the current interpretation of the decision-making process by human beings as "*homo economicus*" fails to account for a more complex reality of the human being making decisions in economics. Therefore, in order to understand the complex reality of human decision-making progress in economics, I propose using a multidisciplinary framework like the biopsychosocial model applied to economics suggested by Cañadas and Giordano (2010).

The university assumes an irreplaceable role in bringing together those scholars who are open to create a multidisciplinary dialogue among theology, philosophy, social, and natural sciences with economics. In sum, it is my argument that studying and teaching economics from an integrative, multidisciplinary perspective with a spiritual dimension may offer profoundly positive possibilities for the field, academe, and society at large.

Bibliography

Allais, Maurice. 1953. "Le Comportement de l'homme rationnel devant le risque: Critique des postulats et axiomes de l'école Américaine". *Econometrica* 21: 503–546.
Alvey, James. 1999. A Short History of Markets as a Moral Science. *Journal of Markets and Morality* 2(1): 55.
Anderson, Bruce, and Philip McShane. 2002. *Beyond establishment economics. No thank-you Mankiw*. Halifax: Axial Press.
Benedict XVI. 2009. Encyclical letter *Caritas in Veritate*. Vatican: *Libreric Editrice Vaticano*.
Ben-Arye, Eran, Gil Bar-Sela, Moshe Frenkel, Abraham Kuten, and Doron Hermoni. 2006. Is a biopsychosocial-spiritual approach relevant to cancer treatment? A study of patients and oncology staff members on issues of complementary medicine and spirituality. *Supportive Care in Cancer* 14(2): 147–152.
Bruni, Luigino, and Robert Sugden. 2007. "The Road not Taken: How Psychology was Removed from Economics, and How It might be Brought Back." *The Economic Journal* 117(2007): 146–173.
Busino, Giovanni. 1964. "Note bibliographique sur le Cours." In *Epistolario*, ed. V. Pareto, 1165–1172. Rome: Accademia Nazionale dei Lincei.
Cañadas, Alejandro, and James Giordano. 2010. "A Philosophically-Based Biopsychosocial Model of Economics: Evolutionary Perspectives of Human Resource Utilization and the Need for an Integrative, Multi-Disciplinary Approach to Economics. *The International Journal of Interdisciplinary Social Sciences* 5(8): 53.
Canterbery, E.Ray. 1995. *The Literate Economist*. New York: Harper Collins.
Crespo, Ricardo. 1998. Is Economics a Moral Science? *Journal of Markets and Morality* 1(2): 201.
Ellsberg, Daniel. 1961. "Risk, Ambiguity and the Savage Axioms." *Quarterly Journal of Economics* 75: 643–669.

Engel, George L. 1977. "The Need for a New Medical Model: A Challenge for Biomedicine." *Science* 196:129–136. ISSN 0036–8075 (print)/ISSN 1095–9203 (web) doi:10.1126/science.

Fábrega, Horacio. 1997. *Evolution of Sickness and Healing*. Berkeley: University of California Press.

Flanagan, Owen. 2002. *The Problem of the Soul: Two Visions of Mind and How to Reconcile them*. New York: Basic Books.

Giordano, James. 2009. "Neurotechnology, Evidence and Ethics: On Stewardship and the Good in Research and Practice." *Practical Pain Management* 10(2): 63–69.

Giordano, James. 2010. "Neuroethics – Coming of Age and Facing the future." In *Scientific and philosophical perspectives in neuroethics*, ed. James Giordano and Bert Gordijn. Cambridge: Cambridge University Press.

Giordano, James, Joan C. Engebretson, and Roland Benedikter. 2008. "Pain and Culture: Considerations for Meaning and Context." *Cambridge Quarterly Review Healthcare Ethics* 77: 45–59.

Glimcher, Paul. 2002. Decision, Decisions, Decisions: Choosing a Biological Science of Choice. *Neuron* 36: 233–332.

Glimcher, Paul. 2003. *Decisions, Uncertainty and the Brain: The Science of Neuroeconomics*. Cambridge, MA: MIT Press.

Gregg, Samuel. 2001. *Economic Thinking for the Theologically Minded*. Boston: University Press of America.

Griffiths, Brian. 1984. *The Creation of Wealth*. London: Hodder and Stoughton.

Hoover, Kevin. 2001. *The Methodology of Empirical Macroeconomics*. Cambridge: Cambridge University Press.

Kahneman, Daniel, and Amos Tversky. 1979. "Prospect Theory: An Analysis of Decision Under Risk". *Econometrica* 47: 263–291.

Menger, Carl. 1963. *Problems of Economics and Sociology*. Urbana: University of Illinois Press.

Robbins, Lionel. 1952. *An Essay on the Nature and Significance of Economic Science*. London: Macmillan.

Samuelson, Paul A. 1938. "A Note on the Pure Theory of Consumer's Behaviour." *Economica* 5(17): 61–71.

Sarno, John E. 1991. *Healing Back Pain: The Mind and Body Connection*. New York: Hachette Book Group.

Sulmasy, Daniel P. 2002. "A Biopsychosocial-spiritual Model for the Care of Patients at the End of Life." *The Gerontologist* 42(suppl 3): 24–33.

Hayek, Friedrich A von. 1962. "The Moral Element in Free Enterprise". In *The morality of capitalism*, ed. Mark W. Hendrickson, 49–57. New York: Irvington-on-Hudson.

Mises, Ludwig von. 1966. *Human Action: A Treatise on Economics*, 3rd ed. Chicago: Henry Regnery.

Neumann, John von, and Oskar Morgenstern. 1944. *Theory of Games and Economic Behavior*. Princeton: Princeton University Press.

Chapter 10
Ethical Dimensions of Finance

Lord Brian Griffiths of Fforestfach

The financial crisis which started in 2007 has been a devastating experience. It exposed incompetence, ethical failures and regulatory weaknesses on a scale which could not have been imagined. The banking systems of one country after another were bailed out by government intervention which involved taxpayer support on a massive scale. The public anger has been tangible, and the political response in terms of bank levies, bonus taxes and the threat of draconian reforms not surprising. Prompt action by governments and central banks helped avert another Great Depression, but the crisis has been followed by a Great Recession with a high cost in terms of reduced real output (world GDP fell at an annualized rate of 6%) and higher unemployment.

For many economists, bankers, civil servants and politicians, the financial crisis has been viewed in purely technical terms. It is similar to some huge systems failure, a massive brown out or some gigantic mechanical breakdown. One of the lasting contributions of Pope Benedict XVI's *Caritas in Veritate* is to show that the crisis is not simply an economic phenomenon but has much deeper roots and implications. It has ethical and cultural dimensions which are not only critical to understanding what happened but also in indicating the way forward (Benedict XVI 2009b, 21). It is this which I wish to explore in this chapter.

For me there are two key questions to be answered: What went wrong and what are the challenges we face going forward?

L.B. Griffiths of Fforestfach (✉)
Vice-chairman of Goldman Sachs International
Goldman Sachs International, London, UK
e-mail: brian.griffiths@gs.com

M. Schlag and J.A. Mercado (eds.), *Free Markets and the Culture
of Common Good*, Ethical Economy 41, DOI 10.1007/978-94-007-2990-2_10,
© Springer Science+Business Media B.V. 2012

10.1   What Went Wrong?

10.1.1   Different Perspectives

The question 'what went wrong?' can be answered from a number of perspectives. One is economic. For many economists, bankers, civil servants, central bankers and politicians, the financial crisis has been viewed in purely technical economic terms. The banks were undercapitalized. They priced risk incorrectly. They made bad lending decisions. They held far too little liquidity. They failed to value their assets at market prices. They had compensation structures which rewarded short term risk taking, not long term value creation. Some banks were too big or too important a part of the system to fail. They had to be rescued at the taxpayers' expense.

The fact that some banks were too big to fail meant they attracted a higher credit rating and lower funding costs. If these banks were to engage in risky activities, they knew there was a safety net to rescue them, which in turn was an incentive to take ever greater risk. The result has been a 'heads we win, tails you lose' culture in which gains are privatized and losses socialized.

Some banks were more prudent than others. But no bank can say that it is exempt from any wrong. If governments had not rescued the banks, directly or indirectly, such was the panic at the height of the crisis that I believe the entire banking system of Western countries would have collapsed. Banks would have had to close their doors to the public, and cash machines would have remained empty. Until normal service was resumed, we would have been thrown into a world of barter.

For this state of affairs, the banking system must accept its share of responsibility.

It is important, however, that the failures within the banking system are seen as part of a wider picture. The years leading up to the crisis were a period of unprecedented prosperity. In the United Kingdom, we had 16 years of quarter-by-quarter continuous economic growth, accompanied by low inflation and full employment.

The average price of houses rose from 4 ½ times average earnings to more than 9 times average earnings. The euphoria this created meant that irresponsible lending was matched by irresponsible borrowing. In the mid-1970s, the ratio of consumer debt (mortgages, hire purchase, credit cards) to household income was roughly 40–50%. By 2000, it had risen to more than 100%, and by the time of the crisis had reached 170%, higher than the United States and every European country.

The build-up to the crisis was not simply a British phenomenon. It was global and was driven by three exceptional factors.

First, there is China. In 1978, Deng Xiaoping dispensed with socialist economics and set China on a totally different path, embracing the market economy and opening it up to the rest of the world. As a result, for the past 30 years the Chinese economy has grown at around 10% each year. Second, in 1989, the fall of the Berlin Wall led to the end of the Cold War, the breakup of the Soviet Empire and political and economic freedom for East European countries. Third, in the early 1990s, India began to liberalize its economy from the interminable licenses, quotas and planning approvals which were the legacy of British Fabianism, the so-called 'license raj'.

If one of these changes alone had taken place, it would have been significant. For all three to occur over a similar period was similar to sighting a black swan. It resulted in more than two billion people from the former Soviet empire, India and China entering the world economy as producers and consumers, something with which we in the Western countries have still to come to terms.

It was the growing prosperity of this era which led Gordon Brown, the then UK Chancellor of the Exchequer, to say with confidence that the economics of boom and bust had finally been abolished. Among the US politicians, including Democrat and Republican Presidents, members of Congress and officials of public agencies (especially those connected with Fannie Mae and Freddie Mac) urged banks to increase lending to poorer families, the so-called subprime market, so that the American dream of home ownership could become a reality for low income families and ethnic minorities. One reason housing in the US was such an attractive investment is that house prices had not fallen once in 70 years.

As global prosperity grew in the years leading up to the crisis, so did global imbalances. The savings rate in China was around 40% while in the US it fell to zero. This was not because the Chinese are by nature more thrifty than Americans, but because China is a younger population without a developed welfare state and national health service, hence the need to save. Oil prices rose from $25 per barrel in 2000 to nearly $150 a barrel in 2008. These savings created a huge balance of payment surpluses in China and oil producing countries and correspondingly a huge balance of payment deficits in the US, the UK and continental Europe. These in turn resulted in enormous inflows of money, especially to the US. Because the world was awash with money, interest rates fell to their lowest level for decades, prompting a search by investors for higher returns. This in turn led banks to create a spate of leveraged buy-outs and the mis-pricing of risk, all of which resulted in an enormous bubble in asset prices. This financial structure became extremely complex, and because complexity is the enemy of transparency, even professional investors found it difficult to understand.

The reason I have gone into such detail on the buildup of debt and the global imbalances in the years leading up to the financial crisis is to show its complexity. The banking system played a crucial part in creating the crisis, and this is no attempt to exonerate it from what it did wrong. A fuller understanding of the crisis, however, would also assign major roles to other key participants: first, politicians (for encouraging bank lending to subprime customers in housing), then central bankers (who kept interest rates far too low for far too long), third the rating agencies (which assigned triple A ratings to a large number of securities which turned out to be backed by mortgages in default), then the regulators (who failed to recognize the growth in leverage in the banking system) and finally the general public (who were delighted to carry on borrowing). The economic causes of the crisis therefore are complex, global and involve all the key players in the financial system as well as the borrowing public.

Another perspective from which to view the crisis is the ethical. The success of the boom years created euphoria. Success, however, easily leads to excess. In my experience of the City in the post-war years, excess and questionable business practices have been a feature of all periods of boom. Just think of the fringe bank crisis of the mid-1970s involving London and County Securities, Cedar Holdings and Triumph Investment Trust which followed the boom of the Heath years or the Guinness affair, Maxwell, Blue Arrow, Polly Peck and County Bank which followed the boom of the mid-to-late 1980s. Success tends to produce hubris, lax accounting standards, cutting corners, dishonest practices and eventually fraud.

The financial crisis began with the failure of subprime borrowers in the US to repay their loans. Yet these loans were widely known as 'no doc loans' (no documentation), 'liar's loans' and 'ninja loans' (no income, no jobs, no assets). When they applied for loans, borrowers were either not asked or failed to disclose their current and potential income, employment, assets and debts. This was not a technical problem in banking or in the market for home mortgages: it was an ethical failure by the mortgage companies that made the original loans. These loans were subsequently repackaged by banks as mortgage bonds and more sophisticated derivative products. Those banks which knew the loans had no documentation must also share responsibility for the ethical failure.

The crisis also raises the question of the meaning of *caveat emptor*, namely 'let the buyer beware'. In a market made up of professionals, all of whom, if they so choose have access to relevant information, *caveat emptor* is a legitimate assumption to make regarding market practice. With hindsight, it is clear that the highly complex products which were introduced in the years leading up to the crisis were not fully understood even by professionals. What duty of care should we expect of those institutions selling such products?

Ethical failures have not been confined to subprime lending and the credit markets. The US Securities and Exchange Commission, which regulates financial markets, has embarked on enquiries into at least 20 Ponzi schemes as well as into a number of major US financial institutions. The Chairman and CEO of a major Irish bank were forced to resign following a failure to declare loans made to them by the bank itself, which they moved to other banks over the quarterly reporting periods. Subsequently, the Irish banking regulator and other senior figures in the financial sector resigned. In Iceland, following the collapse of the banking system, the state prosecutor launched an investigation into potential criminal activities including market manipulation, inside trading and breach of trust with shareholders. In Switzerland, one of its largest banks has reached an agreement with the US tax authorities to release the names of US citizens who opened accounts with them, because the US tax authorities suspect them of evading taxes.

A third perspective of the cause of the crisis is broader than both the economic and the ethical, namely the moral and spiritual values of our society, which is an issue raised by playrights, novelists, politicians, theologians and church leaders.

Sir David Hare is one of Britain's leading playwrights and his play *The Power of Yes* which was put on at the National Theatre last year is subtitled *A dramatist seeks to understand the financial crisis*. The central theme of the play is the way the financial crisis led to the death of an idea, namely that markets embody wisdom and decency. The underlying premise is that capitalism as we know it is an economic system driven by a culture of fear and greed. In one of the early scenes, a financial journalist blurts out 'It's greed, isn't it? It's pure greed', to which Harry, a city lawyer, responds 'People literally driven insane by greed'. Financial innovation, record profitability, mega bonuses, securitization are all presented as having created ever greater hubris. Later the comment is made that despite the crisis bankers still 'don't think they've done anything wrong. No one feels apologetic. These people genuinely believe they're the masters of the universe'.

Church leaders have been equally critical. The Bishop of Manchester said that 'what has brought the world to its current financial distress has a lot to do with sheer greed and selfishness' (McCulloch 2008, 2). He has spoken of 'the greedy over-reaching' of the banking and financial sectors and of 'their confidence that they were secure and untouchable, their (to the rest of us) bizarre reward structures that shouted their forgetfulness of ordinary people'. The Archbishop of York, in an address to the Church of England Synod, stated that we have all been led to the worship of Mammon (Sentamu 2010) while Pope Benedict XVI declared that greed lies at the root of all evil, and it is this which is the source of the current global economic crisis (Benedict XVI 2009a).

Even people familiar with finance have been just as critical. Paul Dembinski, a professor at the University at Fribourg and Director of the *Observatoire de la Finance* in Geneva, has argued that greed has become a passion, so strong that it threatens to undermine the very structures whose cornerstone it had once been, namely markets (Dembinski 2009, 63–64). Over the past 30 years, the process of 'financialization' has led to the triumph of transaction based banking over relationship banking (Dembinski 2009, 86). Alan Greenspan, the former Chairman of the Governors of the Federal Reserve System in the US, stated in a testimony before the Senate Banking Committee that *infectious greed* has become a threat to world finance (Greenspan 2002). The basis for these observations was not that individuals have become greedier in this generation than in the past but that the avenues through which greed can be expressed have grown so enormously.

One interesting aspect of all these criticisms is the use of the word greed. In the Christian tradition, greed is one of the seven deadly sins. St Paul writes of greed being idolatry (cfr. Eph. 5:5, Col. 3:5), which for Jews and Christians is the most heinous of all sins. In the Old Testament, idolatry is expressly forbidden in the first commandment, 'You shall have no other Gods before me' (Exod. 20:3). Many Jewish and Christian theologians view the first commandment as the foundation of the whole law.

In the teaching of Jesus in the Gospels, there are a number of instances in which money is singled out as a barrier to entering his Kingdom. In his conversation with a rich young man, Jesus urged the youth to sell everything and then went on to observe because of the person's response, 'How hard it is for the rich to enter the Kingdom of God. It is easier for a camel to go through the eye of a needle than for a rich man to enter the Kingdom of God' (Lk. 18:24, 25). In the Sermon on the Mount, Christ presented his disciples with a clear choice, 'You cannot serve God and Mammon'. In the story of the rich man and Lazarus, the rich man's wealth led him to be unconcerned with the needs of the poor (Lk. 16:19–31). In the parable of the rich farmer, whose success led him to expand his investments and adopt a philosophy of life 'take life easy, eat, drink and be merry', Jesus prefaces the story by saying 'Watch out! Be on your guard against all kinds of greed for a man's life does not count in the abundance of his possessions' (Lk. 12:15). In each of these instances, money, wealth and possessions are not condemned out of hand. They are examples of people for whom money was an idol. They trusted in money, not in God, and this affected the way they related to other people.

The early Church Fathers were equally condemnatory: 'greed is an illness of the soul', 'the worst type of decay' wrote John Chrysostom (1889) while Cyprian warned that luxurious wealth consists of 'merely gilded torments' (1889, 12). The charge that the financial crisis was fuelled by greed on the part of bankers therefore is one no Christian can dismiss lightly.

10.1.2   Was the Banking Crisis Caused by Greed?

I have been and continue to be reluctant to use the word greed in connection with the financial crisis, not because of undying loyalty to the banking industry nor because of self-interest, but because it is used so readily, without careful thought or definition. It requires little critical analysis to quote from some e-mail shot off by a trader in an investment bank to his girlfriend as an ego trip or some outrageous compensation accorded to a banker whose bank had to be rescued and then conclude that the system as a whole and those who work in it were simply driven by greed.

This raises the question of what is greed. I have never met anyone who admitted to being greedy. From a Biblical perspective, greed is when enough is never enough. It is about accumulation, but it is also about motivation. We cannot judge someone as greedy simply because they own a large house, a yacht or receive a large bonus. The evidence we have in the Gospels suggests that Nicodemus and Joseph of Arimathea while wealthy were not greedy.[1]

At the level of society as a whole, greed as idolatry finds expression in a consumerist culture and ideology that propels people to continue accumulating wealth beyond what they need. Consumerism is a culture dictating that enough is never enough. An important distinction must be made between this greed and the legitimate aspirations of individuals and family to improve their material well being and to care for those dependent on them.

10.1.3   Where Does that then Leave the Bankers?

Of course some bankers are greedy, possibly a greater percentage than in certain other professions. But in my experience the defining characteristic of bankers is not greed: it is the ambition to be the best at what they do, to be the top of the league table, to give the best advice to clients, to execute transactions flawlessly, to provide

---

[1] Cf. Matt. 27: 57–60; Jn. 3: 1–21; 7: 50–51; 19: 38–40.

first class research, to achieve the best returns on assets under management. When pursued to the exclusion of all else and without regard to God, this too is an idol. When it is not pursued in this way, it is a service for the common good and an important contribution to creating prosperity and reducing poverty.

10.1.4 In Response to the First Question, What Went Wrong?

– First, the economic causes of the crisis are complex and involve not just the banks but politicians, central banks, regulators rating agencies and the general public: a failure to recognize this will create the conditions for the next crisis.
– Second, the crisis exposed a lapse of ethical standards and an inadequate duty of care which was surprisingly widespread.
– Third, the growth of consumer debt and the bonus culture in a long period of economic prosperity suggests that the roots of the crisis extend deep into a post-modern and materialistic culture.

10.2 What Are the Future Challenges?

We now come to the second question posed at the beginning: what are the challenges we face going forward? Five can be suggested.

10.2.1 Regaining Trust in Banks

The first challenge is that the public must regain trust in banks. The banking system must once again acquire legitimacy. It must be perceived by the public to be sound. It must be so structured and banks so managed that the public have confidence that their deposits are secure, that they are not being shortchanged by conflicts of interest and that they are being provided with services they require at competitive prices.

An essential pre-condition to restore trust in banks is that the public must believe that banks make a contribution to the common good, that they exist not just for the benefit of their management, employees and shareholders but for the good of us all.

At one level, it is clear that the banking system plays a vital role in any modern economy and that it contributes to the good of all. It operates the payments system within countries and between countries. It provides cash machines, checking services, various kinds of deposits, overdrafts, foreign currency and money transfer facilities. It attracts deposits through providing a variety of savings accounts which it then lends on to individuals, companies and governments. Less obvious from the perspective of the general public is that it stands as an intermediary between saving and investment. In this process, it prices risk and transforms risk. Through commodities markets and the use of derivatives, it allows companies, governments and financial institutions to hedge against risk, such as airlines hedging the price of fuel or manufacturing companies the price of steel. All of the major banks also raise funds for corporations, municipalities and governments by issuing bonds and securities and making secondary markets in these instruments. The growth of derivative markets in recent decades has increased the efficiency of these markets. In recent decades, banks have raised funds for growth industries ranging from tech companies to alternative energy sources and green companies.

At the same time as it is clear that no modern economy could operate without a sophisticated banking system, it is also clear, following the financial crisis, that certain reforms must be made. One area of reform is an increase in the minimum capital and liquidity requirements which banks are required to hold. Banks have already taken steps to put their own house in order by de-risking their balance sheets, replacing short term funding by long term funding and changing the structure of remuneration. The Basel Committee has proposed through Basel III higher capital requirements for banks, and doubtless more reforms will follow in this area.

Next there is the problem of moral hazard: namely systematically important financial institutions which are either too big or too interconnected to fail. There is a widespread belief that the management of these institutions, those who invest in them and those who are counterparties to their trades believe that these institutions have effective government backing and so would not be allowed to fail. However, such a belief is an incentive for such institutions to take excessive risk. As a result of the financial crisis there has been increased consolidation among systematic institutions, which further increases the importance of the issue. Various reform options exist to deal with this problem: the separation of retail and investment banking, the establishment of 'narrow' banks, restrictions on banks' ability to undertake proprietary trading and engage in private equity and the separation of risky from less risky activities within banks, short of breaking them up.

A further set of challenges relates to competition. There is a strong prima facie case that competition in retail banking in the UK is restricted due to the market share of the largest four banks, especially in the area of current accounts. The key to reform is to encourage new entrants into the market as well as possibly requiring certain banks to divest themselves of some of their branch businesses.

The Chairman of the Financial Services Agency, the regulator until now of banks in the UK, has stated that many of the activities of investment banks, far from being for the common good, are 'socially useless activity' (Turner 2009).[2] The evidence for this extraordinary claim is excessive financial invention, the complexity of new products and the increased trading which occurred in the decade before the crisis in foreign exchange, oil futures and interest rate derivatives. Until that time, credit

---

[2]To read the interview in which Lord Adair Turner made this remark, see *Prospect*, issue 162, 27 August 2009; the full account can be found online at http://www.prospectmagazine.co.uk/2009/08/how-to-tame-global-finance/.

instruments, with the exception of bonds, did not have options, futures and derivative markets in a similar way to foreign exchange equities. The decade before the crisis, which saw the development of asset-backed securities, credit default swaps and interest rate swaps, should be thought of as a catching-up process enabling credit markets to have similar features to other financial markets. In any market, the more finessed a product becomes through endless small improvements, the less the marginal value of those improvements. To suggest, however, that even though there are willing buyers and sellers and these markets are active following the crisis, they are nevertheless 'socially useless,' is an extraordinary autocratic statement without any real evidence.

10.2.2 Values and Cultures

The second challenge follows from the fact that the financial crisis was not a purely technical issue. It was not just the breakdown of a financial machine which could be corrected simply through regulatory re-engineering. Structural reforms, although essential, will never be sufficient. The cultures of financial institutions which reflect their values are critically important. A culture is not the same as a set of business principles or corporate values. All major banks, including those which went bust and those which were rescued, had comprehensive statements of business principles: putting their clients first, integrity and honesty, excellence in service provision, respect for individuals, honouring diversity and corporate social responsibility. Business principles are the ideal to which a bank aspires.

A culture is what happens in practice, the way a bank does business, and one key test of a bank's values is what business it is prepared to turn down, even though it may be profitable and legal and within regulatory guidelines. What the financial crisis exposed was the difference between principles and practice.

The problem was that in the euphoria of the boom years these principles and values were not nearly robust enough to prevent bank management from sailing too close to the wind. Chuck Prince, who was then Chief Executive Officer of Citibank, summed up the dilemma well when he said 'As long as the music's playing you have to get up and dance'. In a highly competitive world there is a great deal of commercial logic behind his comments. In the build-up to the crisis, the bad decisions and poor judgments of bankers resulted from values and cultures within financial institutions in which the pursuit of profit and personal reward became too dominant. Acting within the law and maximizing profit and shareholder value are not enough. Banks must ask more searching questions. What do we exist to do? Is it just to make money? Or is there a larger purpose? Is being legal and profitable the only criteria for business decision? If business principles are to be the basis of commercial decisions there are times when the chief executive has to insist, 'now is not the time to get up and dance'.

Building up a culture is not easy. It takes time and needs to be attended to each day in countless small decisions. There are no easy levers to pull. Values and culture require moral energies which the market left to itself will not produce. They originate from outside the market place. These values must be clear and explicit. Leadership is crucial to the process. The leader is the embodiment of the values of an organization. It is he or she who sets the tone in a way no one else can. The values must be championed above all by the chief executive and supported by senior management. Everyone in the bank as well as clients and regulators need to see that management and employees 'walk the talk'. Breaches have to be dealt with immediately, the most serious requiring the most difficult choice, namely dismissal.

One intriguing question is whether one can have ethics without virtue. Many years ago I was asked to teach ethics in the business school of a very distinguished university. My response was that I believed ethics was about right and wrong and that teaching ethics was not therefore about intellectual games and puzzles in which one changed one of the initial conditions and analysed its implication. In response to my question, I was told that the university, although having a religious foundation many years ago, was now secular and felt it inappropriate to teach in this particular way. For banks, the issue is how to recruit, promote and nurture first class leadership which recognizes virtue as the essential pre-condition for implementing business principles.

10.2.3 Banking Compensation

The third, and perhaps the most contentious issue for the future, relates to bank bonuses or more generally bank compensation. The charges against the banks on this count are many and varied. One is that bonuses are in principle wrong and that people should be hired to do a job for a specified sum of money comparable to the way clergy, civil servants, school teachers, doctors and judges are paid. Another is that the sums involved are simply outrageous, which suggest that there is no relationship between effort and reward, let alone any moral justification. A third is that a compensation structure which involves a large cash element based on a single year's performance, with no deferred element or equity component, will encourage short term risk taking and discourage long term wealth creation, and so misalign the interests of bank executives and their shareholders. In addition large bonuses are being paid out by banks which have been bailed out by tax payers or have indirectly benefited from tax payer support. Finally, at a time when unemployment is rising bankers should show more restraint.

My starting point in tackling this issue is that a market economy, with all its challenges, remains the most effective way to create prosperity and jobs in this and other countries. One of the key markets in any economy is the labour market of which the labour market in financial services industry is but a part. The distinguishing characteristics of the financial services market are that it is global, attracts highly talented individuals, demands high energy and commitment and offers high compensation. It is also risky. Banking is a cyclical business, and in a market downturn, banks typically lay off many staff.

In the past, the structure of compensation in banks has been open to legitimate criticism. The cash element was too large and the equity and the deferred element too small. There were guaranteed multi-year bonuses. There was no claw-back if successful performance was short lived. The interests of employees and shareholders were not well aligned. In some cases, compensation was related to an individual's profit and loss in a given year with little regard for how the bank as a whole performed. It was dissatisfaction with issues such as these which led the UK government in 2009 to impose a special tax on bank bonuses.

Since the crisis, governments and regulators as well as banks themselves have taken steps to address these criticisms and to draw up a set of principles for determining bankers' compensations. The crisis exposed the weaknesses in the compensation structures of banks, and so it is perfectly legitimate for politicians and regulators to draw up principles which banks should follow in setting compensation. In the UK, the Financial Services Authority has published a set of principles with which they expect banks to comply and is diligent in enforcing them.

It would be a great mistake, however, if regulators or governments were to set levels, ranges or ceilings on specific compensation levels. Highly talented individuals are in demand internationally and are not restricted by geography. Moreover, if there were attempts to cap individual compensation, it would simply provide incentives for the best people to switch to other areas of the financial sector which are less closely regulated, such as hedge funds, or to set up their own less regulated businesses. Most importantly, regulators do not have sufficient knowledge of the day-to-day business of banks or of the individuals concerned to be able to make judgments about an individual's compensation.

If the past is any guide to the future and even if governments and regulators in all countries adopt and implement commonly agreed principles, such a structure will still allow the most talented traders, deal makers and senior executives to earn large rewards. Governments could levy higher taxes. But if they do, there is a risk they will reduce the size and profitability of their banking industry with a loss of jobs and tax revenues.

An appeal for voluntary restraint will certainly have some impact, but only in the short term. Over a longer period, restraint will prove difficult to sustain because of the nature of competitive markets. Those banks which exercise restraint longest will find staff moving to other institutions. Some may question whether the markets in which the banks operate are genuinely competitive, a perfectly legitimate issue best addressed by the 'competition authorities'. My conclusion therefore is that there are certain actions governments can take in relation to bankers' pay, but given the globally competitive markets in which banks operate, the resulting bonuses and differentials will still remain large.

10.2.3.1 Where Then Does that Leave a Christian Conscience?

Alongside the seven deadly sins of the medieval Church were the seven traditional virtues, one of which was generosity. I believe that generosity, even reckless generosity, certainly sacrificial generosity is one of the true hallmarks of a Christian lifestyle. In the words of Jesus 'From everyone who has been given much, much will be demanded' (Lk. 12:48). Wealth brings its responsibilities. St. Paul in his letter to Christians in Corinth urged them to excel in giving, basing his exhortation on the example of Jesus himself: 'for you know the grace of our Lord Jesus Christ, that though he was rich, yet for your sakes he became poor, so that you through his poverty might become rich' (2 Cor. 8:9). This is a demanding standard but one which must be addressed.

A Christian perspective will also emphasize that we are all children of God by reason of our common humanity. We are all different, and so while equality of income is not a Christian ideal, neither are persistent and large disparities of wealth. While governments may feel frustrated at what they can do in the short term to address the issue, long term substantial differences in income and wealth is something about which Christians can never feel relaxed. Alistair Darling, who as Chancellor of the Exchequer introduced the levy on bank bonuses in the UK in 2009, has admitted that it failed to change the pattern of pay in banking. He did, however, add something important, 'What I wanted to do was to send a message to them (i.e. bankers) that we all live in the same world together' (Robinson 2010).

10.2.4 The Role of Debt

A fourth issue raised by the crisis is the role of debt in our society. The financial crisis has exposed the astonishing scale of debt in our society: consumer debt, the indebtedness of governments and the excessive leverage of banks. In the two decades leading up to the crisis in the UK, the aggregate debt of the UK corporate, financial and household sectors as a percentage of GDP increased by more than sixfold.

Debt is an issue on which the church has been outspoken for centuries. For the first 1,500 years of its existence, the Christian Church opposed usury, that is, the making of loans for profit. The injunction of Jesus was to 'lend, expecting nothing in return'. Usury was condemned by the Church Fathers, Greek (Clement of Alexandria, Cyprian of Carthage, Basil the Great, Gregory of Nyssa and John Chrysostom) and Latin (Ambrose, Jerome and Augustine). It was also condemned by medieval theologians such as St.Thomas Aquinas and reformers such as Martin Luther. In the many Church councils organized in Europe during the medieval period, usury was expressively forbidden.[3]

In this the Church followed not only the injunction of Jesus (Lk. 6:34, 35) but also the practice of ancient Israel in which usury was forbidden within Jewish society. However usury was not forbidden between Jews and those outside the community. Charging interest was not a sin comparable to theft, murder or adultery. It was outlawed, because it was comparatively easy for lenders to exploit privileged or

---

[3]To read more, see Langholm (1992).

even monopoly positions which in turn would lead to a permanent underclass and so damage the fabric of society. This confirmed the wisdom of Proverbs, based on careful observation of what happened in the world namely that 'the borrower is servant to the lender' (Prov. 22:7).

Credit markets are a valuable part of any modern economy, because they allow people to borrow and lend. Even if it were practical, which it is patently not, there is no case for returning to the precepts of medieval theology. There is, however, the question of proportion. In periods of prosperity, it is easy for borrowing to get out of hand – household mortgages worth 125% the value of a property, excessive leverage by banks, with ratios of lending to capital of 50:1 and government debt as a percentage of GDP greater than most investors would judge prudent.

This raises the question of whether there is a case for applying caps or ceilings in these markets. Should individuals be allowed to borrow up to a certain percentage, say only 80%, of the value of a property? Or should the leverage of banks should be no greater than, say, twelve times capital, or should the ratio of government debt to GDP be no greater than 60%, which was the conventional wisdom and one of the fiscal rules in the UK and continental Europe? Any caps or ceilings will of necessity be arbitrary. In a relatively free and open economy, new instruments, new markets and new institutions will be created to circumvent such caps and so the subject will need to be revisited every so often. Because of the excessive growth of debt in our society, however, and its disastrous consequences, I believe that the reintroduction of ceilings or rules is desirable.

10.2.5   The Challenge of Culture

The challenges which have been examined have ranged from immediate practical issues such as greater transparency, bonuses and debt to issues of culture and values and matters of public policy. There is one final issue which springs from the heart of the Christian faith. What is the end of the world of money? What is the goal that the city is striving to reach? What is the object of our ambition? After all the assets have been managed, the advice given and the transactions completed, what then? Will our response be 'vanity of vanities, all is vanity' (Ecclesiastes 1:2) or will we feel we have contributed to the common good 'to the building' of a city that has lasting foundations?

St. Augustine lived through a far greater crisis than we have – the collapse of the Roman Empire and the sacking of Rome itself by the barbarian hordes from the north. The pagans argued that the cause of this was the spread of Christianity and the neglect of their own gods. In his masterpiece *The City of God*, Augustine refuted this by arguing that the course of human history could be explained by the rivalry between two cities, the earthly city and the *City of God*, the *civitas terrena* and the *civitas Dei*.

> Two cities have been formed by two loves: the earthly city by the love of self, even to the contempt of God; the heavenly city by the love of God, even to the contempt of self (Augustine 1887, Bk XIV.Ch.28).

For Augustine, the earthly city found its apotheosis in Babylon and Rome and the heavenly city in the Church, which, despite its shortcomings, was still the body of Christ. The question this raises is whether the activities of the banks and financial markets, when inspired not just by profitability but by the common good, shape the earthly city of which we are a part so that it anticipates and prefigures the eternal and heavenly city, the *City of God*. That I believe is the ultimate challenge which we in the financial sector face.

Bibliography

Augustine. 1887. City of God. In *Nicene and Post-Nicene Fathers, First Series*, vol. 2 (trans: Marcus Dods), ed. Philip Schaff. Buffalo: Christian Literature Publishing Co.

Benedict XVI. 2009a. General audience. http://www.vatican.va/holy_father/benedict_xvi/audiences/2009/documents/hf_ben-xvi_aud_2009 0422_en.html. Accessed 22 Apr 2009.

Benedict XVI. 2009b. Encyclical *Caritas in Veritate*. Vatican: Libreria Editrice Vaticana.

Chrysostom, John. 1889. "Homily 18 on Ephesians". In *Nicene and Post-Nicene Fathers, First Series*, vol. 13 (trans: G. Alexander), ed. P. Schaff. Buffalo: Christian Literature Publishing Co.

Cyprian of Carthage. 1889. "Epistle I to Donatus". In *Ante-Nicene Fathers*, vol. 5 (trans: E. Wallis), ed. A. Roberts, J. Donalson, and A.C. Coxe. Buffalo: Christian Literature Publishing Co.

Dembinski, Paul H. 2009. *Finance: Servant or Deceiver? Financialization at the Crossroad*. Hampshire: Palgrave Macmillan.

Greenspan, Alan. 2002. *Testimony of Alan Greenspan, Federal Reserve Board's Semi-Annual Monetary Policy Report to the Congress before the Committee on Banking, Housing, and Urban Affairs, U.S. Senate*. Washington, D.C.

Langholm, Odd. 1992. *Economics in the Medieval Schools. Wealth, Exchange, Value, Money & Usury according to the Paris Theological Tradition, 1200–1350*. Leiden/New York/Köln: E.J.Brill.

McCulloch, Nigel. 2008. "Bishop Nigel's thought for the month: Lessons from the crunch". *Crux* 38(11): 2.

Robinson, Gwen. 2010. "Bonus supertax failed, says Darling". *The Financial Times*, September 2, 2010.

Sentamu, John. 2010. The way to come closer to God is to be generous and honest towards everyone, Presidential Address to the General Synod. http://www.archbishopofcanterbury.org/2932. Accessed 10 July 2010.

Turner, Adair. 2009. "How to tame global finance". *Prospect*, August 27, 2009.

Chapter 11
Financial Markets: A Tool for Transferring and Managing Risk?

Michel Baroni

11.1 Introduction

During the three last decades, financial markets have developed on a substantial scale in many countries, especially in the United States, Europe and Asia. If we include OTC markets of traded products, we can assert that financial markets are present worldwide, even in the less developed world where raw materials markets are often the most important ones. This means that more and more wealth is exchanged between an ever growing number of participants. If primary markets like stock markets permit wealth creation, derivatives markets that first appeared in the 1980s play a different role, which consists primarily in risk transfer. Risk management may be considered as one of the most important topics for corporate management today, not only for the financial sector but also for the industrial sector as a whole. The growth of all kinds of risks is probably the phenomenon that best characterizes the last few years of economic history. These risks, if they are not managed, can have a significant impact on our economic decisions and lead to large losses, as we have seen with numerous companies. From this perspective, financial markets that allow the buying and selling of risk play a truly constructive role. Specific risks, whether individual or corporate, can usually be sold to insurance companies, but more general risks are often difficult to sell, partly because they are difficult to define and accurately quantify.

In this chapter, we analyze how these risks, when they are identified, can be transferred using financial markets. However, we also highlight that these very risk transfers may also create more systemic risks, as shown by the recent financial crisis.

M. Baroni (✉)
ESSEC Business School, Paris, France
e-mail: baroni@essec.edu

M. Schlag and J.A. Mercado (eds.), *Free Markets and the Culture of Common Good*, Ethical Economy 41, DOI 10.1007/978-94-007-2990-2_11, © Springer Science+Business Media B.V. 2012

Following R. Shiller (2003, 19–66), we firstly analyze different kinds of risk, determine how they are translated into economic risk, and assess to what extent they can be managed. We then propose through the example of the real estate market a model for successfully transferring this type of risk. And finally, we analyze the impact of these transfers on the markets by considering the speculation they may encourage and the new systemic risks they may engender.

11.2   Risks Are Growing but Often Remain Hidden and Are Not Easy to Hedge

11.2.1   Individuals Face Unidentifiable Risks

R. Shiller (2003, 32–45) highlights the fact that when we talk of risk and finance, the critical economic risks that we as individuals face remain substantially hidden. We are aware of a very small part of the risks we are facing. This author is of the view that we do not have a good understanding of the nature and breadth of these risks. It is commonly admitted in economic theory that, for an individual, his labor's income corresponds more or less to his marginal product, that is, the contribution of his labor to the output of his employer after taking into account the contributions of all other workers. It means that our income is dependent on the abilities of others and is sensitive to the reactions of others to changing environments. When joining a company and becoming employees, we may have the impression that these risks have been eliminated. But this is clearly an illusion, because the income of the company is subject to similar factors and depends on the reactions of competitors and of other companies in the production chain to market changes. If this complexity has always existed, the sources of risk are now much more numerous because of the increased number of participants.

Karl Marx's theory of communism proposed that the means of production influencing the income of individuals should be under common ownership in order to avoid the risk of being at the mercy of other people who would have the capacity to modify the factors determining the marginal product of the workers. However, this attempt to mutualize individual risks came up against practical issues and has been abandoned by most of the countries inspired by this economic theory, including some of those countries which remain Communist in name, for example, China and Vietnam. In fact, for most of the world today, an individual's labor is sold in free markets.

R. Shiller (2003, 34–36) notices that consequently, the problem of individual income risk is still with us, and yet it is not really debated in public forums. Neither business leaders nor politicians talk about major economic risks. They prefer predicting a shining future for everyone. Small crises appear frequently in one sector or another. In these cases, redistribution is often the easiest way for politicians to find quick solutions. Taking money from one group to give it to another is an income transfer and a zero-sum game from the perspective of the government budget but not necessarily in terms of risk management. Imagining a social policy in terms of risk management is undoubtedly more difficult than distributing public manna when a sudden need appears. Government policy needs to identify the economic risks and try to fully understand them. Some of them can be accurately measured and priced in the insurance market. Others are too difficult to measure or belong to the field of solidarity; for such risks other solutions have to be found.

Usually, individuals face risks they consider impossible to hedge. In fact, they receive very little help in identifying these risks and in measuring them. For instance, we speak very little of the major risk of becoming unemployable. The causes that can lead to a situation of unemployment seem too abstract, complex, or dependent upon too many factors. Very often, due to lack of sufficient information, we prefer to ignore risk and adopt a conservative behavior. This attitude can lead to poor decisions and loss of opportunities.

11.2.2 New Technology Creates Risk

There is no doubt new technology has changed our way of life, principally in the most developed countries. At the global level, productivity has strongly increased over the past 40 years. The debate is still open among the economists as to the relationship between productivity and technology. For instance, Kneller and Stevens (2003), considering 80 countries over 30 years, show that differences in productivity across various countries exist, because countries vary in the degree of efficiency with which they are able to use available technology.

Moreover, if we consider all the new jobs created by new technology, it is obvious that new wealth has been created. However, we cannot neglect the other side of the coin. A lot of jobs have also been destroyed by the invasion of technology into the productive and service industries. If we take GDP growth as an indicator of wealth creation, the correlation between technology and wealth can also be established.

New technology has caused many other economic risks which are often collateral or systemic as well as unexpected by the designing engineers. Let us think, for example, of the social networks born from Web 2.0 technologies and their impact on the communication policy of governments. Rumors now play a huge role in public opinion. As a piece of information is spread all over the planet, almost immediately through Internet technology at no cost, a small lack of transparency on the part of a politician or a company may destroy almost instantaneously a reputation built up with great effort over several years. To quote R. Shiller (2003, 57), new technology is never an unambiguously good thing. Unanticipated consequences have to be considered carefully, in particular by risk managers.

11.2.3 Most Risks Are Not Easily Diversifiable

Individuals usually face risks they cannot diversify. Of course, some kinds of diversification exist, but in some cases, capturing all the systematic risk is unavoidable. For example, employees of a company specialized in producing toy cars know they are very dependent on fashion. If another company's toy car becomes more fashionable, the company's market may disappear very quickly, and the company may even collapse. Employees who have measured this risk know they have to adapt their skills to be able to work for another company in the same sector or even in another industry. In this case, we would say that training may be the way to manage unemployment risk. But we also know there are various factors involved in finding new employment, such as the inflexibility of the labor market, the employee's skills and age, etc.

If we now take the example of a homeowner, he has to take responsibility for changes in the price of his house or apartment. Most owners occupy their homes, and the capital they have invested in it is a substantial part of their assets. Diversifying their assets is not possible in practice. In this very common case, owners are sensitive to the specific risk of their asset but also to the systematic risk of the real estate market which they cannot hedge.

These two examples show that some very common risks cannot be hedged by insurance. It is difficult to imagine insurance policies which hedge the risk of a decrease in real estate prices in a specific area due to a population change, even if it would be possible to write such insurance policies from a technical point of view. R. Shiller (2003, 65–66) suggests that managing such risks has to be done with large national aggregates (national incomes or GDP, for instance). But, to be more thorough, we think that the transfer of every systematic risk that can impact significantly the behavior of individuals should be studied by risk analysts in various institutions. This ambitious project aims at the extension of financial markets such that they can efficiently provide liquidity for various levels of risks for which liquid markets do not exist at present. As markets for these types of risk need to deal with a large amount of collected data, a high level of information technology is obviously required. These markets, where we can buy and sell different types of risks faced by individuals, might be a great help to individuals but also to investors who can use these products to manage the risks they need to manage.

11.3 Managing Risks by Transfers

11.3.1 Derivatives Markets for Hedging Risk

As seen in the previous section, having the possibility to sell an entire risk or a part thereof is undoubtedly a way to change the behavior of individuals and institutions facing risk. The role of insuring certain types of risks cannot be always played by insurance companies for various reasons. Either the risk is too specific and the premium is too difficult to compute, or it is too systematic and insurance companies would need to hedge it, which may not be possible. At this point, financial markets may be able to play a useful role. Even if derivatives markets are mainly used by professionals, we can easily imagine that they could help individuals to hedge their risks, directly or indirectly. Equity options offer a possible hedge against movements in stock prices. Futures and forwards are used to help hedge the risks linked to interest or exchange rates. Credit derivatives price default risk and are extensively used to hedge against credit risk. All these products are bought or sold in organized markets or as OTC products, very often through brokers or financial institutions. Other financial techniques like securitization allow companies to manage risk by selling risk into a liquid market and allow institutions to construct portfolios which are designed to be an approximation of the systematic risk they face.

All these markets are zero-sum markets and allow many risk transfers. Their main role consists of hedging risk, and the products traded in these markets are essentially used by professionals. Even if they were originally created for hedging, they can also be used to take speculative positions depending on future expectations. We will deal with this dual use of these products in the next section.

11.3.2   An Example of Risk Management in Real Estate

To illustrate how risk management can be implemented with indices and derivatives markets, we take the example of the risk linked to the valuation of real estate assets. Most individuals in developed countries are exposed to real estate risk. To some extent, it can be considered as one of the main financial risks for the middle class, because of the significant part of their assets represented by real estate.

As suggested by R. Shiller (2003, 118–120), the key step in being able to manage real estate risk consists of collecting information on prices and constructing an index. Many methodologies for constructing real estate indices are available. Clearly, methodologies representing the whole market based on transaction prices inspire more confidence than those based on expert valuations. But we have to take into account two specific characteristics of the real estate market: properties are not traded regularly, and one property is different from another. These two characteristics exclude the choice of a standard methodology such as that used for stock markets where a series of quotes is the only source of the index. In this context, a repeat-sales method (two transaction prices for each property are required to construct the index) seems the most appropriate.

Baroni et al. (2007) proposed a repeat-sales index methodology and applied it to a Paris dataset. The results show that this index is very similar to the Case & Shiller is the common name of the index. However, it differs from the latter by the methodology, which uses preselected economic and financial variables. Real estate price returns are computed from the repeat-sales transactions and are associated with their corresponding returns for the economic and financial variables. Hence, for each observation composed of two transactions of the same asset, a return vector is constructed. Then, each real estate return is explained by the other returns, using a linear regression. Finally, the index is constructed from the time factor series, which are determined by a principal component analysis as a linear combination of variables.

The main advantage of this index is that it uses factors that are systematic, not linked to specific kinds of properties. For instance, for the Paris real estate market, trends and volatility of all segments (residential, office, retail, etc.) are mainly driven by three explanatory variables: the evolution of the residential rent index, the unemployment rate, and short-term interest rates. If this index is recognized by financial institutions and professionals as representative of the systematic risk of real estate, it can be used to construct derivative products.

For example, insurance companies could sell contracts to their customers which hedge against a decrease in house or apartment values due to a general price decrease in a particular city. The systematic risk would be transferred to the insurance company which in turn could hedge it by using a futures contract on this index. Similarly, the index could be used by an investor who would like to increase or decrease his risk exposure to real estate. By swapping a part of his portfolio risk with real estate returns provided by the index, he can buy or sell real estate returns without holding real estate assets. This kind of swap already exists, in particular for the IPD index, and a substantial OTC market has been created for this financial product. Index options can also be created to provide any individual or company with a way to hedge systematic risk due to a variation in the level of real estate prices.

These three examples show to what extent collecting information, creating indices and financial products can help to manage real estate systematic risk, one of the major risks to which almost all of the population is exposed, directly or indirectly (e.g., through pension funds).

11.3.3   Financial Innovations Make More Risk Transfers Possible

If we consider the variety of new financial products available today, we can find numerous examples, similar to real estate hedging, where derivatives markets fulfill the major function of risk transfer. However, risk management today generally is a matter for professionals only and covers only commodities and financial products. The role of futures markets is predominant. Even if these markets were created in the seventeenth century, their use for financial assets began only around 30 years ago. At present, all developed countries have organized futures markets. Their basic function consists of reducing or eliminating a risk by hedging, that is, creating a risk that offsets the main risk. To work well, these markets need products which are very precisely defined (maturity, delivery date, delivery terms), but they also need a reasonably large trading volume, with regular bid and ask quotations. Consequently, contracts have to be well designed at their creation to answer real needs. However, the strength of the futures markets is that they can be easily standardized; participants can hedge risks even if they do not hold the underlying asset, or they can sell a product they do not wish to deliver. In fact, very few futures contracts lead to physical delivery. So the number of participants may be much larger for futures markets than for spot markets, and consequently, prices may be keener due to traded volume. In practice, the design of the product is a key issue for futures contracts.

As seen in the previous paragraph, real estate markets are a good example of where futures contracts on an index could be an efficient way to transfer systematic risk. Furthermore, there are a lot of other fields where the same mechanism could be used. For example, let us consider the special case of the labor market where economic sectors and professions represent many different systematic risks. A market in labor market derivatives will depend on the capacity to collect information, then to construct indices, and finally to organize a futures market where bid and ask quotations are sufficient to ensure liquidity. R. Shiller (1998, 52–77; 2003, 121–138) has also suggested the creation of macromarkets to transfer risk of GDP growth which impacts the economic life of all individuals.

Obviously, futures are not the only solution financial markets can provide to transfer risk. Options markets can do the same, and index options, in particular, can also help to hedge systematic risk. However, options pricing is very sensitive to volatility. Consequently, using index options requires the volatility of the underlying index to be robustly estimated. To some extent, possible sellers or buyers of these options must be convinced of the accuracy of the volatility estimates to be willing to participate in these markets. Choosing the right index methodologies is the key to success for these products.

Collateralization and securitization also have to be mentioned as tools for transferring financial risk. These techniques generally aim to reduce the owner's risk by selling it to the market. They have been widely used in recent years, especially from 2004, and the risk has been sold to investors through structured products. For example, the volume of CDOs (Collateralized Debt Obligations[1]) increased fivefold between 2004 and 2006, reaching a valuation of more than 500 billion dollars in 2006, 50% of which was subprime debt. In this case, it is obvious that risk transfer was huge. Yet, this massive resort to financial markets has not canceled the systematic risk the initial lenders have sold to the markets. The investors who bought these securities did not seek to hedge their own risk but to capture the high returns apparently offered. Their behavior corresponds to pure speculation, and with hindsight, it is clear that most investors underestimated the risk they assumed.

So, we can conclude that derivatives markets and products, while making risk transfers possible, are a double-edged sword. They can be efficient risk management tools, aiming to provide more security, but at the same time, they can foster the

---

[1]Collateralized debt obligations (CDOs) are a type of structured asset-backed security (ABS) whose value and payments are derived from a portfolio of fixed-income underlying assets. CDOs securities are split into different risk classes, or tranches, whereby "senior" tranches are considered the safest securities. Interest and principal payments are made in order of seniority, so that junior tranches offer higher coupon payments (and interest rates) or lower prices to compensate for additional default risk.

development of products which, even if they contribute to market liquidity, also foster speculation. The recent financial crisis has revealed that the development of such products can create a systemic risk when their volumes become very large and when the purchasers of such products do not fully understand the risk they are assuming.

11.4   Risk Transfers and Unwanted Effects

11.4.1   Futures Markets and Speculation

Critics of futures markets are numerous when considering speculation. The debate is not new, because futures markets cannot work without speculation, in the sense that the market equilibrium cannot usually be reached only by hedging operations. Speculators are those who do not use derivatives to hedge their physical positions but who wish to maximize their potential gain through the expected variation of prices. Since the nineteenth century, governments and politicians have denounced speculation, because it supposedly distorts market prices. This criticism has been particularly pronounced for commodities. For example, oil prices increased strongly over the period 2006–2008, and many voices were raised in criticism of the impact of speculation on prices. C. Pirrong (2010) analyzed this issue by comparing the arguments generally used in the criticisms with the figures provided by the Commitment of Traders reports and those produced by the Commodity Futures Trading Commission (CFTC) in the United States. In theory, there is no reason for speculation to distort prices. Most futures speculators offset their positions before maturity, so it is difficult to imagine how their actions could affect prices. In practice, the main argument in favor of a significant impact on prices due to speculation is very simple: when the speculators expected an increase in oil prices in 2006, they bought many more futures contracts than they sold, thereby driving up prices, and so, speculation caused prices to rise. In fact, considering the net positions of noncommercial participants (suspected to be speculators and not hedgers) as a proxy to measure the influence of speculation, C. Pirrong (2010), estimates that only 2.56% of the oil price increase was due to speculation. Furthermore, extending his analysis to other assets, he shows that dramatic increases in demand, combined with a relatively stable supply, better explain the price increase than speculative positions. He concludes that the direct evidence of a relationship between speculative activities and price movements is weak. According to Pirrong (2010), introducing position limits lacks an empirical basis. Such limits on speculation will not lead to more efficient pricing in commodity markets but may have an opposite effect and constrain the derivatives markets' most important functions: risk transfer and price discovery. Moreover, constraining speculation will reduce market liquidity, resulting in more volatile markets, thereby pushing up the price of risk.

Thus, speculation which is intrinsically linked to derivatives markets may also be considered as a dampener of risk prices; proposed regulations should take into account this economic function.

11.4.2 Derivatives Markets and Systemic Risk

During the recent financial crisis, derivatives markets were accused of having played a key role in triggering the crisis. As risk transfer markets, they fostered both the diffusion of risks and their concentration. Diffusion means that risks were stretched over all developed countries through financial markets, and concentration means that some financial institutions (investment banks, monoline insurers, etc.) took long positions on specific derivatives products (CDOs, ABS,[2] MBS,[3] CDS,[4] etc.). In an interesting analysis of the beginning of the banking crisis that he calls the "Panic of 2007," G. Gorton (2009) describes how additional risk has been created by a nexus of off-balance sheet vehicles, derivatives, securitization, and, in addition, the growth of the repo (repurchase agreement) market. When US housing prices did not rise as expected, this chain of securitized and derivatives products could not be penetrated by most investors and counterparties to determine the location and size of the risks they held. When financial intermediaries realized they lacked information, they refused to deal with one another, and the liquidity crisis in this market began. An important part of the information story is the introduction in 2006 of the ABX[5] indices, OTC synthetic indices of subprime risks, which plummeted in 2007 and revealed the risk of subprime bonds. The crisis was characterized by a loss of information due to the complexity of the chain of products. That means it became impossible for investors in CDOs or other complex instruments to penetrate the chain backward and value it on the basis of the underlying assets. Even if ABX indices fulfilled their role, they concentrated the information on subprime bonds, without any way to work backward. Moreover, investors purchased tranches of CDO, SIV[6]

---

[2] An asset-backed security (ABS) is a security whose value and income payments are derived from and collateralized (or "backed") by a specified pool of underlying assets.

[3] A mortgage-backed security (MBS) is an asset-backed security or debt obligation that represents a claim on the cash flows from mortgage loans through a process known as securitization.

[4] A credit default swap (CDS) is a swap contract in which the protection buyer of the CDS makes a series of payments (often referred to as the CDS "fee" or "spread") to the protection seller and, in exchange, receives a payoff if a credit instrument (typically a bond or loan) experiences a credit event.

[5] The ABX is a credit derivative swap contract that pools lists of exposures to mortgage-backed securities.

[6] A structured investment vehicle (SIV) is an operating finance company established to earn a spread between its assets and liabilities like a traditional bank. A lot of SIVs were created before the 2008 crisis.

liabilities, etc., without knowing exactly what was known by the structurers. Hence, the information in this market was asymmetric.

Even if our purpose is not to describe in detail the entire chain from the initial borrower to the final product sold to an international investor (for more detail, see Gorton 2009), it appears obvious that the separation between the originator, the distributor, and the residual claimants of the loans played a significant role in the subprime crisis. With this mechanism, incentives to responsible behavior disappeared, and it contributed to the lack of information on the risk. In parallel, the repo market dried up, creating a serious crisis of liquidity, because banks refused to take in repo RMBS[7] and, in general, all the ABS. The systematic risk of subprime mortgages was transformed into a systemic risk where the counterparties lost confidence in each other and suspected one another of possibly defaulting.

To conclude on this topic, we can assert that the triggering of the financial crisis was due in greater measure to the lack of information and irresponsibility in the originator-to-investor process than to the derivatives markets themselves. The investors could not short their positions using the ABX contracts, because the underlying assets were very difficult to price. To some extent, we could say the subprime panic had its origin in a banking panic, which was essentially due to a lack of relevant information and asymmetric information.

11.4.3 Regulation, Volatility, and Financial Innovation

One effect of the crisis is that most people and governments are convinced more regulation is necessary to prevent future financial disasters. The legitimacy of such an approach is not questioned, considering the seriousness of the damage incurred. But, as we can deduce from the previous paragraph, new regulations will have to focus on the systemic risk, which is primarily dependent upon the availability and the quality of information regarding derivatives products and markets. The aim of new rules must not discourage financial innovation if it is agreed that such products and markets allow risk transfer. As developed in the first section, risk growth means individuals and companies will have more and more risk to exchange, but they cannot rely only on the insurers, especially when the risk to hedge is systematic.

Obviously, this issue is not trivial. If we consider, for example, the impact of closeout,[8] netting,[9] and collateral[10] on systemic risk in the derivatives market,

---

[7]Residential mortgage-backed securities (RMBS) are a type of bond commonly issued in American security markets. They are a type of mortgage-backed security which is backed by mortgages on residential rather than commercial real estate.

[8]The closeout is the right of a counterparty to unilaterally terminate contracts under certain specified conditions.

[9]Netting is the right to offset amounts due at termination of individual contracts between the same counterparties when determining the final obligation. Netting legislation covering derivatives exists in most countries with major financial markets.

[10]Collateral used in derivatives markets remains under the control of the counterparty and may be liquidated immediately upon a covered event of default.

the result is mixed. Bliss and Kaufmann (2006) demonstrate that even if these techniques have been adopted to reduce the systemic risk of the derivatives markets, it is not entirely clear that they have reached their objective. According to these authors, they can increase liquidity and depth of the market and facilitate the end users' ability to manage market risks. But netting and collateral may both increase and decrease systemic risk. They increase it by permitting the concentration of dealers but decrease it by providing means of managing counterparty risks. Closeout, however, can be a source of systemic risk by making it more difficult to manage the distress or insolvency of a major dealer. In this perspective, we can consider that the present situation for some OTC derivatives markets is riskier because of the reduced number of dealers after the crisis. Through this example, we can conclude regulatory protection rules may be a two-edged sword to use with caution.

A last issue often evoked when considering the role of derivatives markets is that they may tend to increase the preexisting volatility of a financial market. Gulen and Mayhew (2000), after having surveyed the abundant literature on this topic, examined the impact of the introduction of stock index futures on stock markets' volatility in 25 countries. They found that in most countries, volatility tends to be lower in periods when open interest in stock index futures is high. They also demonstrated that markets in most countries are significantly more integrated with global markets after the introduction of stock index futures. Even if heterogeneity characterizes the analyzed markets, these results show that there is no evidence that derivatives markets create volatility in underlying cash markets; in fact, they may even reduce it. According to Gulen and Mayhew (2000), new derivatives markets clearly increase the liquidity and quality of information in existing financial markets. In the thought of R. Shiller (2010), it is this liquidity and quality of information that ultimately propels economic growth.

11.5 Conclusion

We have considered how the present life of individuals has become riskier and to what extent these new risks can be managed. Our conclusion is that we are often ill-equipped to manage the fundamental risks that we defined with financial words as "systematic risks". Being nondiversifiable, these risks, which derive from the market for our professional work, the real estate market, or the GDP of the country where we are living, are difficult to measure and to hedge. However, solutions using financial markets were then suggested, and we chose the example of real estate to show that risk measurement is possible through indices under certain conditions and that futures contracts can be constructed to hedge this risk. For risks linked to the GDP growth, R. Shiller has suggested the creation of macromarkets. In the same vein, Barnett et al. proposed index-based risk transfer products to fight against chronic poverties. All these suggestions, more or less advanced in their application, have in common the conviction that financial markets may be used to improve the life of individuals and better serve society.

Finally, we have analyzed the possible unwanted effects of risk transfers on the financial system. The role of speculation on the derivatives markets must also be considered in terms of liquidity and price discovery, and from this perspective, may have a positive effect. Naturally, this position does not take into account the risk speculators run with their own capital, and this risk has to be considered when analyzing all stakeholders. It is essentially in this context that regulation has to be implemented. We then concluded that systemic risk induced by derivatives markets is not necessarily caused by the development of derivative products. Information plays a central role in helping investors to understand the risks they assume in order to avoid systematic risk, which is supposed to be managed by derivatives markets, being transformed into systemic risk. We suggest that new rules of regulation focus on collecting the appropriate information in order to make it available for all the market participants. The quality of the necessary information is probably the major challenge to make risk transfers efficient through financial markets and create a source of growth for the maximum benefit of society.[11] Knowing more about risk, with more means to measure it through the creation of indices and to transfer it using derivative products, can make a meaningful contribution to innovation.

Acknowledgment The author wants to thank Paul Nagy for his comments, suggestions, and reviews of this chapter.

Bibliography

Bailey, M.J., R.F. Muth, and H.O. Nourse. 1963. A regression method for real estate price index construction. *Journal of the American Statistical Association* 58(304): 933–942.

Barnett, B.J., C.B. Barett, and J.R. Skees. 2008. Poverty traps and index-based risk transfer products. *World Development* 36(10): 1766–1785.

Baroni, M., F. Barthélémy, and M. Mokrane. 2007. A PCA factor repeat sales index for apartment prices in Paris. *Journal of Real Estate Research* 29(2): 137–158.

Baroni, M., F. Barthélémy, and M. Mokrane. 2008. Is it possible to construct derivatives for the Paris residential market? *Journal of Real Estate Finance and Economics* 37(3): 233–264.

Benedict XVI. 2009. *Encyclical Letter Caritas in Veritate , 65.*

Bliss, R.R., and G.G. Kaufman. 2006. Derivatives and systemic risk: Netting, collateral, and closeout. *Journal of Financial Stability* 2: 55–70.

Case, K.E., and R.J. Shiller. 1987. Prices of single family homes since 1970: New indexes for four cities. *New England Economic Review* 87: 45–56.

Gorton, G. 2009. The subprime panic. *European Financial Management* 15: 10–46.

Gulen, H., and S. Mayhew. 2000. Stock index futures trading and volatility in international equity market. *Journal of Futures Markets* 20(7): 661–685.

Kneller, R., and A. Stevens. 2003. The specification of the aggregate production function in the presence of inefficiency. *Economics Letters* 81(2): 77–81.

Pirrong, C. 2010. No theory? No evidence? No problem! *Regulation* 33(2): 38–44.

Shiller, R. 1998. *Macro markets, creating institutions for managing society's largest risks.* Oxford: Oxford University Press.

Shiller, R. 2003. *The new financial order: Risk in the 21st century.* Princeton: Princeton University Press.

Shiller, R. 2010. Crisis and innovation. *Journal of Portfolio Management* 36(3): 14–19.

---

[11] Quality of information and transparency are not only technical recommendations but also constitute an ethical requirement (cf. Benedict XVI 2009, 65).

Part II
Social Responsibility,
Entrepreneurship and Virtues

Chapter 12
Ministering to the Pioneers of Prosperity

Andreas Widmer

12.1 Humanitarian Aid Is Not Economic Development

Nine years ago, I became the CEO of a business strategy–consulting firm. The company was founded by business professors from Harvard University and focused on private sector business strategy in developing markets.

I was exposed to the aid sector and its efforts to foster economic growth. Drawing from my business expertise and my Catholic faith, I increasingly began to disagree with aid strategy. Much of the current aid strategy does not consider a market-based solution. I found our current aid efforts deeply dehumanizing, violating the dignity of the very people we are trying to help.

Most people think of development as humanitarian aid or disaster relief. Indeed, humanitarian aid is a Christian nonnegotiable (Lk. 10:25–37), and it is our natural reaction to disaster: we want to feed the hungry, heal the sick, and shelter the homeless (Mt. 25:36). The world's reaction to the earthquake in Haiti, the civil war in Darfur, and floods in Pakistan is a litmus test of our common capacity for human compassion.

Churches in particular have a proud and effective tradition of administering charitable aid. The charitable NGO and philanthropic sectors in the United States alone are an annual $300 billion industry (Giving USA Foundation 2010), but few people differentiate between humanitarian aid and economic development (Tonkowich 2009).

Once the most urgent issues are resolved, life returns to some form of normalcy. The immediate danger of dying is over, and people want to go back to work. We call this economic development. This is a major part of what many aid organizations like USAID or DFID understand as their core mission, but many churches and private NGOs also focus on economic development.

A. Widmer (✉)
Chairman of Seven Fund, Inc, Seven Fund, Inc., Cambridge, USA
e-mail: andreas_widmer@email.com

M. Schlag and J.A. Mercado (eds.), *Free Markets and the Culture*
of Common Good, Ethical Economy 41, DOI 10.1007/978-94-007-2990-2_12,
© Springer Science+Business Media B.V. 2012

For example, the world gives Africa a lot of aid but does not do business with Africa. Here are some numbers that illustrate what I mean: the population of Africa makes up 12%, or 1/8, of the world's population. According to William Easterly, since 1949, US \$2.3 trillion in aid was given by donor countries to the developing world. In the last 50 years, Africa has received around US \$1 trillion, roughly \$5,000 per African living today. Twenty-nine percent of worldwide aid is given to a continent with 1/8 of all people. That is about 1/3. On the other hand, foreign direct investment into Africa only amounts to 1.4% of worldwide activity, or 1/71 (Griffiths and Tan 2007, 9). The world gives Africa a lot of aid but does not do business with Africa.

Why is it that all this aid money has had so little effect? Why has not more progress been made? The reasons are many and complex, but a few simple points stand out.

The World Bank has estimated that 60% of all foreign aid stays within donor countries (Griffiths and Tan 2007, 5). These funds are used to pay for consultants to purchase nationally produced goods and for transportation costs. As in any industry, the basic truth applies: if poverty is your business, more poverty means more business. The remaining 40% of foreign aid that goes to the emerging countries to help build the local economy is far outweighed by corruption and the anti-competitive impositions put on African business.

Farm subsidies in the European Union, United States and Canada, and the US steel tariffs totaling over \$300 billion per year are larger than the combined national income of sub-Saharan Africa and dwarf the \$50 billion given in aid each year (Stern 2002).

Europe subsidizes its agriculture to the tune of some \$35–40 billion per year, even while it demands that other nations liberalize their markets in regard to foreign competition.

Dairy subsidy in the EU is \$2.50 per cow per day. (Japanese cows live even better: they receive an average of \$7.50 per day.) (Stern 2002)

While economic aid amounts to around \$70–100 billion per year, poor countries pay some \$200 billion to the rich each year.

Sub-Saharan African countries, where aid constitutes over 10% of GNP, remain the poorest in the world (Birdsall 2007, 15). Countries with some success in combating poverty, such as India and China, depend little on aid (less than 1% of GNP in both countries.)

Sub-Saharan Africa's share of world trade declined from 6% in 1980 to only 3.5% in 2008 (ONE.org 2009). Is that because there are no entrepreneurs in Africa? Is it because Africans are worse at business than we are? Is it because they do not want investments?

Economic development is a complex issue in which culture, aid, economics, and politics all play a role. Some key barriers to development are that local entrepreneurs are often discouraged by their own society, ignored by economic development groups, and lack access to reasonable financial capital vehicles to help their firms grow. These are unfortunate circumstances, because the best way to fight poverty is through investment, not aid.

The most effective poverty fighters are entrepreneurs: people who build local SMEs employing 10–500 people. Entrepreneurs bring about long-term employment, create the middle class, help the local community to flourish, and enable our local churches to function. I realized that entrepreneurs have unique qualities when I first went to Africa to advise companies on business strategy.

12.2   Entrepreneurs Are Pioneers of Prosperity

I was blessed with a wonderful career and the opportunity to have worked with some of the best entrepreneurs in the United States. I was sharing my knowledge with emerging market entrepreneurs and noticed some commonalities: they were the very same kind of people that I worked with in the US high-tech sector, and they could bring about the same kind of economic transformation and general prosperity for their countries if given the chance to grow such companies.

Take Ariff Shamji of AAA Growers in Kenya (www.aaagrowers.co.ke). His company serves the market of premium and ready-to-eat vegetables in Europe and Africa – grown, packaged, and shipped from a few farms in Kenya. He employs over 2,000 people, and they have schools and medical facilities on their company campus.

Or Tokunbo Talabi, who against all odds started a security printing company in Nigeria 12 years ago (www.superfluxnigeria.com). He employs 300 people, and 17 out of the top 24 banks in Nigeria are his customers. His company has also gained the confidence and trust of four national governments to print their ballots and government checks. Talabi's employees have been trained to become experts in security printing in Africa and around the world.

Or Carolina Lopez, who built up her father's transportation business in Nicaragua (www.adenica.com). She turned the 24-day wait for products at customs into 24 hours. This might not sound like a watershed event, but the value that her company creates in the local economy is almost immeasurable: with a 24-day wait, you cannot import fresh food, but with 24 hours, you can. The financing needed for those 24 days prohibits many low-margin products from entering the country, and the strain of having a 24-day delay in shipping suffocates a country's competitiveness.

These three entrepreneurs and all other entrepreneurs have five simple traits in common:

They are not afraid of taking risks. To them, taking rational risk is opportunity.

They embrace competition. To them, competing is the fastest way to learn.

They embrace failure and see failure not as a setback, but as leading them a step closer to eventual success.

They are economically motivated, but their model of an economic win leaves everyone around them better off. And the money they make always finds its way back into their next prosperity-generating idea.

They are people of action, not just words. They are people in motion, not stagnation. They strive for excellence in whatever they do.

12.3   The Missing Middle

Economic growth is caused by wealth creation, specifically wealth creation by SMEs (Schmienann 2009). Yet, aid organizations are afraid to get involved in a project where someone might make money. A middle class is required for society to develop and for churches to become financially independent. SME entrepreneurs are the key building block, but the hurdles for them are real. Most businesses fail because they are too small and undercapitalized. But even if they fail, they contribute. People who have been previously employed in another company start 75% of all new businesses.[1] The single biggest requirement for Foreign Direct Investment (FDI) is investor confidence in the macroeconomic policy and stability of the country. Transparency, good governance, and an effective legal system are all necessities for attracting investments. If we want businesses to grow, we have to create an environment where they can flourish. Consider the difficulty of something as simple as the process of setting up a business: someone once told me that it takes up to 45 different signatories in the Congo to start a new business (Griffiths and Tan 2007, 11). If that is true, then most reasonable business owners are either going to move into the informal sector or move their business to another country. The World Bank suggests that future funding should be made conditional on cutting the time and cost of business start-up.[2] A good idea!

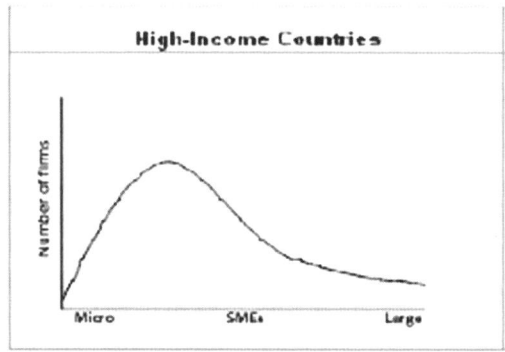

Source: Center for International Development at Harvard University.

Note: This is merely a graphical illustration; it does not reflect specific statistics

In the European Union, it is estimated that more than 20 million SMEs (with up to 250 employees) (Schmiemann 2008) accounted for over 80 million jobs. In the United States (where small firms are defined as those having fewer than 500 employees), 99.7% of all firms fall into the "small business" category, accounting for half the nation's jobs and contributing to more than 50% of nonfarm GDP (Basefsky and Sweeney 2006). In developing countries, this SME sector is almost entirely missing, comprising only 16% of GDP and 18% of employment, which is a major contributor to the cycle of poverty.

---

[1] See Small Enterprise Assistance Funds website: http://seaf.com/impact.htm
[2] See Doing Business: Measuring Business Regulations website: http://www.doingbusiness.org/

Low-Income Countries

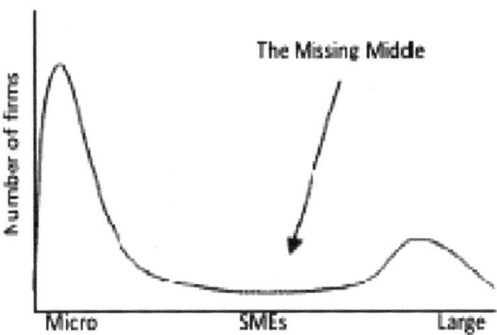

Note: This is merely a graphical illustration; it does not reflect specific statistics

A key issue that contributes to the lack of focus on this problem is our common definition of poverty. In his encyclical *Solicitudo Rei Socialis*, John Paul II argues for a new definition of what it means to be poor. If we measure poverty as living on any number of dollars per day, we state the problem in a most unfortunate and demeaning way. Leaving the "problem statement" at this one-dimensional definition produces narrow and unsustainable attempts at a solution (e.g., redistribution of wealth and donor/recipient dependency mentality). We need a more nuanced definition of poverty because it is within the definition of the problem that we can find the most effective solution.

The late pope suggested that a better definition of poverty is that to be poor is to be excluded from networks of productivity and exchange (John Paul II 1991, 34). Poverty, in other words, is exclusion from the sources of wealth produced by the free economy. This way of thinking is a very fruitful definition that can lead to a myriad of more effective solutions and efforts.

In my estimation, the mental model that underlies the $1-a-day definition is a zero-sum game view of the economy. While this view undergirds many of today's poverty fighting efforts, it is blatantly false. Prosperity is created when business transactions happen, and business can create more money through trade. To increase overall prosperity, it is an increase in business activity that is needed, not a redistribution of wealth.

Many current efforts call for and create separate solutions for the poor – fair trade initiatives, third world shops, handouts rather than integration, and dumping rather than trade. This reinforces John Paul II's assessment that the poor are excluded from the worldwide networks of productivity and exchange. What is called for is solidarity (John Paul II 1991, 34, 41). The West needs to integrate the poor into the existing worldwide networks of productivity and exchange, not create separate networks for the poor (John Paul II 1991, 33). For example, an increase in trade among African countries by less than 5% would yield more than $70 billion in annual income to the local economy (Ayodele 2008). This simple step would exceed in value the yearly foreign aid the continent receives.

Let us not regard the poor as a problem – let us regard them as people with potential. We are challenged to think of the marginalized and the poor not in terms of threat or burden, but in terms of potential and opportunity. This approach will produce diametrically opposed policies (cf. John Paul II 1991, 28 and Benedict XVI 2009, 28). Many of today's solutions try to do away with the poor through abortion and birth control rather than by actually eradicating poverty itself. We should not eliminate poverty by exterminating the poor. That remedy proves worse than the problem; moreover, not only is it wrong, it is also ineffective.

By and large, the West is afraid of the poor, regarding the poor as ignorant masses that need to be managed. The attempt is being made through our government policies to "manage" poverty with government programs and decrees with little effect. We ignore the fact that solving poverty is really done through the creation of wealth. The best wealth creators are SMEs, our own engines of prosperity, not NGOs, not multilateral institutions, and definitely not governments. If SMEs grow, the workforce has good and secure jobs, the local economy grows, a middle class can flourish, and a local basis of philanthropy evolves. In short, regions and countries become economically self-sufficient. But much of this depends upon the moral culture of the local entrepreneurs:

Do they act out of a stewardship mindset?
Have they been catechized?
Do they have a strong and active relationship with Christ?
Do they see their talents and their work as gifts from God?
Do they have an explicit moral culture?

What is the Church's role and responsibility in this? Catholics should not complain if the business elites are immoral and secular if we have not reached out and evangelized. After all, it is the business of the Church to form the moral conscience of people. If they grow in business without adequate spiritual guidance, people fail to see a deeper meaning in their work and their money.

What Can the Church Do?

We can build on what we have. Every parish has entrepreneurs, and there are many more aspiring business owners with talent in the congregation. Unfortunately, very few ministry efforts reach out specifically to them, and as a result, many entrepreneurs have either fallen away from the faith or do not know how to put it into practice at work. They seek deeper meaning, but they do not have the tools and the education to find it in their religion. This unmet need represents a substantial opportunity. The Church has a rich spiritual and theological patrimony with which to minister to and nurture business people and entrepreneurs. The first step is to get them involved by getting involved with them. This implies a Catholic "SME ministry" which:

Evangelizes entrepreneurs
Forms the conscience of business leaders (cf. Benedict XVI 2009, 68)
Furthers initiative and self-reliance

Helps the faithful to see the spiritual meaning of their work
Promotes solidarity among Catholics worldwide

The Church has a lot to offer to entrepreneurs, and entrepreneurs have a lot to offer to the Church, not only in developed economies but also and particularly in the developing world. Many financially poor parishes today rely on outside donations to substitute for a lack of local benefactors, making their financial situation unsustainable and precarious. This does not have to be the case forever. Dependence on foreign donations in emerging economies would ease with an increase of the local middle class. In effect, helping create such a middle class is in the interest of the local parish evangelistically, pastorally, and financially.

Why should the Church become involved in this? Why should the Church care about entrepreneurship and business? First of all, it is our responsibility to minister to all of our brothers and sisters according to their needs (Catechism of the Catholic Church, 831). Evangelization should extend to every part of society, especially those lay faithful with civic and economic influence. It is a matter of applying and promoting the social doctrine of the Church to business and the economy. Entrepreneurship provides wonderful opportunities to apply the principles of subsidiarity and solidarity. Furthermore, a business vocation properly lived out teaches and puts into practice an example of stewardship and the universal destination of goods. It itself is a tool for further evangelization and the common good.

The opportunity for inculturation is ideal: work and competition correspond with the dignity of the human person. The Christian message promotes a culture of self-realization and excellence at all levels but specifically at the level of everyday work of the lay faithful. The Church has always advocated helping the poor not merely by having a heart but also having a mind for the poor.

12.4 Entrepreneurship and Spirituality

The Call of the Entrepreneur, by Fr. Robert Sirico, the founder of the Acton Institute, is a wonderful guiding point for SME ministry efforts (Sirico 2007). Father Sirico writes that entrepreneurship is a spiritual vocation: entrepreneurs make something out of nothing. And whenever we humans do so, we know that God is present in that action because only God can do so – thus, he invites us to be cocreators and to become coworkers in his vineyard to build his Kingdom. George Weigel summarized this point very well in his 2004 Tyburn lecture when he said: "Through our work, John Paul urges, we do not simply make more; we become more. Thus work has a spiritual dimension, and when we identify our work and its hardships with the work, the passion, and the death of Christ, our work participates in the development of the Kingdom of God. This is at the core of how we should approach any kind of development" (Weigel 2004).

Many government and NGO efforts lack this view, which Pope Benedict calls integral human development (Benedict XVI 2009, 68 and Paul VI 1967, 14), and the fruits of their efforts are therefore in danger of hurting more than they help.

What should Catholic SME ministry entail?

What I propose is not a coherent movement but an idea that can be picked up locally at the parish or diocesan level by concerned Catholics, lay and ordained. Its implementation and focus can be manifold and happen inside or outside the structure of the parish or diocese. However, the goal is always the same: integrating faith and work and evangelizing the private sector of the economy.

The Peruvian economist Hernando de Soto, in his latest work on the developing world, wrote: "It is teeming with entrepreneurs" (Soto 2003, 4). This leads us to inquire how that entrepreneurial spirit can be unleashed so that the poorest of the poor can live in dignity.

I believe that SME ministry will be well received by both the laity and clergy and bear much fruit in evangelization. Entrepreneurs are very receptive to the Christian message. Through their work, they are well aware that there is more to life than meets the eye.

They realize that the human person transcends; in their interactions with employees, they realize that there is more to the human person than meets the eye.

They know that truth exists independent of them; every business owner knows to trust the profit and loss statement more than their perception of whether the company is doing well.

They are spiritual seekers; staying motivated to run a business requires a certain spirituality, a belief in a transcendent goal.

They yearn to be ministered to; a review of the most popular business leadership books reveals that guidance on how to integrate one's life and maintain a deeper purpose is a key need in this population.

A Catholic SME ministry effort would not only help entrepreneurs gain access to networks of productivity and exchange but would also help them grow spiritually and develop their skills. SME ministry has three parts:

1. Spiritual formation, guidance, and counseling
2. Business expertise, planning, pitching, and process (skill development)
3. Access to networks of productivity and exchange, e.g., providing a network of access to mentorship, financial resources, and trade relationships (through worldwide lay "solidarity initiatives," for example)

The ministry I propose aims in particular to:

Provide the person with a spiritual understanding of their business vocation.
Promote a stewardship-based entrepreneurial culture.
Make available technical, business, and entrepreneurship education and knowhow.
Explain human dignity, subsidiarity, and solidarity and provide specific examples of what these mean in the work environment.

Create local groups of entrepreneurs for members to support, pray, network, and
  grow together.
Create a Christian entrepreneurship curriculum to be taught at local churches and
  schools to educate entrepreneurs and middle management and inspire the faithful
  to start and grow businesses as well as discover a deeper spirituality through
  work. Only participants in this curriculum would qualify to participate in the
  international network and mentorship programs.
Establish an international network of lay Catholic entrepreneurs and SME leaders
  to share best practices and encourage collaboration, trade, and potentially even
  investments among themselves (what I would call a "Lay Solidarity Initiative").

Reading *Caritas in Veritate* and *Centesimus Annus*, I am left with the impression
that both popes suggest that knowing how to solve poverty and not doing so is tantamount to a moral failure. Each one of us has many opportunities and in fact a
Christian duty to put into practice our knowledge of how to solve poverty:

Continue effective humanitarian aid (Benedict XVI 2009, 19).
Demand economic development that consists of a process different from
  humanitarian aid (Benedict XVI 2009, 19).
Integrate the poor into networks of productivity and exchange (Benedict XVI
  2009, 35).
Promote trade, not aid, so that jobs are created rather than dependency (Benedict
  XVI 2009, 16).
As individuals, consider investing in emerging market SMEs (Benedict XVI
  2009, 35).
Participate in, promote, or create an SME ministry effort (Benedict XVI
  2009, 35).
Act in a way that links life ethic and social ethic (Benedict XVI 2009, 15).

> The Church has always held that economic action is not to be regarded as something
> opposed to society. In and of itself, the market is not, and must not become, the place where
> the strong subdue the weak. Society does not have to protect itself from the market, as if the
> development of the latter were *ipso facto* to entail the death of authentically human
> relations. Admittedly, the market can be a negative force, not because it is so by nature, but
> because a certain ideology can make it so. It must be remembered that the market does not
> exist in the pure state. It is shaped by the cultural configurations, which define it and give it
> direction. Economy and finance, as instruments, can be used badly when purely selfish ends
> motivate those at the helm. Instruments that are good in themselves can thereby be trans-
> formed into harmful ones. But it is man's darkened reason that produces these conse-
> quences, not the instrument per se. Therefore it is not the instrument that must be called to
> account, but individuals, their moral conscience and their personal and social responsibility.
> (Benedict XVI 2009, 36)

The whole church, ordained and lay, should become involved in engaging and
forming current and future business leaders in an effective fashion. Their ability to
create jobs and economic progress and the Church's ability to provide them with
spiritual meaning and moral understanding forms the cornerstone of success.
Prosperity comes from within.

Bibliography

AAA, Growers. 2010. Growers, http://www.aaagrowers.co.ke/.

Adenica, http://www.adenica.com/.

Ayodele, Thompson. 2008. "Food Aid will not Help Africa". *The African Executive*, June 2008. http://www.africanexecutive.com/modules/magazine/article_print.php?article=3212.

Basefsky, Stuart, and Sean Sweeney. 2006. Employment Relations in SMEs: The United States. Cornell School of Industrial and Labor Relations. http://www.ilr.cornell.edu/international/news/upload/BERLIN%20SME%20report.pdf. Accessed 5 Dec 2006.

Benedict XVI. 2009. Encyclical letter *Caritas in Veritate*. Vatican: Libreria Editrice Vaticana.

Birdsall, Nancy. 2007. Do No Harm: Aid, Weak Institutions, and the Missing Middle in Africa (Working paper). Center for Global Development. http://www.cgdev.org/content/publications/detail/13115. Accessed 8 March 2007, 15.

Catholic Church. 1993. *Catechism of the Catholic Church*. 1993. Vatican: Libreria Editrice Vaticana.

Doing business: Measuring business regulations, http://www.doingbusiness.org/.

Giving USA Foundation: The Center on Philanthropy at Indiana University. http://www.givingusareports.org/free.php.

Griffiths, Brian, and Kim Tan. 2007. *Fighting Poverty through Enterprise. The Case for Social Venture Capital*. London: TBN.

John Paul II. 1991. Encyclical letter *Centesimus Annus*. Vatican: Libreria Editrice Vaticana.

ONE. 2009. Trade and investment. http://www.one.org/c/us/issue/98/.

Paul VI. 1967. Encyclical letter *Populorum Progressio*. Vatican: Libreria Editrice Vaticana.

Schmiemann, Manfred. 2008. "Enterprises by Size Class", *Eurostat*, 31/2008. http://epp.eurostat.ec.europa.eu/cache/ITY_OFFPUB/KS-SF-08-031/EN/KS-SF-08-031-EN.PDF. Accessed 25 March 2008.

Schmiemann, Manfred. 2009. "SMEs were the main drivers of economic growth between 2004 and 2006", in *Eurostat*, 71/2009. http://epp.eurostat.ec.europa.eu/cache/ITY_OFFPUB/KS-SF-09-071/EN/KS-SF-09-071-EN.PDF. Accessed 8 Sep 2009.

Sirico, Robert. 2007. *The Call of the Entrepreneur*. Grand Rapids: Acton Institute.

Small Enterprise Assistance Funds, http://seaf.com/impact.htm.

de Soto, Hernando. 2003. *The Mystery of Capital: Why Capitalism Triumphs in the West and Fails Everywhere Else*. New York: Basic Books.

Stern, Nicholas. 2002. Dynamic Development: Innovation and Inclusion, Speech at the Center for Economic Studies (CES) in Munich, November. http://team.univ-paris1.fr/teamperso/page/files/BM%20Nicholas%20Stern.pdf.

Superflux International Limited, www.superfluxnigeria.com.

Tonkowich, Jim. 2009. "'A mind for the poor': Avoiding the Traps," Crosswalk.com. http://www.crosswalk.com/news/commentary/11606128/. Accessed 16 July 2009.

Weigel, George. 2004. The Free and Virtuous Society: Catholic Social Doctrine in the Twenty-First Century, Fourth Annual Tyburn Lecture at Tyburn Convent, Marble Arch, London. http://www.eppc.org/publications/pubID.2107/pub_detail.asp. Accessed 19 May 2004.

Widmer, Andreas. 2009. "A Mind for the Poor". In *In The River They Swim: Essays From Around the World on Enterprise Solutions to Poverty*, ed. Michael Fairbanks, Malik Fal, and Marcela Escobari-Rose, 28–34. West Conshohocken: Templeton Press.

Chapter 13
Corporate Social Responsibility in the Encyclical *Caritas in Veritate*

Antonio Argandoña

The encyclical *Caritas in Veritate* (CV) contains a scant two allusions to *corporate social responsibility* (CSR).[1] In paragraph 40, after referring to the freedom enjoyed by business owners and managers in choosing their investments and the location of their businesses and the dangers this entails for the proper moral functioning of companies, Benedict XVI adds that "there is also increasing awareness of the need for greater social responsibility on the part of business. Even if the ethical considerations that currently inform debate on the social responsibility of the corporate world are not all acceptable from the perspective of the Church's social doctrine, there is nevertheless a growing conviction that business management cannot concern itself only with the interests of the proprietors, but must also assume responsibility for all the other stakeholders who contribute to the life of the business: the workers, the clients, the suppliers of various elements of production, the community of reference" (Benedict XVI 2009, 40). And in paragraph 45: "Today we hear much talk of ethics in the world of economy, finance and business. Research centers and seminars in business ethics are on the rise; the system of ethical certification is spreading throughout the developed world as part of the movement of ideas associated with the responsibilities of business towards society" (Benedict XVI 2009, 45).

These two brief references suggest that the encyclical notes the existence of the "movement of ideas" known as "corporate social responsibility"; that it attributes to this movement a fundamentally ethical content; that it finds in CSR ideas that are useful and acceptable (e.g., the broadening of the goals of the firm in line with

---

[1] This study is part of the activities of the "la Caixa" Chair of Corporate Social Responsibility and Corporate Governance at IESE Business School.

A. Argandoña (✉)
IESE-Business School, Barcelona, Spain
e-mail: AArgandona@iese.edu

stakeholder theory) along with others it considers unacceptable; and that it also sees in CSR a set of instruments or techniques (specifically, ethical certifications) whose moral value it does not pronounce upon. Elsewhere, the encyclical appears to give CSR the stamp of approval when it states that "solidarity is first and foremost a sense of responsibility on the part of everyone with regard to everyone, and it cannot therefore be merely delegated to the State" (Benedict XVI 2009, 38).

This brief reference to CSR in the encyclical reflects fairly accurately certain features of that "movement of ideas" as it exists today. The first thing to be noted is that the encyclical does not contain a generally accepted definition of CSR. This is only to be expected, given that what we call CSR has been approached from at least four different angles:

1. Ethical: Companies have a responsibility for the effects their actions have on themselves and on their environment, and this responsibility is ethical, not legal (or not only legal).
2. Social: Companies are "citizens"; they relate to other "citizens," i.e., people and communities, and must respond to the expectations and demands of these stakeholders and of society in general.
3. Strategic: As economic institutions, companies are oriented to creating value for their owners and so must combine the assumption of their social responsibilities with what is presented as their fundamental economic function (Porter and Kramer 2006). CSR is therefore a means of creating value for the owners of companies (and for society as a whole?).
4. Instrumental: CSR is valued for the results it achieves, and companies must measure those results and show accountability (including through the certifications alluded to in Benedict XVI 2009, 45).[2]

As we pointed out earlier, the encyclical *Caritas in Veritate* is only marginally concerned with CSR. Its subject is *human development*, "the authentic human development [that] concerns the whole of the person in every single dimension" (Benedict XVI 2009, 11). Yet if human development is the goal of economic and social activity, it must logically also be the goal of companies, at least in general terms, and so must be the model for the responsibilities to be assumed by companies, constituting their CSR. At the very least, CSR must be compatible with that ultimate goal of the economy and society. This implies that we should find some indications in the encyclical as to the nature of CSR, from the point of view of Catholic social doctrine.

In what follows, I shall try to present what, in my opinion, could be a valid interpretation of CSR in the perspective of *Caritas in Veritate*. It may not be the only interpretation that could be deduced from the encyclical, but it is one that

---

[2]CSR is sometimes presented from other angles, which are superposed on those mentioned here. For instance, people talk about descriptive CSR (how companies actually behave in relation to their social responsibilities), normative CSR (how they should behave), and instrumental CSR (what tools they have at their disposal). Cf. Donaldson and Preston (1995).

I believe is compatible with the encyclical and also consistent with the ideas of other Christian and non-Christian authors (though not all of them).[3] The danger of this exercise is that of forcing the views of the Pope into line with my own personal ideas on CSR, which is why I must insist that this is my personal interpretation. In what follows, therefore, references to the encyclical must be understood not literally.

13.1 CSR Is an Ethical Responsibility

As we said earlier, the encyclical chooses to interpret CSR from the perspective of its *ethical dimension*. Just a few paragraphs before paragraph 40, cited above, the Pope reminds us that "locating resources, financing, production, consumption and all the other phases in the economic cycle inevitably have moral implications. Thus every economic decision has a moral consequence" (Benedict XVI 2009, 37). So if all actions and omissions in companies (all human actions, in fact) have moral content, then they all give rise to moral responsibilities, which business owners and managers must assume.[4] In paragraph 40, the Pope points out that this sense of responsibility is disappearing because "it is becoming increasingly rare for business enterprises to be in the hands of a stable director who feels responsible in the long term"; or because "the so-called outsourcing of production can weaken the company's sense of responsibility towards the stakeholders – namely the workers, the suppliers, the consumers, the natural environment and broader society"; or because "today's international capital market offers great freedom of action" to place funds wherever the return is highest, independently of other responsibilities; or lastly, because "in recent years a new cosmopolitan class of managers has emerged, who are often answerable only to the shareholders generally consisting of anonymous funds which de facto determine their remuneration" (Benedict XVI 2009, 40).

It is in this context, then, that the Pope observes that "there is also increasing awareness of the need for greater social responsibility on the part of business" (Benedict XVI 2009, 40). So we can say that the encyclical understands CSR as *the whole set, or part of the set, of moral responsibilities that companies must assume for all their actions and omissions, insofar as such actions and omissions have an ethical content.*[5]

---

[3] I do not propose to extend the scope of this study to other documents of the Church's social doctrine, which will be referred to only marginally in what follows.

[4] This point of view is not widely shared: "many people today would claim that they owe nothing to anyone, except to themselves" (Benedict XVI 2009, 43).

[5] Corporate social responsibilities would presumably differ from that set of moral responsibilities in that they would be publicly and formally assumed by the company in the eyes of society (hence their designation as "social responsibilities"), which would entail commitments of transparency, disclosure, accountability, etc. Argandoña (2008), Argandoña and Weltzien-Hoivik (2009).

That CSR has an ethical content is accepted by some authors, but not by all. Specifically, those who take the social, strategic, and instrumental approaches mentioned earlier either do not accept this ethical dimension or else reduce its sense and scope. Similarly, most definitions of CSR make no reference to any ethical content.[6] In fact, the points on which most definitions agree are that CSR is voluntary (without coercion by the State), that it concerns a range of stakeholders, and that it is played out in three areas: the economy (value creation, efficiency, results, profits), society (both inside companies, i.e., employees, and outside companies, i.e., local communities or society as a whole), and the natural environment.[7]

13.2 Not Just Any Ethics Will Do

As we said earlier, the encyclical considers that CSR is ethical but adds that "the ethical considerations that currently inform debate on the social responsibility of the corporate world are not all acceptable from the perspective of the Church's social doctrine" (Benedict XVI 2009, 40).[8] *What those acceptable ethical approaches (theories and praxis) are* is explained in paragraph 45: "the economy needs ethics in order to function correctly – not any ethics whatsoever, but an ethics which is people-centered [...] On this subject the Church's social doctrine can make a specific contribution, since it is based on man's creation 'in the image of God' (Gen. 1:27), a datum which gives rise to the inviolable dignity of the human person and the transcendent value of natural moral norms" (Benedict XVI 2009, 45). The ethics in question is not, therefore, an ethics established from outside; rather, the economy "is ethical, not merely by virtue of an external label, but by its respect for requirements intrinsic to its very nature" (Benedict XVI 2009, 45).[9] We shall come back to this later.

---

[6]For an extensive list of definitions of CSR, see Mullerat (2010).

[7]This is not the place to analyze why many authors do not emphasize the ethical nature of CSR, a subject that has not been tackled in the literature. For some, CSR is a "watered down" alternative to business ethics, which is seen as an advantage, as it avoids the need, on the theoretical plane, for a solid moral foundation as well as the challenges that putting it into practice would entail. For others, CSR is a technical management tool that has been humanized through the introduction, from outside, of certain restrictions on what a company can and must do to maximize its profits, in the form of social action, good environmental practices, human resources policies, voluntary self-restraint, etc. Lastly, for yet others, ethics is no more than a set of social conventions or norms that change over time and geography, so that companies merely need to know what society expects or demands and act accordingly in order to avoid problems (acquire social legitimacy) or be successful, based on a cost-benefit analysis.

[8]If CSR is established on incorrect ethical principles, it will lead to perverse outcomes, which also occur when it is demanded that the economy not be subject to morals (Benedict XVI 2009, 34). That is to say, CSR cannot be morally neutral.

[9]In the same way as "it was not just a matter of correcting dysfunctions [of the market] through assistance [to developing countries]" (Benedict XVI 2009, 35), Benedict XVI clearly would not accept a conception of CSR as a means of validating ethically inappropriate behavior through philanthropic activities or social action.

13.3   It Is Not Derived from Abstract Principles

The encyclical offers no details as to what those responsibilities might be, but it is clearly not referring to a theoretical set; nor are the responsibilities derived solely from *abstract principles or rules*, but from the application of such principles or rules to the context in which companies operate, "namely the workers, the suppliers, the consumers, the natural environment and broader society" (Benedict XVI 2009, 40),[10] in accordance with Catholic moral theology and, therefore, depending on how those responsibilities are understood by the owners, investors, entrepreneurs, and managers of each company, in accordance with the latter's rightly formed conscience.[11] *Caritas in Veritate* notes, for instance, that many managers are aware of the "profound links between their enterprise and the territory or territories in which it operates" (Benedict XVI 2009, 40) and that "the requirements of justice must be safeguarded, with due consideration for the way in which the capital [to be invested abroad] was generated and the harm to individuals that will result if it is not used where it was produced" (Benedict XVI 2009, 40). This means that, beyond any abstract principle, business decisions must take into account circumstances of place, time, prior relations, and expectations that may have been created.

In other words, CSR *is not an objective list* of responsibilities established by society, experts, or stakeholder groups based on certain preferences, expectations,

---

[10]The encyclical does not refer to stakeholder theory, but enumerates the parties most commonly included in this theory (Benedict XVI 2009, 40). Although the Pope states that "business management cannot concern itself only with the interests of the proprietors, but must also assume responsibility for all the other stakeholders who contribute to the life of the business" (Benedict XVI 2009, 40), he is not, it seems to me, saying that the purpose of companies is to create value for all stakeholders or to serve stakeholders' interests. He is merely quoting the position of certain authors, which seems compatible with the view that Benedict XVI expresses elsewhere in the encyclical regarding the purposes of companies, and which in any event requires that the interests of all concerned be taken into account.

[11]Proprietors, investors, entrepreneurs, and managers are the agents mentioned in paragraphs 40 and 41 of CV insofar as they are responsible for decision making in organizations. By proprietors, Benedict XVI seems to mean the people who hold or share ownership of companies and are responsible for managing them; the encyclical laments, for example, that "it is becoming increasingly rare for business enterprises to be in the hands of a stable director [owner] who feels responsible in the long term (…), for the life and the results of his company" (Benedict XVI 2009, 40). The law gives investors the right of ownership of companies and thus also the power to make ultimate decisions, appoint managers, and control the economic surplus; the Pope recalls, for instance, that "investment always has moral, as well as economic significance […] What should be avoided is a speculative use of financial resources that yields to the temptation of seeking only short-term profit, without regard for the long-term sustainability of the enterprise [and] its benefit to the real economy" (Benedict XVI 2009, 40). Entrepreneurs are those who carry out the "business enterprise" (Benedict XVI 2009, 41), i.e., who create start-ups, in the various forms the encyclical recognizes. And managers make decisions in the name and on behalf of the proprietors; the encyclical laments, for example, that "a new cosmopolitan class of managers has emerged, who are often answerable only to the shareholders, generally consisting of anonymous funds which de facto determine their remuneration" (Benedict XVI 2009, 40).

or social demands. Nor are the responsibilities deduced rationally by such external observers, or even by business owners and managers themselves, from certain general principles; rather, they are recognized and assumed by the people who must make decisions in companies, in accordance with their well-formed conscience, based on certain objective rules, the nature of the goods sought through the action, and the overall circumstances of time and place. For example, identifying what is good or bad at any given moment calls not only for natural knowledge of that good but also for experience and judgment about the chances of achieving it (Rhonheimer 2001).

An agent can only do this, however, if over the years, he has developed his capabilities not only to carry out morally right actions but also to know what actions are right and what the chances are of carrying them out successfully, which will depend on the agent's personal capabilities (acquired through the virtues he has acquired in his life) and the capabilities of his environment (the organization and the other people in it and their virtues). That is to say, the definition of social responsibilities will *vary from firm to firm*, depending not only on the company's environment and history but also on the *degree of moral development of the people* who make up the firm.

It may be objected that these conclusions are not stated in the encyclical as clearly as we have stated them here. Yet that is the immediate consequence of the Christian conception of ethics that naturally emerges from the encyclical.[12] An important consequence of this conception of ethics is that there must be *a Christian conception of CSR*, at least insofar as Christian business owners know more about ethical rules and have different experiences and judgments, and also different capabilities: "a non-Christian ethos will reduce what is Christianly obligatory to what is humanly possible and so will only incompletely detect the true possibilities of human action" (Rhonheimer 1987, 936).

13.4   CSR Derives from the Firm's Purpose or Objective

One implication of all the above is that a person's view of the ethical responsibilities of companies derives from his view of the *purpose or objective of the firm*. The encyclical does not offer a detailed account of that purpose, although it does state that the purpose is not to maximize profit. It draws attention, for example, to "the temptation of seeking only short-term profit" (Benedict XVI 2009, 40), as against "the long-term sustainability of the enterprise, its benefit to the real economy and attention to the advancement, in suitable and appropriate ways, of further economic initiatives in countries in need of development" (Benedict XVI 2009, 40). So it would seem that Benedict XVI conceives of the firm as (1) a human

---

[12]Cf., for example, Abbà (1992) and, applied to business ethics, Pérez López (1993), Williams (1986).

community (2) aimed at providing a service to society through the production of useful goods and services, (3) efficiently (as an economic enterprise it is justified in generating a surplus or profit: CV no. 21), (4) so that its sustainability or continuity over time is assured,[13] (5) and collaborating directly in the common good of society (Benedict XVI 2009, 7). This outline gives us the general responsibilities, which individual business owners and managers will have to specify in their particular company, place, and time.[14]

The encyclical goes further, however, and proposes "a profoundly new way of *understanding business enterprise*" (Benedict XVI 2009, 40) by explaining the role of the "logic of gift" and the "principle of gratuitousness." This may have important consequences for the conception of CSR, so although this is not the place to elaborate on these ideas,[15] a few reflections are called for.

The encyclical suggests that there is an implicit "division of labor" between the market (oriented to efficiency), the State (aimed at redistribution), and civil society (operating on the principles of gratuitousness and fraternity) (Benedict XVI 2009, 38). But it states that this distribution of roles is inappropriate if it is understood strictly. Specifically, "economic activity [the market, the firm] cannot prescind from gratuitousness, which fosters and disseminates solidarity and responsibility for justice and the common good among the different economic players" (Benedict XVI 2009, 38). "What is needed, therefore, is a market that permits the free operation, in conditions of equal opportunity, of enterprises in pursuit of different institutional ends [and this] requires that shape and structure be given to those types of economic initiative which, without rejecting profit, aim at a higher goal than the mere logic of the exchange of equivalents, of profit as an end in itself" (Benedict XVI 2009, 38). Action is required "on gradually increasing openness [...] to forms of economic activity marked by quotas of gratuitousness and communion" (Benedict XVI 2009, 39), "with shifting of competences from the 'non-profit' world to the 'profit' world and vice versa" (Benedict XVI 2009, 41).

What the Pope is proposing is the coexistence in the market of a broad range of economic organizations, from privately owned companies aimed exclusively at profit to State owned companies, including "traditional companies which nonetheless

---

[13]The concept of sustainability that underlies the encyclical, both at firm level and at country or global level, is not exclusively ecological. Many authors prefer to talk about economic, social, and environmental sustainability rather than CSR, perhaps because sustainability is, or at least appears to be, more specific, or because it is further removed from moral interpretations (which make some people uncomfortable), or because it lends itself more readily to the use of instruments (measurement, audit, reporting, etc.). The treatment of environmental problems in *Caritas in Veritate* (Benedict XVI 2009, 48ff) is much broader and less deterministic than most other analyses.

[14]Like other documents of Catholic social teaching, the encyclical states clearly that "economic action is not to be regarded as something opposed to society" (Benedict XVI 2009, 36); if on occasion "the market can be a negative force," this is "not because it is so by nature, but because a certain ideology can make it so. [...] It is shaped by the cultural configurations which define it and give it direction" (Benedict XVI 2009, 36). Cf. also John Paul II (1991, 42).

[15]The author has dealt with this subject in Argandoña (2010).

subscribe to social aid agreements in support of underdeveloped countries, charitable foundations associated with individual companies, groups of companies oriented toward social welfare, and the diversified world of the so-called 'civil economy' and the 'economy of communion'" (CV 46). Essentially, it is a matter of ending the domination of private for-profit companies in order to make room for a different form of organization, "one which does not exclude profit, but instead considers it a means for achieving human and social ends" (Benedict XVI 2009, 46). This is not a reference to social action, because "whether such companies distribute dividends or not [...] becomes secondary in relation to their willingness to view profit as a means of achieving the goal of a more humane market and society" (Benedict XVI 2009, 46). So that "without prejudice to the importance and the economic and social benefits of the more traditional forms of business, they [the new forms] steer the system toward a clearer and more complete assumption of duties on the part of economic subjects. And not only that. The very plurality of institutional forms of business gives rise to a market which is not only more civilized but also more competitive" (Benedict XVI 2009, 46).

This may have importance for CSR if we understand that the Pope is talking about different types of organizations that compete (or cooperate) with one another in the market; that pursue different goals, regardless of their legal form (Benedict XVI 2009, 46) and what they do with their profits (Benedict XVI 2009, 46); that assume different responsibilities (i.e., have different forms of CSR); and that try to overcome the deficiencies of the system as we know it today.

13.5 CSR Is Based on Justice and Charity

If CSR has an ethical content, it will naturally assign an important role to the virtues. A socially responsible company is one that is run on ethical lines; in other words, virtues are practiced in it, and CSR is *a manifestation of that practice of the virtues*. Prominent among those virtues, of course, is *justice*, as one of the "criteria that govern moral action" (Benedict XVI 2009, 6). If "every society draws up its own system of justice" (Benedict XVI 2009, 6), companies must be built on justice, especially commutative justice (Benedict XVI 2009, 35). Social responsibilities cannot be exercised where justice is not lived out.

Yet the encyclical also suggests that CSR includes, above all, *charity*, which "goes beyond justice [...] but it never lacks justice, which prompts us to give the other what is 'his' [...] but I cannot 'give' what is mine to the other, without first giving him what pertains to him in justice. [...] On the one hand, charity demands justice: recognition and respect for the legitimate rights of individuals and peoples. [...] On the other hand, charity transcends justice and completes it in the logic of giving and forgiving" (Benedict XVI 2009, 6). Because "if the market is governed solely by the principle of the equivalence in value of exchanged goods [i.e., by relations of commutative justice in the market], it cannot produce the social cohesion that it requires in order to function well" (Benedict XVI 2009, 35). "The 'earthly city' is promoted not merely by relationships of rights and duties, but to an even greater and more fundamental extent by relationships of gratuitousness, mercy, and communion" (Benedict XVI 2009, 6): "without gratuitousness, there can be no justice in the first place" (Benedict XVI 2009, 38). And this defines a scope of CSR that goes well beyond the approaches adopted in many companies.

13.6 It Is Voluntary

If CSR is ethical, it must be *voluntary*, that is, based on the freedom of the agent and not subject to the compulsion of law or the coercive apparatus of the State.[16] In this, the encyclical coincides with most definitions of CSR. But voluntary does not mean optional. Ethical responsibilities have the "obligatoriness" of morality, i.e., that which is required for the good of the human person, for the good of the others involved, for the common good of society, and, in the case of companies, for survival. CSR, like development, can be said to be "a vocation, a call addressed by free subjects to other free subjects in favor of an assumption of shared responsibility" (Benedict XVI 2009, 17) – which is not to say that the ethical responsibilities to which CSR refers must not sometimes be made obligatory by law or regulation, without this making them any the less moral responsibilities.

13.7 It Is Centered on the Human Person

If authentic human development is "to promote the good of every man and of the whole man" (Benedict XVI 2009, 18), CSR must be oriented toward that objective, "the *centrality of the human person*" (Benedict XVI 2009, 47), of all men and women as part of "a single family" (Benedict XVI 2009, 53), because "the primary capital to be safeguarded and valued is man, the human person in his or her integrity" (Benedict XVI 2009, 25). Obviously, no individual company is responsible for the good of all men, nor for the integral (material and spiritual) good of man. But the conception of a company's moral responsibilities must take all this into account.

---

[16]The encyclical recognizes the traditional functions of the State in Catholic social teaching, but does not develop them in detail (Benedict XVI 2009, 24ff). On this subject, cf. John Paul II (1991, 40) and the Pontifical Council for Justice and Peace (1994, 351–355).

For example, CSR must play *a subsidiary role* because "the human person by nature is actively involved in his own development" (Benedict XVI 2009, 68). Certainly, subsidiarity, which the encyclical presents as "an expression of inalienable human freedom" (Benedict XVI 2009, 57), above all in relation to the State, can be applied to other organizations as well. So firms must consider their CSR policies as "a form of assistance to the human person" that is offered "when individuals or groups are unable to accomplish something on their own, and it is always designed to achieve their emancipation, because it fosters freedom and participation through assumption of responsibility." Accordingly, "subsidiarity respects personal dignity by recognizing in the person a subject who is always capable of giving something to others." And "by considering reciprocity as the heart of what it is to be a human being, subsidiarity is the most effective antidote against any form of all-encompassing welfare state" (Benedict XVI 2009, 57), which may occur not only in the State but also in other intermediate organizations such as companies.

The application of the principle of subsidiarity to CSR has a wide range of implications. CSR programs must count on the capabilities of all those involved, seeking not so much to solve people's problems as to put people in a position to solve their problems for themselves, because "the people who benefit from [development programs] ought to be directly involved in their planning and implementation" (Benedict XVI 2009, 47). CSR must therefore *respect the freedom* of those involved and rely on *their participation*,[17] which is far removed from the conception of CSR as a set of techniques, or a form of organization, or a structure: "no structure can guarantee this development over and above human responsibility" (Benedict XVI 2009, 17).

To the extent that CSR recognizes rights in stakeholders, it also identifies duties in them: "the sharing of reciprocal duties is a more powerful incentive to action than the mere assertion of rights" (Benedict XVI 2009, 43). Rather than talking about the social responsibility of companies, therefore, we should be talking about a whole set of responsibilities at all levels of society, ethical responsibilities that are *shared and reciprocal*, including the responsibilities of companies to their stakeholders, and of stakeholders to companies and to one another (Argandoña 2008)[18]: "integral human development is primarily a vocation, and therefore it involves a free assumption of responsibility in solidarity on the part of everyone" (Benedict XVI 2009, 11).

---

[17]The encyclical offers some suggestions for international development programs which, by analogy, are applicable to CSR programs. For example, "solutions need to be carefully designed to correspond to people's concrete lives, based on a prudential evaluation of each situation" (Benedict XVI 2009, 47), etc.

[18]Environmental protection, for instance, is a responsibility of companies, but also of their customers, suppliers, employees, managers, and owners. It will be the company's task to identify and specify the environmental duties that fall within its responsibility, but the company will also need the participation and involvement of all in order to perform those duties.

13.8 It Implies a Conception of the Role of Firms in Society and of the Common Good

If CSR comprises the responsibilities that companies assume voluntarily, not coercively, yet as part of their ethical duties, it somehow entails a conception of the *role of firms in society*, which in turn implies a *conception of the common good*, i.e., "the good of 'all of us', made up of individuals, families and intermediate groups who together constitute society [...] a good that is sought not for its own sake, but for the people who belong to the social community and who can only really and effectively pursue their good within it" (Benedict XVI 2009, 7). In any case, the role of firms in society cannot be detached from the conception of the firms' purpose or objective, mentioned earlier.

13.9 It Is Not to Be Identified with Social Action or Philanthropy

CSR, as presented in the encyclical, is evidently not to be identified with *social action or philanthropy*.[19] The charity that presides over the encyclical from its very first paragraphs is not mere "sentimentality" (Benedict XVI 2009, 3), but a solid virtue that has its origin in God (Benedict XVI 2009, 5). The ethics that inspires CSR is virtue ethics, very different from philanthropy. Certainly, the encyclical stresses the role of *solidarity* – "solidarity is first and foremost a sense of responsibility on the part of everyone with regard to everyone, and it cannot therefore be merely delegated to the State" (Benedict XVI 2009, 38) – but the concept of solidarity in Catholic social teaching is not equivalent to social action or distribution of goods. It includes, of course, "the sharing of goods and resources, from which authentic development proceeds," but this sharing is made possible "by the potential of love that overcomes evil with good (cf. Rom. 12:21), opening up the path towards reciprocity of consciences and liberties" (Benedict XVI 2009, 9). These relations clearly place solidarity far beyond any such sharing of goods.[20]

In any case, the content of CSR is not confined to the acquisition and distribution of material goods, as "authentic human development concerns the whole of the person in every single dimension" (Benedict XVI 2009, 11). It includes "having more"

---

[19] The encyclical contains a very brief reference to the "charitable and educational activities" of the Catholic Church, but points out that the Church's public role is far more ambitious (Benedict XVI 2009, 11). In *Deus caritas est*, the references to the Church's social support activities are more extensive (Benedict XVI 2005, 19ff).

[20] In paragraph 35, it is stated that "without internal forms of solidarity [...], the market cannot completely fulfill its proper economic functions" (Benedict XVI 2009, 35). These "internal forms" of solidarity obviously cannot refer to philanthropy.

(Benedict XVI 2009, 18), but it must not be limited to "mere accumulation of wealth"; rather, it must be "at the service of higher goods" (Benedict XVI 2009, 11), including openness to transcendence ("God is the guarantor of man's true development" Benedict XVI 2009, 29) and spiritual growth (Benedict XVI 2009, 76).

This thesis may seem utopian when applied to an economic institution such as a firm, whose goals appear to be purely material. As we have already pointed out, however, a company's goals include, but go beyond, the purely material, and its responsibilities are also moral, shunning both the "types of messianism which [...] always build their case on a denial of the transcendent dimension of development" (Benedict XVI 2009, 17) and the kind of spiritualism that refuses to acknowledge the role of companies in the satisfaction of human needs and the progress (including material progress) of humanity. The responsibilities included in CSR therefore also relate to people's intrinsic motives, such as the satisfaction of a job well done, participation in social relationships (the "category of relation": Benedict XVI 2009, 53), or the acquisition of knowledge and operational capabilities. Above all, however, they also include the development of attitudes, values, and virtues, i.e., "higher goods" (Benedict XVI 2009, 11), so as to achieve "the good of every man and of the whole man" (Benedict XVI 2009, 18; see also Pérez López 1993). Firms can therefore be expected to have a conception of CSR that does not hinder integral human development in all its dimensions but that contributes positively, where possible, to all of them.

This means that CSR cannot consist merely in achieving results, much less purely material results. As an ethical responsibility, its goal is the improvement of people, starting with those who put CSR into practice and continuing with the rest, i.e., those that benefit from it. In relation to "the 'technical' worldview that [...] is now so dominant that truth has come to be seen as coinciding with the possible," the encyclical points out that "when the sole criterion of truth is efficiency and utility, development is automatically denied" (Benedict XVI 2009, 70).

13.10   It Demands Committed Leaders

The conception of CSR underlying *Caritas in Veritate* is humble, unpretentious, and conscious that "the conviction that man is self-sufficient and can successfully eliminate the evil present in history by his own action alone has led him to confuse happiness and salvation with immanent forms of material prosperity and social action" (Benedict XVI 2009, 34). It does not claim to solve all problems, nor does it offer definitive solutions. It leaves each person to be "the main agent of his own success or failure" (Benedict XVI 2009, 17).

CSR is part of the organizational and managerial task of owners, entrepreneurs, and managers shared by all the people in the company and other stakeholders. To them, the following words from the encyclical can be applied: "development is impossible without *upright men and women*, without financiers and politicians whose consciences are finely attuned to the requirements of the common good.

Both professional competence and moral consistency are necessary" (Benedict XVI 2009, 71). The encyclical concludes that "[d]evelopment needs Christians with their arms raised towards God in prayer, Christians moved by the knowledge that truth-filled love, *Caritas in Veritate*, from which authentic development [the authentic corporate social responsibility] proceeds, is not produced by us, but given to us. For this reason, even in the most difficult and complex times, besides recognizing what is happening, we must above all else turn to God's love. Development requires attention to the spiritual life, a serious consideration of the experiences of trust in God, spiritual fellowship in Christ, reliance upon God's providence and mercy, love and forgiveness, self-denial, acceptance of others, justice and peace" (Benedict XVI 2009, 79).

Bibliography

Abbà, Giuseppe. 1992. *Felicidad, vida buena y virtud*. Barcelona: Ediciones Internacionales Universitarias.

Argandoña, Antonio. 2008. Ethical foundations of corporate social responsibility. In *Responsabilità sociale d'impresa e nuovo umanesimo*, ed. Emilio Bettini and Flaviano Moscarini, 31–56. Genoa: Sangiorgio Editrice.

Argandoña, Antonio. 2010. From action theory to the theory of the firm, Barcelona: IESE, *Working Paper*, WP-855, April.

Argandoña, Antonio, and Heidi von Weltzien-Hoivik. 2009. Corporate social responsibility: One size does not fit all. Collecting evidence from Europe. *Journal of Business Ethics* 89(3): 221–234.

Benedict XVI. 2005. *Encyclical letter deus caritas est*. Vatican: Libreria Editrice Vaticana.

Benedict XVI. 2009. *Encyclical letter caritas in veritate*. Vatican: Libreria Editrice Vaticana.

Donaldson, Thomas, and Lee E. Preston. 1995. The stakeholder theory of the corporation: Concepts, evidence, and implications. *Academy of Management Review* 20(1): 65–91.

John Paul II. 1991. *Encyclical letter centesimus annus*. Vatican: Libreria Editrice Vaticana.

Mullerat, Ramón. 2010. *International corporate social responsibility. The role of corporations in the economic order of the 21st century*. Alphen: Kluwer Law International.

Pérez López, Juan A. 1993. *Fundamentos de la dirección de empresas*. Madrid: Rialp.

Pontifical Council for Justice and Peace. 1994. *Compendium of the social doctrine of the church*. Vatican: Libreria Editrice Vaticana.

Porter, Michael E., and Mark R. Kramer. 2006. Strategy and society: The link between competitive advantage and corporate social responsibility. *Harvard Business Review* 84: 78–92.

Rhonheimer, Martin. 1987. Moral cristiana y desarrollo humano. Sobre la existencia de una moral de lo humano específicamente Cristiana. In *La Misión del Laico en la Iglesia y en el Mundo*, ed. Augusto Sarmiento, Tomás Rincón, José M. Yanguas, and Antonio Quirós, 919–938. Pamplona: Eunsa.

Rhonheimer, Martin. 2001. Is Christian morality reasonable? On the difference between secular and Christian humanism. *Annales Theologici* 15(2): 529–549.

Williams, Oliver F. 1986. Can business ethics be theological? What Athens can learn from Jerusalem. *Journal of Business Ethics* 5: 473–484.

Chapter 14
The Ethical Anchoring of Corporate Social Responsibility and the Critique of CSR*

Stefano Zamagni

In this chapter, two specific questions are dealt with: one, how robust are the critiques against corporate social responsibility (CSR), and the other, which ethical anchoring is capable of offering more solid support for CSR? I will not deal with the history of CSR, a rather recent history all told that usually begins with the pioneering contribution of Bowen in 1953 which contains an early definition of CSR (Chirielieson 2004), nor will I comment on the reasons for which, with the development of globalization beginning in the end of the 1970s, the problematic nature of CSR has exploded onto the scene (Zamagni 2003). Nor will I confront, finally, the contents of corporate social responsibility, what is understood by CSR and the ways of implementing it at the level of firm praxis (Sacconi 2004).

I would like to observe that, notwithstanding the plethora of studies and debates that have taken place over the course of the last quarter century, there still exists no commonly accepted definition of CSR. We are still at the phase of the "privatization" of the definitions, which is at the origin of many interpretative problems and grave miscomprehensions that cause quite often bitter and useless polemics. The fact is that a definition makes sense only if it becomes the common property of a scientific community, since the nature of a definition in a particular field of knowledge is that of a public good. Indeed, the idea of a private definition is an oxymoron.

---

*"The Ethical Anchoring of Corporate Social Responsibility" is republished from L. Zsolnai (ed.), *Interdisciplinary Yearbook of Business Ethics*, vol. 1: 31–51. Oxford: Peter Lang, 2006. A somewhat different version of this essay was published in Italian (Zamagni 2005).

S. Zamagni (✉)
University of Bologna, Bologna, Italy
e-mail: bruna.bordoni@unibo.it

M. Schlag and J.A. Mercado (eds.), *Free Markets and the Culture of Common Good*, Ethical Economy 41, DOI 10.1007/978-94-007-2990-2_14,
© Springer Science+Business Media B.V. 2012

14.1   On the Robustness of the Critique of CSR

It should not be surprising if, among experts in the economic disciplines, but not only, the *fin de non recevoir* still dominates regarding the themes of CSR – it is a fact that the theoretical economic literature, for example, is all but mute about the causal reasons and effects of CSR – and the critiques of the very idea of CSR are frequent, not to mention of its actual application. After more than a century of pronouncements on the thesis of axiological neutrality of economic science, that is, of the affirmation according to which there exists a sphere of social relations – those that take place in the market – that do not need to be subjected to any external ethical judgment what I have just said comes to no surprise. Is it not perhaps true that economic behavior, that of the firm in particular, is in and of itself oriented toward the good, inasmuch as the firm produces value? It follows that economic behavior is different from every other type of human behavior because it eludes morality without, though, being contrary to it. As we will see later, it was the impressive development of the market economy itself and of its most important institution, the firm, that sent into crisis that consoling image that has allowed, for a long time, the economist to work "undisturbed" by concerns of an ethical nature. But it is a fact that such a realization has not yet become common within the profession notwithstanding the mass of events and facts that should indicate a change in course.

Before moving on to the examination of the criticisms of CSR and to their confutations, it is, however, opportune, not to mention intellectually honest, to recognize the positive aspects, the elements of truth contained in those criticisms. I will indicate three. In a recent essay, Beltratti (2003) discusses the case of socially responsible investing – essentially, ethical finance – under the hypothesis that voluntarily renouncing to invest in certain stocks results in lower returns. The problem studied in the paper is that of deciding under which conditions such an investment is capable of changing the equilibrium of the system. The relevance of the problem is that rational agents will accept socially responsible behavior only if, operating this way, they believe they will be able to modify the final equilibrium of the system through the induced effects of their behavior on prices in the stock market and on the curve of equity yields. Let us not forget, in fact, that the familiar hypothesis of rational behavior implies that one aims to maximize the objective for which one acts, but not that that objective must necessarily be profit or one of its variants. Well, Beltratti demonstrates that there is a critical threshold for the level of socially responsible investments, below which the particular objective pursued is not reached. What is the meaning of this result? To suggest that, if the number of firms that accept to adhere to the CSR project does not reach the critical mass, the risk is of reinforcing what the skeptics say, according to which, at the end of the day, what wins in the market is the combination of acquisitive behavior and instrumental rationality on the part of economic agents.

A second element of truth that emerges from the criticisms of CSR is that CSR can sometimes serve as a screen that allows unscrupulous firms to eliminate their rivals or to reduce their competitive force. In brief, the argument is as follows.

Let us assume that on the market, there operate two types of firms, those opportunists and those intrinsically motivated by CSR. Let us assume in addition that the critical consumers, which are today increasing in number everywhere, are willing to reward the latter type of firm and sanction (through boycotts and condemnation campaigns) the former. In situations of this type, it is possible that opportunistic firms decide to behave initially in a manner that is even "more ethical" than the others with the aim of marginalizing them on the market so that they can then eventually return to their old behavior. Let me observe that such eventualities will be all the more probable the more public institutions – such as governments or public agencies – intervene in the process of CSR offering incentives and various forms of economic advantages to firms that agree to conform to the guidelines determined by the public institution. In this case, the heterogenesis of the ends would be assured: CSR would become an instrument for crowding out, that is, for pushing aside the virtuous firms and increasing the monopolistic rent of the opportunistic firms.

Finally, the critics of CSR are right when they denounce the danger that socially responsible behaviors can conceal a dangerous trade-off, namely, a trade-off between moral commitment and social commitment. As we know, the specific logic of CSR is to combine – in the sense of the *ars combinatoria* – the logic of pure business (which says that the only thing that counts for the firm is the economic result as measured by its profit) and the logic of pure philanthropy (which suggests the firm must commit a part of its profits to socially important uses). It is typical of CSR to reject the celebrated dichotomy of J. S. Mill between the laws of production of wealth and the laws of distribution of wealth. A firm is not socially responsible which, while it produces wealth ignores the defense of human rights, the respect for the moral integrity of people, etc., and then becomes compassionately generous in the moment of the distribution of the wealth produced. The noted historical cases of A. Carnegie and J. D. Rockefeller of the USA at the end of the nineteenth century are, along with many others, eloquent examples of what it means, in practice, to accept Mill's dichotomy (Zunz 2002).

Well, the danger that I hinted at above is that with the social commitment, that is, corporate philanthropy, falsely confused with CSR, cynical managers can cover up the absence of moral scruples. And because the capacity for philanthropic donations is correlated to the size of the firm, it could happen that the large pressure groups are able, more easily than the smaller groups, to "buy" the good reputation that is considered necessary to them, except changing the strategy when the competitive scenario becomes particularly severe. One example will make the point clearer. In Enron's *2000 Report on Social Responsibility*, one reads: "We want to work to promote reciprocal respect with the communities and stakeholders that are touched by our activities. We treat others as we would like to be treated." Everybody knows, today, how the celebrated "golden rule" has been applied by Enron!

Let me return to the main argument. What do we find deep down inside the mother of all criticisms of CSR? The vivid affirmation by Friedman that sees in CSR a grave threat to the capitalist system: "Few tendencies can threaten the foundations of our free society like the acceptance by top managers of a social responsibility that goes beyond making as much money as possible for their shareholders"

(Friedman 1962, 133). This thesis has been further advanced in a famous *New York Times* article of September 1970, with the evocative title "The only responsibility that corporations have is to increase profits," in which one reads: "the shortsighted vision is even exemplified in the speeches of businessmen on social responsibility… here, as happens with price and wage controls, businessmen seem to reveal a *suicidal impulse*. The real social responsibility of the firm is to obtain the highest profits – obviously in an open, correct, and competitive market, producing wealth and work for all in the most efficient way possible".[1] (italics added)

More recently and moving in the same direction, Steinberg, in an influential volume writes: "The aim of the firm is not to promote the public good…. If the *nature* of the goods or services or the *mode* in which they are produced has priority over the long-term maximization of value for the shareholder, then the activity in question *is no longer a business activity*" (Steinberg 2000, 36; italics added), and a few pages later: "Just as you have prostitution when you have sex for money, instead of for love, a company prostitutes itself when it pursues love or social responsibility instead of money" (Steinberg 2000, 42).

We must admit that this thesis is not without a certain intellectual appeal. Though, as we will see, it is much less solid than it seems. The central point of the thesis is in the following line of reasoning. The market is the place in which the coordination of economic activity happens through voluntary cooperation. This is due to the fact that "both parties to an economic transaction benefit from it, provided the transaction is bilaterally voluntary and informed" (Friedman 1962, 13). It follows then that when two (or more) parties, in the absence of cheating and coercion, that is, in the condition to choose freely, give life to an economic transaction, those parties also agree to the consequences that derive from that transaction. It can be noted that here lies the ethical justification, in economics, of consequentialism. The notion of consent founded on free choice is well expressed by Posner when he writes: "It is my contention that a person who buys a lottery ticket and then looses has 'consented' to the loss so long as there is no question of fraud or duress" (Posner 1981, 94; quoted in Peter 2004). Therefore, outside of these cases, choosing means giving one's consent, and giving consent means to legitimize. As Peter argues (2004), the market does not therefore need to ask for certificates of legitimacy since the market is capable of self-legitimizing. This is not the case, for example, with the State that – as Peter (2004) observes – needs the approval of the citizens via democratic elections in order to be able to use coercion, which is the way it achieves its objectives.

We are now at the point of arrival of the reasoning: because the firm is the most important institution of the market, the self-legitimacy of the latter is automatically extended to the self-legitimacy of the former. This is why the only social responsibility of the firm is to create wealth and increase profits, respecting the rules of the game. Also because – the critics of CSR add – of objective cognitive limits, the firm

[1] The synthesis of Friedman's thinking on the theme discussed here can be found in Friedman (1993).

is unable to gauge the real interests of its various classes of stakeholders. Citing A. Smith (incorrectly because out of context), who, in *The Wealth of Nations,* had written: "I have never seen that much good has been done by those who declare to do business for the public good" (Book IV, chap. 2), these critics conclude that the only wise thing to do is to let each business – that knows best its own interests – to maximize profit. It will be up to the shareholders, to whom the profits go, to decide freely whether to destine part or all of them to socially useful ends. The more the firm remains a profit machine, the more the cause of the common good is served.

What does not fit in this apparently persuasive argument? First of all, it is not always necessarily true that freedom of choice postulates consent. I agree with Peter (2004) that this would be the case if the choice were not constrained, as is typically the case in economics. The subject that voluntarily (i.e., with no coercion) offers his organs for sale to reduce his suffering due to poverty and hunger certainly would not consent to the consequences that would stem from this act. Free choice has a legitimizing force only if the set of the alternatives among which the agent has to choose is also under the agent's control or, at least, is part of the agent's choice problem. If the menu of choice is given – as it is the case in reality – that condition is certainly not satisfied. In other words, for the prospect of uncoerced choice to found consensus, one requires that everyone agree to the constraints on which each person acts.

As is well known, the centrality of the category of consent is typical of the contractualist school of thought from Hobbes up until Rawls included. The idea is that if I have signed a contract with you – let us say a labor contract – to do something that I no longer want to do, you can always respond: "but then you were in agreement, now you are obligated." That is to say, consent is the foundation of obligation, not simply a procedure to implement or regulate it. However, Rawls (1971) majestically argued that in order that from consent obligation can be born, it is necessary that constraints under which the parties to the social contract make their free choice should be accepted by both. In other words, that which is requested is a justification – legitimacy is not enough – for the constraints, a justification that is agreed upon by all who take part in the social contract. Only if we can show that the subjects have given their consent (or would have a reason for giving their consent) for a certain institutional setup, then one can argue that the agreement is just and therefore obligatory. Now, it is not difficult to understand why this condition is never met in practice in our market economies. Indeed, the freedom of choice describes the absence of any coercion coming from others. It has to do with the *possibility* of choice, which says nothing about the *capability* of choice. This is the message stemming from the work of Sen (1988) when he reminds us that the *use* of freedom is in some way essential to its definition. In arguing that freedom consists in the ability to realize self-determined ends, Sen (1999) incorporates a substantive claim into his analysis of freedom: an agent's freedom is directly linked to what opportunity he/she has to realize his/her ends. It follows that the opportunity set an individual is presented with is as important to evaluating its freedom as it is its autonomy in decision making.

More can be said on the issue at stake. The syllogism on which Friedman's thesis rests – that the market is self-legitimizing and that the firm is the main pillar of market; ergo, the firm is also self-legitimizing – takes for granted something which is in reality not so, that is, that the organizational principle of the market is the same as that for the firm. Which is not the case, because while the market postulates horizontal and symmetrical relationships among all that take part to it – if it was not like this, the contract could not be its principle instrument – the internal organization of the firm is founded, today as yesterday, on the principle of hierarchy, so much so that command is the firm's main instrument. This is a point that R. Coase had already clearly illustrated in his celebrated essay, *The Nature of the Firm*, in 1937, when he argued that the firm and the market are two alternative institutions, a point that has been recently reiterated by Zingales: "Governance is synonymous with the exercise of authority, management and control. These words sound strange, however, when they are used in the context of a free market economy. Why do we need any form of authority? Is it not, by chance, true that the market is responsible for the efficient allocation of all the resources without the intervention of authority?" (Zingales 1998, 497). I therefore conclude that the most insidious weapon that the critics of CSR have at their disposal is truly blunted.

Now, I will pass to the second aporia present in the reasoning that I am examining. Even if we leave aside the first aporia, the anti-CSR thesis would make sense, and would even have a bit of weight, *if* the markets, both of inputs and outputs, were perfectly competitive; *if* income distribution were equitable, at least in the minimal sense of allowing everybody to participate in the market game; and *if* the preferences of the economic agents went unchanged with respect to the carrying out of the economic activity. Well, the same economic textbooks teach us that these are three very heavy conditions, none of which are ever satisfied in a real economy. In particular, it is well known that preferences do indeed change endogenously. Whenever this is the case, it might happen that the individual finds itself forced by rationality to follow a course of action which, by the agent's own standards, is inefficient, that is, reduces its wellbeing. As shown by Yaari (1977), if in an exchange process an agent, even if it is endowed with perfect information and perfect foresight, is in a position where behaving inefficiently is the only rational thing to do, then the exchange process contains an ethical fault. Arrow's paper (1973) by providing a very effective account of the reasons, why the three conditions above are never met, contains (perhaps) the first economic justification for enterprise ethical codes. It would be proper, at this stage, to shed some light on the paradox that the anti-CSR line of thought brings us to.

An antique idea of economic science, one that has touched almost all schools of thought – but not, for example, the Austrian school – is that which sees the economy as a separate space, different from both the political space and the space of civil society. Where does this idea reveal itself? In the conviction on the basis of which the economic variables (prices, quantities, income, asset values, etc.) can fluctuate from one period to the other and can be impacted on by events in the fields of politics and social relations. But, in the long-run, such variables tend however to approach their standard of reference, determined by market fundamentals, as one would say in the current jargon. There are different theories that explain how these standards are determined, but the conviction is that prices and market magnitudes cannot go too far, or indefinitely, from their specific attractor, whatever it may be.

Clearly, only a conception of the economic system as a field of human interaction separate from the rest of society can give meaning to propositions of this kind. Because in the same moment in which we speak of *market fundamentals*, we affirm that the market possesses its own dynamic, not disturbed by the other social dynamics. In fact, if it were not like this, how could we speak of market "fundamentals?" Today we know that this is not the case, but this is not my point. Rather, my point regards the above-mentioned paradox. The anti-CSR thesis presupposes, for its own validity, the existence of both perfectly competitive markets (first condition) and market fundamentals (third condition). But if this were the case, in a long-run competitive equilibrium, profits would be zero, as Leon Walras already demonstrated in 1874 with his theory of general economic equilibrium. That is like saying, that in order to be right, Friedman and the other scholars that see themselves in his position – the only social responsibility for a firm is to increase profits – must presuppose conditions under which firms do not attain any more profits!

Finally, I come to a third aporia inherent in the argument of the CSR critics. These authors all agree on one point: that the pursuit of profit by the firm must happen with full respect for the rules of the economic game and in particular of the legal norms in vigor. If we think well enough about it, this is just circular reasoning. It is clear, in fact, that *if* the rules of the economic game were complete; *if* the processes of lawmaking were able to follow, quickly enough, the evolution of the economic happenings in phases of accelerated social dynamics like the one we are living in; and *if* all this were assured, then it would be true that it would make no sense to talk about CSR. But the necessity of CSR is born by the fact that these circumstances are never met, as everyone knows. It is exactly because the contracts are basically incomplete and because markets do not always exist that agency problems and problems stemming from abuse of authority on the part of those who possesses the residual rights of control emerge in reality (Sacconi 2003).

To put it another way, it is of course true that allowing the firm, which definitively knows its own good better than anyone else, to pursue it freely and then leave it up to the market to direct individual interests toward the common good, would be an intelligent strategy. But this is true only if the economic game were played inside *civil* and *just* institutions, as the tradition of the civil economy, long before A. Smith, had understood and explained (Bruni and Zamagni 2007). It is when civil and just institutions do not yet exist, or they are incomplete and imperfect, that the pursuit of the common good requires something more and different from the mere pursuit of interest. In a well-known passage, Smith writes of the "obvious and simple system of natural liberty" where each one "is left perfectly free to pursue his own interest in his own way" and to interact with others by bringing "both his industry and capital into competition with those of any other man." However, Smith puts a double constraint to his account. The first, which is most of the time overlooked, is the requirement that the individual is free to pursue his own interest "as long as he does not violate the laws of justice." The one constraint is a constraint of social benefit: although each one "intends only his own gain ... he is ... led by an invisible hand to promote an end which was no part of his intention... By pursuing his own interest, he frequently promotes that of the society more effectually than when he really intends to promote it." Thus, Smith places the self-interest behavior within the double constraints of justice and of social benefit. This is why a truly socially responsible firm is that which cooperates to define a civil ethic that will be able to favor the emergence of forms of organizational condensation from which civil and just institutions can emerge. Acting in respect of *given* rules is not enough, when those rules need to be changed.

14.2 The Ethical Anchoring of CSR

That the concept of responsibility finds, today, many difficulties in being accepted, let alone applied, is all told understandable. On one hand, globalization is increasing, in unprecedented ways, the distance between action and the ultimate consequences of the action. One thinks about the impact of processes of mergers and acquisitions on the phenomenon of "short-termism": firms fearing takeovers tend to pay scarce attention to all that does not have a return in the short run – including social responsibility. On the other hand, the new technologies that connote the third industrial revolution tend to reduce the sense of responsibility in so far as they tend to increase the number and typology of the unpredictable consequences of the actions. The notion of responsibility is strictly connected to that of accountability. Responsible is one who knows how to manage situations, adequately evaluating their risks and results. But the current technological changes render this exercise ever more difficult, if not impossible. As Baumann wrote: "today, the organization in its own is a tool for canceling responsibility" (Baumann 1992, 225). Therefore, it should not be surprising if there are still many doubts, first of all cultural, with regard to CSR on the part of both academics and business people.

In what follows, I will critically examine the four ethical theories that – often unknown even to many of their users – hold up the various positions on CSR present in the current debate.

14.2.1 Personal and Firm Ethics

Why should the firm ever act in a *socially* responsible way if no canon of economic rationality exists that justifies that behavior? Is it not perhaps sufficient a personal ethics based on the principle of intentionality that reduces ethical questions to interpersonal relations? According to the ethics of intentions – upon which many critics of CSR base their arguments – an action is defined as good when it conforms to two rules: the proximate rule (conscience) and the remote rule (the law). The person who, harmonizing conscience and the law, behaves accordingly, commits a morally good act. It is the intentions, and not only the consequences, of action that must come under the definition of ethical behavior. That is like saying, the ends justify the consequences. This is where the famous expression, that sums this up nicely, comes from: *good business is good ethics*. The firm that turns a lot of profit is also highly responsible because, creating wealth, it allows well-intentioned people to pursue their goals. There is no better illustration of this way of thinking than Andrew Carnegie, the great American philanthropic capitalist, whose methods of doing business were anything but civil. In his *The Gospel of Wealth* of 1889, one reads: "Wealth concentrated in the hands of one man alone is the result of the labor of an entire community and must go back to that community in one way or another. The rich person is the custodian of a fortune, and that must be at the disposal of the common good, and his career *must be divided into two parts*: acquisition and distribution" (Cited in Picard 1999, 26; italics added).

What is the principal limit of such an ethical theory? That it does not give enough weight to the induced and indirect effects of individual actions. If my activity, though guided by good intentions, generates negative externalities that fall on other subjects, the act which was subjectively just becomes objectively, that is ideopraxically unjust. Deciding to entrust my savings to a financial institution so that it maximizes my rate of return is a just act according to the criteria of the proximate and remote rule. But if that institution invests my savings in any one of the many illicit ways, the act in question is objectively censurable. This means that the anticipation of the effects of an action is an integral part of ethical behavior. More in general, the fact that the firm operates today in a system in which it is the globalized market that constrains, more than ever before, the economic agents is not a sufficient reason for freeing them from their social obligations. Also because one cannot want that the market is, at the same time, the place of maximum entrepreneurial freedom and such a constraining place that it renders firms socially irresponsible. Thinking in this way would bring us to a pragmatic contradiction.

14.2.2 Enlightened Self-Interest

An ethical theory that seeks to remediate some of the deficiencies just highlighted is that of *enlightened self-interest*. Because of the tight interconnection between external environment and the firm, if it wants to compete successfully in the long term in the market, cannot avoid taking into consideration the needs of the context in which it operates, and in particular those of its stakeholders. Just as that version of utilitarianism known as social utilitarianism suggests, *good ethics is good business*. This is like saying ethics pays in one way or another. Cochran wrote to explain the difficulties of development in the western United States in the second half of the nineteenth century: "the low level of business ethics among many American entrepreneurs was a grave impediment both to economic efficiency and raising capital" (Cochran 1964, 96). The famous economic historian Rostow (1961) pushes himself so far as to claim that the root cause of the Great Depression was a lack of ethical behavior on behalf of the economic leadership.

The ethical theory in question represents certainly a step forward but too short of a step to be interesting. Reducing social responsibility to just another constraint to the strategic management of the firm, the enlightened self-interest approach inverts the natural order of things. Instead of being a presupposition or a guideline for economic action, ethics becomes in fact a consequence of economic success. An explanation should be attempted. According to this theory, ethical behavior is visualized as a superior good in the sense that the demand for such a good grows at a larger rate than income and vice-versa. (The demand income elasticity is larger than one.) The more people become rich, the more the need, or the demand, for ethical behavior grows, and vice-versa. Consider now the case of a firm that competes on the global markets and that intends to put CSR procedures into practice. If its rivals, through illicit behavior (e.g., the use of child labor) are able to lower production costs and therefore the selling price, there will be a reduction in income for the firm in question. The latter will then lower the demand for ethical behavior until this is brought in line with average behavior. In situation of this type, the strategy that Shleifer (2004) suggests adopting is to accelerate, as quickly as possible, the process of income growth, through an intensification of the levels of competition and without too many moral scruples (better to use child labor, e.g., than to see people die of hunger). The increase in the disposition to "pay" for higher ethical levels would come as a consequence.

But if ethics is simply a by-product of economic growth – Marx would have said a superstructure of the economic structure – what sense would there be in talking about CSR? And why speak ever of ethical behavior as an ulterior constraint under which to maximize long-run profits if ethics is a consequence of economic results? As it can be understood, the above line of reasoning is opposite to the great Socratic message according to which virtue is not born out of riches; on the contrary from virtue itself derive all the riches and all the other good things to men.

14.2.3 Ethics of Responsibility

The moral theory, currently more in vogue in studies of CSR, is the ethics of responsibility as interpreted by the well-known stakeholder model. We can consider Max Weber the father of such a theory who, in his celebrated essay, *Politics as a Profession,* indicates the ethics that must characterize "he who wants to place his hands on the gears of history" (Weber 1969, 101). Adding, a few pages later, that responsibility is the "willingness to respond to the *foreseeable* consequences of one's actions" (Weber 1969, 109). To the Weberian formulation of the ethics of responsibility, Jonas (1990) has added an important qualification. Basing his idea on a "heuristic of fear," Jonas does not consider it sufficient to stop only at the foreseeable consequences; one must go further and take into account the *possible* consequences of its actions. The appropriate imperative for the new type of human action is, for Jonas: "to act in such a way that the effects of your action are compatible with the continuation of an authentically human life." From the Kantian imperative "you can, because you must," we pass to "you must, because you can."

It is not difficult to understand the meaning of Jonas' qualification. Limiting oneself only to the control of the foreseeable effects of one's actions is too little in economic contexts in which the *proprium* of the entrepreneurial function is to continuously generate unforeseeable effects. On the other hand, is it not perhaps in this – as Schumpeter had acutely anticipated – the basic difference between entrepreneur and *rentier* or bureaucrat? Think, in addition, about the possibility, which is enormously greater today with respect to the past, of so-called "rational errors" made by the firm. As experience suggests, the cost of such errors too often exceeds the monetary value of the capital conferred by shareholders. In cases like this, the calculation of the foreseeable consequences does not constitute a solid anchoring for the notion of responsibility. (Think about the corporate scandals of Enron and Parmalat, among the many others.)

Well, it is on such a foundation that stakeholder theory affirmed itself, beginning in the 1960s. In the words of its most representative exponents, Evan and Freeman (1988): "We believe that the legal, economic and moral challenges to the current theory of the firm require a revision in an essentially Kantian perspective. This means that each group of stakeholders has the right not to be treated as a means oriented toward some end, but must participate in the determination of the future direction of the firm." (Evan and Freeman 1988, 101). It follows that the objective of the firm is not the maximization, under constraints, of profit, as is the case in the shareholder theory. The latter defends the position according to which the shareholders, being ultimately responsible for the destiny of the firm, have the right to a special and different consideration with respect to other classes of stakeholders. Rather, "the authentic objective of the firm… is that of operating as a vehicle for *coordinating* the interests of the stakeholders" (Evan and Freeman 1988, 104, italics added).

The primary task of management is therefore to operate for the realization of a balancing of different interests: "Management is the bearer of a financial relationship that links it closely to the stakeholders as much as to the firm as an abstract entity. Management is asked to act in the interest of the stakeholders as if it was an agent of theirs and must act in the interest of the business to guarantee its survival, safeguarding in the long-term the shares of each group" (Evan and Freeman 1988, 104). Finally, in a very recent essay, Freeman, after having reaffirmed that "the firm is a *nexus of relationships* among groups that have an interest in its activities," adds: "The firm has to do with the world in which clients, families, employees, investors (shareholders, bondholders, banks), local community, and managers interact and create value. To understand the firm, one must understand how these relationships function" (Freeman 2004, 1). From this follows the conclusion that the central objective of stakeholder theory is that of studying how to make the interests of the various stakeholders move in the same direction. "The creation of value and not the conflict of value is the metaphor of reference" (Freeman 2004, 1).

But how to achieve the compatibilization of the interests of all those who, inasmuch as they are bearers of specific investments (finance capital, human capital, trust, social capital, etc.), cooperate within the firm for the creation of value? In other words, how is to respond to the objections of many, and in particular of M. Jensen and K. Goodposter,[2] according to whom a multi-stakeholder model of governance would leave the managers confused, without the so-called bottom line which can be utilized to evaluate their performance?

As Sacconi (2004) indicates, the response is the social contract among all the stakeholders as a *normative* device for defining the contents of CSR. The Rawlsian contractualist version of stakeholder theory, as opposed to the original Kantian version, is capable of supplying a criterion for judgment, not only of the legitimacy of the firm as an institution, but also of its strategic management. Asking the interested subjects if they would give their consent to being part of a firm in a state of nature in which they were guided only by enlightened self-interest – and not also by conventions and traditions – Rawlsian contractualism allows for the identification of a bargaining equilibrium. The fundamental property of such an equilibrium is that each stakeholder would accept it in order to cooperate voluntarily, given that it would be the expression of an impartial procedure in which the moral equality of all the participants would be assured. The normative force of contractualism is, therefore, in linking justice (or equity) to consensus without renouncing the rational calculus. In formal terms, instead of maximizing the profit function, the firm maximizes the function that represents the solution to the negotiation game among all the stakeholders. Sacconi (2003) demonstrates how, under reasonable conditions, such a solution exists, in general.

Everything is okay, then, regarding the possibility of using CSR as a model of enlarged governance of the firm? Not quite, because once the fiduciary obligations of the firm regarding its stakeholders are identified, there still remains the problem of their practical application. What is to guarantee, in fact, that the obligations decided upon in the social contract will be effectively met? Let us assume that following the deliberative process that brought the stakeholders to agree to the social contract, the firm decides to give itself an ethical code or something similar. What is to assure that the self-imposition of some canon of behavior fixed in the ethical code is, in reality, respected? The answer the literature is able to give is based on the mechanism of reputation: the firm that self-inflicts the sanctions called for by the ethical code following defective behavior will see its reputational capital grow in the eyes of all of its stakeholders, and this will improve its economic performance, for obvious reasons.

As Sacconi has observed (2004), things would happen this way if it were not for the fact that the reputational mechanism suffers from grave cognitive fragility. It would require that the awareness of the stakeholders, and in particular of the consumers and civil society, were perfect, in order that they would be able to decide if that which was supposed to have been done was done. On the other hand, one cannot forget that the ethical horizon of contractualism is always that of axiological

---

[2] The "paradox of the stakeholder" of Goodpaster goes like this: on the one hand, the manager is paid by the shareholders so that he looks out for their best interests (that is to maximize profit); on the other hand, the manager must act so as to balance the interests of all (Goodpaster 1998).

individualism; according to which the normative foundation is the impartial agreement of rational individuals. In other words, in the contractualist view, rational individuals realize that it is in their interest – whatever that may be – to agree on common norms of behavior to avoid phenomena such as free-riding, shirking, and the many difficulties of coordination. This is tantamount to say that the ethical code is visualized as a *rational constraint* that the firm imposes on itself. It is nonetheless always a constraint. And therefore if, given the contextual conditions, there is a chance of transgressing the norms without penalty, that is, without tarnishing the firm's reputation, this will occur.

14.2.4 Ethic of Virtues

It is at this point that the fourth ethical theory to which I referred at the beginning of the section comes into play. This is the ethic of virtues, as Adam Smith, on the heels of the line of thought inaugurated by the civil humanists in the fifteenth century, elaborated in his fundamental work *The Theory of Moral Sentiments (1759)*. The institutional structure of society – says Smith – must favor the dissemination among citizens of the civic virtues. If economic agents do not already embody in their structure of preferences those values that they are supposed to respect, there is not much to be done. For the ethic of virtues, in fact, the enforceability of the norms depends, in the first place, on the moral constitution of individuals; that is of their internal motivational structure, much before any system of exogenous enforcement. It is because there are stakeholders that have ethical preferences – that attribute, that is, value to the fact that the firm practices equity and works for the dignity of people *independently* of the material advantage that can be derived – that the ethical code could be respected *also* in the absence of the mechanism of reputation. And that there are subjects endowed with ethical preferences is, today, a fact documented by a dispassionate observation of reality, other than by experimental research.[3]

Consider, to give just one example, the relationship between a company and its employees. As is well known, this relationship can assume the forms of the "social exchange" or "market exchange." In the former case, immaterial elements like loyalty, honesty, and attachment to the mission enter into play. These elements cannot be negotiated, since they are nonverifiable. In the latter case, everything passes through the definition of "optimal" schemes. Now, there is nobody who does not realize that there is a great difference, as far as the company performance is concerned, between the two types of relationship. But it is evident that the worker will accept to enter into a "social exchange" instead of a "market exchange" only if the firm will appear to him to be a moral subject that believes in and puts into practice the principle of reciprocity.

---

[3] For a review, see Fehr and Fischbacher (2002) and the essays in Sacco and Zamagni (2002).

The point worth highlighting in particular is that the key to the ethic of virtues is in its capacity to resolve the opposition between self-interest and interest for others, between egoism and altruism, by moving beyond it. It is this opposition, child of the individualistic tradition of thought, that prevents us from grasping that which constitutes our own well-being. The virtuous life is the best not only for others – like the various economic theories of altruism would have it – but also for us. This is the real significance of the notion of common good, which can never be reduced to a mere sum total of individual well-beings. Instead, the common good is the good of being in common. That is, the good of being inserted into a structure of common action, which is exactly what the firm represents.

Viola (2004) suggests that common is the action that, in order to be carried out, requires both the *intentional* coming together of many subjects (and of which all the participants are aware) and of intersubjective relationships that lead to a certain unification of efforts. More precisely, three are the elements that distinguish a common action. The first is that it cannot be concluded without all those who take part being conscious of what they are doing. The mere coming together or meeting of many individuals is not enough. The second element is that each participant in the common action must retain title, and therefore responsibility, for that which he does. It is exactly this element that differentiates common action from collective action. In the latter, in fact, the individual's identity disappears, and with him disappears also personal responsibility for that which he does. The third element is the unification of the efforts on the part of the participants in the common action for the achievement of the same objective. The interaction among many subjects in a given context is not yet common activity if they follow diverse or conflicting objectives. Therefore, the firm, in as much as it possesses all three of these elements, is a common action.

Diverse are the types of common action in relation to the object of commonness. The commonness, in fact, can realize itself around the means or around the ends of the action itself. When the commonness is extended to the end of the action – as happens in the firm – the final result of the action has the nature of a true joint product. This means that it is de facto impossible to determine the specific contribution of each stakeholder. This was attempted more than a century ago by the neoclassical theory of distribution of income with the principle of marginal productivity of factors, but with rather scarce success as we know, nowadays (Screpanti and Zamagni 2005). Note that while in the contract – which is another example of common action – the commonness is limited to the means (each party accepts that the other will pursue his/her own ends, even if the ends are not the same), in the firm the end is realized through common action. This is why in the firm cooperation – and not coordination – is the principal form that intersubjectivity assumes. The contracts have to be coordinated, but the stakeholders in a firm must cooperate if they want to achieve an optimal result. The question then arises: how is one to positively resolve a problem of cooperation? Bratman (1999) gives a convincing response, when he outlines the following three conditions. In the first place, each participant in the common action assumes that the intentions of others are relevant, and therefore worthy of respect, and knows that this is reciprocal. This is the condition of "mutual responsiveness." It is not enough that the members intend to do the same activity; they must want to do it together. In the second place, each person commits to a joint activity – even if for different reasons – and knows that the others also intend to do the same. This means "commitment to the joint activity," in which it is de facto impossible to quantify the specific contribution of each person to the joint product. Finally, each person commits to helping others in their efforts so that the final result will be the best possible "(commitment to mutual support)." Reciprocal aid must manifest itself while the joint activity is being carried out, not *a latere*, not at the end of the activity. Such a commitment should not be confused with self-interest nor with disinterested altruism. There being a connection of interests, by providing help to others one pursues one's own interests.

Now, we can appreciate the specific value that the ethic of virtues offers us, that is, to liberate us from the obsessive Platonic idea of good, an idea that says there is an a priori good from which an ethic is extracted to be used as a guide to our actions. Aristotle – the initiator of the ethic of virtues – in total disagreement with Plato, indicates for us instead that the good is something that happens and that is realized through activities. As Lutz (2003) puts it, the most serious problem with the various theories of business ethics stemming from the individualistic tradition of thought is that they are not capable of offering a reason for "being ethical." If it is not good for us to behave ethically, why do what is recommended by ethics? On the other hand, if it is good for us to "be ethical," then why would it be necessary to offer managers incentives for doing that which is in their own interest to do? The solution to the problem of moral motivation of managers is not that of setting constraints (or providing incentives)[4] for acting against their self-interest, but to offer them a more complete understanding of their own well-being. Only when ethics becomes part of the objective function of the agents does moral motivation cease to be a problem, because we are authentically motivated to do that which we believe is best for ourselves.

This is why cultivating civic virtues is the undeniable task not only from the point of view of citizenship – something known for a long time – but also from the point of view of CSR. Since institutions, contrary to what the theorists of market fundamentals think, influence economic performance also in the long term, the task is to intervene in the institutional setup of society in order to encourage – and not penalize, as happens stupidly today – the largest possible dissemination of civic virtues through education and actual deeds. The results will then follow, notwithstanding what the skeptic thinks. For the skeptic, the managers, under pressure from the movement of ideas that have come about around CSR, will attempt to imitate or mimic behavior inspired by the ethic of virtues, though continuing to not really believe. This way – the skeptic reasons – market competition will select, according to the circumstances, those corporate cultures which are founded on those values that will demonstrate to be most profitable. Today, we know, both theoretically and

---

[4] One observes that an incentive, like a constraint, is always the expression of a relationship of power. That which changes is only the form with which the power is expressed.

empirically, that things do not proceed this way. The "cynical" manager who, without believing it, behaves like a "virtuous" manager, sooner or later will begin to perceive himself/herself as *homo reciprocans* – just as the theory of self-attribution teaches (Schlicht 2002) – stopping from behaving in a merely opportunistic way. Therefore, if the market is capable of "recompensating" in a coherent way what I call the civil culture of the firm, in the long run both the dispositional and the motivational structure of the economic agents – managers included – will adapt as a consequence. This is not an insignificant advantage of the approach of moral evolution according to which the affirmation of the values of CSR ultimately depends on the process through which these values are edified as virtues.

Bibliography

Arrow, Kenneth J. 1973. Social responsibility and economic efficiency. *Public Policy* 21: 303–318.

Baumann, Z. 1992. *Modernità e Olocausto*. Bologna: Il Mulino.

Beltratti, A. 2003. Socially responsible investment in general equilibrium. Milano: Fond. Eni Enrico Mattei Working Paper.

Bratman, M. 1999. Shared cooperative activity. In *Faces of intention*, ed. M. Bratman. Cambridge: CUP.

Bruni, L., and S. Zamagni. 2007. *Civil economy*. Oxford: P. Lang.

Buchanan, J., and G. Tullock. 1962. *The calculus of consent*. Ann Arbor: University of Michigan Press.

Chirieleinson, C. 2004. L'evoluzione del concetto di corporate social responsibility. In *La responsabilità sociale di impresa*, ed. G. Rusconi and M. Dorigatti. Milano: F. Angeli.

Cochran, T.C. 1964. *The inner revolution*. New York: Harper & Row.

Evan, W., and R.E. Freeman. 1988. *Ethical theory and business*. Englewood Cliffs: Prentice Hall.

Fehr, E., and V. Fischbacher. 2002. Why social preferences matter. The impact of non-selfish motives on competition, cooperation and incentives. *The Economic Journal* 112: C1–C33.

Friedman, M. 1962. *Capitalism and freedom*. Chicago: University of Chicago Press.

Friedman, M. 1993. The social responsabilità of business is to increase its profits. In *An introduction to business ethics*, ed. G.D. Chrissides and J.H. Keler. London: Chapman.

Freeman, R.E. 2004. *Stakeholder theory: the state of the art*. University of Virginia, Working Paper.

Good Paster, K. 1998. Business ethics and stakeholder analysis. In *Corporations, persons and morality*. New York: Free Press.

Jonas, H. 1990. *Il principio responsabilità*. Torino: Einaudi.

Lutz, D. 2003. Beyond business ethics. *Oikonomia* 2: 1–15.

Peter, F. 2004. Choice, consent and the legitimacy of market transactions. *Economics and Philosophy* 20: 1–18.

Picard, J.F. 1999. *La Foundation Rochefeller et la Recherche Midicale*. Paris: PUF.

Posner, R. 1981. *The economics of justice*. Cambridge, MA: Harvard University Press.

Rawls, J. 1971. *A Theory of Justice*. Cambridge (Mass): Harvard University Press.

Rostow, E.V. 1961. To whom and for what ends is corporate management responsible? In *The corporation in modern society*, ed. E.S. Mason. Cambridge, MA: Harvard University Press.

Sacco, P., and S. Zamagni (eds.). 2002. *Complessità relazionale e comportamento economico*. Bologna: Il Mulino.

Sacconi, L. 2003. L'autoregolazione dell'economia via norme etiche. *Etica e Economia* XIII: 1–2.

Sacconi, L. 2004. Responsabilità sociale come governance allargata d'impresa. In *La responsabilità sociale dell'impresa*, ed. G. Rusconi and M. Dorigatti. Milano: F. Angeli.

Schleifer, A. 2004. Does Competition destroy ethical behaviour? National Bureau of Economic Research, Working Paper 10269.

Schlicht, E. 2002. Social evolution, corporate culture and exploitation. Forschungsinstitut zur Zukunft der Arbeit GmbH (IZA) DP GS1.

Screpanti, E., and S. Zamagni. 2005. *An outline of the history of economic thought*. Oxford: Oxford University Press.

Sen, A. 1988. Freedom of choice: Concept and content. *European Economic Review* 32: 280–299.

Sen, A. 1999. *Development as freedom*. New York: Random House.

Steinberg, E. 2000. *Just business ethics in action*. Oxford: Oxford University Press.

Viola, F. 2004. *Il modello della cooperazione*. Palermo: Mimeo.

Weber, M. 1969. In *Il lavoro intellettuale come professione*, ed. A. Giolitti. Torino: Einaudi.

Yaari, M. 1977. On Endogenous changes of preferences. Erkantis, XX, 3.

Zamagni, S. 2005. La critica delle critiche alla CSR e il suo ancoraggio etico. In *Guida Critica alla Responsabilità Sociale e al Governo d'impresa*, ed. L. Sacconi. Roma: Bancaria Editrice.

Zamagni, S. 2003. L'impresa socialmente responsabile nell'epoca della globalizzazione. *Notizie di Politeia* 72: 28–42.

Zingales, L. 1998. Corporate governance. In *New Palgrave dictionary of economics and law*. London: Macmillan.

Zunz, O. 2002. *Perché il secolo americano?* Bologna: Il Mulino.

Chapter 15
Can CSR, Market Efficiency, and Financial Rewards Interact Positively in Periods of Crisis?

Youssef El-Khalil

15.1 Corporate Social Behavior in Economic Theory, Religion, and Philosophy

Although generally perceived as a recent notion, corporate social behavior (CSB), corporate citizenship, and corporate social responsibility (CSR), as it is variously called, ought not to be understood as alien to the concept of the market.

The market is not an invention but a social institution that has developed with time, continuously adjusting, reacting to developments, accommodating to aspirations, bending to realities, and incorporating new concepts while periodically introducing and amending formal rules, regulations, and laws.

As a model, the "perfect market" incorporates essential notions to function well. Efficiency and the smooth functioning of the "market mechanism" require a set of assumptions entailing that economic agents meet on equal terms, that perfect information prevails, that no prejudices exist, that a large number of institutions prevail, and that free entry to and free withdrawal from the marketplace are assured. As all economists very early learn, these assumptions are necessary to ensure a perfect competition in which all economic agents are "price takers," none of whom is big enough to be able to affect market prices. Economists are also taught that when the so-called necessary assumptions prevail, resources are allocated in the most efficient way; society will be placed on its "production possibility frontier," and Pareto efficiency will be reached where utility shall be maximized as the utility of any one agent could not be increased without decreasing that of another.

Y. El-Khalil (✉)
Executive Director, Banque du Liban, Central Bank of Lebanon, Beirut, Lebanon

Lecturer, American University of Beirut (AUB), Beirut, Lebanon, London
e-mail: ykhalil@bdl.gov.lb

M. Schlag and J.A. Mercado (eds.), *Free Markets and the Culture of Common Good*, Ethical Economy 41, DOI 10.1007/978-94-007-2990-2_15,
© Springer Science+Business Media B.V. 2012

Furthermore, economics has recognized, since Adam Smith, the existence of "externalities," which occur whenever the economic activities of agents affect others without those others being compensated – in the case of the production of negative externalities – or sharing in the costs – in the case of positive externalities. Adam Smith suggested governments should intervene to "internalize" externalities by curbing negative externalities (e.g., pollution) or increasing the production of positive ones (e.g., inventions). Nobel Prize laureate, Ronald Coase, proved about two centuries later that externalities could be internalized without government intervention if rights were well defined and the costs of negotiation were affordable (Coase 1960). Economists proposed the "NEW" (Net Economic Welfare) concept more than 40 years ago. An alternative to GDP, to the latter is added the negative values of the environmental and human harms undertaken during the process of production and the positive values of unpaid labor.

The above assumptions, rules, and concepts can easily be conceived as paving the way to the chapters of intervention that characterizes social corporate behavior. People meeting on equal terms means decreasing all kinds of differences pertaining to race, color, connections, social status, or inheritance that can favor one economic agent with respect to another. Perfect information prevailing is associated not only with prices but with technology and education. Free entry to the marketplace means access to credit and to free local and international trade. Price takers can best be identified with small- and medium-sized enterprises in today's terminology whereas negative externalities mostly fit within the chapter of damage to the environment. These factors provide for the major features of programs with which SCB is associated in the realms of education for the vulnerable, equal opportunity hiring programs, microcredit, fair trade with less developed countries, environmental programs, and responsible corporate behavior in general.

Praise of action in favor of the social good is not limited to economics. Religion in general imposes ethical codes of action on believers. The Old Testament, the Gospel, and the Quran abound in precepts imposing a code of conduct in which a just, uncorrupted attitude, complemented by sympathy toward the other, is required from the abiding follower.

The encyclical letter *Caritas in Veritate* stresses the integration of truth and charity within Christianity. Establishing peace and justice requires adhering to the divine project as incarnated by Christ. To be able to go beyond sentimentalism and in order to have a universal outreach, our behavior has to be guided by the binding together of Truth and Logos. Christian action, according to this logic, casts together Love and Reason in order to achieve the divine project (Benedict XVI 2009).

For Islam, justice is a key word from which other essential concepts derive. The word "balance" appears in many a Surat in the Quran, with the meaning of the word stretching from direct physical accurate weighing for the trader to the divine's just weighing of the mortal's deeds on earth in order to be judged in the aftermath. The importance of justice is ultimately illustrated by the fact that the "just" is one of God's holy names. Man, in his earthly life, is ordered to be "just" in commerce, in his testimony, when treating his peers and family, when distributing charity, etc. Social justice for Islam stems from three values: the principle of absolute spiritual liberation from subjection and humiliation, the principle of equality in rights, and the principle of social solidarity. From these three principles derive Islam's social policy of providing basic needs to the needy and defending the vulnerable through a complex system of taxation and redistributive spending (El-Khalil 2009).

Philosophy, from its side, has always pondered about the causes and effects of altruism in its seemingly contradictory aspect of serving self-interests and serving the other, with clear links to biological, psychological, and socioeconomic dimensions. In answer to Hobbes' positions toward the human attitude, David Hume and Adam Smith see morality at the heart of man. Altruism goes beyond a one-to-one relationship and becomes a dynamic interaction with the "other" as a human being. Altruism is seen as a reflection of man's ability to project oneself in the misery of the other and to identify oneself with him. Do we help the other in expectation of reciprocity? Not for Hume and Smith, who stress the gratification and the joy of giving. As the famous saying of Adam Smith puts it: "And hence it is, that to feel much for others and little for ourselves, that to restrain our selfishness, and to indulge our benevolent affections, constitutes the perfection of human nature...As to love our neighbor as we love ourselves is the great law of Christianity, so it is the great precept of nature to love ourselves only as we love our neighbor, or what comes to the same thing, as our neighbor is capable of loving us" (Smith 2002, Chap. V). It may be that altruism, as an intrinsic tendency, acts as a mechanism for self-preservation of humanity.

15.2 The Integration of Corporate Social Behavior in Business Management

Philanthropy, which used to be traditionally linked to the public relations department in a typical corporation, has ceded its way to CSR, which is now often initiated and fostered by CEOs. By 2008, the majority of the FTSE companies were publishing CSR annual reports, while virtually all global corporations had a CSR policy or department (The Economist 2008a). It is not uncommon anymore for giant retailers (Marks and Spencer) to announce medium-term plans with dozens of projects ranging from promoting education in Third World countries to cutting down on CO_2 emissions or increasing an offering of organic food (The Economist 2008c).

Corporate social behavior emerged as a "branded" concept in the 1990s. Globalization, with its spectacular increase in international trade, has been characterized as well by the unprecedented surge in the ability to exchange information. This, in turn, has participated in the increase of citizen awareness with respect to issues concerning poverty and the environment on local as well as global levels. Consumers have become more sensitive to matters relating to nutrition, public health, pollution, working conditions, and gender relations that influence their consumption behavior more and more.

The reputation risk, which has always been embedded in the list of risks, suddenly was placed at the top of the list as facts pertaining to a particular development

Table 15.1 Risks faced by the modern manager

Reputation risk
Financial risk
Market risk
Liquidity risk
Operation risk
Balance sheet risk
Regulatory risk
Location risk
Human risk
Technology risk
Foreign currency risk

Table 15.2 Factors dictating CSR management

Consumer's awareness of globalization and Third World issues
Consumer's awareness of environmental issues
Shareholder's better access to information
Shareholder's requirements for more transparency and better governance
Taxpayer's awareness
Employees' frustration
Regulatory pressure
Emergence of new technologies, trends, and expectations

could now be more easily filmed, scrutinized, and circulated through traditional and modern media. Catching a scandalous event on camera no longer necessitates more than a cell phone, and circulating it on a megascale is cheaper and faster than ever through podcasts, blogs, and YouTube, while the traditional media is always eager to recuperate it and take it to more elevated and often better documented levels (Table 15.1).

The reputation risk that faces the modern enterprise imposes challenges on both the sales and equity sides of business as modern consumers and shareholders can inflict damage on both the revenue and the value of a firm by shying away from its products and shares. Moreover, it is no longer sufficient that a company ethically manages its own production; care and scrutiny must be given to the reputation and behavior of the company's suppliers, outsourcing counterparts, and direct or indirect contractors. Valdez and British Petroleum (BP) and oil spilling, BP and the questions raised with respect to the technical and quality standards of the drilling companies with which it contracted, Gap and Nike and the Asian sweatshops, GlaxoSmithKline and the availability of HIV medicine to poor countries, Google and freedom of information in China, Blackberry and freedom of communication in the Gulf countries, McDonald's and obesity, and pesticides and genetically modified products are all contemporary examples of how the reputation risk can affect both the value and the profits of a firm (Table 15.2).

CSR, moreover, needs not only to be exercised in managing, preventing and reacting to reputation risk, or promoting a corporate citizenship image that can increase sales, it can also trigger research and development in specific fields that may create opportunities for the enterprise. Toyota's hybrid cars, in this case, have provided a vital market breakthrough together with a valuable green image for the company. New environmental regulations, moreover, constitute incentives for firms to invest in research and in new technologies that decrease the costs of production while at the same time improving their social responsibility image. US corporations' support for environmental issues has increased to 29% in 2009, from 19% only 2 years before (Veleva 2009). This has, without doubt, been affected by the stricter regulatory settings and the more generous incentive schemes for green technologies on one hand, together with the increased citizenship awareness toward environmental issues on the other.

15.3   The Behavior of Corporate Social Behavior in a Recession

CSR, other things equal, should be negatively affected by an economic recession as CSR spending is related to a corporation's profits and equity levels. This spending, however, can also be boosted by a "shift" in supply due to an increase in awareness or other factors playing in favor of corporate citizenship. The end of the decade is witnessing a context where governments, consumers, and investors request more environmentally friendly technology and products, employees and shareholders mark their frustration caused by layoffs and dire return on investment, and the general public manifests its distrust in business, requesting more transparency and social responsibility from the corporate world. This undoubtedly puts more pressure on corporations that need to foster even more their public images in order to compete better at times of lower profit making.

Four surveys on the "State of Corporate Citizenship" were undertaken in the USA since 2003. The last one covers 2009, thus allowing for an interesting comparison of CSR behavior between the recession and expansion years.[1]

The 2009 survey shows that although the recession is heavily felt – three quarters of the companies declare either a decreased (49%) or an unchanged (26%) level of revenues – chief executives give more importance to CSR than previously; 54% of respondents state that corporate citizenship is even more important during a recession. Reputation, after having ranked second in previous surveys, now shares first place (70%) with company traditions and values, as a driver for corporate citizenship. Many of the executives' perceptions have to be seen in the light of the scandals that have characterized the markets in recent years. Corporate citizenship according to the surveyed is manifested by ethical business practices (91 points), by treating and valuing employees well (81 points) and by managing and reporting finances accurately (76 points). Treating employees well in times of recession can have a

---

[1] A biennial survey of CEOs from small, medium, and large size companies in the USA, funded by the Hitachi Foundation. For a presentation of the survey results, see Veleva (2009).

positive effect on labor productivity and retain good talent while at the same time boosting the corporation's reputation. Although philanthropic support and donations decreased in dollar amounts for 38% of companies since such donations are linked to profits, the number of companies entertaining such donations remained remarkably the same between 2007 and 2009. It is interesting to note that large companies did not see a drop in donations; they either maintained or increased their support, a reminder that size counts with respect to CSR. Forty-four percent of large companies, as in 2007, presented volunteering opportunities for employees, 33% reported an increased hiring from poor communities (up from 23% in 2007), and 31% reported increased participation in improving community conditions, compared to 29% in 2007. Of notable interest is the increased integration of CSR in the business strategy. Senior executives are increasingly convinced of the business rewards associated with corporate citizenship. In three quarters of the surveyed companies, it is the CEO who leads CSR. Forty-three percent of companies declare that CSR is integrated into their business planning process. This ratio increases to 61% for large companies, two-thirds of which declare having written policies about corporate citizenship (Veleva 2009). As the EIU puts it, "During an economic expansion, corporate citizenship is an opportunity…in an economic downturn it can be a vital competitive advantage" (Economist Intelligence Unit 2008).

15.4 Managing Corporate Social Behavior Efficiently

The complexity of CSR is taking it beyond the sheer domain of communication into matters affecting the cost structure of the enterprise and its revenue stream as well as its equity and risk management. It goes beyond the classical sphere of the firm's decision-making to cover nontraditional matters such as outsourcing and the social image of suppliers. Good management of CSR requires its being embedded at the heart of decision-making as an important part of the corporation's organizational structure. Prestigious MBA programs (Columbia, Harvard) are devoting increasing space to CSR in their curriculum or are straightforwardly offering programs in CSR or NGO management. It might not be a coincidence that the initiation of CSR as a distinct element of management came from successful individuals in sophisticated specializations such as the software industry.

An efficient managerial approach affects various aspects of spending on CSR-related activities. Efficiency requires not only minimizing the costs on such spending but also having the maximum impact from the money spent. Corporations are keener on supervising, acquiring better technology, and auditing, ensuring the feasibility and often the sustainability of projects than was generally the case with traditional philanthropy. Responsible social spending has more and more to pass through disciplined spending.

The sheer size of large corporations also brings to discussion considerations related to economies of scale. The latter describes the situation where companies, by producing a larger volume of output, can spread their fixed costs (such as salaries and rent) on a higher quantity of output and would thus decrease their cost per unit of output. Economies of scale can also be met through alliances, partnerships, and mergers through which volumes are increased and synergies built.

Such interaction is possible within the social investment field. Alliances of different forms can be built between two corporations, a corporation and an NGO, a corporation and a government, a corporation and an elected body, and in bilateral or multilateral groupings.

Muhammad Yunus describes the success story of a partnership between Groupe Danone and the Grameen Group to establish a food-producing venture, the aim of which is to manufacture healthy food, at low price, to improve the diet of rural Bangladeshis, especially children. Yunus dwells on the experience by developing the concept of social business. "It's a business designed to meet a social goal. In this case, the goal is to improve the nutrition of poor families in poor Bangladesh. A social business is a business that pays no dividends. It sells products at prices that make it self-sustaining. The owners of the company can get back the amount they've invested in the company over a period of time, but no profit is paid to investors in the form of dividends. Instead, any profit made stays in the business-to finance expansion, to create new products or services, and to do more good for the world" (Yunus 2007, xvi).

More modest but well-illustrating and more market-oriented experiences exist on a global level. The Association for the Development of Rural Capacities (ADR), a developmental organization in Lebanon, emerged in a postwar-fragmented country where efforts of the government mainly focused on the reconstruction of the infrastructure to the detriment of other developmental issues, notably poverty in rural areas. ADR dwelt on a major characteristic of fragmented Lebanon: the existence of "islands" of efficiency in a country which lack communication and synergy. The association dwelt on its interaction with banks, universities, and municipalities in the execution of its programs. It introduced the first microcredit program of partnership between a commercial bank and an NGO to the country (and probably to the Arab world) in 1997. At first, the bank was only interested in the public relations image of the program which started serving the fishermen in the old city of Tyre. As the program was expending in volume and scope, however, the bank increasingly realized the business aspect of it. The experience was replicated by other players since then, and it is the situation today that more than two-thirds of microcredit in Lebanon is served by partnerships between commercial banks, NGOs, and microfinance institutions.

The essential synergies through such partnerships are straightforward and well accepted by now. Traditional banking does not serve microborrowers well as their small average loan size involves much higher overhead, requiring a bigger number of credit officers and managerial costs. In addition, banks in general, when introduced to microfinance, have to penetrate markets of which they know little and serve clients with no documented credit history, who, in addition, have no collectable collateral to present. In contrast, NGOs know better the borrowers and the regions they serve, can hire a larger number of credit officers for a loan portfolio of the same size, and charge higher interest rates which are usually not in the range of commercial banking lending rates.

As for the benefits to ADR, those came on different levels. Entering into a partnership with a bank required it to develop its organization structure, upgrade its accounting and IT systems, hire legal consultants, and abide to certified audit. It simply took the NGO to the higher sphere of corporate behavior. Financially, the partnership with the bank allowed for a cheaper cost of funds. Costs of delivery and payback were decreased furthermore by serving the clients through the cash windows of the bank or through post offices in villages not served by the banking community.[2] Another reward for ADR has been to witness some of its clients graduating from being nonbankable to becoming bankable clients with good credit histories and an eligibility to bigger loans, thus helping achieve one of the organization's goals, that of decreasing the marginalization of individuals in rural Lebanon. All of these factors permitted a decrease in the interest rate charged on the end users and on their cost of transportation. The synergies of the alliance thus permitted gains to the three stakeholders, namely, the bank, the borrowers, and the NGO.

Experiences of cooperation in microfinance have abounded during the past 15 years. The financial system, due to its accumulated experience and the support of IT developments, has been increasingly integrating microfinance either by acquiring NGOs and microfinance institutions or by developing its own systems. Such integration illustrates an interesting experience of how CSR, on a global level, can develop into an integrated business activity.

Another experience of ADR, outside the realm of finance, was the construction of a housing compound for the fishermen of Tyre, one of Lebanon's poorest income groups. To prepare the project, the School of Architecture at the American University of Beirut (AUB) was approached, and the point was made that Lebanon lacks projects of low-income housing, that such projects would prosper in the future, and that AUB's students, by working on preprojects, would benefit from a rare exposure in the country while at the same time serving their community well, the latter being one of AUB's declared missions. At a later stage, and after land was donated, academicians and students from the Harvard School of Design adopted the project which earned wide international recognition.[3] This partnership, while allowing AUB and the Harvard School of Design to exercise CSR, gave students an important professional experience and contemporaneously provided the fishermen with high-quality and safe low-income lodging. In parallel, achieving such a high-profile scheme was an important landmark to ADR, allowing it to acquire high-quality design at minimal cost.

Synergy with CSR can also be produced through partnerships between corporations and the public sector. Satyam Computers, an Indian consulting giant, provides

---

[2] ADR introduced to Lebanon the practice of delivering microfinance through the country's postal system/LibanPost.

[3] Hashim Sarkis from the Harvard School of Design was responsible for the architectural design of the project which has won several awards. It has received the Cityscape certificate for public housing, was selected for the PHAIDON Atlas of Contemporary Architecture, received a design award from the Boston Society of Architects, and was one of 11 projects selected by the MoMA Small Scale Big Change exhibition, besides being published in several architectural journals, including Harvard Design Magazine, Architectural Record, and Metropolis.

different sanitation programs in the state of Andhra Pradesh. It has also partnered with the government to establish the "Emergency Management and Research Institute" (EMRI) to create a single emergency line. Instead of having to call different numbers depending on the nature of the hazard or the emergency they face, EMRI developed a system through which the 70 million people of the state could access a unified emergency service through a single telephone number. (The Economist 2010).

Although CSB as a distinct aspect of corporate behavior is emerging within the developing world, the experience is relatively recent. On a global level, the idea of "fair trade" is increasingly affecting international commerce between rich and poor countries. The scope for an increased corporate citizenship in the latter group, however, is affected by the weak-prevailing regulatory and supervisory structures. As experience shows, CSB is better fostered in markets where government supervision and incentives in favor of transparency, donations, green economics, and other CSB components prevail.

15.5   Future Scope for Corporate Social Behavior

CSB is fundamentally linked to profits. The higher the profit level, the higher the ability of corporations to engage in CSB. What is more interesting, however, is the latter's multiple effects on revenues, costs, and value. By being attractive to consumers, it can increase revenues through improving a company's social image. In parallel, it can decrease costs when corporations – by polluting less or adopting green technologies, for example – escape taxes and benefit from subsidies. The reputation risk, in a world of increased scrutiny and unmerciful consumer and investor pressures, furthermore, can make CSB failures particularly costly and make stock value vulnerable to negative social perceptions. The increased engagement of high executives and the integration of CSB in the chore of corporate decision-making are manifestations of its greater integration as an essential component of business. It affects decision-making and strategy on all levels from procurement to sourcing and distribution. While economic expansion periods can afford more spending on CSB, recessions require even more focus on the latter as it is in dire times that a company needs to be more competitive and to earn a better market image. It might increasingly be the case that the quality of CSB of a company is a component of the quality of its management in general.

The business approach to corporate citizenship can positively affect the execution of social projects by imposing discipline, cost minimization, and sustainability and can thus increase the efficiency of social spending. CBS execution, from an economic point of view, enjoys economies of scale. This is triggering various kinds of ventures between companies, governments, municipalities, and NGOs. Corporations increasingly seek NGOs for their know-how in certain themes as well as their presence in regions and sectors that are targeted by CSB. Some experiences suggest increased integration or even acquisitions, especially in microfinance.

A danger that arises is a potential detachment of NGOs from their missions into trendy projects that may suit better the interests of the company. Worries are increasingly raised with respect to CSR. "What happens when profits and CSR do not go together? What about when the demands of the marketplace and the long-term interest of society conflict? What will companies do?....If they were to accept reduced profits to promote social welfare, the owners would have reason to feel cheated and consider corporate social responsibility as corporate financial *irresponsibility*" (Yunus 2007, 17).

The recent attention given to CSR has to be identified as well within its political context. The last four decades, particularly and since the emergence of Thatcherism, have seen a general decrease in the role of government in industrially advanced countries because of the well-known concerns about inefficiencies commonly associated with the public sector. This, by and large, has been accompanied by an increase in the size of NGOs. The trend might continue in the near future as OECD countries are giving priority to fiscal restructuring. While declaring that deficit reduction is the most urgent issue facing the country, the British prime minister promises "radical redistribution" of power from government to communities and people to reverse decades of overcentralization (Cameron 2010). Similarly, development aid has been increasingly channeled through NGOs in a will to boost civic society's dynamism and to counter corruption often manifested by governments in Third World countries. The polemics linked to an excessive decrease in government role, however, are well known in economic theory. The "perfect market" recognizes room for necessity for government intervention, in case externalities are produced, when competition is threatened or when redistributive policies are addressed. Having governments shying away from such responsibilities and overrelying on market players through CSB or other channels might take society further away from optimality.

Bibliography

Benedict XVI. 2009. Encyclical letter *Caritas in Veritate*. Homebush: St. Pauls.
Cameron, David. 2010. Cuts programme will help economic success. *British Broadcasting Corporation*. http://www.bbc.co.uk/news/uk-10847659?print=true. Accessed 3 Aug 2010.
Case, K., R. Fair, and S. Oster. 2008. *Principles of Economics*. Upper Saddle River: Prentice Hall.
Coase, Ronald H. 1960. "The Problem of Social Cost". *Journal of Law and Economics* 3(1):1–44.
Economist Intelligence Unit. 2008. Corporate citizenship: Profiting from a sustainable business. http://graphics.eiu.com/upload/Corporate_Citizens.pdf. November.
El-Khalil, Youssef. 1996. Sustainable banking and Insurance: Incorporating the Environmental Risks. Near East Workshop Private Sector Intervention in the Environment Agenda in Lebanon, Amman.
El-Khalil, Youssef. 2010. Equitable and Social Development: The Role of NGOs in Lebanon. Presentation of the seminar on the Social Impact of Economic Reforms in Lebanon, organized by IPALMO – Rome, the Lebanese Parliament, Beirut, July.
El-Khalil, Youssef. 2009. Commentaire sur la Lettre Encyclique 'Caritas in Veritate' du Souverain Pontife Benoit XVI, Charité et Raison Génèrent Justice et Efficacité Economique. Seminar on Caritas in Veritate, Rome, November.

Fleishman-Hillard. 2007. Rethinking corporate social responsibility. http://fleishmanhillard.
    com/2007/05/09/rethinking-corporate-social-responsibility-2007/Accessed 9 May 2007.
Globescan. 2008. CSR monitor. www.globescan.com. Accessed Sep 2010.
Golin, Harris. 2009. The buck stops-and starts-here: Corporate citizenship as a strategic business
    opportunity for the financial services industry. http://www.golinharris.com/resources/gh/flash/
    The%20Buck%20Stops%20Here.pptx.pdf. Accessed Sep 2010.
Halal, W. 1998. *The New Management: Bringing Democracy & Markets inside Organizations*. San
    Francisco: Berrett-Koehler Publishers.
Makower, Joel. 2009. The state of green business 2009. http://www.greenbiz.com/news/2009/02/02/
    state-green-business-2009-green-economy-gains-currency. Accessed 2 Feb 2009.
Smith, Adam. 2002. *The Theory of Moral Sentiments by Adam Smith*. Cambridge: Cambridge
    University Press. Originally printed in 1759.
The Economist. 2008a. Ethical capitalism: How good should your business be? http://www.economist.
    com/node/10533974/print. Accessed 17 Jan 2008.
The Economist. 2008b. A survey of corporate social responsibility. Just good business. http://
    www.economist.com/node/10491077/print. Accessed 17 Jan 2008.
The Economist. 2008c. Do it right. Corporate responsibility is largely a matter of enlightened self-
    interest. http://www.economist.com/specialreports/PrinterFriendly.cfm?story_id=10491124.
    Accessed 17 Jan 2008.
The Economist. 2010. Solutions for the digital networked economy. http://www.economist.com/
    sponsor/bt/index.cfm?pageid=article2. Accessed 20 Aug 2010.
Veleva, V. 2009. *The State of Corporate Citizenship 2009: The Recession Test*. Boston College
    Center for Corporate Citizenship. Vatican: Libreria Editrice Vaticana.
Yunus, M. 2007. *Creating a World without Poverty: Social Business and the Future of Capitalism*.
    Jackson: Public Affairs.

Chapter 16
Capitalism and Social Change: Some Thoughts on How to Change the World

Alan M. Webber

16.1 Where Are We?

The world today is suffering – and so are far too many of the people who live in it.

There are, of course, still days of wonder, days of pure physical beauty, of incomparable natural glory, days of great human achievement and accomplishment, days of noble individual and group generosity, days of transcendent interpersonal charity, days of innovation and creativity, days of magical artistic performances, and days of inspired thought and brilliant action.

All of that is true, and yet, looking at the arc of the world over a period not of days but of decades and even millennia, it is impossible not to conclude that things are badly out of order. It is not just a matter of keeping track of a few basic indicators. Or of expressing a sense of concern for some of the ways in which the earth and millions of people on earth suffer in a variety of serious and deplorable ways.

What we need to consider are ways in which life on earth is in consistent, ongoing jeopardy – life-threatening jeopardy.

A recent book, *The Greatest Challenges of Our Time*, by László Szombatfalvy (2010) identifies what the author considers four major challenges that could permanently alter – or even end – life on earth as we know it: environmental degradation, climate change, poverty, and war and violence. In a series of chapters on each challenge, he chronicles how far we have traveled, often without real thought, careful analysis, or precise numbers, toward our own undoing.

A.M. Webber (✉)
Co-founder of Fast Company. Former Editorial director and Managing editor
of "Harvard Business Review
Fast Company, Harvard Business Review, New York, USA
e-mail: alanwebber@mac.com

M. Schlag and J.A. Mercado (eds.), *Free Markets and the Culture
of Common Good*, Ethical Economy 41, DOI 10.1007/978-94-007-2990-2_16,
© Springer Science+Business Media B.V. 2012

For example, as a result of environmental degradation due to industrialization and the overutilization of natural resources, today 2.5 billion people face a serious water shortage. According to Szombatfalvy, a shortage of water causes the death of 6,000 people per day, mostly children (Szombatfalvy 2010, 17). At the same time, population growth is seriously taxing the world's ability to feed itself. Today, the global food supply has enormous challenges to feed 6.8 billion people; in the next 50 years, the global population is projected to increase to between nine and ten billion people.[1]

The challenge of global climate change has been well chronicled since the release of former Vice-President Al Gore's award-winning film, "An Inconvenient Truth," as has the failure of the nations of the world to arrive at a serious international agreement that would curtail CO_2 emissions and begin a long and difficult journey to a more sustainable approach to producing and consuming energy, food, and other contributors to climate change.

The numbers on war and violence are as staggering as those related to the water and food supply. In 2008, worldwide spending for military weapons reached $1,454 billion. Interestingly, for comparison purposes, the poorest 40% of people on earth live on approximately this same amount of money, while global aid to developing nations stands at around 7% of what the world spends on weapons (Szombatfalvy 2010, 30).

But it is the chapter on poverty that is easily the most troubling. As Szombatfalvy points out, more than 2.5 billion people live on less than $2 per day. Almost 20% of humanity lives on a maximum of $1.25 per day, and about the same number lives on a maximum of $2 per day. The mathematics of poverty are staggering. Approximately 900 million people suffer chronic malnutrition – a polite way of saying they gradually starve to death. Eleven billion people lack clean drinking water; two billion people lack hygienic toilet facilities, which lead to other diseases; ten million children die each year because of malnutrition, dehydration, or diarrhea (Szombatfalvy 2010, 34). Those are some of the global numbers; we will come back shortly to reflect on what they tell us.

But first, it is worth taking a look at the numbers concerning the United States of America – the wealthiest nation in the world – and arguably the wealthiest nation in the history of the world.

In a recent column in the *New York Times*, Bob Herbert totaled up the statistics on poverty in contemporary America: last year, nearly 44 million Americans were living in poverty, more than 14% of the population, and an increase of four million people from the year before. And poverty is not spread equally in America, any more than wealth is. More than 25% of the black and the Hispanic population in the United States is poor; more than 15 million children in the United States are living in poverty. Nor are the trends encouraging: in 2009, median family incomes were actually 5% lower than that had been in 1999. As for wealth, it is as unequally apportioned as the poverty: in 2005, more than 21% of US national income was

---

[1] Although Szombatfalvy is right that the world has difficulty in feeding itself, this is more generally thought to be due to a distribution problem, rather than a lack of food. The world is actually dealing with an inverse of the demographic problem feared by Malthus, with a drop in the population making it difficult to maintain social security systems in First World countries and an adequate labor force in Third World countries. This is exactly where good sustainable development comes in.

earned by only 1% of all Americans. Today, the top quintile in America actually owns 84% of the nation's wealth (Herbert 2010).

This disproportionate distribution of wealth and poverty has staggering consequences. For example, despite spending more money on health care than any nation on earth, life expectancy in the United States is lower than South Korea and the United Kingdom, and on a par with Greece; the United States ranks third in male obesity and eighth in female obesity; and America is twentieth in the world in child well-being, behind Greece, Poland, and the Czech Republic. In another category, which is not unrelated to poverty, the United States currently has more than 2.3 million people in prison, 800,000 more people than China.

Another consequence of poverty in the United States is the creation of an unbreakable cycle of poverty. As Tony Judt writes in *Ill Fares the Land* (Judt 2010), young women who live in the poorest states in America are more likely to become pregnant as teenagers than young women in wealthier states. Moreover, children of the poor in the United States are likely to do worse in school than wealthier children and end up in lower-paid jobs – if they get jobs at all. In addition, while absolute poverty is a huge problem for people and society, perhaps more important is the spread between the haves and the have-nots. Judt writes, "The wider the spread between the wealthy few and the impoverished many, the worse the social problems: a statement which appears to be true for rich and poor countries alike. What matters is not how affluent a country is but how unequal" (Judt 2010).

Just as important may well be what people *think* is the distribution of wealth in their country.

A recent study in the United States determined that Americans *think* that the top quintile of the population holds 59% of the wealth and would *like to see* the top quintile hold 32% of the wealth to be more equitable – a distribution more like Sweden than the United States. In fact, as mentioned previously, the top quintile in the USA holds 84% of the nation's wealth. According to some estimates, the top 1% of Americans today hold nearly 50% of the wealth.

The costs of such exaggerated economic inequality are, in fact, more than just economic. As Tony Judt notes, "Inequality is corrosive. It rots societies from within" (Judt 2010).

But what neither Judt nor Szombatfalvy take on is the actual nature of the deep underlying problem that these statistics register. Neither seems willing or even interested in arguing about the connections that make the numbers so powerful and chilling. In Szombatfalvy's case, he neglects to make the case that it is poverty that drives the other three great global challenges. And Judt sees the issue of economic inequality as a political problem requiring a political solution.

What seems clear to me, at least, is that the numbers and arguments marshaled by both men suggest something deeper; their data, if we were talking about something more easily grasped by the human mind, one company, say, rather than the entire world or the United States, would be evidence of a widespread system failure.

If a corporation had numbers like those presented by these writers – or any number of other equally concerned observers of the current world situation – we would all declare that company in dire peril. If we were business school professors, we would rub our hands in glee at the prospect of taking apart the obvious failings of the business. We could point at unsustainable business practices, a ridiculous misuse of resources, terrible human resources practices, an abuse of customers, and an almost willfully self-destructive strategy.

What kind of company would use up its necessary materials in a way that would render it out of business in the near-term future? What kind of company would treat its people so poorly that the employees it needs to have in order to perform are uneducated and the customers it needs to buy its goods and services impoverished?

This is a company that is locked in a downward cycle, a systems failure where every part of the system reinforces the ultimate failure of the whole of the parts!

Faced with a company like this, we would look at the underlying source of the problem: we would want to know what is the system that is behind the system failure.

In this case, the answer seems both obvious and, for obvious reasons, also unspeakable.

The system that is the source of the problem is capitalism.

Interestingly, the system that is the source of the solution is also capitalism.

16.2   What Seems to Be the Problem?

While he is unwilling to name the problem, Tony Judt is brilliant in describing the nature of the problem. "Something is profoundly wrong with the way we live today," he writes. "For thirty years we have made a virtue out of the pursuit of material self-interest: indeed this very pursuit now constitutes whatever remains of our sense of collective purpose. We know what things cost but have no idea what they are worth" (Judt 2010).

In fact, it is a lot worse than that. Because of the way we practice capitalism – at least the American version of capitalism – we do not even know with accuracy what things actually cost.

But we will come to that in a minute when we enumerate some of the foundational problems with contemporary capitalism.

First, it is important to understand the choices that we have when it comes to economic systems, that is, the choices other than capitalism.

Even today, communism – the god that failed – has its adherents. Realistically, however, communism has two fatal flaws. First, to the extent that has been tried as a system, it has failed and failed miserably. It simply does not work as an economic system: it cannot produce anything even close to what it theoretically promises, it cannot operate as it theoretically should, and finally, while it has not worked in the past, it bears even less relevance in a world based increasingly on innovation, creativity, entrepreneurship, knowledge, speed, and widespread technological change. Second, and perhaps even more tellingly, communism, as we have seen it attempted over the years, seems to produce the exact opposite of what it says it is for: far from producing social and economic equality, it has brought into existence tyranny, despotism, dictatorship, and totalitarianism.

Socialism, for its part, also has its adherents today. And while it has suffered a less extreme track record of abject failure than its big brother, communism, it is fair to say that increasingly nations that have embraced socialism as an economic and political system are now starting to walk away from it. It has not delivered the results it once promised. And even more toxically, it has delivered some results that are importantly undesirable, most significantly a form of "learned helplessness": people who have grown up under the influence of socialism tend to exhibit behavior that suggests that the task of taking care of their needs, wants, and desires should and inevitably will fall to someone or something else, the "the state" or "them" or some unnamed general collective. It is hardly a mind-set or behavior pattern designed to solve large-scale social and economic problems.

Which leaves capitalism.

What is the matter with capitalism – particularly the American version?

First, in the context of the first part of this chapter, it is fair to say that the biggest problem with capitalism is that by its very nature, it seems to require poverty, an observation most astutely made by Nobel Prize recipient Muhammad Yunus in his book, *Creating a World Without Poverty.*

"Unfettered markets in their current form are not meant to solve social problems and instead may actually exacerbate poverty, disease, pollution, corruption, crime, and inequality," Yunus writes. "The negative impact of unlimited single-track capitalism is visible every day – in global corporations that locate factories in the world's poorest countries, where cheap labor (including children) can be freely exploited to increase profits; in companies that pollute the air, water, and soil to save money on equipment and processes that protect the environment; in deceptive marketing and advertising campaigns that promote harmful or unnecessary products" (Yunus 2008, 5).

In the wake of the recent global economic meltdown, it is relatively easy to enumerate some of the most dangerous and cynical practices that have come to dominate the contemporary form of American capitalism.

Start with what has become the generally accepted definition of capitalism's purpose: for most large-scale, publicly traded companies, there is one overriding "definition of victory" – the company's stock price. Indeed, for at least several decades now, the default definition taught at leading MBA programs in America's top business schools says that the job of the CEO and the top management team is "shareholder value creation." In other words, corporations exist to make their shareholders richer.

This overriding definition leads to a number of attendant practices.

First and foremost, it has made profit maximization the basis for judging corporate performance. And profit maximization has meant a short-term orientation, a quarter-by-quarter metric that judges executive and corporate achievements in blocks of 3 months at a time.

By definition, this system requires a company to grow continuously and relentlessly, no matter how large it already is. Corporate leadership demands higher numbers from its employees every year and then judges performance strictly on the basis of the employees' ability to "hit the numbers."

This, in turn, almost inevitably leads to a number of unintended consequences. To drive better numbers and achieve higher profits, companies reflexively refuse to accept as many costs of doing business as they can. In economic terms, they treat as "externalities" things that accrue to the public's interests – things like sound environmental practices, long-term human resources investments, and social costs of doing business. In fact, most companies, while mouthing the piety that "our people are our most valuable asset," in practice account for their people as an expense, not an asset. Which means that they are quick to cut people, resort to layoffs, employ part-time employees whose health-care costs they do not pay for, and adopt other cost-cutting practices that help improve the short-term, bottom-line results that, in turn, drive up the stock price. (Not to mention a willingness to condone sometimes unethical and even illegal practices in the name of producing quarterly earnings.)

Another pernicious unintended consequence is the decoupling of the real cost of doing business from the price consumers pay for the goods and services they consume. A classic example of a false pricing signal that has major economic, social, environmental, and political implications is the cost of gasoline at the pump in the United States. Energy, in general, and oil, in specific, cut across virtually every dimension of life today. Because the world's economy is carbon-based, oil exploration, recovery, refining, and use end up playing a role in every one of the four great challenges enumerated by Laszlo Szombatfalvy.

That said, it seems almost unthinkable – and certainly irresponsible – that Americans today pay approximately $2.70 at the pump for a gallon of gasoline. That is a price that certainly does not reflect the real costs of oil; it certainly does not represent the replacement cost of each gallon; it does not include the environmental cost of the gasoline; and as some observers have argued, to be more accurate, it does not but should include the military budget of the United States since so much of America's foreign policy over the last several decades seems predicated on doing whatever is necessary to assure the US economy has access to relatively cheap and plentiful supplies of oil.

If these are the sins of capitalism – at least as it has come to be practiced in America – then what are its redeeming qualities?

It has one. But that one is so significant, so powerful, and so vital that it represents capitalism's saving grace: capitalism is a living system. Alone among the economic systems that are available for organizing human conduct, capitalism has in its core, in its DNA, the capacity to change and evolve, to respond to changing conditions and circumstances.

As Joyce Appleby writes in her history of capitalism, *The Relentless Revolution*, "Probably the most striking feature of capitalism has been its inextricable connection with change – relentless disturbances of once-stable material and cultural forms. More than promote change, it offered proof that the common longings of human beings for improvement could be achieved. It opened up to a significant proportion of men and women in the West the possibility of organizing their energy, attention, and talents to follow through on market projects like forging a new trade link or meeting an old need with a commercial product" (Appleby 2010, 329).

She goes on to say, "The novelist Tom Wolfe commented recently that we were witnessing 'the end of capitalism as we know it.' That's a statement that could have been made many times in the past two centuries, for capitalism is a system constantly reinventing itself, a set of prescriptions peculiarly open to disruption, a work in progress" (Appleby 2010, 334).

And finally, in coming to terms with capitalism and its strengths and weaknesses, she writes, "Critics look for structural changes that will undermine capitalism as a system. They often underestimate the two enduring strengths of capitalism, encouragement of innovation and a capacity to create new wealth along with the real satisfactions that wealth brings to a growing population of recipients."

"The shame in the flourishing of capitalism is the stark inequality between nations and regions of the world. Measures of well-being like life expectancy, family purchasing power, and children's nutrition reveal greater inequalities than fifty years ago" (Appleby 2010, 363).

Which raises the question: if capitalism is to morph again to meet the problems associated with its success, where can we look for changes that will help capitalism itself solve the challenges that now confront the world, most importantly, the challenges of poverty and social change?

16.3   Can Capitalism Heal Itself?

This is a true story.

A few years ago, I was invited by one of America's largest privately held companies to address the CEO and his top executives. The theme was leadership and change: how the world was changing, and what leaders needed to do to adapt to the new competitive realities.

At the end of my talk, the CEO thanked me and then took up the theme. But he made it more pointed.

"Looking at the United States today, in business, government, organized religion, and non-profits," he challenged his executives, "who would you say has real moral authority?"

By "moral authority," he meant a leader whom anyone in the room would follow with absolute confidence and a leader who would speak with real conviction, with genuine concern for the larger public good, rather than for self-interest. In other words, who was a shining example of a leader with utter integrity?

The room fell silent. For a good five minutes, no one spoke.

At the end of that time, it was clear that no one in the top ranks of that company could think of a single American leader in business, government, organized religion, or nonprofit organizations who fit the criteria of a leader with "moral authority."

Today, when Americans look at the three major institutions that could, arguably, provide the leadership necessary to tilt capitalism in a new, more sustainable direction, the answer that was given in that room appears to be the answer most Americans give in general. As the *New York Times*' Bob Herbert reports in the same September 17, 2010 column on the storms in the US economy, according to a recent national poll, the mood in America toward major institutions is beyond skeptical: "Glum and distrusting, a majority of Americans today are very confident in – nobody" (Herbert 2010).

Let us start with attitudes toward business, the leaders who are most directly in charge of the conduct of capitalism.

In 2008, before the utter implosion of Wall Street and the financial system of the United States and the world, only 11% of Americans said they had "a great deal of confidence" in the people in charge of major corporations; 35% said they had "hardly any confidence."

Then in 2009, as the economy crumbled, requiring the federal government to bail out banks and major industrial enterprises, such as General Motors, a survey of Americans found that 70% said that people on Wall Street were not as honest and moral as other people. When asked to rank the honesty and ethics of different occupations, business executives ranked near the bottom; on a list of most admired professions, "business executive" came in at 21 out of 23 choices.

Is it reasonable to expect business executives to embrace changes to the system that they have gone to school to learn, in which they have worked and from which they have prospered? Will they embrace a different way of keeping score other than their company's stock price? Will they begin to make the case for more accurate market price signals or for carrying the true costs of the way they do business on their own books?

What about the federal government? If capitalism is to be redirected, can we expect the government to provide the leadership to invent new regulations and requirements that will lead to a "kinder, gentler" form of capitalism, a capitalism that solves global problems, rather than causing them?

Not if the American people's assessment of their government is correct. According to recent surveys, only 23% of Americans believe that the federal government reflects the will of the people; for the last 5 years, the Congress' approval rating has been under 29% – and this past summer, it dropped to 19%. At the other end of the spectrum, 86% of Americans agree with the assessment that the government is "broken."

Much of this mistrust of government comes from a deep disaffection from the role that money plays in politics: interestingly, the ranking of occupations by honesty and ethics puts "lobbyists" at the bottom, even lower than business executives. Because of that, it seems a great leap to imagine that America's elected officials, who depend on campaign contributions to get and hold onto their jobs, will suddenly find the courage or imagination to produce regulations that could alter the trajectory of American capitalism – even if they so wanted. It is an equally large stretch to think of the precise regulations that would make a significant difference to how business gets done.

Are we left with organized religion as a force for change?

Unfortunately, these are not good times for organized religion in America, which may well be one of the most religious, or at least most spiritual, nations on earth. Again, the survey data reveal a great and growing disaffection on the part of ordinary Americans and their affiliation with and practice of organized religion.

According to one recent survey, 34 million Americans have given up on organized religion. Nor do Americans feel a sense of permanence in their religious affiliations: 44% of Americans have left the faith they were raised in for another religion – or none at all. In fact, among Americans between the ages of 18 and 29, a full 25% say they do not belong to any faith; among all Americans, 16% have no religious affiliation (Pew Research Center 2008).

But what may be more disturbing is the significant erosion that has taken place in the way Americans regard the role of religion in the world. In 1998, 33% of all Americans agreed with the statement, "Religion brings more conflict than peace." Ten years later, that figure had doubled to 66% (Hout and Fischer 2009).

So can we expect organized religion to change capitalism? Do the main religions of the world have the knowledge, expertise, and practical skills to guide capitalism in a new and different direction? Do these religions have the appetite for the argument? Do they have the belief systems and teachings that would contribute to alleviating poverty – or are they, in a number of significant respects, part of the problem, rather than part of the solution?

As Muhammad Yunus writes in *Creating a World Without Poverty*, "Institutions and policies that created poverty cannot be entrusted with the task of eliminating it. Instead, new institutions designed to solve the problems of the poor need to be created" (Yunus 2008, 12).

What kinds of institutions is he talking about?

What kinds of institutions are we seeing come into existence to make a difference in the world?

16.4 The Rise of Social Entrepreneurship and Hybrid Capitalism

Consider the stories of three individuals, Mohammad Yunus, Bill Strickland, and Rosanne Haggerty.

Mohammad Yunus was an economics professor who one day found himself walking through the village of Jobra when he encountered Sufiya Begum, an impoverished woman who was making bamboo stools in her front yard. No matter how hard she worked, she could not escape poverty because the only source of money for her work was a moneylender, who not only loaned her the money for her bamboo but also set the price for buying her stools. She was in many ways a metaphor for poverty: a woman locked in a vicious cycle from which she could not escape (Yunus 2008, 45–46).

That episode led Yunus to create the Grameen Bank, and with it a new approach to escaping poverty that has benefited not only the people of Bangladesh but poor people all over the world.

Bill Strickland was a poor black kid in Pittsburgh, Pennsylvania, who would not have graduated from high school were it not for the intervention of one man: a white ceramics teacher who captured Bill's youthful imagination. In the ceramics class,

Bill learned more than pottery; he learned about art, jazz, and architecture, and most important, he learned the value of learning.

He barely got into college at Pittsburgh, and when he graduated, he took over a struggling program for at-risk kids in the same neighborhood in Pittsburgh where he had grown up. Using the lessons he had learned in that one ceramics class, he developed a school curriculum that used arts and crafts to teach kids all kinds of subjects – and to teach them not to give up. Today, Bill's program has been "franchised" in similar schools across the United States and around the world – and his own program has grown to include job training for unemployed adults, whose work development is paid for by companies looking for skilled employees who want to work. Moreover, Bill's programs are housed in a spectacular building in Pittsburgh designed by a protégé of Frank Lloyd Wright (Strickland 2007).

Rosanne Haggerty went to one of America's elite colleges. But rather than use her education to go to Wall Street or join a prestigious company, she went to work for a nonprofit organization committed to fighting homelessness. After a short time there, however, she grew discouraged. The organization did not really want to end homelessness, it merely wanted to work within acceptable boundaries, which guaranteed the continued existence of both homelessness and the nonprofit.

Determined to end chronic homelessness in New York City, Rosanne set up her own organization. She succeeded in converting a crack-house hotel in the heart of Times Square into housing for chronically homeless men and women and developed a new and innovative approach to ending homelessness – and a whole new business model to pay for it. Her program has grown in scope and scale to include more hotels in New York and expanded to one of the city's most distressed neighborhoods, where poverty spawns a host of other social ills. Her model has been adopted in cities across America, and Rosanne has consulted to advocates for the homeless around the world. Remarkably, today there is only one chronically homeless person left in Times Square.

All three of these individuals have much in common.

None is a recognized expert in the field in which they have chosen to work.

None has the credentials, according to conventional wisdom, to do what they have done.

None was supported by the powers-that-be, or the existing institutions in their field.

None began on a large scale, supported by large amounts of money or traditional investments.

None experienced immediate success or enjoyed overnight celebrity.

None "got it right" the first time; all of them had to adjust, adapt, and tinker with the organizations they invented.

None of them has left the organization they started; all of them recognized that making deep, permanent, system change was the work of a lifetime, not a quick fix or short-term undertaking.

None of them did it for the money, or the fame, or the glory.

All of them surrounded themselves with talented, capable individuals who could help them develop and grow their idea, and make it better.

All of them stayed "close to the ground," in touch with the communities they were serving so as to be able to change and adapt with the changing needs and demands of the "customers."

All three of them began as small "petri-dish-size" experiments; they kept what worked, changed what did not, and grew slowly and carefully based on trial and error.

Today, all three are celebrated success stories.

Muhammad Yunus is the recipient of the Nobel Peace Prize. Bill Strickland and Rosanne Haggerty are both recipients of MacArthur "Genius" Grants in the United States.

But even more important, all three are examples of social entrepreneurs. And it is social entrepreneurs – and social entrepreneurship – that more than anyone or anything else holds genuine promise for developing a form of capitalism that can solve real social problems.

The power of social entrepreneurship is its ability to cut the x-y axis of capitalism and social problems on the diagonal, thereby achieving the best of both worlds.

From the world of capitalism, social entrepreneurship takes the premise that new ideas, innovation, fresh thinking, and new business models can capture both the imagination and the wallet of the market. Social entrepreneurs, like any entrepreneurs, embrace the test of the marketplace. They want their innovations to work, to achieve real results, and to gain real customers, supporters, and adherents. They want the market to vote "yes" for their idea and to provide the operating capital and financial support to enable the idea to take hold, grow, and prosper. They believe, in other words, in the part of capitalism that embraces the market mechanism and rewards innovation and entrepreneurship.

But what they do not accept in their practice of capitalism is a one-dimensional definition of success. They do not believe that stock price or shareholder value creation is the true measure of an organization's performance. Far from it.

Rather, they devote their application of capitalism to solving social problems. From issues of poverty, homelessness, the environment, education, disease, literacy, and other human crises that diminish, demean, and threaten life on earth, particularly for the most vulnerable people on the planet, social entrepreneurs apply the creativity and discipline of the market to make a positive difference. They are global and local. They are individuals pursuing with a passion a cause that they care deeply about, usually in a community of which they are a part, and doing it with the economic discipline of the market. At the same time, they are learning from other social entrepreneurs around the world, forming a loose network of people and organizations committed to making a difference on a global scale, when all their efforts are aggregated.

They are change agents, but not abstract do-gooders. They are entrepreneurs, but not narcissistic wealth machines.

They represent the best of both worlds.

At the same time, they are able to act both top-down and bottom-up. Because they are entrepreneurs, they do not need the permission of large-scale institutions or existing organizations to take action. They can operate as low-cost, low-risk grassroots start-ups. And because they respect the principles of capitalism, they can attract the support and the backing of organizations that wish to affiliate with and lend support to worthy and possibly profitable causes.

As Paul Hawken writes in *Blessed Unrest: How the Largest Movement in the World Came Into Being and Why No One Saw It Coming*, "in contrast to the ideological struggles currently dominating global events and personal identity, a broad non-ideological movement has come into being that does not invoke the masses' fantasized will but rather engages citizens' localized needs. This movement's key contribution is the rejection of one big idea in order to offer in its place thousands of practical and useful ones. Instead of isms it offers processes, concerns, and compassion. The movement demonstrates a pliable, resonant, and generous side of humanity. It does not aim for the utopian, which itself is just another ism, but is eminently pragmatic" (Hawken 2007, 18).

Because there is no one right way to be a social entrepreneur, or to support social entrepreneurship, this movement is finding all kinds of expression. There are venture capitalists who want to back innovative solutions to pressing social problems that stand to make a healthy return on the investment – not profit maximization – but a healthy blend of profit and social gain. There are consulting firms setting up units to advise and counsel would-be social entrepreneurs, courses in colleges and universities to teach students how to become a social entrepreneur, think tanks devoted to studying and amplifying the work of social entrepreneurs, and conferences designed to bring together the growing community of social entrepreneurs and give them a large tent under which to gather.

In addition, existing philanthropies are studying the work of social entrepreneurs to see if there is a better, more strategic use of their funds than writing checks for charities: what if it makes more sense and ultimately gets better results to make an investment in a social business? Large multinational companies are backing social entrepreneurs in their start-ups and learning to imitate them in the way they shape new, innovative products and services to the poorest, neediest markets. And increasingly, governments, strapped for funds to do the things they already do and overwhelmed by demands to speak to new, pressing needs, are partnering with social entrepreneurs to find workable answers that do not require the expenditure of more tax dollars.

What makes the movement of social entrepreneurs so remarkable is its inherent flexibility – the way it takes full of advantage of the strengths of capitalism – while blunting the system's weaknesses. Social entrepreneurs are finding backing from some of the world's most prestigious organizations: the World Economic Forum in Davos, the Skoll Foundation, the Omidyar Network, TED, Ashoka, the Acumen Fund, to name just a few. Nor is it simply an American phenomenon. There are social entrepreneurs on every continent and in almost every nation in the world. Social entrepreneurs are working to keep alive the hunter-gatherers of Africa, to assist the oppressed in the Middle East, and to offer support to disadvantaged and abused women around the world, just to name a few. Even in nations where it is difficult to be a traditional entrepreneur, the unique contribution made by social entrepreneurs has opened doors of opportunity. All around the world, social entrepreneurs can operate freely and openly without anyone's backing and often achieve real and lasting results by replicating the "petri-dish" strategy of Muhammad Yunus, Bill Strickland, and Rosanne Haggerty.

Will it be enough to change the world? Can it create a new trajectory for capitalism, produce a new direction that will heal the world?

That is not a question that has ever found an easy answer. It may not even be the right question.

Perhaps a more apt question is "Can anyone produce a better, more hopeful, more human solution to address the planet's ills?" Is there anything more likely to generate local and global solutions, to tap into the hopes and aspirations of more people, to harness more human energy and more willing investment capital than the growing movement of social entrepreneurs?

If there ever was a movement that corresponded to Margaret Mead's visionary quote about change, it was social entrepreneurship. Mindful of the constant need for individuals to make a difference in the world, Margaret Mead said, "Never doubt that a small group of thoughtful, committed citizens can change the world. Indeed, it is the only thing that ever has" (Lutkehaus 2008, 261).

Bibliography

Appleby, Joyce. 2010. *The Relentless Revolution: A History of Capitalism*. New York: W. W. Norton.

Hawken, Paul. 2007. *Blessed Unrest: How the Largest Movement in the World Came into Being and Why No One Saw It Coming*. New York: Viking.

Herbert, Bob. 2010. "Two different worlds". *The New York Times*, September 17, 2010. http://www.nytimes.com/2010/09/18/opinion/18herbert.html.

Hout, Michael, and Claude S. Fischer. 2009. "The Politics of Religious Identity in the United States, 1974–2008," Presentation for *American Sociological Association*, Berkeley: University of California. 9 Aug 2009.

Judt, Tony. 2010. *Ill Fares the Land: A Treatise on our Present Discontents*, New York: Penguin Press. Quoted from http://amcatholic.wordpress.com/author/blackadderiv/.

Lutkehaus, Nancy C. 2008. *Margaret Mead: The Making of an American Icon*. Princeton: Princeton University Press.

Pew Research Center. 2008. *U.S. Religious Landscape Survey. Religious Affiliation: Diverse and Dynamic*. The Pew Forum on Religion and Public Life. http://religions.pewforum.org/pdf/report-religious-landscape-study-full.pdf.

Strickland, Bill. 2007. *Make the Impossible Possible: One Man's Crusade to Inspire Others to Dream Bigger and Achieve the Extraordinary*. New York: Crown Business.

Szombatfalvy, László. 2010. *The Greatest Challenges of Our Time*. Stockholm: Ekerlids Publishing House.

Yunus, Muhammad. 2008. *Creating a World Without Poverty: Social Business and the Future of Capitalism*. Jackson: Public Affairs.

Chapter 17
The German Social Market Economy: Challenged by *Caritas in Veritate*

Andrea M. Schneider

17.1 The German Social Market Economy: Challenged by *Caritas in Veritate*

"The functioning of a free market economy depends on sound cultural and ethical foundations." For earlier thinkers like the moral philosopher and father of economics Adam Smith this was self-evident. He was an expert on human action as well as on business action and had no difficulties in studying the economy with a holistic approach. After the division of the academic disciplines ethics and economics shortly after Adam Smith, however, a partial approach gained momentum and is still prevalent. Economists and businessmen developed economic standards, ethicians and philosophers ethical standards for the market. We evidently lost a lot due to this segmentation. It might even have contributed to the emergence of the financial crisis in 2008.

Although there has been a growing body of literature on business ethics, dialogue of the academic disciplines should not be a privilege of the few but an imperative for all economists and for all dealing with business and economics.

There is a lot to learn from the insights of earlier thinkers who followed such a holistic and interdisciplinary approach. This was the fact for the precursors and founding fathers of the German Social Market Economy. Since they are not so well known outside of Germany, a closer look at their writings could be an interesting contribution to an international and interdisciplinary discussion – especially given the fact that they were strongly influenced by the Catholic social teaching of their time.

A.M. Schneider (✉)
Cabinet office of the Federal Chancellor Angela Merkel
Bundeskanzleramt, Berlin, Germany
e-mail: andreamschneider@web.de

M. Schlag and J.A. Mercado (eds.), *Free Markets and the Culture of Common Good*, Ethical Economy 41, DOI 10.1007/978-94-007-2990-2_17,
© Springer Science+Business Media B.V. 2012

17.2   Normative Foundations of the German Social
Market Economy

The history of economics and its schools of thought show that economic theories and especially concepts of economic and social orders reflect their specific cultural and historical background; they contain specific assumptions concerning the nature of man, the role of the State, and the evolution and functioning of institutions. Additionally, they are based on specific value systems. In order to understand diverging concepts of liberalism, it is worthwhile and necessary to choose a holistic approach.

The theoretical, anthropological, and normative foundations of the German Social Market Economy can best be understood by first examining the historical and cultural background.[1] During the second half of the nineteenth century, socialism was at Germany's doorstep. It became a reality in other countries. On the other hand, Germany experienced periods of laissez-faire liberalism with a weak State governed by economic stakeholders. This era brought prosperity and poverty, social progress and problems, and hope and despair. The strongly diverging political forces favoured strongly diverging options for the future. World War I and sanctions after the war made arguments for any direction only fiercer.

This was the background and the experiences of the country when during World War II different groups of professors of economics, law, and sociology – many of them working at the University of Freiburg – and some theologians came together to discuss their moral obligation in this time of war and of Nazi dictatorship. They debated fundamental ethical questions such as the moral obligation vs. the moral prohibition as Christians to resist the regime or to murder the tyrant. They discussed encyclicals and Christian ethical principles.

Most of all, they discussed what should be done after the war. Which economic and social order would be best fit for a truly free and just society? Which order would be best suitable for the human person?

The groups met and wrote secretly; some members paid for this with their lives, their ideas being a great danger to the Nazi regime. Others contributed with writings from exile. Dietrich Bonhoeffer[2] approached one of these groups on behalf of the Confessing Church – a Protestant schismatic Church that arose in opposition to Nazi efforts to nazify the German Protestant Church. He asked them to develop a program and general principles outlining how to organize a State on Christian ethical principles after the war in a way so as to ensure world peace. Their program became one of the fundamental contributions to the design of the Social Market

---

[1] See Schneider (2004, 57ff).

[2] Dietrich Bonhoeffer (1906–1945) was a German Lutheran pastor and theologian who had participated in the German Resistance Movement against the Nazi regime. He was arrested in 1943 and executed in Flossenbürg concentration camp on April 9, 1945, for his involvement in the attempt to assassinate Adolf Hitler on July 20, 1944. He was a founding member of the Confessing Church.

Economy. Some authors and also members of other groups later on played an active part in the first West German government where they could use their considerations for the practical installation of what was to be called "Social Market Economy" ("Soziale Marktwirtschaft").

Seeing this background, it is no surprise to find many statements on human dignity and freedom, on justice and equity, and on ethics and culture in the writings of group members and of scholars influenced by them.

The Social Market Economy has many pioneers and founding fathers. Alfred Müller-Armack, Alexander Rüstow, Wilhelm Röpke, and Walter Eucken are among the best known and most influential.

They had a lot in common. All of them had a good understanding of the human person and of human action. Almost all had done a thorough analysis of history and of crises of societies. They were convinced that human dignity is of the highest value while freedom is the highest goal for a person and a society to achieve. The development of the human person and of a humane society should be the yardstick for the economic order, for society, and for the progress of a society. They were convinced that institutions matter and that the political, economic, and social order we live in brings either the best or the worst out of human beings. Their ideas strongly reflect the Protestant and Catholic social teaching of their time, *Rerum Novarum* being one important source of inspiration.

The founding fathers were representatives of what is nowadays called Ordoliberalism[3]. They developed very similar concepts of a liberal economic and social order. These concepts all involved a free market economy, understood as an intentionally organized economic order, embedded within a strong legal, cultural, and moral framework with a strong State to safeguard freedom and social progress.

Alfred Müller-Armack, an economist and sociologist, worked for Ludwig Erhard, Germany's first minister of economics who enacted the Social Market Economy. Müller-Armack invented the term Social Market Economy in 1946 (see Müller-Armack 1962/1976c, 296)[4]. He was convinced that a free market economy was the most efficient way for a nation to achieve a high level of living standard not only for a few but for everybody. But for a market economy to be efficient and – very important – *accepted* in the long run, it had to be balanced with social progress for the whole of society (see Müller-Armack 1956/1976b, 243ff). If the uncertainties of life caused by sickness or unemployment were not taken into account, they would be destructive to creativity and efficiency. A high level of income inequality would give rise to fundamentalists on both the left and the right of the political spectrum. It would cause social tension, which would undermine civil peace, social life, and democracy.

---

[3] Ordoliberalism is a German version of neoliberalism. Many German and German-speaking economists of the time called themselves neoliberal. However, the term "neoliberalism" in Germany today is broadly used in a pejorative way and equated with laissez-faire liberalism. Historically, it is a renewed ("neo") version of classic liberalism that explicitly rejects the notion of laissez-faire liberalism.

[4] First date refers to original year of publication. Second year refers to year of edition used.

Moreover, it would undermine a basic trust and a sense of cooperation within the society as well as diminish compliance to formal rules and informal norms. High levels of inequality would be destructive to the economy and the society as a whole and in the end to freedom itself. Thus, the ideals of freedom and of justice were to be necessarily balanced (see Müller-Armack 1948/1981, 90ff).

Müller-Armack relied on the writings of Rüstow, Röpke, and Eucken:

Alexander Rüstow was a social scientist and an economist. He emphasized the need to define "freedom" not only as a set of rights but as a duty. Man has an obligation to strive for his own freedom and for the freedom of others (see Rüstow 1963a/1963b, 307).[5] Rüstow passionately argued for economic freedom. Free markets and competition are highly efficient in generating economic growth. Furthermore, economic freedom is the necessary basis for political freedom and freedom of man in general (see Rüstow 1963a/1963b, 78). However, economic freedom has no use of its own and the economy no superiority: "We believe that there are uncountable things which are more important than the economy: family, community, the State, all forms of social integration as well as humanity, furthermore religion, morality, aesthetics, shortly: the humane, the cultural. All these big areas of humanity are more important than the economy" (Rüstow 1963a/1963b, 77).[6]

But none of the other areas of life can exist without the economy: "Primum vivere, deinde philosophari" (Rüstow 1963a/1963b, 77). If the basic material needs for a dignified life are not available, all of these areas cannot unfold. The true purpose of the economy is to serve these higher values. It should therefore be the "servant to mankind."[7] Politics should aim at the "vita humana," at a life in dignity and vitality. The purely materialistic social policy of the nineteenth century should be turned into a "vital policy," seeking to support the human person and their well-being, a well-being which extends beyond the economic situation (see Rüstow 1952, 8; 1955, 70; 1957, 215ff; 1963a, 82f; 1963b, 68).

The economist Wilhelm Röpke, like Rüstow and Müller-Armack, criticized the laissez-faire liberalism of the nineteenth century, which had made the economy first and absolute, in response to a purely materialistic and utilitarian ideology. As a consequence, laissez-faire liberalism had led to a cult of productivity and materialism, a "defect of the vision of the soul" (Röpke 1958, S. 151; see also Röpke 1947, 11ff). According to Röpke, a materialistic society denies a hierarchy of fundamental values and humiliates the human being in unbearable ways.

Laissez-faire liberalism underestimates the moral preconditions of the market economy, and it overestimates the self-regulative abilities of markets. Markets and competition do not produce a reservoir of morals but consume it. Moral reserves are produced within families and other communities outside the market

---

[5] See also Eucken (1952/1990, 178) where he stresses that men have lost the feeling for what freedom is and for its value. We rediscover this thought in CV where Benedict asks us to reflect on "how rights presuppose duties, if they are not to become mere licence" (Benedict XVI 2009, 43).

[6] All subsequent quotes, whose original is in German, have been translated by the author.

[7] See the article with the same title by Rüstow (1963a/1963b).

(see Rüstow 1955, 64). Laissez-faire liberalism negates the fact that the market economy cannot be left to itself. It is "no creation of nature" but a "highly fragile artefact of civilization" (Röpke 1942/1948, 87). The market economy needs a reasonable commercial law, an efficient market control, and a strong State. The government should concentrate on designing and adjusting the economic and social order and should not interfere in the economic process.

In addition, the market needs a minimum of virtues such as honesty in business affairs (see Röpke 1958, 170). Even more so, for Röpke it was clear: the market economy needs an anthropological-sociological framework (see Röpke 1957, 1959, 10). He described the type of society in which the market economy should be embedded as the following: "The market economy, and with it social and political freedom, can thrive only as a part and under the protection of a bourgeois system. This implies the existence of a society in which certain fundamentals are respected and color the whole network of social relationships: individual effort and responsibility, absolute norms and values, independence based on ownership, prudence and daring, calculating and saving, responsibility for planning one's own life, proper coherence with the community, family feeling, a sense of tradition and the succession of generations combined with an open-minded view of the present and the future, proper tension between individual and community, firm moral discipline, respect for the value of money, the courage to grapple on one's own with life and its uncertainties, a sense of the natural order of things, and a firm scale of values" (Röpke, cit. in Gregg 2010, 14).

Müller-Armack, Rüstow, and Röpke all agreed strongly with Walter Eucken who had emphasized the need to see the economic order as being interdependent with the political, legal, social, and cultural order. He pledged for "thinking in orders" (see Eucken 1952/1990, 13–16, 19ff). All areas of life are interdependent, and politics has to bear this in mind in all affairs.

When Ludwig Erhard introduced the Social Market Economy based on the writings of these precursors and his own ideas, there was hardly anyone in favour. It was some years before the Christian Democratic Party included it in its political program. The Social Democrats remained sceptical until the mid-1950s. Having seen the destruction, the public was in favour of central planning as were the Allied powers. However, Erhard strongly believed in the power of free enterprise as the only way out of destruction. He therefore abolished an array of restrictions to free markets in West Germany literally overnight, against advice and without permission of the US authorities.

As a politician and economist he was convinced that "to be responsible for economic policy means to be responsible for the whole nation." The enormous economic problems after World War II could only be solved "if with the market economy we succeed not only to benefit some social classes but to ensure and continuously enhance a dignified living standard for the entirety of the nation" (Erhard 1957/2000, 134). This is why Erhard found a Social Market Economy without a rigorous policy of price stability (see Erhard 1957/2000, 15) inconceivable since it is the people with small income and savings that suffer most when inflation rises. The yardstick for good or bad economic policies should not be dogmas or interest groups but exclusively the human person, the consumer, the nation. "An economic policy can only be considered good if and as long as it is absolutely beneficial and beneficent to mankind" (Erhard 1957/2000, 133). In this sense, Erhard was rather a "Minister for the Common Good" than a "Minister for Economic Affairs."

He compared the role of the State to the primary referee of a football match. The referee designs the rules of the game, watches over the rules, and does not interfere "as long as the economy does not provoke an interference" (Erhard 1957/2000, 138). It might not be a surprise that this latter specification was interpreted very differently over the years – with changing governments – and is gaining quite some momentum in the current financial crisis.

The foundations of the Social Market Economy are rooted in economic theory just as much as in sociological, historical, and anthropological theories of the person and of humanity. Without going into the details, it is evident that many statements of the founding fathers comply with Catholic social teaching and with Benedict XVI's *Caritas in Veritate*:

First of all, the holistic approach to the human person and to society where free economic activity and entrepreneurship is more than work but an expression of freedom. This conforms to Benedict's statements on work as an "actus personae" which goes beyond an economic significance (see Benedict XVI 2009, 41). Entrepreneurship is at the heart of the Social Market Economy; people use their personal freedom to take initiative and to produce and trade.

Therefore, a free market economy is the best way to reach high levels of living standards. It is furthermore not only an economic phenomenon but also a cultural achievement. The economy should not take supremacy over other areas of life and should be a "servant to mankind." For the market economy to be efficient, it needs to be balanced with social progress. This implies a certain amount of redistribution of income by the State.

A strong State has a central role in devising the rules for the free market as well as for the achievement of the common good. Political, economic, and social institutions and structures are instruments for freedom and for economic and human development. Institutions influence behaviour, and they shape values and virtues.

Institutions matter. However, they are not sufficient. The functioning of the free market depends upon cultural and ethical foundations. It depends upon certain virtues such as creativity and innovation, trust and fairness, which cannot be supplied by the market. The market economy consumes, rather than produces, morals. Institutional ethics and individual ethics need and complement each other.

Most of the founding fathers even agreed that the regeneration of values and virtues can only be done by an inner strength that only religion and faith can bring about (see, e.g. Müller-Armack 1952/1976a, 238). Although the formation and regeneration of values and virtues was crucial for them, it was given little attention in the years to come. When the financial crisis hit Germany and caused fervid discussions on causes and remedies, it did not cause a general crisis of the Social Market Economy. In fact, acceptance rates that had declined over the years suddenly rose. The crisis did cause some discussion on ethics and principles and a small renaissance of the fundamentals of the original concept. Some realized that it was the neglect of some of the basic elements and the gap between theory and practice that was part of the problem.

17.3   Practical Experiences

How did the Social Market Economy practically do? Where are we today? The German *Wirtschaftswunder*, the strong economic growth in West Germany after World War II, had shown what economic freedom and entrepreneurship could bring about – just as Ludwig Erhard had expected. He refused to accept the term "German miracle," because he saw the success of his economic policy as the "consequence of the honest effort of a whole nation" (Erhard 1957/2000, 157), of individuals who were finally allowed to use their initiative and energy, creativity and knowledge freely. Poverty and hunger were overcome quickly in the years after World War II, and a considerable level of living standards was reached. Social security systems were developed and refined over the years. Germany's economy today is internationally competitive, with a well-elaborated social safety net.

The acceptance of the Social Market Economy in West Germany, however, was only minimal after World War II, where people in the midst of destruction and chaos favoured a more centralized system relying on plans and subsidies rather than on individual initiative. It took years to be accepted, and in the end it was success rather than theory, which made the difference. Thus, acceptance was fairly good although never really strong and declining over the years. However, it was evident for everybody in West Germany that capitalism was, to put it simply, "better than socialism" because of what could be observed happening on the other side of the Iron Curtain.

Much more than the general public, it was the entrepreneurs and business people who broadly accepted the basic philosophy and principles of the Social Market Economy – and not only the free market aspect but the social justice aspect as well. The association of German employers describes the general philosophy of good corporate governance as "the combination of acting right morally and economically" (BDA 2006). Labour unions and employer associations have a strong foundation in the German constitution and can rely on a long tradition of strong partnership. During the years 2007 and 2008, the social partners of the chemical industry jointly developed a Common Ethical Codex of Conduct and a catalogue of common action reinforcing this Codex on the company level (see Chemie-Sozialpartner 2008).

This rather strong commitment to the Social Market Economy, however, seems to be in contrast to a rather weak public estimation of entrepreneurs. To do business and to gain profit is not always seen as a form of personal achievement. In addition, the strong tradition of social partnership is hardly seen and valued by the general public.

For the people in the GDR, the picture was quite different. They suffered the destruction of capital stock, the decay of cities and buildings, the pollution of nature, and the lack of fundamental rights. The success of the West German Social Market Economy and the prospect of a life in prosperity was therefore one of the main driving forces of the peaceful revolution of 1989. The D-Mark was the symbol for prosperity and for freedom of choice. However, it was primarily the powerful idea of freedom that drove people on the streets. People were driven by the desire to express themselves freely, to take initiative, to engage in free economic activities, to be able to take care of their own lives, and achieve a life in prosperity. Finally, they were driven by a sense of solidarity to achieve it together, with and for everyone.

On October 3, 2010, Germany celebrated 20 years of reunification. Nobody could have foreseen how long it would take for East Germany to recover from 40 years of socialism. However, a lot was achieved within 20 years, and notwithstanding many errors and imperfections, reunification can be considered a success story, and not only economically. In any case, it was a major turning point in the history of Germany and of Europe.

Only a few had predicted the collapse of communism. As early as 1891, Pope Leo XIII rejected socialism in *Rerum Novarum* and uncovered its underlying fatal mistake as a misconception of the nature of man where "the autonomous subject of moral decision disappears" (John Paul II 1991, 13, see Leo XIII 1891, 17). The person is suppressed by mechanisms of control, bureaucracy, and mistrust. The human being is robbed of its uniqueness and its unique dignity, of its creativity and responsibility. Human beings are robbed of the means to establish a truly humane community.

Leo's predictions have been confirmed by the events of 1989. Socialism failed, because it misjudged the nature of man. Its anthropological foundation was a deep mistrust in the human person. This pessimistic view could only lead to a totalitarian system, where the interest of the individual is subordinated to the interest of all, where individual freedom is more and more repressed by force, rules, and controls. Such a system violates the human rights for free enterprise, for private property, for economic freedom. It makes people passive; it discourages free initiative, creativity, and the sense of achievement. It denigrates the "basic virtues of economic life, such as truthfulness, trustworthiness and hard work" (John Paul II 1991, 27). Where the freedom of the person is thus violated, the social order cannot long be stable. The collapse of communism has often been called "the victory of freedom." Human rights and human nature cannot be suppressed forever.

The process of reunification consumed a lot of resources. However, it cannot be held responsible for all problems that followed. Germany went through periods of weak growth and high unemployment, political inconsistencies and reform blockages. Many deficits and culprits were identified over the years, not all of them addressed by politics: There is a predominance of the economic sector and a materialistic tendency which cannot be denied. The high level of public indebtedness limits the scope for investment in education, research, infrastructure, and the future in general. The welfare system shows disincentives for work and individual effort – economic freedom and social justice were not always well balanced. For some, *freedom* today is a set of rights without duties. For others, *solidarity* is a set of rights without duties.

Germans find it hard to tolerate almost any level of inequality of income or widening of the income gap. It seems that it is not so much inequality that people condemn but a missing connection of individual effort and individual income. Bonuses and golden handshakes for failures therefore do not only contradict economic standards such as personal accountability, they systematically undermine trust and acceptance.

The year 1989 could have been a good occasion to reflect upon the development of Germany, of the progress of the economy and the society, and upon its basic foundations, etc. It was only partially done and possibly all strength had to be gathered for the process of reunification, for building up a country which lay in shambles. However, a closer look at the writings of the founding fathers would have helped a self-critique, since it would have shown that many of these problems arose because of a neglect of basic fundamental principles.

The founding fathers of the Social Market Economy themselves were highly critical from the start. They saw a gap between theory and practice. As early as the 1950s, they criticised the materialistic turn the Social Market Economy and society had taken as well as the cult of consumerism and increase of the living standard as the primary goal (see, e.g. Röpke, 1958, 151 and Rüstow, 1955, 70). They worried about the rise of the budget deficit, the burden of taxes, and the size of the welfare state. They were especially troubled by the neglect of values and moral foundations.

Twenty years after reunification and 60 years after the introduction of the Social Market Economy, the financial crisis of 2008 was an important opportunity for reflection, especially concerning cultural and moral foundations. The crisis has made it clear that personal responsibility is more than observance of the law. It has shown that institutional ethics cannot do without personal responsibility. It has shown that any State, any society, any business, and any economic order can do without a certain amount of ethical conduct for a while. However, it will lose acceptance and efficiency in the long run. It is running the risk of major crises.

This is why today we see a renaissance of *Ordnungspolitik* – of a strong State that sets the rules of the game – as well as a renaissance of personal liability. For the founding fathers liability was a crucial criterion for economic success. It was neglected for decades. Economic failure has brought it back onto the table.

17.4 Challenges by *Caritas in Veritate*

Catholic social teaching influenced the foundations and inherent values of the Social Market Economy in the early twentieth century. It contributed greatly as well during the late twentieth century. Many important encyclicals on economic and social affairs were published, such as *Sollicitudo Rei Socialis* and *Centesimus Annus*. However, at least in Germany, they were perceived only in a limited circle of academics. Only a few economists were in dialogue with theology, philosophy, or the other social sciences.

However, today there is a chance for change. Today, many see that the financial crisis is not only caused by market failure or by State failure but also by a moral crisis. This has opened a window of opportunity for Church teaching to play a larger role in the ongoing discussions.

As Benedict XVI emphasises in *Caritas in Veritate*, the world is in need of a profound cultural renewal; it needs to rediscover fundamental values on which to build a better future. "The different aspects of the crisis, its solutions, and any new development that the future may bring, are increasingly interconnected, they imply one another, they require new efforts of holistic understanding and a new humanistic synthesis. (…) The current crisis obliges us to re-plan our journey, to set ourselves new rules and to discover new forms of commitment, to build on positive experiences and to reject negative ones. The crisis thus becomes *an opportunity for discernment, in which to shape a new vision for the future*" (Benedict XVI 2009, 21).

His new vision for the future includes a sustainable development that involves the integrity of creation and the responsibility for future generations and accepts responsibility not only on the national but also on the global level. He is very precise in his definition of a truly humane development on the global level and talks about the fight against poverty, hunger, and disease, and about free movement of labour or freedom of religion.

Caritas in Veritate offers much food for thought, not only for theologians. It offers many important impulses for adjustments and enhancement of Germany's Social Market Economy and for liberal economic and social orders in general. Here are just two aspects where the teaching of the Church could contribute to current discussions:

(1) The market, the State, and the principle of solidarity
Pope Benedict XVI points out the danger of the predominance of the economic sphere and the danger of seeing profit as a goal in itself: "Profit is useful if it serves as a means towards an end that provides a sense both of how to produce it and how to make good use of it. Once profit becomes the exclusive goal, if it is produced by improper means and without the common good as its ultimate end, it risks destroying wealth and creating poverty" (Benedict XVI 2009, 21). However, not only wealth is destroyed, as we witnessed in the financial crisis. Benedict taps into John Paul II's line of thought, emphasizing that if man is confused about means and ends, he will be at loss concerning the authentic meaning of life. The founding fathers gave the same warning. However, the question is: How can this confusion be clarified?

Part of the answer might be to return to sound criteria for economic policy, and, indeed, we can see a huge wave of articles and discussions on the question: "Which are the essential criteria for the economic and social order?" During the financial crisis of 2008/2009, an article in *Handelsblatt*, a German newspaper for managers and businessmen, states that the human person should be the primary criterion. But again, what does this mean?

Benedict answers, "The integrated economy of the present day does not make the role of States redundant, but rather it commits governments to greater collaboration with one another. Both wisdom and prudence suggest not being too precipitous in declaring the demise of the State. In terms of the resolution of the current crisis, the

State's role seems destined to grow, as it regains many of its competences" (Benedict XVI 2009, 41). This is what actually happens in many States today, where governments take on a stronger role in setting up the rules of the game – be it for financial markets or for wages paid for managers.[8]

However, a balancing of the role of the market and the role of the State cannot be enough. For Benedict, it is evident that the exclusively binary model of market-plus-State does not guarantee the common good: "The economic sphere is neither ethically neutral, nor inherently inhuman and opposed to society. It is part and parcel of human activity and precisely because it is human, it must be structured and governed in an ethical manner" (Benedict XVI 2009, 36). He further explains: "In fact, if the market is governed solely by the principle of the equivalence in value of exchanged goods, it cannot produce the social cohesion that it requires in order to function well. *Without internal forms of solidarity and mutual trust, the market cannot completely fulfil its proper economic function.* And today it is this trust which has ceased to exist, and the loss of trust is a grave loss" (Benedict XVI 2009, 35).

Thus, Benedict stresses the importance of solidarity and trust *within* the market and the need to *civilize* the economy: "authentically human social relationships of friendship, solidarity and reciprocity can also be conducted within economic activity, and not only outside it or 'after' it" (Benedict XVI 2009, 36). Due to the financial crisis, he can find stronger support even among economists who might have rejected this notion prior to September 2008.

Benedict sees a way to civilize the economy in the existence of various types of business enterprise, which are neither purely private nor purely public. These types contradict the exclusively binary model of market-plus-State, which – in his eyes – is corrosive of society. These types of economic activities, which are often based on solidarity, build up society. They are marked by quotas of gratuitousness and communion, which cannot be established by the law but can grow in civil society without being restricted to it. They foster solidarity between citizens, participation, and adherence as well as actions of gratuitousness. This logic of "gratuitousness" is in contrast to the logic of "exchange" of the market and to the logic of the "duty" of State law. "It is from their reciprocal encounter in the marketplace that one may expect hybrid forms of commercial behaviour to emerge, and hence an attentiveness to ways of *civilizing the economy*" (Benedict XVI 2009, 38).

In fact, we see a rising interest in social entrepreneurship in many countries. The business model of social entrepreneurs is to solve social problems. Profit is a means for social innovation. In this respect, an entrepreneur is not purely defined as the head of a company but can be anyone who pursues an economic, social, or political innovation.

This is not completely new. The solution of the social question of the nineteenth century and the development of German social policy would not have been

---

[8] As a consequence of the short-term profit orientation that contributed to the financial crisis, the German government introduced rules concerning compensation for managers. Compensations now have to take long-term sustainability into account.

possible without pioneers in the Church and in civil society like Adolph Kolping (1813–1865) or Johann Hinrich Wichern (1808–1881). Furthermore, the founding fathers of the German Social Market Economy were aware of the danger of the dualism and the exclusiveness of market and State; they therefore stressed the interdependence of all aspects of life. They knew that public spirit and gratuitous commitment are necessary for the functioning of the market and for the enhancement of the society.

Benedict follows this line. Solidarity and gratuitousness are not only necessary outside the economy and outside for-profit businesses, but they are also necessary within: "The great challenge before us (…) is to demonstrate, in thinking and behaviour, not only that traditional principles of social ethics like transparency, honesty and responsibility cannot be ignored or attenuated, but also that in *commercial relationships* the *principle of gratuitousness* and the logic of gift as an expression of fraternity can and must *find their place within normal economic activity*. This is a human demand at the present time, but it is also demanded by economic logic. It is a demand both of charity and of truth" (Benedict XVI 2009, 36).

In the long run, this approach to the economy and to society might be a chance for a new paradigm. If the variety of entrepreneurs within the market, the civil society, and the State would cooperate rather than only coexist, they could create networks of partners. In Germany, for example, there are networks of for-profit and non-profit companies, of Churches and associations, and of local and federal State authorities in order to cooperate for better child protection. Personal relationships and trust between partners striving towards the same goal is the essential ingredient for effectiveness. These commitments can be expected not only to have strong positive impact on the level of trust among these partners and in society but also to have strong positive repercussions within the companies.

The existence of a variety of non-profit and low-profit companies and organisations can have a positive effect on the State as well. Here, usually the logic of "public obligation" is ruling. There exists a principle of "giving"; however, it is imposed by the State, for example taxes. Where taxes flow to the support of weaker members of the society, it is a form of institutionalized solidarity. Although the need for a transfer system is usually not denied, the way it is designed has led to broad discussion.

Pope John Paul II strongly criticised the so-called welfare state. In his perspective, a State that takes upon itself responsibilities that are the genuine competence of individuals, families, neighbourhoods, or other social groups is exaggerating its role and distorting the principle of subsidiarity. By intervening directly, the welfare state discourages human initiatives and energies. By offering material assistance *in humiliating ways*, the welfare state reduces the needy to mere *objects* of assistance – without helping them to escape their precarious situation by promoting their dignity as persons. This type of State stands in the way of families and social networks that can offer solidarity and familiarity instead of dis-integration and anonymity. In these types of welfare states, "people lose sight of the fact that life in society has neither the market nor the State as its final purpose, since life itself has a unique value which the State and the market must serve" (John Paul II 1991, 49). We can find quite some signs of this loss of direction in many if not all welfare states that fit this description.

The Church's social doctrine refuses the notion that solidarity should be *totally* delegated to the State. On the contrary: "Solidarity is first and foremost a sense of responsibility on the part of everyone with regard to everyone and it cannot therefore be merely delegated to the State. While in the past it was possible to argue that justice had to come first and gratuitousness could follow afterwards, as a complement, today it is clear that without gratuitousness, there can be no justice in the first place" (Benedict XVI 2009, 38).

This means that any solution to social problems cannot be purely materialistic. Solidarity is the expression of relationship. Social policy and economic policy have to follow the same criteria: the *human person* and his dignity. For example, respect is gratuitous as is trust and partnership. It is *gratis* but it bears fruit, it brings profit – economically and socially.

(2) The meaning of progress
If the market and the State can transcend their limited logic of today, a different, broader kind of *progress* might be possible. In Chap. 2 of *Caritas in Veritate*, Pope Benedict XVI states that progress of a merely economic and technological kind is insufficient. "Development needs above all to be true and integral. The mere fact of emerging from economic backwardness, though positive in itself, does not resolve the complex issues of human advancement, neither for the countries that are spearheading such progress, nor for those that are already economically developed, nor even for those that are still poor, which can suffer not just through old forms of exploitation, but also from the negative consequences of a growth that is marked by irregularities and imbalances" (Benedict XVI 2009, 23).

In *Centesimus Annus*, John Paul II warned that possibility of man choosing to idealize the economy and the creation of wealth is a danger of today's capitalist systems: "It is not wrong to want to live better; what is wrong is a style of life which is presumed to be better when it is directed towards 'having' rather than 'being'" (John Paul II 1991, 36). This is not a general criticism of the market mechanism but of an ethical and cultural system which forgets that the economy is only one aspect of life, which becomes confused about means and ends, which gives a central place to consumerism, and which is thus alienated from its human existence and at a loss about the authentic meaning of life (see John Paul II 1991, 39).

In the decades since the concept of GDP (Gross Domestic Product) was introduced, there have been waves of discussions about the explanatory power of this indicator. Nobel laureate Simon Kuznets who developed the concept in the late 1930s warned early on not to overstretch its informative value. However, over the years GDP has become the most important indicator – not only for the performance of the economy but also for the level of individual well-being and the progress of society. Within developed countries, the rate of economic growth, of unemployment, and of inflation have become the predominant indicators in public discussions and the primary goals of political action.

This notion is presently being questioned. There is a new wave of international debates and activities that question the idealization of economic growth. OECD, the

EU-Commission, the UN, the World Bank, some governments, and some scientists discuss what is the idea of the progress of society, how it can be measured, and how it can be fostered. They all look for a new, more sophisticated concept of "well-being" or "progress beyond GDP." Some countries like Canada or Ireland already have national reports on the progress of society that cover a wide range of indicators. Alongside economic indicators are measures for the condition of social life, education, nature, and subjective measures of life satisfaction and happiness.

We are far from reaching a stage where spiritual aspects of progress are touched. But to ask the question – what is progress – and to discuss it on a national and international level in an interdisciplinary dialogue is a grand step forwards. This discussion is an open and ongoing process in which the Church could and should take an active part. The Church has much to contribute, especially concerning the meanings of "development" and "progress." In *Caritas in Veritate*, Benedict states: "The truth of development consists in its completeness: if it does not involve the whole man and every man, it is not true development." This is the central message of *Populorum Progressio*, valid for today and for all time. Integral human development on the natural plane, as a response to a vocation from God the Creator, demands self-fulfilment in a "transcendent humanism which gives [to man] his greatest possible perfection: this is the highest goal of personal development" (Paul VI, cit in: Benedict XVI 2009, 18).

He goes a step further: *"Development must include not just material growth but also spiritual growth*, since the human person is a 'unity of body and soul' [*Gaudium et Spes*, 14], born of God's creative love and destined for eternal life. The human being develops when he grows in the spirit, when his soul comes to know itself and the truths that God has implanted deep within, when he enters into dialogue with himself and his Creator. (…) *There cannot be holistic development and universal common good unless people's spiritual and moral welfare is taken into account*, considered in their totality as body and soul" (Benedict XVI 2009, 76). In this, he would find strong support by the founding fathers of the German Social Market Economy, who strongly advocated the need for meaning and faith, values and virtues for a person's life and for society as a whole – a notion rarely mentioned in public by economists today.

17.5   Final Remarks

Benedict XVI begins and concludes his encyclical with a reference to *Populorum Progressio*. He cites Pope Paul VI, who emphasised that man cannot bring about his own progress unaided, because by himself he cannot establish an authentic humanism. "Only if we are aware of our calling, as individuals and as a community, to be part of Gods family as his sons and daughters, will we be able to generate a new vision and muster new energy in the service of a truly integral humanism. The greatest service to development, then, is a Christian humanism that enkindles charity and takes its lead from truth, accepting both as a lasting gift from God" (Benedict XVI 2009, 78).

In this, Paul VI reminds us of the imperfection and limits of all endeavours of man vis-à-vis his Creator. "Without God man neither knows which way to go, nor even understands who he is" (Benedict XVI 2009, 78). Humanity thus presupposes humility – a truth that believers and non-believers can certainly agree on, which has strong implications for political advisors and for policy makers. During World War II, this truth was self-evident to those who had gathered to discuss a political, economic, and social order for Germany.

To Benedict, this truth has a particular implication for Christians: "*Development needs Christians with their arms raised towards God* in prayer, Christians moved by the knowledge that truth-filled love, *caritas in veritate*, from which authentic development proceeds, is not produced by us, but given to us" (Benedict XVI 2009, 79). Thus, for Christians, in order to move closer to "the common good," it is essential not to stand still with acquired knowledge but to constantly challenge it. As the social teaching of the Church is growing and elaborating by continuously reading the signs of the times in the light of Scripture and open to the logic of the Spirit, our understanding of human nature and of the economic and social order best fit for human nature and for the common good is growing. There is a great deal that the social teaching of the Church and economic thinking inspired by it has to offer to the public debate. The insights into human nature and the need for a holistic approach to human nature, progress, and development are among some of the most important contributions they can make.

Bibliography

Benedict XVI. 2009. *Caritas in veritate* (*CV*). Vatican: Liberia Editrice Vaticana.
Bundesvereinigung der Deutschen Arbeitgeber – BDA. 2006. 'Wirtschaften mit Werten - Für alle ein Gewinn'. http://www.bda-online.de/www/arbeitgeber.nsf/res/429D78F12B75374BC1257 4EC00310B05/$file/Wirtschaft_mit_Werten.pdf.
Chemie-Sozialpartner. 2008. *Verantwortliches Handeln in der Sozialen Marktwirtschaft.* www. chemie-sozialpartner.de/vereinbarungen/soziale-marktwirtschaft/wittenberg-prozess/.
Erhard, Ludwig. 2000. *Wohlstand für alle*. Düsseldorf: Econ Verlag.
Eucken, Walter. 1990. *Grundsätze der Wirtschaftspolitik*, 6th ed. Tübingen: Mohr (Siebeck).
Gregg, Samuel. 2010. *Wilhelm Röpke's Political Economy*. Cheltenham: Edward Elgar.
John Paul II. 1991. *Centesimus annus* (*CA*). Vatican: Liberia Editrice Vaticana.
Leo XIII. 1891. *Rerum novarum*. Saint Mary-of-the-Woods: Aurora Press.
Müller-Armack, Alfred. 1976a. Stil und Ordnung der Sozialen Marktwirtschaft. In *Wirtschaftsordnung und Wirtschaftspolitik*, 2nd ed, ed. Alfred Müller-Armack, 231–242. Bern: Haupt Verlag.
Müller-Armack, Alfred. 1976b. Soziale Marktwirtschaft. In *Wirtschaftsordnung und Wirtschaftspolitik*, 2nd ed, ed. Alfred Müller-Armack, 243–249. Bern: Haupt Verlag.
Müller-Armack, Alfred. 1976c. Das gesellschaftspolitische Leitbild der Sozialen Marktwirtschaft. In *Wirtschaftsordnung und Wirtschaftspolitik*, 2nd ed, ed. Alfred Müller-Armack, 293–315. Bern: Haupt Verlag.
Müller-Armack, Alfred. 1981. Vorschläge zur Verwirklichung der Sozialen Marktwirtschaft. In *Genealogie der Sozialen Marktwirtschaft*, 2nd ed, ed. Alfred Müller-Armack, 90–109. Bern: Haupt Verlag.
Röpke, Wilhelm. 1947. *Das Kulturideal des Liberalismus*. Frankfurt: G. Schulte-Bulmke.

Röpke, Wilhelm. 1948. *Die Gesellschaftskrisis der Gegenwart*, 5th ed. Erlenbach-Zürich: E. Rentsch.

Röpke, W. 1958. *Jenseits von Angebot und Nachfrage*, 2nd ed. Erlenbach-Zürich: E. Rentsch.

Röpke, Wilhelm. 1959. Marktwirtschaft ist nicht genug. In *Hat der Westen eine Idee?* Tagungsprotokoll, vol. 7, 2nd ed, ed. Aktionsgemeinschaft Soziale Marktwirtschaft, 9–20. Ludwigsburg: M. Hoch.

Röpke, Wilhelm. 1960. Wirtschaft und Moral. In *Was wichtiger ist als Wirtschaft*, ed. Alexander Rüstow et al., 17–31. Ludwigsburg: M. Hoch.

Rüstow, A. 1952. *Der Mensch in der Wirtschaft, Umrisse einer Vitalpolitik*. Heidelberg: Lutzeyer.

Rüstow, Alexander. 1955. Wirtschaftsethische Probleme der sozialen Marktwirtschaft. In *Der Christ und die Soziale Marktwirtschaft*, ed. M. Patrick, 53–74. Stuttgart/Köln: Kohlhammer.

Rüstow, Alexander. 1957. Vitalpolitik gegen Vermassung. In *Masse und Demokratie*, ed. Albert Hunold, 215–238. Stuttgart: Erlenbach-Zürich.

Rüstow, Alexander. 1961. Paläoliberalismus, Kommunismus und Neoliberalismus. In *Wirtschaft, Gesellschaft und Kultur, Festgabe für Alfred Müller-Armack*, ed. Fritz.W. Meyer et al., 61–70. Berlin: Duncker & Humblot.

Rüstow, Alexander. 1963a. Menschenrechte oder Menschenpflichten? In *Alexander Rüstow – Rede und Antwort*, ed. Walter Hoch, 296–313. Ludwigsburg: Hoch.

Rüstow, Alexander. 1963b. Wirtschaft als Dienerin der Menschlichkeit. In *Alexander Rüstow – Rede und Antwort*, ed. Walter Hoch, 76–91. Ludwigsburg: Hoch.

Schneider, Andrea. 2004. *Ordnungsaspekte in der Nationalökonomik*. Bern: Haupt Verlag.

BCC

Recent economic development and the financial and economic crisis require a change in our approach to business and finance. This book combines theology, economy and philosophy in order to examine in detail the idea that the functioning of a free market economy depends upon sound cultural and ethical foundations.

The free market is a cultural achievement, not only an economic phenomenon subject to technical rules of trade and exchange. It is an achievement which lives by and depends upon the values and virtues shared by the majority of those who engage in economic activity. It is these values and virtues that we refer to as culture. Trust, credibility, loyalty, diligence, and entrepreneurship are the values inherent in commercial rules and law. But beyond law, there is also the need for ethical convictions and for global solidarity with developing countries. This book offers new ideas for future sustainable development and responds to an increasing need for a new sense of responsibility for the common good in societal institutions and good leadership.

M. Schlag and J.A. Mercado (eds.), *Free Markets and the Culture of Common Good*, Ethical Economy 41, DOI 10.1007/978-94-007-2990-2, © Springer Science+Business Media B.V. 2012

Index

Printed by Printforce, the Netherlands